THE PITTSBURGH THEOLOGICAL MONOGRAPH SERIES

General Editor

Dikran Y. Hadidian

17

Scripture in History and Theology:

Essays in Honor of J. Coert Rylaarsdam

# SCRIPTURE IN HISTORY & THEOLOGY:

## ESSAYS IN HONOR OF J. COERT RYLAARSDAM

EDITED BY

ARTHUR L. MERRILL

and

THOMAS W. OVERHOLT

THE PICKWICK PRESS

Pittsburgh, Pennsylvania

1977

**Library of Congress Cataloging in Publication Data**
Main entry under title:

Scripture in history & theology.

(Pittsburgh theological monograph series ; 17)
"The writing of J. Coert Rylaarsdam, Arthur L.
Merrill" : p.
Includes bibliographical references and indexes.
CONTENTS: Merrill, A. L. The two covenants.—
Sheehan, J. F. X. The prep narrative.—Ahlström, G. W.
King Jehu. [etc.]
I. Rylaarsdam, John Coert, 1906—    II. Merrill,
Arthur L. III. Overholt, Thomas W., 1935—
IV. Series.
BS540.S36              220.6              77-12106
ISBN 0-915138-32-8

J. COERT RYLAARSDAM

# CONTENTS

## PART I. AN APPRECIATION

## PART II. UNDERSTANDING SCRIPTURE

PART III.  INTERPRETING SCRIPTURE

PART IV.  BIBLIOGRAPHY

## J. COERT RYLAARSDAM

John Coert Rylaarsdam was born in Lismore, Minnesota, on
November 24, 1906, the son of Cornelius and Marie Aarsen Rylaarsdam.
He received his education at Hope College (A.B. 1931), New Bruns-
wick Theological Seminary (B.D. 1938) and the University of Chicago
(Ph.D. 1944). He did special work in Arabic at Princeton University
(1935-36) and in theology at Cambridge University (1938-39). Central
College of Pella, Iowa, conferred upon him the Doctor of Divinity,
honoris causa, in 1960.

His teaching career began in 1931 in Basra, Iraq, where he
was instructor in English in the American School for Boys for four
years. This was followed by four years as Professor of Old Testament at New Brunswick Theological Seminary from 1941-45. Professor Rylaarsdam joined the faculty of the Divinity School of the
University of Chicago in 1945 and served there until 1972 when he
became Professor emeritus. Since 1971 he has been Professor in
the Theology Department at Marquette University.

He has been co-editor of The Journal of Religion, consulting
editor for The Encyclopaedia Britannica, and editor for the first
three volumes of Guides to Biblical Scholarship: OT Series. He
has also served on the editorial boards of Studia Post Biblica
and Biblical Research. Dr. Rylaarsdam has served on various study
groups of the World Council of Churches, including the Commission
on Worship. He delivered the Rauschenbusch Lectures for 1957 at
Colgate Rochester Divinity School, and lectured at the John XXIII
Institute at St. Xavier College in 1967.

Professor Rylaarsdam is married to Harriet Loring Worcester
and has two children, John and Katherine. His home is in Chicago,
Illinois.

# CONTRIBUTORS

GÖSTA W. AHLSTRÖM is Professor of Old Testament and Ancient Palestinian Studies in the Divinity School and the Department of Near Eastern Languages and Civilizations of the University of Chicago, Chicago, Illinois.

WILLIAM A. BEARDSLEE is Professor of Religion at Emory University, Atlanta, Georgia.

GLENDON E. BRYCE is Assistant Professor of Old Testament at Princeton Theological Seminary, Princeton, New Jersey.

HARRY M. BUCK is Professor of Religion Studies at Wilson College, Chambersburg, Pennsylvania.

GRACE EDWARDS was Assistant Professor of Religion and Philosophy at Milwaukee-Downer College, Milwaukee, Wisconsin, and since 1957 resides in Athens, Greece.

DONALD E. GOWAN is Associate Professor of Old Testament at Pittsburgh Theological Seminary, Pittsburgh, Pennsylvania.

ROBERT M. GRANT is Carl Darling Buck Professor of Humanities in the University of Chicago and Professor of New Testament and Early Christianity in the Divinity School, Chicago, Illinois.

WALTER HARRELSON is Professor of Old Testament in the Divinity School of Vanderbilt University, Nashville, Tennessee, and a Director of the Ecumenical Institute for Advanced Theological Studies in Jerusalem.

ARTHUR L. MERRILL is Professor of Old Testament Theology at United Theological Seminary of the Twin Cities, New Brighton, Minnesota.

LESTER V. MEYER is Associate Professor in the Department of Religion at Concordia College, Moorhead, Minnesota.

THOMAS W. OVERHOLT is Associate Professor of Philosophy, Program in Religious Studies, at the University of Wisconsin-Stevens Point, Stevens Point, Wisconsin.

WALTER E. RAST is Professor of Old Testament and Palestinian Archaeology at Valparaiso University, Valparaiso, Indiana.

ARNOLD B. RHODES is Professor of Old Testament at Louisville Presbyterian Theological Seminary, Louisville, Kentucky.

GEORGE W. SCHREINER is one of the ministers of the United Church of the Medical Center, which serves the Chicago West Side Medical Center, including the medical schools and schools of nursing of the University of Illinois and Rush-Presbyterian-St. Luke Hospitals, Chicago, Illinois.

JOHN F. X. SHEEHAN, S. J., is chairman of the Theology Department at Marquette University, Milwaukee, Wisconsin.

CLYDE CURRY SMITH is Professor of Ancient History at the University of Wisconsin-River Falls, River Falls, Wisconsin.

SHEMARYAHU TALMON is Professor of Biblical Studies and Dean of the Faculty of Humanities at the Hebrew University of Jerusalem, Israel.

JAY A. WILCOXEN is Associate Professor of Bible at the Divinity School of the University of Chicago, Chicago, Illinois.

RAYMOND B. WILLIAMS is Associate Professor in the Department of Philosophy and Religion at Wabash College, Crawfordsville, Indiana.

# ACKNOWLEDGMENTS

The essays which make up this volume were contributed by former students and colleagues of J. Coert Rylaarsdam. To them we extend our thanks for their diligence in meeting deadlines and their efforts on behalf of this project through which we seek to honor Dr. Rylaarsdam as a person, teacher and scholar.

Grateful acknowledgment is hereby made to the publishers for permission to quote from the following works:

To Atheneum Publishers, New York, for permission to quote from Claude Levi-Strauss, Tristes Tropiques c 1973.

To Basic Books, Inc., Publishers, New York, for permission to quote from Claude Levi-Strauss, Structural Anthropology, translated from the French by Claire Jacobson and Brooke Grundfest Schoepf c 1963.

To William B. Eerdmans Publishing Co., Grand Rapids, Michigan, for permission to quote from William Stringfellow, Count It All Joy c 1967.

To the Hamlyn Publishing Group Ltd., Middlesex, England, for permission to quote from F. M. Powicke, Modern Historians and the Study of History c 1955.

To Harper & Row, Publishers, Inc., New York, for permission to quote from Jürgen Moltmann, Theology of Hope c 1967 SCM Press, Ltd., London; and from Gerhard von Rad, Old Testament Theology, Volume I c 1962 Oliver & Boyd, Ltd., Edinburgh.

To the Macmillan Company, New York, for permission to quote from Dietrich Bonhoeffer, Ethics c 1955 Macmillan Publishing Co., Inc.; c SCM Press, Ltd., 1955.

To Orbis Books, Maryknoll, New York, for permission to quote from Gustavo Gutierrez, A Theology of Liberation c 1973.

To Pantheon Books, a Division of Random House, Inc., New York, for permission to quote from Ivan Illich, Medical Nemesis c 1976.

To SCM Press, Ltd., London, England, for permission to quote from Brevard S. Childs, Memory and Tradition in Israel c 1955.

To the University of Chicago Press, Chicago, Illinois, for permission to quote from Claude Levi-Strauss, The Savage Mind c 1966 Weidenfeld and Nicolson, Ltd.

Grateful acknowledgment is also made to the Trustees of the British Museum, who hold the copyright, for permission to use the photograph of the Black Obelisk of Shalmaneser III on the cover.

Our thanks go to Dikran Y. Hadidian for his willingness to include this volume in the Pittsburgh Theological Monograph Series and his assistance in bringing the project to fruition. Our thanks also to Barbara Jean Merrill for her work in preparing the indices.

Purim    5737
March 4, 1977

Arthur L. Merrill
Thomas W. Overholt

PART ONE:

AN APPRECIATION

# THE TWO COVENANTS: THE THOUGHT OF J. COERT RYLAARSDAM

## Arthur L. Merrill

The appointment of J. Coert Rylaarsdam to the faculty of
the Divinity School of the University of Chicago in 1945 marked
a distinct shift in the understanding of biblical studies
there. Until 1942 the Biblical Field had been placed within
the Humanities Department of the University so that the Bible
and related documents could be studied as historical phenomena
without the pressure of ecclesiastical control. The historical
studies of Scripture, however, were becoming more and more
distant from the preparation of persons for ministry, and Dean
Ernest Colwell was concerned that the theological dimensions
were being neglected. For this reason Rylaarsdam was appointed
to the Biblical Field as Professor of Old Testament Theology.
It was Colwell's creation and organization of the Biblical
Field as an integral component of the faculty of theology
that established the agenda for Rylaarsdam's life and work as
a scholar of the Old Testament.

This is not to say that other personal and social factors
had no influence in his life and studies. His upbringing and
education within the Reformed tradition, expressed through the
Reformed Church of America, introduced into his thought the
strong theocentric focus and the commitment to the "protestant
principle" that persists throughout his writings. His
experience as a missionary teacher contributed to his deep
awareness of the multi-faceted nature of the Near Eastern
world. His participation in pulpit and pew of an Episcopal

church was both the expression of and the occasion for his strong emphasis on the objective character of the community of faith. His encounter with Israel both as an historical fact and as a present reality brought awareness of the difficulties of using the OT as merely a Christian book.

It was the quest to understand what it means to be a theologian of the OT that appears to inform his writing and teaching throughout his scholarly career. He had been trained and stood in the tradition of those of the so-called "Chicago School" who equated truth with the historical method, and who affirmed that empirical, analytic and synthetic research was the only basis for and the only legitimate starting point of theological understanding.[1] In such an historical approach the goal was to reconstruct the ancient world that had produced the Scriptures and thereby find its true meaning. The procedure of the historical method stripped the past of its authority and the method itself became a surrogate for the authority of the Scriptures. The historical method taken to its extreme produced a historicism which tended to deny any contemporary relevance to the Scriptures and replace the truth of the Bible with the self-evident truth of the method being used.

The challenge to such a position came externally and internally. From the Continent came the neo-orthodox theologies of Barth and Bultmann, which challenged not only the method but its deepest assumptions, claiming that the search was being carried out at the wrong locus. And internally the challenge came from the character of the Divinity School as an institution founded to produce persons for the ministry of the church. The historical method had failed to explicate the relevance of the Scriptures, either theologically or culturally, and thus biblical studies had become virtually obsolete. It is this latter factor that appears to have influenced Rylaarsdam in his quest to define the meaning of OT Theology. Throughout

his professional career the concern for the ministry of the
community of faith has been a dominant factor.  In a graduate
school which tended to focus on those students enrolled in
the doctoral program he was always concerned that the professional program not be slighted.  In dealing with students
he showed as much concern for the neophyte preparing for
ministry as for the brilliant doctoral candidate.

It is out of this blend of influences and concerns that
Rylaarsdam developed his own unique definition of Old Testament
Theology.  He wrote:

> The theologian of the Old Testament is an historian
> and a critic.  He is neither an antiquarian nor an
> apologist.  His method is dialogical.  Taking his
> stand in the Old Testament, he listens to all move-
> ments that appeal to it, for they may call his
> attention to something in it he has overlooked, and
> he tries to provide all with a critical response
> that measures the particular use each makes of the
> Hebrew Bible against its broad ethos and outlook.[2]

He never repudiated the historical and philological methods in
which he had been trained, but he sought an understanding of
the OT that would be both faithful and relevant.  He accepted
neither historicism nor neo-orthodoxy, considering both to be
merely apologists for positions which had already been established on external bases.  Rather he was concerned to develop
and articulate the theological relevance and function of the
Scriptures in a way that would have them inform the contemporary
discussion.  He therefore neither wrote a history of the
religion of Israel, though he was deeply interested in the forms
and meanings of Israel's religion, nor developed a biblical
theology in the more technical sense.  In what appears to be
a self-description he wrote, "the relationship between description and theology is not a formal one, controlled by an
a priori inclusive hermeneutical program.  It is personal,
occasional, informal, and usually eclectic."[3]

The authority of the Scriptures thereby lies within itself and is to be effective only in the careful descriptive and historical task of revealing what the text itself has to say. On that basis the biblical theologian becomes the critic of all those movements which appeal to the Scriptures, and has one's own understandings of the received traditions of synagogue or church challenged.

This view of the Scriptures informs and undergirds all of Rylaarsdam's work. In a great variety of his publications this understanding appears as the guiding principle and lends thematic unity to a diversity of concerns. In the process his work shows a consistency and logical development that is not apparent in the casual perusal of his writings. In his various tasks as teacher, preacher, lecturer, and writer this unity shines through luminously. There is at the same time a certain chronological development which is important to note. This development in neither unilinear nor does the chronology itself dominate the process, for throughout his work one comes upon the same recurring themes and concerns. Yet his ultimate contribution is the result of that development.

## I. NATURE AND GRACE

J. Coert Rylaarsdam began his scholarly career with his doctoral dissertation, later published as Revelation in Jewish Wisdom Literature.[4] This volume, along with the work of Helmer Ringgren,[5] can be said to have laid the groundwork for the present appreciation and study of wisdom literature in the OT, and the deutero-canonical books.[6] The study of the wisdom materials had been opened up by the publication of the "Teaching of Amen-em-opē" by Wallis Budge in 1923 and the subsequent study of the literature from a comparative viewpoint. The recognition that the biblical material could no longer be studied in splendid isolation raised profound theological questions, some of which were extremely disquieting to those who held what might be termed "orthodox" views. Questions of authority and revelation were to be raised in a way that even the earlier controversies over the historical-critical method had not raised.

Read from today's perspective, this small volume does not appear to be very radical, yet it defined the starting-point for all successive views of the wisdom literature. It begins by establishing that Hebrew wisdom, in its methods and forms, its social context and moral stance, was deeply embedded in the context of the Ancient Near East. Thus Hebrew wisdom begins as a "secular" task, partaking by its nature in the world in which it was born. This literature, however, is not only "secular", for it is taken over by the national religious tradition, ultimately to be submerged by and lost in rabbinism which identified wisdom with the Torah. This process is traced not only in the Hebrew Bible but also into the deutero-canonical books.

Rylaarsdam then went on to examine the theological implications of this development. He notes that from the beginning there are both optimistic and pessimistic views held by the wisdom writers. He compared the optimism of the wisdom writers with that of the prophetic literature and came to the conclusion that the difference between them grew out of divergent views of revelation. The prophets held to a vertical view of revelation in which God takes the initiative; the wisdom writers studied the way of life in nature and history. The former is "subjective" and the latter "objective." It is only in the later stages of the development of the wisdom tradition that the two become blended, so that not only does one seek wisdom, but Wisdom herself seeks out humans to teach them her meaning. "As the human search recedes, emphasis upon the divine initiative grows."[7] Wisdom is then no longer a part of the order of creation but belongs to a transcendent order.

When the natural and empirical wisdom fails, one has two
alternatives: to be pessimistic, doubting and despairing of
ever knowing and fully finding, or to seek a transcendent
faith. Human ability and initiative ever contend with the
divine transcendence. There is an ever present tension between natural human freedom and a sovereign divine rule. To
stress either side of the dialectic to the extreme is to contribute to its opposite. "The tension did not snap, for there
was always an overlapping of nature and grace."[8]

This tension which he discovered within the wisdom tradition
of Israel became the key for understanding the contemporary
scene. In both his introduction and conclusion the contemporary
religious discussion is noted. The "humanism" of the classical
liberal position with its emphasis on the empirical and ex-
perimental is set over against the "supernaturalism" of the
neo-orthodox position, as exemplified by Karl Barth, with his
emphasis on the "irrational and transcendental." The wisdom
literature points out that the tension between transcendence
and freedom is as real for the order of grace as for the order
of creation. It is in the dialectic of these two that the
Christian lives out a life of faithfulness, aware that neither
is the ultimate solution to Christian existence and faith.

This correlation of nature and grace led Rylaarsdam to
two further areas of interest and study. One was the meaning
of creation in OT Theology and the other a concern for the
meaning of worship. The former is not so much marked by specific
articles or a monograph as by a continuous concern that the fullness of "biblical realism" be expressed. That was engendered
not only by the spurious use some had made of the Bible as
natural science, but also by the more serious question of the
meaning of nature for the life of faith. Because our age has
so been dominated by the concern for history, we have tended to
ignore the significance of nature.

Admittedly Rylaarsdam began with the common assumption that
Israel's confession of God as the ruler of nature is an inference

from her confession of his rule in history. The affirmations of
the community of faith that God is One and that he is "Creator of
heaven and earth" do not permit us to draw a sharp line between
history and creation. The world, ha'aretz, is the sign of God's
sovereignty and the unity of history and nature is to be found in
the universality and authority of God. Further a creation faith
is the incentive for human action and the basis for an imperative
in the life of faith.[9] As he was fond of saying to his classes,
"Incarnation is not a scandal for the Jew." For the Incarnation
points to continuities in time and space which are part and parcel
of the OT faith. The crisis in our understanding of Creation
focuses in the function of the world of time, space and matter
for God. That crisis finds its answer not in a Christocentric
interpretation of the faith, but in a basically theocentric
perspective, in the biblical persistence in focusing on the
action of God in the empirical world. It is that objective and
universal Word of God in nature and history that must be apprehended
in any talk about God's revelation.

This line of thought comes to its clearest expression in his
work on the Song of Songs, which began in the Layman's Bible
Commentary[10] and was later developed in an article.[11] In the
Song of Songs, Rylaarsdam finds evidences of a universal Eros,
AHABAH, which corresponds to the universal Wisdom or Logos, HOKMAH.
The Song of Songs has its validity in its celebration of this
natural erotic force. He lamented that this dimension was lost
in the ongoing reinterpretation of the Song of Songs by both
Israel and the Church where it was reduced to a metaphor for
the divine-human relationship, and subsumed under the basic rubrics
of redemption. He hoped that the scholarly recovery of the Song
of Songs as a series of lyrics about a mystery of nature in
which humans share might become a basis for recovering the affirmation of God as Creator.[12]

The other major development in his concern for the revelation
of nature and grace is expressed in his deep and abiding interest
in the meaning of worship.[13] This is not only the consequence of
his commitment to the church and his role as an ordained minister

in the service of the Church and her Lord, but also of his understanding of worship as the clue to the discovery of the deepest
dimensions of Israel's faith and self-understanding.  His series
of articles in <u>The Interpreter's Dictionary of the Bible</u> stand as
a monument to this concern.

For Rylaarsdam the forms and meanings of Israel's worship
are resident not only in what Israel says, but also in what she
does.  Therefore he pointed to the <u>Shema</u> as a clue to the fact
that the meaning of Israel's worship was grounded in the Unity
of God.  That theocentric focus was also to be seen in the actions
of Israel's feasts and fasts.  The proclamation of the one Lord
in his power and goodness was the key to unlocking the significance
of the varieties of expression and the developments of the divergent
forms of worship.[14]

Such a view of worship leads to seeing it as an objective
reality which is a manifestation of the will and purpose of God.
Its central function is to mediate the grace of God, for the
effective meaning of worship is not in the natural processes or
in any of the human actions that are its component parts.  On the
other hand, this guards against falling into any personal or
pietistic understanding of worship.  Such a "subjectivism" is
not to be discerned in Israel's worship, for her faith lies in
the reality of the One who both created the world and established
the community of faith.  On the other hand, it guards against
viewing worship as something done for its own sake.  The effectiveness of the ritual and its accompanying words can never be
separated from the divine action which gives it its rationale.[15]
This is not to deny that even this objective view of worship has
its own ambiguity.  It still functions as both a form of self-
dedication to the divine reality and of self-preservation.[16]
However all worship points to the faithfulness of the Lord who
instituted the various forms of worship.

Therefore worship in ancient Israel is to be seen both as
commemoration and anticipation.  It celebrates both creation and

the release from bondage. Israel's existence is a gift from the
Lord and that gift is to be celebrated and enjoyed in both history
and nature. At this point Rylaarsdam did not accept either the
earlier understanding of the festivals of Israel by Wellhausen
nor the more recent interpretations which have focused on the
process of "historicization". For as he says, "Both Wellhausen
and the current movement overlook the fact that the so-called
process of historicising of the agricultural feasts did not constitute a displacement of their significance as observances of
natural processes."[17] Any attempt to maintain a sharp line of
demarcation between history and nature is to be resisted, for
each and every festival contains both elements and, though the
line between them may be blurred, neither is ultimately dissolved
in the other. Both history and nature have attached to them a
revitalizing significance that must be discerned in Israel's
worship.

The festival celebrations of Israel are not only commemoration
but also anticipation.[18] The action and triumph of God is not
only a past event, but also the hope of Israel. The faithful
observance of Israel's worship is indispensible to the fulfillment of the promise and is resident in the words and actions of
that ritual. Thus fasting is not only an act of mourning for
disaster that is already at hand but also an act of repentance
to avert further disaster.[19] The Passover is celebrated before
the exit from Egypt. Hence the effectiveness of worship lies
not in itself but in the faith that God has chosen to use it.
Therefore Israel's worship is always, when true to itself,
eschatological in nature, both celebrating the triumph of God
as an actual fact, in both history and creation, and also pray-
ing for and celebrating an anticipated triumph. Its finality
is based solely on the adequacy of God's action.[20]

## II. FAITH AND HISTORY

Though we may say that Rylaarsdam's thought begins with the concern for nature and grace, that concern leads immediately and directly to another which occupied the central part of his life and work as a theologian of the OT, the concern for faith and history. His many lectures in congregations, colleges and seminaries, including the prestigious Rauschenbusch Lectures at Colgate Rochester Divinity School, tended to return again and again to this theme. In articles and his commentary on Exodus he wrestled with the question of how one might reconcile what at times appeared to be diametrically opposite concerns. For no matter how much he was interested in the dimensions of nature and the creation faith in Israel, Rylaarsdam at heart never let go of the notion that the Bible bears witness to a faith which holds that God discloses himself by means of and in relation to the events of history. The whole structure of the Biblical testimony points to this perspective. For those who wrote them, the Hebrew Scriptures were a record of the character and deeds of God in history, and as such were written in the form of a history.

This view of the Scriptures set the hermeneutical problem in a very characteristic way for his time. There were two ways in which one could read the Bible.[21] On the one hand, it could be read primarily as a record of a specific religious tradition. As such it was a cultural product of a "historic faith," participating in all the ambiguities and relativities of history. It thereby served a basically educational function in so far as it was a cultural object. On the other hand the community of faith has taken the Bible as a book of revelation. As such it is an authoritative resource for life and faith within the community that so regards it. It is not a mere record of the past, but a present dynamic reality in which God confronts human beings. It is the relation of faith and history that defines the hermeneutical issue, for the community of faith has had

difficulty in reading the Bible in both ways at the same time, so
that the one could inform and serve the other. Liberalism tended
to read the scriptures only as a cultural object. Orthodoxy
tended to regard it as only an authoritative book of faith.

Yet both liberalism and orthodoxy were seen to fall prey to
the same error: the tendency to regard revelation as static and
propositional. As a historical book the Bible appeared to display
only endless varieties of religious experience that had no unity.
There was no basis for finding a unity that could transcend the
polarities of "prophetic faith" and "priestly religion." Liberalism therefore tended to look elsewhere for its categories of
meaning and understanding while the orthodox tried to maintain
the identity of fact and faith.[22]

In this respect Rylaarsdam was very appreciative of critical
historical scholarship for its contribution to the smashing of
any simple identification of fact and faith, and also of the
so-called "neo-orthodox" scholars who attempted to maintain the
paradoxical character of the relationship of faith and history.
For orthodoxy and liberalism there was no gap between fact and
faith. Fact demanded faith and the dependence of faith on fact
was absolute. That revelation is not a static form with a
stable content but a dynamic action of God's self-disclosure
as an historical action which is existentially apprehended as
a source of faith and inspired response, became the basis for
his reconstruction.[23]

Yet increasingly Rylaarsdam found the "neo-orthodox"
stance unacceptable as a definition of what it meant to be an
OT theologian. First of all, as has been more recently pointed
out by Brevard Childs and Langdon Gilkey, the Biblical Theology
Movement attempted to find the facts of faith in the "Acts of
God." Like the old orthodoxy, it was seeking to close the gap
between fact and faith. It did not take the awareness of the
paradox seriously enough.[24] And secondly, it lost the inter-
dependent and reciprocal relationship between the kerygmatic
and critical functions of the Bible. This led to the danger

of knowing the "kerygma" of the Bible and of not being able to subject that understanding of the kerygma to the full dimensions of the Bible itself. Thus the neo-orthodox movement was seen as falling into the ever-present danger of placing its interpretation of the Bible at the service of the theological perspective of the interpreter. "Biblical scholarship cannot be identified with the function of the Bible in the Church."[25]

Therefore "it is imperative for the biblical scholars to read the Bible as a historical record and to provide it with a unifying framework for which all its contents are evidence." Then "history will provide faith with knowledge and faith will sanctify history."[26] The dialectical relationship must always be maintained and that is the task of biblical theology as a historical discipline.

In fact Rylaarsdam never has given us a theological compendium of the OT. Whether such a theological project is any longer possible is of course a legitimate question. But in his commentary on Exodus in The Interpreter's Bible one finds the initial attempt to show what such an undertaking might look like.[27] Here he begins with the affirmation that the Exodus event is the single most important event for the faith of the people of God, called Israel. The life of Israel and its meaning depends ultimately upon this divine action. On the basis of this event the covenant between God and Israel is sealed. To it and from it all other lines in the OT are drawn. On the basis of this event all recognition of the God of Israel is to be made. Here is the revelatory event par excellence, which discloses the action and triumph of God as the center of all life and meaning. The Exodus, as an event of faith, was in Israel the affirmation that its God, the God who had disclosed himself to his people in the act of deliverance was not simply the master of a moment of history but the Lord of all history and of the cosmos.

Therefore it is this event which provides the occasion for attempting the correlation of critical, literary and historical studies with our knowledge of the God who reveals himself as the

"Lord of history" which is, nevertheless, historically mediated.[28] For the Exodus is not a history of early Israel, nor primarily an account of origins. It is rather an exposition of the meaning of that history for Israel. It points to the God of Exodus who in his freedom and sovereignty is powerful and purposeful, as well as moral and intentional in his use of humans to accomplish his purpose.

But that historic memory is combined with Israel's present living experience. For historic revelation always entails a community of faith. Such a community is not held together by a common life, or by common principles and practices, but by the remembrance and celebration of the particular historical event which it affirms as the event of revelation.[29] This event is not to be statically conceived but re-interpreted in each and every age both to undergird the life of the community and to be the basis for re-evaluation and critique.

Thus the Exodus story is not the genetic account of the history of Israel and its folkways, though it points to dimensions of that history. Nor is it the heroic saga of a Moses who delivered his people. Rather the story is the glorification of the Lord of Israel who has gloriously triumphed over the forces of history (the Pharaoh) and of nature (the Red Sea). The story is essentially theocentric in its character and form. History is interpreted not in the usual categories of economic enslavement and politcal tyranny, but in the categories of theology, in terms of the living Lord.

The book of Exodus is so important to Rylaarsdam because it locates revelation in history and that revelation creates a community of faith. This is the meaning of Sinai, the implementation of revelation, for revelation never stands alone and by itself.[30] The community of faith must internalize that revelation and create the forms that reflect their response in faith. It is Sinai that provides Exodus with its enduring meaning and its perpetual re-levance. Sinai stands for the methodical interpretation and im-

plementation of the faith which is the gift of revelation. The
community of faith is neither a mystical fellowship nor the consequence of moral demand. Instead, Sinai stands for the organic
and living relationship that exists between the social and
religious institutions of Israel and the revelatory event.
Further it means that Israel can take all forms and structures
and incorporate them into her faith community. It supports the
"protestant principle" that all things are secular, but they can
also become holy as they are related to the ultimate reality
which gives the community its existence and meaning. It is the
theocentric focus of Israel's faith that permits her to see the
unity of her life in the world.

It is from the viewpoint of the issues raised by the tension
of faith and history that Rylaarsdam moves to a discussion of
the relation of the Old Testament to the New.[31] In most discussions
of this relationship the issue is posed as a problem of the
Church with the OT. The OT may be either seen as a history of
failure and therefore of no revelatory significance for the
Christian (Bultmann), or the concepts and ideas of the OT are
thought to have been superceded and transcended by those of the
New (Liberalism). The bond and tension that relate the Old to
the New are seen by Rylaarsdam as centering on the issue of faith
and history, and that means for him the eschatological dimension.

The crux of the relationship is the problem of the NT.
Though on the one hand it interprets the Christ event as but one
other event in the history of salvation, there is on the other
hand the understanding of the Christ event as eschatological
event. From such a perspective history is swallowed up by faith,
and it is precisely this eschatological perspective that has
become increasingly unintellegible in the present age. The
finality and freedom of God's action were equated with or displaced by the finality of the event itself. The neo-reformation
theologies of Barth and Bultmann emphasized the recovery of the
eschatological interpretation of the Christ event. But, "the
finality of the Christ event remained Christocentric!"[32] And von

Rad, by making the relationship one of promise and fulfillment, merely continued the history of salvation interpretation which did not take seriously the eschatological dimension of the NT.

What raises the issue in a new and critical way is the shift from asking about the relevance of the eschatological faith for this world, to the more "secular" question of the relevance of this world of time, space and matter for the action of the God. We have been taught to read the OT in the light of the New and make it a Christian book, but this does not answer the contemporary question. We must interpret the NT in the light of the Old. Yet even this must not be done in such a way as to undercut the radical eschatological viewpoint of the NT. There is a solution, according to Rylaarsdam, in the radical theocentricity of the Scriptures which holds together both the continuities in time and space and the radical discontinuities that the eschatological perspective demands. Only in such a faith stance can one be open to haʿolam, which is both the world and the future. It is the finality of the Word of God, the decisiveness of his action, which is the constant. Here also is to be located the persistence of the divine purpose. For there is no fulfillment in history which exhausts its source in the ultimate mystery. Hope is possible because of this inexhaustible mystery of the dynamic Word (Act) of God. The continuity of both nature and of the people of God exemplify this mystery and rest on the finality of God in its goodness.

From this viewpoint the NT becomes the best commentary written on the OT. In the light of its eschatological perspective it interprets the faith, pointing to its understanding of the Christ event. The NT has thereby become the book for the new age. The OT reminds the community of faith, however, that only in a theocentric focus can faith and history be taken seriously.

III.  THE TWO COVENANTS

To be an Old Testament theologian is not only to be
grounded in the ethos and mythos of the OT, but also to have
one's understanding informed by the ethos and mythos of one's
own age.  Such a theologian is required to stand with feet
firmly planted in both worlds.  For this reason Rylaarsdam was
often called upon to speak in contexts which were not primarily
"biblical", and his writings are reflective of this dual aspect
of his thought.  He was concerned about race, poverty, education,
the problems of culture, the need for planning.  Yet all of them
ultimately came under the critique of the "biblical perspective",
the discussion being informed by the persistent themes and recurring motifs which informed biblical faith.

There was, however, one area which continued to claim his
concern and energy, the question of Jewish-Christian dialogue,
and throughout his scholarly career he was concerned to explore
avenues which he considered appropriate to the continuation of
that dialogue.  Not only the Hebrew Scriptures but also the
establishment of Israel as a modern state contributed to the
urgency of that question.[33]  Therefore, Rylaarsdam attempted to
participate in and contribute to the dialogue of Jew and Christian.
He was a member of the Colloquium on Judaism and Christianity at
the Divinity School of Harvard University in 1966, and helped to
establish a Jewish-Protestant Colloquium at the Divinity School
of the University of Chicago in 1963.  He was convinced that
history had shown that that dialogue was not only difficult but at
times impossible, and that the responsibility for the breakdown
rested heavily on the Christian.

The presuppositions for such a dialogue were considered to
be the common confession of the one living God and the mutual
recognition of each other's divine vocation.[34]  However, Rylaarsdam
was willing to admit that though the Jew need not recognize
Christianity's claim to its divine call the Christian could never
deny the validity of the Jewish claim.  The traditional view of

Jewish-Christian relationships which rests on a primarily
chronological view of history always tended to deny the vocation
of the Jew.  Christianity, for Rylaarsdam, must always bear its
witness in the context of the living witness of Judaism.  The
mystery of an eternal Israel always confronts the Church to
challenge any attempts to cut off the roots which are the source
of her life.  Therefore any traditional view of promise and
fulfillment tends to deny the Jewish claim to election.  For
this results only in an acknowledgement of debt to the Jew of
the past, and not of the present.

It is out of this concern for the Jewish-Christian dialogue
as well as his study of the Old Testament that Rylaarsdam
ultimately came to the conclusion that the primary categories
which inform the OT are the two covenants.[35]  In this he is not
referring to the categories of Old and New Covenants.  The two
covenants are not to be seen as having primarily a chronological
relationship.  Rather they are grounded in the very life and
existence of Israel and the Hebrew faith.  On the basis of their
paradoxical relationship one can understand both the varieties
of expression in the Old Testament and the differences between
Judaism and Christianity.

The first covenant is the covenant with Israel, the Sinai
and Shechem covenant, representing the basic tension of faith
and history.  The people and the land are the primary symbols
of this covenant, for they point to God's action in the particularities of history.  Here the basic motifs of promise and fulfillment are to be located.  The people of God are called into
being to be the elect nation, living on the land and open to the
future.  The way to transformation is by a reconfirmation of the
past; the future is both open and contingent.  Such a view informs
theological understanding by calling for a recitation of the
mighty acts of God as the avenue to the knowledge of God and
his ways in the world.  Ethically it defines the life of faith
as one of responsibility based on human volition.  The call of

faith is to do the right, to choose the good, to seek forgiveness of sins.

The second covenant represents a different view of faith. Here David and Zion, the King and the Temple, are symbols which reflect eternal verities. They stand for a transcendent world which is reflected in the eschatological tradition. This is the covenant of nature and grace. It is predicated on the world as a primordial past, on the foundation of an eternal order. Here contingency and relativity are overcome by a view of the eternal cosmos which finds its expression in this world. Any transformation in this world can take place only from a renewal ex fonte. The divine human relationship is perceived as rooted in an ontic relationship and predicated on the ancient customary law. The ethical life consists of being reckoned as right and the ultimate concern is to be regarded as sinless.

These two covenants contain tensions which defy complete resolution. They are polar aspects of the divine revelation to Israel. One is grounded in a history of salvation, in a series of divine acts in history, the other in an eschatological perspective which sees the divine reality as both Alpha and Omega. The basic differences can be summarized as: "the primordial and absolute over against the historical and contingent; the orientation to the past versus the orientation to the future; and a decreed divine determinism in tension with assumptions of human freedom and responsibility."[36]

So the shape of OT theology is neither linear nor circular, with a center, but an ellipse which contains two foci. These two foci of nature and grace and of history and faith become the basis for examining the various meanings of faith, both in ancient Israel and in the contemporary world. Within the OT itself we find the two foci being related to each other in a variety of permutations. In their interaction can be discerned the different expressions of the faith. By such a means both wisdom and prophecy can be held together, both history and apocalypticism have their commonalities and differences. Only in such a view can the whole OT be taken seriously as the occasion and source of faith.

In the two covenants J. Coert Rylaarsdam finds the unity of faith that is informed not only by the tensions of nature and grace and of faith and history but also between them. Here is the basis of his reconstructions of the faith of Israel and its relevance to contemporary theological understanding. Here is the uniqueness of his thought and his enduring contribution to both the study of the OT and of theology. Therefore I would take this occasion to express my appreciation of him as scholar, mentor and colleague and to dedicate this volume to him who has always sought to make an honest confession of the Holy Name.

## Footnotes

1. Cf. H. Arnold, *Near the Edge of Battle* (Chicago: The Divinity School Association, 1967) and R. W. Funk, "The Watershed of the American Biblical Tradition: The Chicago School, First Phase, 1892-1920," JBL 95 (1976) 4-22.

2. "...of Old Testament Theology," *Criterion* 11 (1971) 29.

3. "Introduction: The Chicago School - And After," *Transitions in Biblical Scholarship* (Chicago: University of Chicago, 1968) 15.

4. Chicago: University of Chicago, 1946.

5. *Word and Wisdom* (Lund: Ohlssons, 1947).

6. R. B. Y. Scott, "The Study of the Wisdom Literature," Int. 24 (1970) 23.

7. *Revelation,* 73.

8. *Revelation,* 98.

9. Cf. "What is the Ought in Race?," *Criterion* 4 (1965) 14.

10. *Proverbs, Ecclesiastes, Song of Solomon* (Richmond: John Knox, 1964, 135-160.

11. "The Song of Songs and Biblical Faith," *Biblical Research* 10 (1965) 1-18.

12. "Song of Songs," 18.

13. "The Matrix of Worship in the Old Testament," *Worship in Scripture and Tradition* (ed. M. H. Shepherd, Jr.; New York: Oxford University, 1963) 44-76.

14. "Matrix," 45.

15. "Atonement, Day of," IDB, 1. 316.

16. "Feasts and Fasts," IDB, 2. 261.

17. "Matrix," 61.

18. "Passover and the Feast of Unleavened Bread," IDB, 2. 667.

19.  "Feasts and Fasts," 262.

20.  "Matrix," 63.

21.  "Preface to Hermeneutics," _JR_ 30 (1950) 79.

22.  "Preface," 81.

23.  "The Problem of Faith and History in Biblical Interpretation," _JBL_ 77 (1958) 26-32.

24.  "Problems," 29.

25.  "The Recovery of the Bible," _The Chicago Theological Seminary Register_ 46 (1956) 2f.

26.  "Preface," 85.

27.  "Introduction and Exegesis of the Book of Exodus," (_IB_, 1; Nashville, Abingdon, 1952) 833-1099.

28.  "Exodus," 833.

29.  "Exodus," 848.

30.  "Exodus," 841.

31.  "The Old Testament and the New: Theocentricity, Continuity, Finality," _The Future as the Presence of Shared Hope_ (ed. Maryellen Muckenhirn; New York:  Sheed and Ward, 1969) 59-83.

32.  "The OT and the New," 66.

33.  "The Religious Issue of Israel," _Land Reborn_ 12 (1961) 16-19.

34.  "Common Ground and Difference," _JR_ 43 (1963) 261-70.

35.  "Jewish-Christian Relationship:  The Two Covenants and the Dilemmas of Christology," _JES_ 9 (1972) 249-70.

36.  "The Two Covenants," 262.

PART TWO:

UNDERSTANDING SCRIPTURE

# THE PRE-P NARRATIVE: A CHILDREN'S RECITAL?[1]

John F. X. Sheehan, S. J.

During the past generation of OT scholarship it has come to be widely recognized that the Pentateuch incorporates materials which reflect distinctly different cultic occasions in the religious environment of the early Israelites. Von Rad was among the first to argue at length for such a polarity, contending in his famous essay on "The Form-Critical Problem of the Hexateuch" that Deut 6:20-24 and 26:5b-9 are "creedal" formulae representing the core of the Pentateuch and that the Sinai material is "secondary" and "late."[2] Though various aspects of von Rad's interpretation have come under attack,[3] this work exerted an important influence on Pentateuchal scholarship. Martin Noth, for example, argued that at least the Sinai and Exodus traditions were separate and different.[4] Among other things he points out that while Psalm 105 tells the whole Exodus narrative it gives scant mention to Moses and Aaron,[5] that Moses is not mentioned in the historical credo,[6] and that Sinai is seldom mentioned outside the Pentateuch.[7]

There have been other suggestions of a polarity incorporated within our present Pentateuch. One school of OT scholarship finds evidence for gospel and law, kerygma and didache undergirding the oldest cultic memories.[8] We note also Ahlström's judgment that "Jebusite" and "Shilohite" streams of religion flowed together in Jerusalem.[9]

As it happened, I was re-reading the von Rad material at the same time I was reading page-proofs for a collection of essays on the OT more or less united around the theme of the threshing floor.[10] In connection with the writing of those essays, I had had occasion to re-examine some of the Ugaritic material and was struck by a passage in 2 Aqht V which reads:

6.  ...ytb bap t̲g̱r tḥt
7.  adrm. dbgrn. ydn
8.  dn. almnt. yt̲pt. t̲pt. ytm.[11]

The text says of Dan'el, a Ugaritic hero, "He is seated at the mouth of the opening among the noble ones who are on the threshing floor. He gives judgment to widows. He makes judgment for orphans."[12] For a variety of reasons, threshing floors were sometimes used as judicial courts in the ancient Near East.[13] There is extra-biblical evidence for this.[14] That the "threshing floor" is a center for "cultic activity" is also well-known.[15]

At the same time my mind was pre-occupied with another element of Jewish religious life, and from these three strands there began to take shape the central idea of the present essay. There is a well-known reference in the Bar Mitzvah ritual to the gratitude of the father that the son is now responsible for his own sins and that the father is no longer responsible as he was until the lad reached puberty.[16] The writer cheerfully admits that it is a great distance from the Ugaritic threshing floor to the Bar Mitzvah ritual. One is unlikely to be much moved by Rashi's judgment that Bar Mitzvah as a conveyor of obligation was "in the category of biblical laws as it was given to Moses at Sinai."[17] Still there are a plethora of references in Talmudic and Midrashic material to "obligation" beginning at 13,[18] and it is a sound principle of historiography to presume that the dynamic originates at some point earlier than that to which the historian can push his investigation. The idea of "obligation" beginning at 13, which continues even to the present day, can be traced back with certainty to the second century. A tradition that the boy was "obliged" to fast at 13 can be traced back to second temple times.[19] We can safely presume that the idea does not originate at the precise moment when it first becomes accessible to the historian. We must admit, of course, that we simply do not know how much earlier the idea is than our evidences for it. We can presume, however, that it is earlier, and that is sufficient for ur purposes at this juncture.

The idea which emerged from reflection on these strands of
evidence can be stated in the form of three tentative hypotheses:

1. that the Pentateuch as we have it is undergirded by
   two polar liturgies;

2. that these liturgieṣ mirror the differing views of
   religion as presented to adults and to children;

3. that the "adult liturgy" involved much stress on
   obligation, while the children's liturgy was virtually
   "obligation free."

The present paper will examine material generally in connection
with the "children's aspect" of the religion presented in the OT.


I


Before launching into this topic, however, a word should be
said about the "adult liturgy," the liturgy of obligation and
judgment.  While a detailed examination of the "judgment-cult"
lies beyond the scope of this paper, we may mention briefly the
Massah (Exod 17:7; Deut 6:16; 9:22; 33:8; Ps 95:8) and Meribah
(Exod 17:7; Num 20:13; 20:24; 27:14; Deut 33:8; Ps 81:7; 95:8;
106:32) incidents, which seem to indicate the presence of such a
cult.  The antiquity of these stories is indicated by the fact
that although they are dispute and testing stories, there is some
question in their present form on who disputed with whom or who
judged the dispute over what.  A. Klostermann[20] was the first to
point up some of the possibilities here, and the parallel he drew
between a Vorlage of Deuteronomy and the work of the Icelandic
Grágás (laws formulated from the individual decisions of pilgrim
judges) was a bold stroke at the time.  What may have looked like
a "bold stroke" in 1907 when Klostermann wrote looks almost sober
today, however, in light of the work of Parry and Lord which
pointed up parallels between oral composition in 20th century

Yugoslavia and any other oral composition.[21]

There is one other interesting extra-biblical allusion that is helpful here. In the Ugaritic materials, the chief god prior to the emergence of Baal is tpt nhr (Judge River), frequently called Prince Sea (zbl ym). Sea and River in many ancient literatures fall into a pattern of judgment.

For example, Lord observes on Gen 32:22-25:

> There is evidence in older traditions that it was not an angel with whom Jacob struggled but a river spirit whom he had to overcome before the river could be passed.[22]

Jacob is in the company of classical heroes, for Achilles must wrestle with a river and Odysseus struggle with the sea.[23] It is at least interesting to note that Jacob's struggle with the river-- if it was such--does not take place in the P-narrative.

Eduard Meyer has pointed out[24] that Wellhausen was the first to see that Meribah could be related to waters of dispute. His reference is to an edition of the Prolegomena that is not available to the present writer:

> Me Meríbah, das Haderwasser, wird in Wahrheit, wie Wellhausen, Prolog. 348 erkannt hat, das Prozesswasser bedeuten, d.h. die heilige Quelle, an der Gericht gehalten wird; das wird dadurch bestätigt dass die Quelle von Qades, Gen 14.7 gerade zu Gerichtquelle ain mispat genannt wird. ...Massa etwa die Prüfüngsstätte, mag eine benachbarte Lokalität gewesen sein, wo etwa der Zeugenbeweis geführt wurde oder vielleicht der Prozessführende ein Gottesurteil sein Recht zu erweisen hatte.[25]

The usages made of the words and themes of Massah, Meribah, and Qadesh differ in the various sources. Let us cite Pedersen:

> ...it is evident that in the Blessing of Moses (the struggle) is regarded as a fight for the word of Yahweh and his covenant. In this, Levi has disregarded

all consideration for family, for fathers, brothers and
sons and the struggle seems to have been assigned to
Massah and Meribah... In reality, there is every reason
to suppose that Meribah means "legal dispute" and the
two names indicate a place in which sentences were pronounced.[26]

In his study Sacral Kingship Aubrey Johnson finds a number
of OT references to nhr and the struggle between the Divinity and
the "primeval ocean with its multitude of waters and its many
currents,"[27] and sees the Ugaritic conflict: deities, zbl ym and
tpt nhr as part of that. Perhaps this is so, but since "Judge
River" lost the combat, he must have won his title in an earlier
version of the legends. It seems probable that what we have here
is a place where a primeval myth of struggles between deities and
earth-forces, between heroes and bodies of water, came to rest on
an historical memory of "judgments" involving conflicts that took
place between real historical individuals. Such a process is not
a unique one, but is a fairly uniform mode of behavior when myth
and history meet.[28]

The notion of "judgment" is complex, which may explain the
confusion at Massah and Meribah and the varied ideas which Pedersen
and Johnson treat under the rubric of "judgment." But there is
another a priori reason for expecting a cult of judgment, whatever
the nature of that judgment may be. There is always a near perfect
identity between "heavenly" activity and "cultic" activity. Whatever God does in Heaven, he must do also in the liturgy. So if
God is in any sense a Divine Judge in the OT, and he surely is,
then there ought to be some liturgical correspondence to that.
Mowinckel writes:

> To 'what happens' in the cultic drama corresponds what
> happens in Heaven; he that sits enthroned in the Temple
> is the one who sits enthroned up there and sends thunder
> and rain and 'renews the surface of the earth' and with
> awe all kings and persons ought to recognize that he is
> at the same time the god of Israel.[29]

Finally, there is one more suggestion which lends plausibility to the thesis that the OT encompasses a liturgical polarity:
one of the old classics in the study of liturgical texts notes that
one and the same drive sends a man to the theater and to church,
that the church activity originally embraced both entertainment
and obligation. Only the modern age saw the need of separating
these two.[30] One of the new classics, the assembled works of
Claude Lévi-Strauss, insists that "the whole structure of primitive
thought is binary."[31] Therefore, if there is any indication for
the existence of one half of the dichotomy (the judgment cult),
there is good reason to suppose that the second half, the non-
judgment portion, exists as well. It is to this second aspect
that I now turn.


II


If there is a "judgment" aspect, ought there not be a "non-
judgment" aspect? While I was investigating the hypothesis that
there would be evidences in various places of the second half of
the polarity, I came upon Sean McEvenue's The Narrative Style of
the Priestly Writer,[32] which interprets P as "children's literature."[33] McEvenue's study begins with the assumption that Elliger
was correct in its definition of P and Pg.[34] Briefly put, Pg is
the "priestly narrative," the original and older portion of P;
the remainder of P with its complicated legislation is the work of
(a) later author(s). While I have considerable differences of
opinion with both McEvenue and Elliger, it is clear that I lean
heavily on the contributions of the former. At least one other
recent effort, that of Soggin, has been made to find some evidences
for something like a "children's recital."[35] The advantage of
McEvenue's method of approach was that it opened a large block of
narrative material, Pg, for examination. For a number of reasons
one may differ with him, following the contemporary consensus re-

garding the "late" date of Pg.[36] In fact, though, it probably does
not matter whether or not Pg as we have it is late, for it is frequently acknowledged that the present text bears witness to much
earlier material. Van Seters has recently written:

> The question of the relationship of P to the pre-
> priestly sources is an important issue...and one
> which I do not regard as clearly settled. P. Volz
> raised the question forty years ago as to whether
> P was to be considered as an independent narrative
> source, or simply a priestly editor who supplemented
> the earlier corpus with legal discussions, cultic
> institutions and theological discussions.[37]

But even the more complicated "later" discussions may flow from
earlier material. P. J. Budd notes, "direction as a priestly
function must have deep pre-exilic roots. For one thing, it dealt
with issues arising from ancient taboos."[38] Finally, those scholars
who hold for the "principle of coagulation" as an ancient device of
composition, would have to conclude from the name-lists and genealogies in P that it contains very ancient sources, for in this view
all later material "coagulates" around the earliest forms of
material, which are inevitably name-lists and genealogies.[39]

The reasonableness of finding in Pg a locus for a children's
recital which is ancient is further enhanced by von Rad's remarks
on the antiquity of the P material:

> With the Priestly Document, however, the discovery
> that it contains old, and indeed very old, material
> has come as a surprise, considering the wholesale
> late dating earlier attributed to it.[40]

He further notes:

> It is obvious that a body of varied cultic material
> (Ps) has been secondarily inserted into P...[But]
> since this literature in contrast with JE had never
> left the sacral sphere, we have probably to reckon
> with a much steadier process of elaboration.[41]

Given the intrinsic conservatism of religious practice, von Rad's remarks are not surprising. Mowinckel in his Religion und Kultus shows the conservatism of the god of the "judgment cult" who became the God of Israel:

Wir wissen nur, dass [Jahwe] schon vor Moses Zeit in
Kadesch von den Halbnomaden verehrt wurde und in
Verbindung mit Rechtssprechung und Orakelwesen stand,
wie er wohl auch als Spender des Segens der dortigen
Quellen galt. Dann wurde er der Bundesgott Israels,
der Vorkämpfer seines Volkes, der Hüter der alten
Sitte und des Rechts. Im Kanaan hat er dann allmählich
alle die Funktionen übernommen, die man dem Ba$^c$al, dem
Hadad usw. beilegte: er ist Himmelsherr, Spender von
Regen und Fruchtbarkeit, Lenker des Alls, Herr der
Geschichte und der Natur geworden.[42]

In other words, the tendency of the religious dynamic is that it retains everything from the past--except where this contradicts a later and more powerful dynamic.[43] All cult then eventually contains traces of something that no longer makes sense (unless it has been recast slightly to fit a new meaning).

Nor is this innate conservatism, the drive to preserve the archaic or to archaize, limited to what is already demonstrated to be religious and cultic. In a recent work M. Seale argues that the "nomadic" origins of the Hebrew Bible are insufficiently stressed:

It is well known that nomadic institutions and patterns
of culture are remarkably tenacious, persisting for...
thousands of years after a given tribe has settled.[44]

In his preface to the translation of Noth's work, Bernhard Anderson attributes to Gunkel and Dilthey the following view of exegesis:

Exegesis is not a science but an art in which the
critic with sensitivity and imagination seeks to
're-create' (nachschaffen) the situation in life of
the people which find expression in literary works.[45]

Anderson then refers to H. A. Hodges' work on Dilthey. Hodges
sees in Dilthey the judgment that a skilled reader can re-create
or re-experience those very life processes which led to the
printed page. "In the operation of understanding itself, the life-
process is reversed."[46] Perhaps we could put it another way. A
centuries-long progression led to a given text. By contemplating
the text long enough we can come to know not only the meaning of
these lines, but we can re-experience the life-process which produced them. This then is my methodology. For some persons this
process may look much too subjective. They should be reminded,
however, that the OT is not a volume of empirical science, but a
work of art.

One of the most obvious features of P[g] to someone who reads
it at a single sitting is that it is virtually "obligation free."
One's first reaction is disbelief. This is, after all, religious
literature. Is not obligation the very stuff of religious literature?

Not for P[g]. The narrative consists of edifying stories, generally with happy endings. The great partriarchs all die in bed
surrounded in their old age by loving relatives and grandchildren.
Since there is so little stress placed on obligations, the two that
are cited (directly and indirectly) leap off the page at the reader.
The first is blunt enough, "The man-child who is not circumcised
shall be cut off from his people. He has violated the convenant"
(Gen 17:14). There is one further reference to something which
smacks of obligation. When the marriage of Esau with a foreigner
takes place, the commentator notes, "This was a grief to Isaac and
Rebecca" (Gen 26:35). Later the mother of Jacob begins to fear
that the same thing may happen to Jacob and she sighs, "If Jacob
should take a wife from among strangers, then what is my life worth
to me?" (Gen 27:46). It is difficult not to see here a remark aimed
at a special audience, the pubescent male. He is being taught, in
preparation for the rite of circumcision, that relatively soon he
will confront at least two obligations. One is to submit to circum-

cision. The other is to defer to the wishes of the community in his choice of a wife.

These observations take on an added cogency in light of the work of anthropologist Victor Turner and his development of the notion of "liminality," which he borrowed from van Gennep and developed in the following fashion. In most rites of passage the initiands go through a prolonged period of being on the limen (threshhold) of new responsibilities. While in the period of liminality, their obligations are much curtailed. "Ordinary rules and relationships are suspended where they are concerned."[47] It is not that eventual rules and regulations are not to be important for the mature member of the group, but "liminality represents the mid-point of transition in a status sequence between two positions."[48]

It should be pointed out here that the OT itself bears witness to the idea of adolescent circumcision among the Hebrews. At least that is the way Helmer Ringgren understands Genesis 34, Exod 4:25 and Josh 5:2-3.[49] It is difficult to read Exod 4:25 and its reference to Moses as the "bridegroom of blood" in any other way.

> Moses is called a 'bridegroom of blood' (ḥatan dāmîm) after his circumcision. The Hebrew word ḥatan, which designates a relationship through marriage, is derived from a root that in Arabic refers to circumcision.[50]

If ḥatan dāmîm is preparation for marriage, it is surely remote preparation for marriage. It is hard to see circumcision as part of a wedding night ritual!

One of McEvenue's most insightful observations is the following:

> The phrase bᵉ ᶜesem hayyom hazzeh occurs only in priestly literature. In Pᵍ it is used 4 times and always for a day in which a divine command is fulfilled: Gen 7, 13, Noah and his family enter the ark; Gen 17, 23, 26, Abraham carries out the law of circumcision; Ex 12, 41, the Israelites leave Egypt. The expression seems to carry with it the idea of memorable [sic], i.e., a feast day.[51]

McEvenue has correctly seen here an allusion to a type of liturgical event. While Childs has shown clearly that occurrences of the root zkr are frequently indicative of liturgical re-presentation, such are not the only indicators.[52] The notion of "re-presentation" might bear some review here. The least common denominator of the idea, for many religions, is this: a mysteriously "saving event" that is historically past is made somehow to be effectively present. Or as Childs puts it:

> Actualization is the process by which a past event is
> contemporized for a generation removed in time and
> space from the original event. When Israel responded
> to the continuing imperative of her tradition through
> her memory, that moment in historical time likewise
> became an Exodus experience. Not in the sense that
> later Israel again crossed the Red Sea. This was an
> irreversible, once-for-all event. Rather, Israel
> entered the same redemptive reality of the Exodus gener-
> ation.[53]

What Childs has called "actualization" is often called "sacramental re-presentation" in other religious traditions. Precisely because the concept has become so sophisticated in modern theologizing, it is easy to overlook its relatively simple roots in the ancient forms. In modern Roman writing on the Eucharist, it is difficult to overstate the force of "sacramental re-presentation." For Schillebeeckx, "There are two aspects to Jesus' redemptive acts; they take place in history, yet they have a perennial character."[54] In this regard a reading of Bouyer's classic summary of the notion "sacred time"[55] might be helpful. Yves de Montscheuil says in talking of the signe efficace:

> Il semble absurde de dire que la messe produirait
> ce sacrifice de la croix, qui s'est accompli au
> Calvaire. Mais cela doit être bien compris. Au
> Calvaire, le Christ s'est sacrifié personnellement,
> et il a accompli en lui le sacrifice de toute l'humanité
> prédestinée. Ce sacrifice est réellement accompli...

> L'effet de la messe est précisément, si l'on peut dire,
> que ce qui en un sens est déjà fait, se fasse. En
> un sens, elle fait être, elle fait passer en acte
> quelque chose qui appartient au contenu réel du sacri-
> fice de la croix.[56]

There is a simple common denominator in the notion that Childs
finds in the OT liturgies and that de Montscheuil and the others
find in the Christian Eucharist. It is the idea that somehow
the liturgical sacramental system "destroys time," that the
barrier disappears.

As I have said, modern writers on OT theology tend to bring
to the OT liturgies the more sophisticated understanding of the
"time-destruction" idea with which their various denominations
have endowed them. But the notion is, at base, a fairly simple
one. Dorothy Eggan in writing of a "children's liturgy" among
the Hopi Indians points out that it is the role of any such
liturgy to destroy time. This is part of its effectiveness in
the inculcation of values. She describes it as being an effective
substitute for theater, church, school and jail. For those who
conducted the liturgy, "it was a very real substitute also for the
psychoanalytic couch, since in reaffirmation, restatement, and
reliving of beliefs and experience, much doubt and bitterness was
worked out."[57] More important for our purposes, she notes:

> For the learners, related patterns of Hopi philosophy
> and behavior were absorbed in an emotionally charged
> atmosphere which tended to fuse reality and fantasy
> (her emphases) and to make the resulting patterns
> more rewarding for 'ego-synthesis.'[58]

There is a fact of human experience to which we can have re-
course here: it is that "destructiveness of time" is something
that takes place always and easily, not only in structured liturgies
but in the world of child's play and pretense. A number of writers
have pointed to the relationship between fantasy, games, and "destruction of time." Wallach's study of creativity shows the precise

advantage of the fantasy life to be that it can cause time to cease to exist.[59] His survey concludes by showing that the ability to engage in fantasy and reach a kind of timelessness correlates with "inter-action with parents [in a way] that would involve fantasy such as games and storytelling."[60] Piaget gave the name "symbolic games" to those games that specialized in making reality yield to the imagination, games of "representing realities that are out of the present perceptual field."[61] It is more than interesting for our purposes that the ability to fantasize in play is at its apex in the age-group for which our children's narrative would have been written, the early adolescent.[62]

I would like to suggest that what we have then in the narrations which follow $b^{ec}esem\ hayyom\ hazzeh$ are the earliest impositions of "re-enactment." With a little adult encouragement, the child's ability to use fantasy to put time to one side was used by the most ancient Hebrew teachers. With their encouragement, $b^{ec}esem\ hayyom\ hazzeh$, he relives the experience of Noah and his family entering the art (Gen 7:13); $b^{ec}esem\ hayyom\ hazzeh$, he relives the leaving of Egypt with the other Hebrews (Exod 12:41). And then, all too painfully, he relives the experience of the earlier circumcised adolescent males of Abraham's household.

It is in preparation for this that the narrative of encouragement was composed. To give him courage for this, he spent some time in the period of liminality where normal rules do not hold. Therefore there was no need in the most intense period of preparation to take on the obligations of the covenant, and so to devote time in the narrative itself to hearing about the obligations of that covenant. We have noted that in $P^g$ there are two exceptions: 1. to undergo circumcision, 2. to defer to the wishes of the community in the choice of a bride. These could not be put to one side even in the period of liminality, since this limen culminated immediately in the former obligation and in preparation for the second.

Perhaps we have seen enough by now to establish the possibility that the P-narrative has become the locus where an ancient
ritual took up its abode. There are other loci in the OT where
vestigial evidences of a similar ritual occur. We note, for
example, the texts cited by Soggin in the article mentioned
earlier:[63] Exod 12:26; 13:14; Deut 6:20; Josh 4:6; 4:21; and
22:24. All of these passages make mention of young children
asking the question, "what does it mean?", and of hearing
responses which touch on the magnalia dei and, with one possible
exception, avoid the question of any obligation that derives from
those magnalia. Soggin sees all these passages as catecheses, and
liturgical catecheses at that, in which the question is to be asked
by the child and the formulated answer given by the parent.[64] So
are "explained" such diverse traditions as "die Traditionen des
Auszugs, der Landnahme, und des Gesetzes...auch wenn sie wahrschein-
lich, zu Beginn unabhängif von einander standen."[65] (It is beyond
the scope of this article that Soggin sees here the historicizing
of liturgy rather than, as would the present writer, the liturgizing of history.) Only in Deut 6:20 is the question clearly connected
with "personal obligations"; otherwise, the question precedes a
reference to a great historical event or to the sort of magnalia
which ought to be recited in a period of liminality.

To what source do these catechetical questions belong? The
answer is not clear. Soggin cites Martin Noth and Ivan Engnell to
the effect that Exod 12:24-27 and 13:1, 16 are a "deuterono-
mistisch stilisierten Zusatz an J-element."[66] Still, "schon in
sehr früher Zeit" it became embedded into the theme of the
"Hinausführung aus Ägypten."[67] He follows Noth also in seeing
Josh 4:6 and 21 as Deuteronomistic.[68] Josh 22:24 is seen as
probably re-used by P.[69]

It is not necessary for the purposes of this article to dis-
prove all the above. It would be possible for the same ancient

ritual to have been absorbed into more than one source. One wonders, though, at the reasoning which might have led Soggin (and many others) to the Deuteronomistic identification. Was the asking of the question enough to cause these passages to be so identified? Could more of these passages be attributed to Pre-P in some way? One wonders if the Deuteronomistic identification stemmed from the same sort of problem that Wellhausen confronted: because of his late dating of P, he had to use an involuted explanation of the fact that P preserves the old pesach formula celebrated at home and not "before Yahweh." In fact, because so much of P is early, it easily retains the old family pesach.[70]

In another work Soggin described chapters 3-5 of Joshua as an historicizing of liturgy.[71] As I have said, his arguments equally apply to a liturgizing of history, or at least a "heightened" history that becomes liturgy. I suggest that the implications of Soggin's insights are wider than he realized, that the questions here and those cited in his article point back to an adolescent service, probably orally composed, and in the earliest phase of OT composition. I maintain that the "kernel" of the service is detectable and that a cataloguing of the earliest parts of the P-narrative flowing from the service is probably possible, although beyond the scope of this article. The likely existence of the service can be buttressed by theoretical but valid argumentation from what we know of life in earliest "Israel." Moreover, I suggest that diligent search of the OT will probably come up with other echoes of the catechesis which formed part of this ancient service.

At this stage, I suggest a reading of chapters 3-5 of Joshua and a comparing of the liturgical movements and stage directions with a passage from the P-narrative, Exod 14:15-18, 21-23, 26, 28-9. This passage is defined as P-narrative in the strictest sense.[72] It contains rubrics, "stretch forth your rod," v.16, a procession, v.22, a rubric, v.26, the dramatic event, v.28, and a reprise, v.29. But for the lack of an introductory question, this passage could be clearly recognized as the liturgy of which Soggin

spoke in discussing Josh 4:6 and 4:21. Did the original catechetical question about the ceremony's meaning disappear in conflation
with Yahweh's question in v.15, "What does this cry mean?"

There are surely "echoes" of the adolescent narrative in other
texts. Some of them may be quite early echoes, imbedded in later
material. Thus, Psalm 78: "what we have heard and known for ourselves and what our fathers have told us, must not be withheld from
their descendants but handed on to the next generation" (3-4); "He
gave our ancestors strict orders to teach it to their children" (6);
"and these in turn were to tell their own children" (7); and Ps 44:
1-2: "God, we have heard with our own ears. Our fathers have told
us of the deeds you performed in their days, in days long ago."
Deut 32:7-14 is a long paean of positive memories of Yahweh's saving
acts, and we note that it is introduced: "Think back on the days
of old, think over the years through the ages. Ask of your father,
let him teach you; ask your elders, let them enlighten you."

In a classic English translation of Wellhausen, the famous
statement appears, "Not because they sacrifice, but because they
teach do the priests appear as pillars of the religious order of
things."[73] It should be noted here that "priesthood" in the period
which concerns us was surely not the formal office that it later
became. Soggin cites Köhler's observation that in early Israel,
the father of the family was the person responsible for the education of the sons. Joachim Wach had long since recognized that
priesthood is essentially little more than the formalization of
the father's role.[74] Perhaps as certain aspects of priesthood
such as "sacrifice" and "verdict" became more complicated, they
then became the work of professionals. "Instruction" in a pre-
dogmatic theological age could much longer remain the province
of the father of the family.

But the dynamic worked both ways. In Judges 17 we read of the
travelling "Levite" in a story that is hardly redolent of sacerdo-
tal sophistication. Michah urges the young man to "stay and be a
father and a priest to me" (v.10). Budd had suggested that "it is

possible that the priest used narrative as a teaching device."[75]
It is likely. All fathers in ancient Israel so used narrative,
and the priest was a father.

Thus, by reading the P-narrative in a manner suggested by
Dilthey, we see evidences for an adolescent circumcision ritual.
The narrative as a whole came to be used as a teaching device.
In its earlier phase, the emotional fusion of reality and fantasy
made circumcision somewhat easier and the adoption of a value-set
more likely. Since it is written for liminands, the P-narrative
is relatively obligation-free. These liminands fairly easily re-
lived experiences through sacramental re-presentation, since they
were still quite young and accustomed to the time-destruction
that is inherent in childhood games and fantasy.

## Notes

1. This is excerpted from an unpublished paper delivered at the University of Uppsala, Sweden. The paper was written under a grant from the <u>American Council of Learned Societies</u>.

2. G. von Rad, *The Problem of the Hexateuch and Other Essays* (New York: McGraw-Hill, 1966) 1-78.

3. Cf. E. W. Nicholson, *Deuteronomy and Tradition* (Philadelphia Fortress, 1967). The book itself is an attempt to come to terms with some of von Rad's theses. Bibliographical treatment of other such attempts is unusually thorough throughout the book.

4. M. Noth, *A History of Pentateuchal Traditions* (Trans. with an introduction by B. W. Anderson; Englewood Cliffs, N.J.: Prentice-Hall, 1972; German original, Stuttgart: Kohlhammer, 1948). Further references will be cited Noth-Anderson.

5. Ibid., 157.

6. Ibid., 156.

7. Ibid., 60.

8. So does F. M. Cross (*Canaanite Myth and Hebrew Epic* [Cambridge: Harvard, 1973] 83-90) sum up (albeit without approval) the "History-of-Redemption" school.

9. G. Ahlström, *Aspects of Syncretism in Israelite Religion* (Lund: Gleerup, 1963) 9.

10. J. Sheehan, *The Threshing Floor* (New York: Paulist, 1972).

11. C. H. Gordon, *Ugaritic Textbook* (Rome: Pontifical Biblical Institute, 1965) 248.

12. Cf. Deut 10:17-18.

13. Cf. 1 Kgs 22:10.

14. C. H. Gordon (*Orientalia* 12 [1943] 65 n. 1) cites a Nuzu text <u>i-na [ma] ag-ra-at-ti uš-te-si-wa-ni</u> (not his own transliteration, but one from a previously published text) and translates it: "in the threshing floor he hailed me to court." The root of <u>magrattu</u>, Gordon points out, is <u>grn</u> as "threshing floor" in Ugaritic.

15. Cf. for example, Ahlström *Aspects*, 38 n. 3.

43

16. *Encyclopaedia Judaica,* (Jerusalem: Keter, 1972) <u>sub verbo</u> <u>Bar</u> Mitzvah, 243-248. The reference here is in col. 244.

17. Ibid.

18. Ibid.

19. Ibid.

20. A. Klostermann, *Der Pentateuch* (Leipzig: Deichert, 1907) 348-428.

21. A. B. Lord, *The Singer of Tales* (Cambridge: Harvard, 1960).

22. Cf. ibid., 197.

23. Ibid.

24. E. Meyer, *Die Israeliten and Ihre Nachbarstämme,* (Halle: Niemeyer, 1906).

25. Ibid., 55.

26. J. Pedersen, *Israel Its Life and Culture,* (4 vols.; London: Oxford Univeristy, 1926) III-IV, 172. (He may only be following Meyer here.)

27. A. Johnson, *Sacral Kingship in Early Israel,* (2nd ed., Cardiff: University of Wales, 1967) 67 n. 1.

28. Unpublished notes of E. R. Leach are quoted to this effect in *Structuralism: A Reader,* (Ed. M. Lane, London: Cape, 1970) 322.

29. S. Mowinckel, *The Psalms in Israel's Worship* (New York: Abingdon, 1967) I, 174. This same basic notion is developed 114-115.

30. J. Harrison, *Ancient Art and Ritual* (New York: Henry Holt, 1913) 9-10.

31. Cf. E. Leach, *Claude Lévi-Strauss* (New York: Viking, 1970) 92. Cf. 65-7 where the idea is developed in some detail.

32. S. McEvenue, *The Narrative Style of the Priestly Writer* (Rome: Pontifical Biblical Institute, 1971).

33. Ibid., 3-5.

34. K. Elliger, "Sinn and Ursprung der priesterlichen Geschichtserzählung," <u>ZTK</u> 49 (1952) 121-142.

44

35.  J. A. Soggin, "Kultätiologische Sagen und Katechese im Hexateuch," *VT* 10 (1960) 341-347.

36.  McEvenue, *Narrative Style,* 19.

37.  J. Van Seters, *Abraham in History and Tradition* (New Haven: Yale, 1975) 125-126.

38.  P. J. Budd, "Priestly Instruction in Pre-Exilic Israel," *VT* 23 (1973) 7.

39.  T. B. L. Webster, *From Mycenae to Homer* (London:  Methuen, 1958) 185.

40.  G. von Rad, *Old Testament Theology* (New York:  Harper and Row, 1967) I, 232.

41.  Ibid., 233.

42.  S. Mowinckel, *Religion und Kultus* (Göttingen:  Vandenhoeck & Ruprecht, 1953) 43.

43.  C. H. Gordon writes in his review of Von Soden's *Grundriss der Akkadischen Grammatik* in <u>Orientalia</u> 22 (1953) 231, that all ritual texts tend to be linguistically "archaic or archaized."

44.  M. Seale, *The Desert Bible* (London:  Weidenfeld and Nicholson, 1974) 14.  (He goes on throughout the book to prove his point rather well from linguistic evidence.)

45.  Noth-Anderson, xviii.

46.  H. A. Hodges, *Wilhelm Dilthey: An Introduction* (London: Routledge and Kegan Paul, 1944) 122.

47.  Turner's position is so summed up by Aylward Shorter in his *Africal Culture and the Christian Church* (New York:  Orbis, 1974) 205.

48.  V. Turner, "Passages, Margins, and Poverty:  Religious Symbols of Communitas," *Worship* 46 (1972) 398.

49.  H. Ringgren *Israelite Religion* (Philadelphia:  Fortress, 1966) 203.  See also <u>hatana</u> in E. W. Lane, *An Arabic-English Lexicon* (8 vols. London:  Williams and Norgate, 1965) 4. 703-704.

50.  Ibid.

51.  McEvenue, *Narrative Style,* 61 n. 55.

52. B. S. Childs, *Memory and Tradition in Israel* (SBT 37; Naperville: Allenson, 1962).

53. Ibid., 85.

54. E. Schillebeeckx, *Christ the Sacrament of the Encounter with God* (New York: Sheed and Ward, 1963) 55-9. Schillebeeckx differs with much earlier Roman speculation about the nature of the Eucharist. Hence, his argumentation flowing from "sacramental re-presentation" shows how mainstream this material is.

55. L. Bouyer, *Rite and Man* (South Bend: Notre Dame, 1963) 189-206.

56. Y. de Montscheuil, *Mélanges Théologiques* (Paris: Aubier, 1946) 55.

57. D. Eggan, "The Personal Use of Myth in Dreams," *Myth, a Symposium* (Bloomington: University of Indiana, 1958) 66-67.

58. Ibid.

59. M. Wallach, "Creativity," *Manual of Child Psychology* (Ed. P. Mussen, New York: Wiley, 1970) 1259.

60. Ibid., 1261.

61. J. Piaget, "Piaget's Theory" [sic], *Manual of Child Psychology* (Ed. P. Mussen; New York: Wiley, 1970) 708.

62. J. L. Singer, "Imagery and Daydreaming," *Handbook of General Psychology* (Ed. B. Wolman; Englewood-Cliffs, N. J.: Prentice-Hall, 1973) 390.

63. Soggin, "Kultätiologische Sagen."

64. Ibid., 345.

65. Ibid., 345-346.

66. Ibid., 342.

67. Ibid., 343.

68. Ibid.

69. Ibid.

70. Cf. M. Weinfeld, *Deuteronomy and the Deuteronomic School* (Oxford: Clarendon, 1972) 216-217, n. 2.

71. Soggin, *Le Livre de Josué*, (Neuchâtel: de la Chaux Niestlé, 1970) 41.

72. Elliger's version of Pᵍ cited in McEvenue, *Narrative Style*, 189.

73. Budd, "Priestly Instruction," 1. He so quotes Sutherland's 1885 translation. Some German editions make the word "teach" perhaps not totally accurate here. The edition that Sutherland uses is not at the present writer's disposal. In any event, the distinction between "teach," simpliciter, and "give torah-explanation" is not absolutely important for our purposes.

74. J. Wach, *Sociology of Religion* (Chicago: University of Chicago, 1944) 62.

75. Budd, "Priestly Instruction," 6.

# KING JEHU -- A PROPHET'S MISTAKE*
## Gösta W. Ahlström

One morning in the year 841 B.C. a young man wearing a prophet's mantle made his way over the river Jordan and began to climb
through one of the wadies up to the Transjordanian plateau.   He
continued east to Ramoth-Gilead at the so-called "King's Highway."
Reaching the city he had little trouble locating its small fortress,[1] the headquarters of the Israelite army which was then at
war with the Aramean kingdom of Damascus.   He entered the fortress
through the southern gate, and passing the guards' room he found
the officers in the main chamber.   We may imagine that they were
discussing the recent military setback and what strategical move
to take next, or that they were airing their dissatisfaction with
the political situation, which the war had not noticeably improved.
Joram, the king of Israel and commander-in-chief, was not present;
he had been wounded in the battle and thus had left temporarily
for his palace in Jezreel (2 Kgs 8:28f.).

When the young man saw the officers he asked to see their
general, Jehu, in private, claiming to have a confidential message
for him.   Alone with Jehu in a smaller chamber, the prophet poured
out some olive oil from a little flask which he had brought with
him and anointed the general's head with it, repeating the words
which his prophet-master, Elisha, had told him:   "Thus says
Yahweh, the god of Israel, I anoint you king for the people of
Yahweh, for Israel" (2 Kgs 9:6).   Having uttered a few more words,
presumably about Jehu destroying the reigning Omride dynasty, the
young man opened another door and ran away.   When Jehu rejoined
the other officers he told them only that the young man was a
madman (a common description of a prophet in the ancient Near
East)[2] and thus they should pay no attention to his ravings.
But when they finally learned the truth, they paid homage to
their commander by putting their garments on top of the steps and
hailing him as the new king (2 Kgs 9:11-13).   A <u>coup d'etat</u> had
begin.

Jehu wasted no time. He ordered the gates of the city closed to prevent anyone from leaving Ramoth-Gilead to tell the king and the court in Jezreel about the mutiny (2 Kgs 9:15f.). He assembled some of his troops and mounting his war chariot sped quickly toward Jezreel. We may imagine that not far outside the city of Ramoth-Gilead a lonely figure was hurrying in the same direction. Perhaps he hid himself behind some thorny bushes so as not to be seen by the man he had anointed. He had fulfilled his mission, and for the rest of his life he would be a silent spectator of the unfortunate Jehu regime which he, at the behest of his prophet-master, had inaugurated.

When Jehu arrived in Jezreel he promptly killed king Joram and mortally wounded king Azariah of Judah, Joram's ally in the war against the Arameans. He ordered the palace eunuchs to throw the "kingmother," Jezebel, out of a window of the palace to her death so "some of her blood spattered on the wall and on the horses, and they trampled on her" (2 Kgs 9:33). The princes of the house of Omri in Samaria were ordered killed, as were 42 princes of the Judean royal family who were en route to Samaria and Jezreel on a courtesy visit. According to 2 Kgs 10:11, Jehu killed "all that remained of the house of Ahab in Jezreel, all his great men, and his familiar friends, and his priests, until he left him none remaining." But still more blood had to flow. All the priests of the Baal cult are said to have been gathered together in their temple in Samaria and slaughtered, and then the temple of Baal itself was destroyed (2 Kgs 9-10).

The biblical narrator represents these happenings as a religious purge directed by the will of Yahweh. Jehu is seen as the one who rid the country of the Baal cult, the one who saved the worship of Yahweh in Israel.[3] But is this interpretation historically accurate? What actually happened in Israel? What factors lay behind Jehu's bloody revolt? Was there really any general unrest in the country during king Joram's reign as has been commonly supposed?[4] Or was the revolt motivated by the peculiar aspirations of Jehu or of a particular faction or "party" with which he was in sympathy? Killing the entire royal family and court officals, including priests, Yahweh priests as Baal priests, all of whom were state officials (2 Kgs 10:11), suggests that the revolt was primarily political. If so, the later biblical historiographer, in his zealous abhorrence for people whose religious tradition and attitudes were somewhat different from his own, has transformed a political event into a piece of theological propaganda.

In order to get a clearer picture of the events that led to Jehu's military coup we must go back in time and review the political, social, and religious situation in Israel in the time of the Omrides. The founder of the dynasty, Omri,[5] pursued policies oriented toward the West. Israel was a rather small and isolated nation principally occupying the culturally poor central hill-country of Palestine. The industrial and cultural centers were along the coast and the main caravan routes from Egypt to Syria and Mesopotamia. To break this isolation Omri opened the door to the Phoenician world and made a treaty with Tyre, thereby weakening Aram's dominant position in Palestine; this treaty was sealed by a political marriage between his son, Ahab, and Jezebel, daughter of the Tyrian king, Ittobaal. In allying himself with Tyre Omri followed the example of David and Solomon, a fact not mentioned by the biblical narrator,[6] for whom this particular alliance marked the beginning of all the religious problems; such an attitude does not come through in connection with David's treaty with Tyre, however.

With Omri's alliance with Tyre Israel's economy and culture entered a new phase. The Phoenician cities were at the peak of their political and economic importance and expansion (Carthage was founded some three decades after Jehu's revolt).[7] Culturally, the Sidonians (as the Bible calls them) influenced not only the rest of Palestine, but also parts of Cyprus and the Aegean world; Homer's *Iliad* expresses admiration for Phoenician handiwork

(Bk. 23, 740-745). We also find a growing importance of the mer-
chant class in Israel at this time. It has usually been assumed
that the riches which now flowed into Israel went to the upper
classes of society which already had plenty (the crown, the temples,
state officials, etc.), and did not really benefit the masses.
This is not an uncommon economic situation, and there is no way
of telling whether such an unequal distribution of wealth contributed in any way to a popular uprising against Omri's grandson,
king Joram.[8]

In the East Omri conquered Moab and made it a vassal state
(cf. 2 Kgs 3:4 and the Mesha inscription from Dibon found in
1868).[9] Most of the territory north of Moab (i.e., north of the
river Arnon) he incorporated into Israel. This required the
building of some fortresses and cities (including some Levitical,
i.e., administrative, cities, such as Jazer and Heshbon) by Omri
and his successor in order to stabilize the new districts. Whether
Omri won back most of Galilee (territory lost under Baasha;
1 Kgs 15:20) in his wars with Aram-Damascus is doubtful. 1 Kgs
20:34 states that under Omri the Arameans took several cities
from Israel and received the right, in the terms of the peace
treaty, to extablish bazaars in Samaria, the new capital that
Omri built on the hill of Shemer. This location better suited
the king and his Westpolitik,[10] for it was not closed off in the
west as was the old capital at Tirza.

Omri's policies, including the treaty with Tyre, were continued by his son and successor, Ahab, under whom Israel became
one of the most important powers in Syria-Palestine. Ahab inherited from his father the war with the Arameans. After finally
defeating Aram-Damascus he showed leniency toward its captured
king, Bar-Hadad (1 Kgs 20:1ff.). This tipped the balance of power
in Israel's favor. Bar-Hadad had to promise to return to Israel
the cities taken from Omri,[11] and to give Ahab the right to
establish bazaars in Damascus (1 Kgs 20:34). It is probable that
Ahab granted Bar-Hadad his life because he needed him as an ally

in a greater coalition against Assyria which under Ashurnasirpal
II (883-859) and Shalmanezer III (858-824) was becoming more and
more dangerous for the states of Syria-Palestine.[12]  In the battle
at Qarqar in 853 B.C. we see Israel and Aram-Damascus as the two
most powerful members of the Syro-Palestinian coalition against
Shalmanezer III.[13]  The coalition had the "usual" support of Egypt
which sent a small body of foot-soldiers.

In his efforts to establish friendly relations with the
neighboring countries Ahab succeeded in ending the longstanding
strife between Israel and Judah.  A treaty was made between the
two states and sealed by a political marriage between the crown-
prince of Judah, Joram, and Ahab's daughter, Athaliah (2 Kgs 8:18;
2 Chr 21:6).[14]

It is difficult to say exactly when the Moabite king, Mesha,
began his wars of liberation against Israel.  Mesha's inscription[15]
sees to imply that he did so during Ahab's reign; according to
2 Kgs 1:1 and 3:5, however, Moab regained its independence only
after Ahab's death.  Since Ahab probably died shortly after the
battle at Qarqar in 853 B.C.,[16] his preoccupation with the coalition
against Assyria may have given Mesha that opportunity to secede.
The break could have been completed during the reign either of
Ahab's son, Azariah, who ruled only two years, or of his brother
and successor, Joram, who did not fare too well in his war against
Mesha; the latter possibility is supported by 2 Kgs 3:7 which
states that Joram "invited" the king of Judah, Jehoshaphat, to
go to war with him against Moab because Mesha had broken his
vassalage oath.

One should remember that for the narrator (as usual in
biblical historiography) the religious problems are of paramount
importance.  His description of the events is thus both selective
and tendentious.  This explains his statement that Omri and Ahab
did more evil than any other king before them (1 Kgs 16:25, 30),[17]
even though they were, in fact, very successful kings.  He sees
the religious situation in Israel as being totally wrong (i.e.,

different from that of his own time), and thus the kings are "sinful."[18] Jehu's revolt has been remodelled to suit this historiographical bias.

In the biblical account this revolt is set against an almost fanatical struggle between Yahweh supporters and Baal supporters which supposedly reached its climax during the time of Ahab and Jezebel. The narrator does not mention, however, which Baal he is concerned about: the Canaanite-Israelite Baal, or a foreign deity also called Baal by the writer. To specify which Baal he had in mind would certainly have diluted his propagandistic composition. The dramatis personae of this religious struggle, according to the texts, are Ahab's Tyrian queen, Jezebel, and the priest-prophet, Elijah,[19] who has been made the leader of a Yahwistic opposition to the queen's many attempts to promote the worship of Baal and, concomitantly, to arrest the worship of Yahweh. As a matter of fact, the textual material gives the impression that the queen tried to replace Yahweh with her own Baal as the chief god of the nation. This may be an exaggeration, but that there was some kind of conflict seems indisputable.

There are four reasons for interpreting Jezebel's religious activities as the promotion of a Tyrian god, the name of whom the narrator has not cared to give. Firstly, the queen was a daughter of Tyre's king; it would have been natural for her to maintain and propagate her native form of religion in preference to the (in her view) inferior religion of the strange land in which she found herself. Secondly, Ahab had a temple to Baal built in Samaria (paralleling Solomon's building of bamoth for his wives in Jerusalem), indicating that we are dealing with a new god not worshipped in Samaria before. Thirdly, we must consider the fact that, according to 2 Kgs 11:18 (cf. 2 Chr 23:17), the Omride queen of Judah, Athaliah, had a Baal temple built in Jerusalem; its first priest was Mattan, a good Phoenician name meaning "gift." We know that the indigenous Canaanite-Israelite Baal was worshipped in the temple of Solomon until the reforms of king Josiah (622 B.C.), as was the goddess Asherah (2 Kgs 23:4ff.).[20] Athaliah's temple construction in Jerusalem may thus be equated with Ahab's temple construction in Samaria; in both cases it was a sanctuary for the foreign god of a foreign queen.[21] It would hardly be surprising for Athaliah to have carried out the same kind of religious policies in the southern kingdom as her mother, Jezebel, did in the north. Finally, in Elijah's denouncements of the Baal cult in Israel there is no polemic (as by later Yahwists) against the masseboth (stelae symbolizing Canaan's indigenous Baal), the asherim (wooden poles symbolizing the goddess Asherah), or the so-called bamah-sanctuaries where these deity symbols resided. It would thus be a mistake to regard Elijah as a "reform" prophet and compare him with the likes of an Hosea or an Isaiah. Elijah objected not to the age-old Canaanite-Israelite national religion of his time, but to the attempt to make Jezebel's Tyrian Baal an Israelite god.

The fact that Ahab erected a sacred stele to Baal in Samaria (2 Kgs 3:2)[22] further supports the identification of this Baal as a Phoenician deity. The text says that king Joram "put away" this stele,[23] possibly indicating that Joram was somewhat more conservative than his father and reacted against a too obvious or offensive symbol of a god who was not originally or traditionally part of the religion of the country.[24] Since we do not know where the stele had been placed (in a holy precinct?) it would be risky to speculate about its real significance and relation to the Baal temple.[25]

The ritual contest on Mount Carmel between Elijah and the priest-prophets of Baal may also indicate that we are dealing with a non-Israelite god, if the event really occurred at Carmel. When nothing happened to the sacrifice for Baal, no fire came from the deity, Elijah said: "Call louder! For certainly he is a god, but he may be preoccupied or busy, or he is on a journey; perhaps he is sleeping, then he will wake up" (1 Kgs 18:27). This has

been seen as mockery, which it very well may be, but it is not
without a grain of truth. Elijah obviously knew what kind of
god his opponents were sacrificing to, dancing for, and calling
upon. His words may thus provide information about the character
of this Baal. The conclusion has been drawn that the god should
be the Tyrian Melqart because of certain resemblances between
Elijah's sarcastic remarks and the later legend of Herakles-
Melqart and his cultic awakening-resurrection.[27]

When Jezebel's excessive promotion of her Baal cult became
persecution of Yahweh worshippers (1 Kgs 18:4) this naturally
caused a split in the court and the capital. For example, the
chief minister of the royal palaces and estates,[28] Obadiah, is
said to have "feared Yahweh," i.e., he adhered to the old
religious customs of the country. During the persecution of
Yahweh worshippers he had 100 prophets in a cave, 50 at a time,
and also fed them (1 Kgs 18:3f., 13). There was a time under
Ahab, therefore, when it was dangerous to worship Yahweh, and
this, of course, is one reason for the narrator's hatred for
Ahab and his house. But was this also the situation under Joram?
His removal of the sacred Baal stele in Samaria suggests otherwise, and we do not hear of any persecution during his lifetime.
Like his brother and predecessor, Ahaziah, he was given a name
by Ahab with a theophoric component referring to Yahweh;[29] this
is a declaration that the official state religion was Yahwistic
(which does not in itself preclude the existence of other gods in
the same religious system). It should be emphasized that "Church"
and "State" were closely interrelated in this period. Religion
was the ideological base for the king's existence and for his
policies;[30] the religious establishment was an arm of the royal
administration. One might wonder, therefore, why the revolt did
not take place during Ahab's reign for it was a reaction against
Ahab's and Jezebel's religious policy. The reason given by the
narrator is that Ahab "humbled" himself before Yahweh (1 Kgs
21:29). He has thus failed to make this detested monarch a

complete "apostate." This further indicates that other factors
may have been the main causes for Jehu's insurrection.

We are not given any specific information concerning the
cultural and social conditions in Israel during Joram's reign.
One may assume, therefore, that they were very much the same as
existed under his predecessors. We know that Jezebel was alive
and as "kingmother" (gebirah) she could still have been politically
active. The title gebirah refers to an office with its own administration; its holder was thus very much a part of the power
structure.[31] It would have been quite possible, therefore, for
Jezebel to have continued promoting her Baal cult, even though
Joram may not have been an enthusiastic supporter of her evan-
gelism.[32]

The incident with Naboth's vineyard has often been seen as
an indication of moral and social decadence in Israel under the
Omrides,[33] but it could as well be understood as a conflict in
which the royal court did not yield to a private citizen in a
matter of expropriation.[34] If this incident occurred during the
reign of king Joram (cf. 2 Kgs 9:25f.), as some scholars have
supposed,[35] it may have been a factor contributing to Jehu's
revolt. But whether the murder of Naboth really says anything
about religious and moral decadence under Ahab and his sons is
quite another problem; it would be dangerous and arbitrary to
draw such a conclusion from one incident only.

What else do we know about Joram's reign? His war against
Moab was a fiasco. Most of Transjordan was lost to Moab and
Aram-Damascus. The latter kingdom under Bar-Hadad had resumed
hostilities, and his army is said to have once penetrated to the
very walls of Samaria. The long siege[36] caused a severe famine
in the city (2 Kgs 6:24 ff.). The food supply disappeared; desperate, people started to eat their babies.[37] It cost 80 silver
shekels for the pleasure of eating the meager meat of a donkey's
head (usually one did not eat any donkey meat!); it may be noted
for comparison that the ordinary price for a goat was 2-3 shekels,

and that one shekel normally bought over three gallons of fine flour.[38] The siege ended miraculously, according to the biblical narrator, but what actually happened is not known.[39] If this event occurred in Joram's reign (the biblical account does not identify the Israelite king) it would be possible to place it in one of the years when Damascus was being threatened by Assyria; Bar-Hadad would have to return home in a hurry to combat his eastern enemy. Shalmanezer III was again on the march campaigning in Syria in 849, 848, 845, and 841. A likely candidate would be 845, the year Bar-Hadad II probably died.[41] The loss of Moab and the Transjordanian territories, the unsuccessful war against Aram-Damascus together with the Assyrian presence in Hauran[42] east of Gilead could be regarded as reasons enough for Jehu's military revolt.

Another factor sometimes used as an argument for unrest in the country is the extensive building programs of Omri and especially Ahab. The latter continued to build up Samaria (cf. his so-called ivory house; 1 Kgs 22:39)[43] and erected a Baal temple in the city (1 Kgs 16:32). His other building projects include his palace in Jezreel and the fortification and rebuilding of Hazor and Megiddo, to mention a few. Such programs undoubtedly required a huge amount of forced labor.[44] Whether these building projects, however, created any popular revolutionary movements during the time of king Joram is impossible to determine.

Who supported Jehu's coup d'etat? Considering the fact that Joram did not win any laurels through his military activities, it is quite understandable that these activities would have created discontent among his officers, such as Jehu, and court officials, such as the court prophet Elisha, and among geographically isolated, non-urban and thus conservative groups, such as the religious fanatic Jonadeb ben Rechab. When Jehu arrived at Jezreel the eunuchs and court officials took fright and did what he told them.

Especially interesting is the role of Elisha. The Old

Testament pictures him as a parallel figure to Elijah and as such hostile toward the Omride dynasty. The question is: What role might he have played in the events leading to Jehu's rebellion? It is significant that his home was in the capital, Samaria, where he seems to have been a very important individual (2 Kgs 2:25; 5:3; 6:32). He was probably a court prophet who spoke on behalf of other citizens before both the king and the commander of the army (2 Kgs 4:13). We must consider the possibility that he belonged to a "party" in Samaria which had grown dissatisfied with the present regime and wanted a change, and perhaps was looking to Assyria for help against Aram. From 2 Kgs 6:31ff. we learn that there was a conflict between Joram and Elisha;[45] the king threatened to kill the prophet who regarded him as "a son of a murderer." The background of this hostility is not clear, but in the midst of the Aramean siege of Samaria, with the city in the grip of famine, we find the elders of the city (the "city council") meeting with Elisha in his home, perhaps to discuss the precarious situation and possible solutions. The prophet may have been encouraging them and others to favor a change in government. If so, the antagonism between the king and the prophet is quite understandable. The king may have known that the prophet had been undermining his position for some time. If so, this was treason, which explains why the king wanted Elisha killed. As a matter of fact, the elders did take part (willingly or otherwise) in the murder of the princes in Samaria by sending their heads in baskets to Jehu in Jezreel, thereby demonstrating their support and loyalty (2 Kgs 10:5ff.). Consequently, when Jehu later arrived in Samaria no member of the Omri dynasty was left in the capital; all opposition from this quarter had been exterminated.

The picture now begins to come into better focus. In a time of distress certain groups within the military and governmental establishments felt it necessary to change the direction of national policy. Elisha seems to have been an active supporter

of these pro-Assyrian groups.  With Shalmanezer close to Gilead,
if not already on Israelite territory, the time had come to dispose of the king and his (pro-Egyptian?) "party."  This factional-
ism and political maneuvering explains Elisha's relationship with
Jehu.  By anointing Jehu king via one of his disciples he furnished
the usurper with the divine oracle of election which was necessary
in order to ascend the throne.[46]  Jehu's military status, in turn,
provided the power base necessary to make this election a
political reality.

The biblical narrator has utilized the above mentioned undercurrents in order to depict Jehu's actions as willed by Yahweh
through the prophet Elisha.  But he fails to show that there was
any great support among the population for overthrowing Joram
and his advisors; had there been such he would certainly have
mentioned it, for it would have strengthened his case.  Particularly revealing in this regard is 2 Kgs 10:9.  According to this
passage, the people were frightened when they saw the baskets
containing the many ("seventy") heads of the princes murdered at
Jehu's request which were sent from Samaria and placed outside
the gate of Jezreel.[47]  To calm the people he told them that they
were without guilt for this massacre, for he himself had conspired against the king and murdered him.  To this we should add
2 Kgs 9:14 where the narrator laconically states:  "Thus Jehu,
son of Jehoshaphat the son of Nimshi, conspired against king
Joram."  The conclusion can only be that Jehu's revolt was
nothing else but a politically motivated military coup d'etat
which lacked any real popular support.  This also would explain
why it was so bloody.  As a usurper Jehu naturally had to exterminate all members of the Omri dynasty and their adherents in
order to secure the throne.  And to shift the country's foreign
policy he had to dispose of all those who represented the old
policy:  court officials, civil servants, priests, etc., in a
word the anti-Assyrian "party."[48]

With Jehu the kingdom of Israel became a politically weak

59

nation. Gone was its position (attained under Ahab) as a major
power in Palestine. The killing of Jezebel and the other Omrides
effectively broke the treaty with Tyre, and the alliance with
Judah was likewise shattered by the murder of its king and 42
princes. King Jehu "inherited" from Joram the hostility and
warfare with Aram–Damascus. The Syro–Palestinian states were
still threatened by Shalmanezer III. Realistically, therefore,
Jehu understood that the only support he could count on would be
from Assyria. His revolt was thus intended to save Israel from
destruction by the Assyrian army. As a result he became an
Assyrian vassal. One of Shalmanezer III's inscriptions, the
so-called Black Obelisk (now in the British Museum) shows "Iaua
king of Bit-Humri" (i.e., Jehu) among other Syro-Palestinian
kings as one of Shalmanezer's tributary vassals.[49]

Unfortunately for Jehu, Assyrian vassalage did not help in
his dealings with Aram–Damascus and its new king, Hazael, also
a usurper. Jehu stood alone without an ally. During 838–828
Shalmanezer III was occupied in other areas of his empire. Hazael
made the most of this opportunity and "cut off parts of Israel,"
taking Transjordan down to the border of Moab (2 Kgs 10:32f.);
this may be the explanation of the Moabite Mesha's boast that
"Israel perished utterly forever" (M.I. 1.7). It is possible
that Hazael also annexed parts of Galilee; the destruction of St.
VII at Hazor, e.g., has been attributed to an invasion by Hazael
(c. 815-814).[50] Early in the reign of Jehoahaz, the son of Jehu,
(814-798) Hazael went down along the coast of Gath which he conquered; this means that the Israelite army could not stop him
from marching through part of Israelite territory. After taking
Gath Hazael attacked Jerusalem whose king, Jehoash, paid a heavy
tribute (2 Kgs 12:17f.). Aram had now replaced Israel as the
main power in Palestine and as such controlled the caravan routes
in Transjordan and along the coast. As both Israel and Judah had
to pay tribute to the king of Aram–Damascus, they had become for
the moment Aramean vassals.

In making peace with Israel and Jehu's son, Jehoahaz,
Hazael stipulated that Israel could maintain an army of no more
than "50 horsemen, 10 chariots, and 10,000 foot-soldiers" (2 Kgs
13:7). This should be contrasted with the picture given of Ahab's
army at the time of his participation in the coalition against
Shalmanezer III; the Monolith inscription of Shalmanezer credits
Ahab with 2,000 war chariots and 10,000 infantry men.[51] One
cannot get a better illustration of Israel's reduction to near
destruction under Jehu's son. It now was completely at the mercy
of the king of Aram-Damascus.

It is now appropriate to return to the question raised at
the beginning of this study, namely, whether Jehu really did up-
root the so-called Baal cult in Israel as the biblical narrator
would have one believe. He did exterminate those who opposed
his pro-Assyrian policy. This meant that the political ties with
Tyre, one of Assyria's opponents, had to be cut. The representatives
of the Tyrian Baal religion in Israel were naturally regarded as
part of the anti-Assyrian "party," as were some Yahweh priests.
The later narrator of these events, however, has cast them in
the narrow mold of his own religious bias. Jehu has been lifted
from his historical setting and given a position in the writer's
theological history quite different from his actual character and
aspirations. He is depicted as a "pure-Yahwist" of a much later
time; in reality, he was nothing more than a traitorous general
trying to seize power in a politically unstable situation. That
he was not a "pure Yahwist" is evident from his acceptance of
masseboth and asherim and such other traditional Israelite deity
symbols as the Yahweh bulls of Bethel and Dan and the calf of
Samaria.[52] Indeed, the biblical narrator seems to have had difficulty disguising his disappointment with Jehu and his regime. To
the standard complaint that Jehu, like all the northern kings,
did not turn aside "from the sins of Jeroboam, the son of Nebat,
which he made Israel to sin, the golden calves in Bethel and in
Dan" (2 Kgs 10:29)[53] he adds that Jehu "was not careful to walk

in the law of Yahweh, the god of Israel, with all his heart"
(v. 31). Obviously Jehu had not established the form of Yahweh
religion that the narrator embraced and propagated.  It may have
been because that form of religion did not yet exist.[54]

The biblical account of Jehu's revolt is a rather good
illustration of ancient Near Eastern historiographical art.
Its author belongs to the same "school" of historians whose
most famous characters are the great kings of Mesopotamia and
Egypt, kings who in their inscriptions state that they were
always victorious, even though they at least occasionally were
not.  This is history as it should have been.[55]  History as it
was often was quite different.  Taking into consideration all
of the available facts we must, from the perspective of modern
historiography, conclude that Jehu's revolt was a political insurrection legitimized by the prophet Elisha.[56]  In furnishing
the usurper with the oracle of divine election he made a grave
political mistake, for he contributed directly to the future
disasters which soon befell his country.  His candidate for the
throne, Jehu, did not become a blessing for Israel, but just the
opposite!

## Footnotes

*Originally a public lecture given November 2, 1976, sponsored by the Divinity School and the Department of Near Eastern Languages and Civilizations at the University of Chicago. I wish to express my appreciation and gratitude to Mr. W. Boyd Barrick, M.A., for stylistically improving the text.

1. This place has been identified with Tell er-Rumeith in Trans-Jordan where a small fortress (ca. 37m. by 32m.) from the 10th century B.C. was found; N. Glueck, *Explorations in Eastern Palestine* (AASOR 25-28; New Haven: Yale Univeristy, 1951) 98ff.; P. W. Lapp, "Tell er-Rumeith," RB 70 (1963) 406ff. and RB 75 (1968) 98ff.; M. Ottosson, *Gilead: Tradition and History* (ConB, OT Ser. 3; Lund: C.W.K. Gleerup, 1969) 32f.; B. Oded, "Observations on Methods of Assyrian Rule in Transjordania after the Palestinian Campaign of Tiglath-Pileser III," JNES 29 (1970) 179f.

2. J. Pedersen, *Israel* (reprint; Copenhagen: Branner og Korch, 1954) 3-4, 110f.; G. W. Ahlström, "Prophecy," *Encyclopaedia Britannica*, 15th ed.; see also J. Lindblom, *Prophecy in Ancient Israel* (Philadelphia: Fortress, 1962) 57ff.; J. M. Ward, *Hosea: A Theological Commentary* (New York: Harper & Bros., 1966) 157f.; W. L. Moran, "New Evidence from Mari and the History of Prophecy," Bib 50 (1969) 24 n.2; J. J. M. Roberts, "The Hand of Yahweh," VT 21 (1971) 24ff.

3. This is also the picture given by most scholars; see, for instance, W. F. Albright, *Archaeology and the Religion of Israel* (2d ed.; Baltimore: John Hopkins, 1946) 160f. ("Yahwism had, indeed, triumphed politically in the Northern Kingdom with Jehu's victory.") and H. Daniel-Rops, who says that,"Jahweh had gained a dazzling victory in Israel," *Israel and the Ancient World* (tr. K. Madge; Garden City, N.Y.: Doubleday, 1964) 249. Cf. T. Ishida, "The House of Ahab," IEJ 25 (1975) 136.

4. Thus, e.g., John Bright says, "Though we hear of no popular uprising Jehu and his soldiers almost certainly acted in line with what they knew to be popular sentiment;" in *A History of Israel* (2d ed.; Philadelphia: Westminster, 1972) 246.

5. According to M. Noth the name Omri would be an Arabic name, *Die israelitischen Personennamen im Rahmen gemeinsemitischen Namengebung* (BWANT 46; Stuttgart: W. Kohlhammer, 1928) 222 n.7.

6. For an evaluation of Omri and his policies, see among others, C. F. Whitley, "The Deuteronomic Presentation of the House of Omri," VT 2 (1952) 137ff.

7.  D. Baramki, *Phoenicia and the Phoenicians* (Beirut:
Khayats, 1961) 26; S. Moscati, *The World of the Phoenicians*
(London: Weidenfeld & Nicolson, 1968) 114ff.  The emergence of
the Assyrian Empire under Ashurnaṣirpal II is seen by J. D. Muhly
as a phenomenon which possibly "encouraged the Phoenicians to
seek their fortunes beyond the sea," in "Homer and the Phoenicians:
The Relations between Greece and the Near East in the Late Bronze
and Early Iron Ages," *Berytus* 19 (1970) 62.

8.  E. W. Heaton, for instance, considers this one of the
forces behind Jehu's revolt, *The Hebrew Kingdoms* (New Clarendon
Bible, OT 3; Oxford: Clarendon, 1968) 89.

9.  For the Mesha inscription see E. Ullendorf, "The Moabite
Stone," *Documents from Old Testament Times* (ed. D. Winton Thomas;
New York: Thomas Nelson & Sons, 1958) 195ff.; H. Donner and W.
Röllig, *Kanaanäische und Aramäische Inschriften* (3 vols.;
Wiesbaden; O Harrassowitz, 1962-64) Nr. 181; J.C.L. Gibson,
*Testbook of Syrian Semitic Inscriptions* (2 vols.; Oxford:
Clarendon, 1971-73) 1.71ff.; J. M. Miller, "The Moabite Stone as
a Memorial Stele," PEQ 106 (1974) 71ff.; see also, J. Liver,
"The Wars of Mesha, King of Moab," PEQ 99 (1967) 14ff.

10.  A. Alt maintained that in buying the hill of Shemer
Omri intended "to create for the first time in the kingdom of
Israel as close an equivalent as possible to David's royal city
of Jerusalem," in "The Monarchy in the Kingdoms of Israel and
Judah," *Essays on Old.Testament History and Religion* (tr. R. A.
Wilson; Garden City, N.Y.: Doubleday, 1967) 322.

11.  Probably in Bashan and Gilead, according to N. K.
Gottwald, *All the Kingdoms of the Earth* (New York: Harper &
Row, 1964) 63f.  One could perhaps also add northern Galilee.

12.  Cf. W. Schramm, "Assyrische Königsinschriften," WO 8
(1975)37ff.; W. W. Hallo and W. K. Simpson, *The Ancient Near
East: A History* (New York: Harcourt Brace Jovanovich, 1971)
125ff.

13.  See D. D. Luckenbill, *Ancient Records of Assyria and
Babylonia* (2 vols.; Chicago: University of Chicago, 1926) 1. 223,
par. 611; A. L. Oppenheim in ANET (1950) 278f.  See further below.

14.  Concerning Athaliah being the daughter of Ahab or Omri,
S. Herrmann argues that from what one "can gather of her age,
Athaliah was probably Ahab's daughter," in *A History of Israel
in Old Testament Times* (Philadelphia: Fortress, 1975) 226 n.8.

15.  See n. 9.

16. Cf. E. R. Thiele, "An Additional Chronological Note on 'Yaw' Son of 'Omri'," BASOR 222 (1976) 5. According to 1 Kgs 22:40 Ahab died a natural death; see J. M. Miller, "The Fall of the House of Ahab," VT 17 (1967) 313; A. Jepsen, "Ahabs Busse," Archäologie und Altes Testament (Festschrift K. Galling, hrsg. A. Kuschke und E. Kutsch; Tübingen: J.C.B. Mohr, 1970) 149.

17. See, for instance, C. F. Whitley, "The Deuteronomic Presentation of the House of Omri," VT 2 (1952) 137ff.

18. This religious outlook is the basis for the evaluation of the kings of Israel and Judah. One should, e.g., note how King Hezekiah is appreciated: "There was none like him among all the kings of Judah after him, nor among those who were before him," 2 Kgs 18:5. The fact is that this king almost destroyed Judah with his foreign policy, but this of little importance to the narrator who in his Yahwistic zeal measures Hezekiah according to his religious and cultic activities.

19. It is perhaps also possible to see Elijah as a court prophet because "we find him repeatedly at or near the court and seeking involvement," M. A. Cohen, "In All Fairness to Ahab: A Socio-Political Consideration of the Ahab-Elijah Conflict," Eretz Israel 12 (1975) 89.

20. Cf. G. W. Ahlström, Aspects of Syncretism in Israelite Religion (Lund: C.W.K. Gleerup, 1963) 50f., 58f.; cf. R. Patai, The Hebrew Goddess (New York: KTAV, 1967); K. H. Bernhardt, "Aschera in Ugarit und im Alten Testament," Mitteilungen des Instituts für Orientforschung der deutschen Akademie der Wissensch. zu Berlin 13,2 (1967) 163ff.; S. Terrien, "The Omphalos Myth and Hebrew Religion," VT 20 (1970) 330. One should, in this connection, note the occurrence of the phrase "Yahweh and his Ashtoret" on an 8th century B.C. inscription from the Judean fortress at Kuntilet cArjud (Kuntilet Quraiyah) 50km. south of Kadesh Barnea, reported by W. G. Dever at the ASOR and SBL meetings at St. Louis, Mo., 28-31 October 1976. From Beitin (Bethel?) should be mentioned the occurrence of two "Ashtarte" plaques from Iron I, J. L. Kelso, The Excavation of Bethel (1943-1960) (AASOR 39; Cambridge: American Schools of Oriental Research, 1968) 84, par. 338. For the many "Ashtarte" figurines found in the royal Judean palace at Ramat Rachel, see Y. Aharoni, Excavations at Ramat Rachel, Seasons 1959 and 1960 (Roma: Centro di Studi Semitici, 1962) 41f.

21. J. Bright maintains that it is "unlikely that the Tyrian Bacal ever had much following among Judah's conservative population," in History, 249. That may be right, but how does one know anything about the conservative population of Judah?

22. For Phoenician parallels see, for instance, J. Morgenstern, "The King-God among the Western Semites and the Meaning of Epiphanes," VT 10 (1960) 149.

23. In 2 Kgs 10:27 it is said that Jehu removed this stele. This could mean that one has tried to give Jehu more credit than he deserved and King Joram less.

24. His failure to do anything about the Ba'al temple may indicate that this temple (like the bamoth for Solomon's wives) was not a national shrine, but a private chapel for the "king mother" and her co-religionists. The stele, on the other hand, may have had more national implications and was thus considered an excessive or inappropriate innovation by the new king.

25. It may be possible to see this massebah as being obeliskoid or of the Phoenician conical form that occurs, for instance, on a coin from Byblos of Emperor Macrinus (217-218 A.D.) showing the temple, a horned altar, and a conical stele; see the discussion in Th. A. Businck, The Tempel von Jerusalem I (Leiden: E.J. Brill, 1970) 454ff., Abd. 127; cf. also D. Harden, The Phoenicians (New York: Praeger, 1962) 93, fig.101; Moscati, World, 47f. and fig. 4.

26. The contest on Carmel has been disputed by A. Jepsen, who considers it as having taken place in Samaria, "Elia und das Gottesurteil," Near Eastern Studies in Honor of William Foxwell Albright (ed. H. Goedicke; Baltimore: John Hopkins, 1971) 304ff.

27. Cf. Morgenstern, "The King-God," 171ff. For Melqart as a name of a god or a god epithet see Donner and Röllig, KAI 2. 53, Nr. 36 and 203, Nr. 201; see also D. van Brechem, "Sanctuaires d'Hercules-Melqart. Contribution à l'etude de l'éxpansion phénicienne en Méditerranée, I. Gadès, II. Thasos, III. Rome," Syria 44 (1967) 73 ff., 307ff.; W. Culican, "Melqart Representations on Phoenician Seals," Abr-Nahrain 2 (1960-61) 41ff.; R. D. Barnett, "Ezekiel and Tyre," Eretz Israel 9 (1969) 10.

28. Cf. T. N. D. Mettinger, who sees the title "over the house" as a "loan-translation" of the Egyption mr pr wr, Solomonic State Officials (ConB, O.T. Ser. 5; Lund: C. W. K. Gleerup, 1971) 70ff., 79.

29. W.O.E. Oesterley and Th.H. Robinson, A History of Israel (2 vols.; Oxford: Clarendon, 1932) 1. 323. Cf. G. W. Ahlström, "Ahab," SBU 1. col. 32; Cohen, "In all Fairness to Ahab," 89*. Joram's attitude towards Yahweh is clear from 2 Kgs 3:13f. and 6:12 which shows that when Joram asks for the divine will he seeks the Yahweh oracle through Elisha, cf. Y. Kaufmann, The Religion of Israel (Chicago: University of Chicago, 1960) 274.

30. One could here refer to an example from our modern time as an illustration and compare the religions of the ancient Near East

with the government policies of a communist country. A certain
ideology is the basis for all the actions of the government and the
political leader personifies the ideology, cf. Cohen, "In all Fairness to Ahab," 90*f. Translated into Near Eastern concepts this
could be expressed as in the enthronement oracle in Ps 2:7; "You
are my son, I have today given you birth." Thus the kingship is
willed by the deity and the king is "ideologically" part of the
divine sphere. This can also be exemplified with Psalm 72 where
the king is said to be the life giver of his nation, cf. G. W.
Ahlström, *Joel and the Temple Cult of Jerusalem* (VTSup 21; Leiden:
E.J. Brill, 1971) 103ff. With this in mind it should be understandable that the king in principle would not oppose his own god.
That would mean that he would have challenged his own basic function
and position. God and king are two aspects of the same phenomenon:
the existence of the nation and its well-being.

31. H. Donner, "Art und Herkunft des Amtes des Königinmutter
im Alten Testament," *Festschrift J. Friedrich* (hrsg. R. von Kienle,
et al.; Heidelberg: C. Winter, 1959) 106ff.; Ahlström, *Aspects*,
61ff.; Terrien, "Omphaos Myth," 330f.

32. See note 24.

33. Cf. Bright, *History*, 241,246.

34. D. J. Wiseman, "Alalakh," *Archaeology and Old Testament
Study* (ed. D. Winton Thomas; Oxford: Clarendon, 1967) 128. S.
Herrmann sees it as "a clash between legal ordinances rather than
one between individuals," in *History*, 212.

35. Cf. J. M. Miller, "The Fall of the House of Ahab," VT 17
(1967) 317.

36. The fortification walls of Samaria remained almost intact
down to the time of Alexander the Great.

37. For this kind of forced "cannibalism," cf. Deut 28:53ff.;
Ezek 5:10; Lam 4:10; see also A. L. Oppenheim, "'Seige-documents'
from Nippur," *Iraq* 17 (1955) 69ff., esp. pp. 79f. and n34.

38. Cf. M. Rehm, *Die Bücher Samuel* (Würzberg: Echter Verlag,
1949) 86.

39. It should be noted that the texts are not written down for
the purpose of historiography but rather in order to extol the
personality of the prophet Elisha, cf. J. Gray, *I & II Kings* (OTL;
2d ed.; Philadelphia: Westminster, 1970) 512.

40. Luckenbill, *Ancient Records*, 1. pars. 567f., 571, 651-655,
658f.; cf. Hallo and Simpson, *Ancient Near East*, 128.

41. For the kings of Damascus at this time, see F. M. Cross, Jr., "The Stele Dedicated to Melcarth by Ben-Hadad of Damascus," BASOR 205 (1972) 36ff. An incident occurred during this seige which should be noted. When King Joram, during the famine caused by the seige, was once walking on the walls of Samaria, a woman called up to him and asked for help. From the king's answer to her we learn that Yahweh was still the national and main god of Israel. According to the narrator the king answered the women, "If Yahweh will not help you, whence shall I help you? From the threshing floor or from the wine-press?" (2 Kgs 6:26ff.). This answer also clearly shows that the king's cultic functions in the vegetation rituals at these two locations (threshing floor and winepress) were well known and im-portant but of no value as long as Yahweh did not seem to give any help; cf. G. W. Ahlström, "Der Prophet Nathan und der Tempelbau," VT 11 (1961) 116.

42. M. C. Astour connects this with Hos 10:14 mentioning Shalman having destroyed Beth-Arbel (near modern Irbid in Trans-jordan) in "841 B.C.: The First Assyrian Invasion of Israel," JAOS 91 (1971) 386f.

43. For the ivory plaques in Phoenician style which have turned up in the excavations at Samaria (1931-35), see J. W. Crowfoot and G. M. Crowfoot, *Early Ivories from Samaria* (London: Palestine Ex-ploration Fund, 1938).

44. Concerning the internal situation in Israel during this time Bright says that "it evoked tensions that cancelled its beneficial results and created a situation packed with danger," in *History*, 240.

45. H. Schweizer considers this passage to be an addition, in *Elischa in der Kriegen: Literaturwissenschaftliche Untersuchungen von 2 Kön 3; 6,8-23; 6,24-7,20* (SANT 37; Munich: Kösel, 1974) 395ff.

46. Divine election was the ideological basis for kingship in Israel as in other Near Eastern kingdoms. Cf. T. C. G. Thornton, "Charismatic Kingship in Israel and Judah," JTS 14 (1963) 4 f.; R. de Vaux, "Le roi d'Israël, vassal de Yahvé," *Mélanges E. Tisserant*, Vol. I (Studi e Testi 23; Roma: Biblioteca apostolica vaticana, 1964) 121f. (*The Bible and the Ancient Near East* [Garden City, N.Y.: Doubleday, 1971] 152ff.); G. W. Ahlström, "Solomon, the Chosen One," HR 8 (1968) 93 ff.; H. Tadmor, "The People and the Kingship in Ancient Israel: The Role of Political Institutions in the Biblical Period," *Cahiers d'Histoire Moniale* 11 (1968) 14,19; and cf. also K. Koch, "Die Briefe 'prophetischen' Inhalts aus Mari," UF 4 (1972) 68. For a parallel to Jehu's election see the Zakir inscription, Donner and Röllig, KAI, Nr. 202.

47. It is possible that the placing of the princes' heads out-side the city gate is a phenomenon that indicates Jehu having used an Assyrian custom and possibly also that he did it on the instigation

of Shalmanezer III.  That would explain the Assyrian king's blessing
of his revolt.  Arranging the heads of captured enemies outside the
city gates was an Assyrian custom known from the times of Ashurnasirp
II and Shalmanezer III.  The latter states in his inscriptions thàt
he at several places has "erected a pyramid of heads" outside the
gates of the captured city.  See Astour, "841 B.C.," 388 n.6; Luckenbill, *Ancient Records*, 1. pars. 598f., 605; A. L. Oppenheim, ANET, 27

48.  Astour, "841 B.C.," 388.

49.  Luckenbill, *Ancient Records*, par. 590.  It is therefore in
order that it is Jehu who is depicted on the obelisk and not Joram,
as has been suggested by P. K. McCarter, "Yau, Son of Omri," BASOR
216 (1974) 5ff.  It should be noted that the Akkadian phrase bīt
humri (É-humri) in Assyrian sources refers to Israel first from the
time of king Jehu; S. Parpola, *Neo-Assyrian Toponyms*, (AOAT 6;
Kevelaer: Butzon & Bercker, 1970) 82f.  According to H. Tadmor KUR
Bit-Humri means "the land of Bit-Humri" and not the "Omri-land;"
mar Humri, as well as mar Agusi, mar Adini and mar Dakuri is a reference to the king, ("The Historical Inscriptions of Adad-Nirari
III," *Iraq* 35 (1973) 148f.).  For the chronological problems of
the dynasties of Omri and Jehu, see E.R. Thiele, "An Additional
Chronological Note on 'Yau, Son of Omri,'" BASOR 222 (1976) 19ff.

50.  Y. Aharoni in Y. Yadin et al., *Hazor II* (Jerusalem: Magnes,
1960) 37 n. 217; cf. Y. Yadin, *Hazor: The Head of All Those Kingdoms,
Joshua 11:10* (Schweich Lectures 1970; London: Oxford University for
the British Academy, 1972) 169.

51.  Luckenbill, *Ancient Records*, par. 611; Oppenheim, ANET, 279.
For comparison it should be mentioned that Aram-Damascus contributed
1,200 chariots and 20,000 infantry, and that among other nations
Egypt, which was always looked upon as a support against Assyria,
sent as a token 1,000 foot soldiers.  Shalmanezer's army consisted
of ca. 2,000 chariots and ca. 5,500 cavalry horses; cf. M. Elat,
"The Campaign of Shalmanezer III against Aram and Israel," IEJ 25
(1975) 25ff.

52.  Hos 8:5ff.

53.  For the collector of the traditions of 1-2 Kings the
country Israel should never have existed.  Its sin was really that
it had separated itself from Judah and from Yahweh of Jerusalem.

54.  Here one should observe that the prophet Hosea completely
condemns Jehu, saying that Yahweh himself (who was said to have
chosen Jehu) "will punish the house of Jehu for the blood of Jezreel," Hos 1:4.

55.  In order to understand the idea of writing "history" in
ancient times one should note an utterance by Hekataios from

Miletus: "Thus I write as the truth seems to be to me."  See F.
Jacoby, *Die Fragmente der griechischen Historiker I* (Leiden: E.J.
Brill, 1957) 7.

56.  Concerning the problem of charismatic versus dynastic
kingship, the revolt of Jehu cannot be used as an indication for
the existence of a charismatic principle in Israel.  This investigation
may have shown that such a distinction between the Judean kingship
and that of Israel may be artificial.  Jehu did not become king because of the existence of a charismatic principle in Israel.  He
became king thanks to the Assyrian threat.  If that had not existed
Joram may have died in peace as king.

# JEHU AND THE BLACK OBELISK OF SHALMANESER III

Clyde Curry Smith

## I. Prolegomena

> The materials can never all be collected, for they
> can never be known. Problems cannot all be solved,
> for, as they are solved, new aspects are perpetually
> revealed. The historian opens the way; he does not
> close it.[1]

In the consideration of any matter, the historian ought to identify the several levels of reality and of meaning appropriate to
it. Simultaneously, each level needs to be seen in an historical
perspective illustrative of those developments in understanding
which the passage of time and intensity of study have made possible.
Clearly, in the successive statements pertaining to each level the
historian gets beyond the base for the next level; in the picking up
of that next level some overlap cannot be avoided.

The spatial limitations appropriate to an essay and the real
accomplishments of more than a century of scholarship make it
mandatory for a shorthand of sorts to be applied. Thus I will use
the designation BO (or BO Slm III) to refer to the Black Obelisk of
Shalmaneser III (858-824 B.C.E.)[2] whose king is identified in its
own words:

> Shalmaneser, king over all peoples, prince, priest of
> Assur, mighty king, king of all four regions, sun for
> all peoples, leader of all lands; son of Assurnaspirpal,
> august priest, whose priesthood to the gods was pleasing,
> lands in their totality at his feet he caused to bow;
> pure creature of Tukulti-Ninurta, who all his enemies
> slew and overwhelmed like the deluge. (BO 15-21)

In any concern for the interrelationship of assyriological and
biblical materials, it is not inappropriate to come once again to
BO Slm III, since its text, as already noted by S. R. Driver in his

Schweich Lectures of 1909, provided the first long Assyrian inscription to be read in modern times as a result of the archaeological recovery of ancient Mesopotamia.  That achievement belonged
to H. C. Rawlinson; the date was 1850.  Moreover, within the year
a second pioneering scholar, E. Hincks, had discovered among its
epigrams the first extra-biblical reference to an Israelite in
contemporary non-Israelite materials rather than transmitted
tradition, identifying thereby simultaneously that unique portrait
which survives of the reigning Israelite monarch Jehu.[3]  That this
same Jehu should be involved precisely in that coup which T. H.
Robinson defines as Yahweh's activity of "prophetic revolution,"
initiating thereby that movement whose spirit without question
enabled biblical literature not only to come into being but also
to survive antiquity (a theme already well developed by J. M. P.
Smith in his Prophets and Their Times of 1925 with its connecting
references to the Assyrian data) is sufficient justification for
our essay in this volume which seeks to honor an eminent theologian
of the Old Testament of that same Chicago School!

## II.  Levels of Reality

### The base level

It was in the centre of the mound, that one of the most
remarkable discoveries awaited me...  I had business in
Mosul... but had scarcely left the mound when a corner of
black marble was uncovered, lying on the very edge of the
trench.  This attracted the notice of the superintendent
of the party digging, who ordered the place to be further
examined.  The corner was part of an obelisk, about seven
feet high, lying on its side, ten feet below the surface.
An Arab was sent after me without delay, to announce the
discovery, and on my return I found the obelisk completely
exposed to view.  I descended eagerly into the trench,
and was immediately struck by the singular appearance,
and evident antiquity, of the remarkable monument before
me.  We raised it from its recumbent position, and, with
the aid of ropes, speedily dragged it out of the ruins.
Although its shape was that of an obelisk, yet it was flat
at the top and cut into three gradines.[4]

At the base level, as the late J. A. Wilson would have said with sherd in hand in the opening lecture to his class on the history of ancient western Asia, "the only fact is an artifact." This is the level of objective form and of genuine concreteness. Discovered by A. H. Layard late in 1846 BO Slm III, after a hazardous journey, came to the British Museum, where it was accessioned on 4 November 1848 and has long been displayed as one of its greatest treasures.[5]

According to the Oxford English Dictionary "obelisk" as an applied conceptual term derived immediately from its use in Renaissance textual criticism, though it had been known previously to both ancient and medieval scholars, and coming ultimately from the Greek word for "spit" or "squewer." Thus the word was used at the outset of the nineteenth century to describe an Egyptian monumental form of "lofty needles," and it was from that usage that Layard, "with some want of discrimination,"[6] employed the term to denominate this peculiar black basalt, even though the object's exact shape did not fit the typical Egyptian form. There are but four of these Assyrian truncated obelisks, for which the old British Museum description "pyramidion with steps" might be more apt.[7] Subsequent excavation has been able to add only fragments to this corpus. Of these, BO Slm III remains the prime example of its species, having been not only first discovered but also best preserved. The complete list, in order of discovery, is as follows:

1. Black [Basalt] of Slm III, (BM 118885).[8]

2. [Black] Basalt of Anp II (Aššur-nasir-apli, 883-859), discovered by H. Rassam, at Nimrud (BM 118800).[9] It is amazing that two monuments so closely related in both character and location should have suffered such diverse fates, the slightly older being so completely shattered (presumably in antiquity), the other being one of the best preserved.

3. White [Limestone] of an Anp, discovered by Rassam, at Kuyunjik (BM 118807).[10] The bibliography generated over the White Obelisk (hereafter WO) makes clear if nothing else, since it does not solve which king originated the monument, Anp II

or Anp I (1050-1032), how impossible it is to interpret a monument without a connected text, even if the illustrations are reasonably clear.

4. Broken [White Stone (= Gypsum)] of Abk (Aššur-bel-kala, 1074-1057), discovered by Rassam, at Kuyunjik (BM 118898).[11] It was the fragmentary condition of the initial columns of text which generated the earlier controversies pertaining to this monument and the king to whom it should be assigned.

5. Fragments from Nineveh assigned to Anp II or Slm III, discovered by R. C. Thompson, at Kuyunjik.[12] The origin of these and their ninth century date has served to fuel the controversy pertaining to WO. As Reade has commented, "Many small fragments of carved stone, from Aššur, Kalḫu, and Nineveh have been thought to belong to other ninth century monuments of this kind."[13]

6. Fragment joining Basalt of Anp II, discovered by M. E. L. Mallowan, at Nimrud.[14] Of the two best preserved, BO and WO, it is noteworthy that, because of its state of preservation, the assignment of BO has from the beginning been unambiguous, whereas in the case of WO ambiguity and argument yet prevail. Yet in either case the matter is chiefly textual. What most interests us, however, requires a shift in level of reality from the object as a whole in comparison with like artifacts to the initially observable detail, i.e., the panels of relief art upon the obelisk. Yet each shift in level carried with it a broadening, rather than narrowing, of the comparative base.

## The representational level: macroscopic

It was sculptured on the four sides; there were in all twenty small bas-reliefs, and above, below, and between them was carved an inscription 210 lines in length. The whole was in the best preservation; scarcely a character of the inscription was wanting; the figures were as sharp and well defined as if they had been carved but a few days before. The king is twice represented, followed by his attendants;

a prisoner is at his feet, and his vizier and eunuchs are
introducting men leading various animals, and carrying vases
and other objects of tribute on their shoulders, or in their
hands. The animals are the elephant, the rhinoceros, the
Bactrian or two-humped camel, the wild bull, the lion, the
stag, and various kinds of monkeys. Amongst the objects
carried by the tribute-bearers, may perhaps be distinguished
the tusks of the elephant, shawls, vases of the precious
metals, fruit, and bars of metal, or bundles of rare wood.[15]

Our second level of reality is the representational. It is fair
to observe that the twenty panels of BO, the thirty-two panels of WO
insofar as they remain clear, and the six somewhat fragmented panels
of Basalt of Anp II which have to date appeared, are nearly self-
explanatory. A few of the types of animals might require some
discussion, but the impression remains of processions of animals
and/or men, the latter often carrying reasonably recognizable
objects, at least at the general level, moving in an overall
pattern around the four sides within the horizontal bands. Any
connections between bands are quite unclear, though it might be
assumed that one is to "read" panels from top down, or even from
bottom up; the point is that horizontal-around clearly prevails over
vertical-by-face. Consistently on BO, and, as far as one can tell
from the few panels published, on Basalt of Anp II, the processions
move from right to left. Peculiarly, as A. Moortgat has diagrammed,
the activities on WO proceed back and forth.[16] With respect to
divergence of themes from the prevailing passivity of "tributary"
processionals on BO and Basalt of Anp II, WO presents, in Moortgat's
inventory, "warlike expeditions to the mountains, conquests of
strongholds and cities, the offering of tribute to the Assyrian king,
sacrifices in front of the temple, wild animals hunted on foot or
from a chariot."[17] The concerns of this essay make it necessary to
lay aside many of these themes, in order to concentrate on that
central focus which is best identified on what is to us the "front"
face of BO. Similarly, the unique panel of Broken of Abk can be
summarily dismissed, since no processional climax can be presupposed.

The central focus of BO lies in the two panels wherein the exceptions to the prevailing processional movement occur. These are panels one and two from the top of that side which has been designated "primary" or "front"; there the procession, either that of the horizontal band or overall, comes to a halt before a main figure who stands erect and stationary facing right. Behind this figure are two associates or attendants likewise facing right. Before him, he who heads the procession kneels prostrate. That the erect figure should be called the Assyrian king is not surprising. In fact prior to the discovery of BO, Layard had cleared room B of the Northwest Palace, which we know as the main throneroom of Anp II,[18] and had found within a larger bas-relief a scene strikingly similar to the two we discuss here (see below). A listing of such scenes is in order, again arranged according to their sequence of rediscovery.

But in order to arrive at a list of strictly comparable scenes, it is necessary to make a delimiting distinction. The fragmentary panels of Basalt of Anp II and a number of other reliefs also show cessations of processional movement, and again before the royal figure. The distinction lies in the absence of the prostrate figure, and while we shall have need of some cross-referencing, we cannot dwell on those equally interesting alternatives. Suffice it to say that in this other _topos_ there stand at the head of the procession, before the king, groups of what appear to be the king's associates or attendants, after whom come "tributary" figures, be they objects or bearers of that "tribute." With this qualification then, the focal scenes with which I will be concerned are:

1. <u>Wall relief of Tp III</u> (Tukulti-apil-Ešarra, commonly Tiglath-pileser, 744-727) No. 1, discovered by Layard, at Nimrud (Detroit Institute of Arts 50, 32).[19] In spite of the displacement from one palace to another, supportive scenes continuing the theme are probably in evidence on a relief found (later with Tp III No. 2) at wall r no. 1[20] which would belong behind the King facing right as part of his supportive group, including his chariot and horse.

2. <u>Wall relief of Anp II</u>, discovered by Layard, at Nimrud (BM
124537).[21] The kneeling prostrate figure facing left before the
erect king facing right constitutes only the right hand third
of this relief, there being behind the king, also facing right,
his supportive group, including chariot and horse. The total
impression of the original sequences is best obtained from
Meuszyński,[22] though for the upper alone, employing redis-
covered original drawings, see Yadin.[23]
3. <u>Wall relief of Tp III</u> No. 2, discovered by Layard, at
Nimrud (BM 118933).[24] Concerning the wall reliefs on Tp III,
it is interesting to note that similar to those of Anp II the
two frame reliefs were separated by an inscription, of which
Layard made careful copies before sawing it away. The problem
with these also includes, however, the disruption which occurred
in antiquity, for what has appeared from Layard's copies is
that the inscriptions ran sequentially also, as consecutive
annals rather than as Anp II's "Standard Inscription." Such
consecutiveness of inscription helps to guarantee sequence of
relief, though the reconstitution of the "annals" of Tp III
remains a major issue.[25]

A supportive scene continuing the theme of relief TP III no. 2
might be evident on another relief,[26] though there are two
contrasts: the procession was moving from left to right, and
in spite of the somewhat fragmentary condition of the relief
it is evident that the king, who stood <u>facing left</u>, was not
erect, but had his right foot upon the neck of the prostrate
figure.
4. <u>Wall relief of Tp III</u> No. 3, discovered by Layard, at
Nimrud, but abandoned there.[27] Of the lower register there
survives today only the piece showing the king, seated and
facing left (Leyden, A.1934/6 1)[28] though the British Museum
has the upper register, part of a siege scene with females
and a child fleeing in a cart (BM 118882).[29] The drawing makes
clear an original prostrate figure facing right was present,

though partially hidden behind the king's lead attendant. Several additional scenes or scene-fragments preserved in part or only in the drawings might belong to one of the alternate topoi; of these we note relative to the latter, Original Drawing I, pl. IX,[30] because it shows the king seated facing right. There are no further sculptured wall reliefs pertinent to our inquiry; and no other comparable scenes, so far as I could determine, appear in the surviving reliefs from the later neo-Assyrian palaces. But our topos and its alternate do appear in other materials, and in miniaturized version on stone not unlike the wall relief.

5. Reliefs in bronze from gate bands of Slm III, discovered by Rassam, at Balawat (BM 124661).[31] We have already indicated that thematic scenes may be understood as involving a complete register of a given band (the subsequent enumeration will follow that of King's publication). The alternative topos of a processional terminating before the king and without the presence of the kneeling prostrate figure occurs nine times, twice the king stands erect facing right (IIIR1, XIRu),[32] six times he stands erect facing left (IIIRu, VLu, VL1, VILu, VIL1, VIIL1), and once he is seated facing left (IXL1). The prostrate figure also occurs twice, one each with the erect king facing left (XLu) and right (XIIIR1). The overall impression of these bands coming from the same reign as BO weights heavily in the levels of meaning to which we point.

6. Reliefs in bronze from gate bands of Anp II, discovered by Rassam, at Balawat.[33] Band "I" shows the alternate topos with erect king facing right. The remainder of the sixteen bands were re-discovered in the reserves of the British Museum in 1956, but only preliminary reports have appeared, insufficient for our present purposes.[34]

7. Wall painting of Tp III, discovered by Thureau-Dangin, at Til Barsip.[35] A. Parrot incorporates two of these paintings though that which is shown is but parts of even longer scenes

("over seventy feet"); the first represents our alternate topos with king seated facing right, the second shows, albeit in fragmentary fashion, the prostrate figure before the seated king facing right.[36]

8. Reliefs on the [Limestone] Throne-base of Slm III, discovered by David Oates, (IM 65574).[37] Around the outer (north and south) faces of the slabs there are two processional scenes, one left and one right. In each case the procession moves away from that uniquely peculiar front (west) face which appears to show, though this is debated,[38] respectively Marduk-zakir-šumi I (circa 854-819)[39] and Slm III, the kings of Babylonia (left of center, facing right) and of Assyria (right of center, facing left), "shaking hands," a "symbolic gesture" the significance of which remains unexplained.[40]

Concerning the two tributary processions, each representing our alternate topos, they terminate near the back of their respective faces, close to the east wall, when the movement encounters the erect king facing into oppositely moving lines; hence the king faces right on the north scene, left on the south.

It has become customary to divide neo-Assyrian art into three phases, for each of which two Assyrian kings are identified as chiefly responsible:  early with Anp II and Slm III, middle with Tp III and Sar II (Šarrukin, commonly Sargon, 721-705), and late with Sn (Sin-ahhe-eriba, commonly Sennacherib, 704-681) and Asb (Aššur-ban-apli).[41]  But such a division of the final two hundred fifty years of the imperial Assyrian state is simply a reflection either of its principal figures or of the chanciness of archeological discovery, or both. When, however, we look for and at a particular element in that art, such as the portraying of a figure kneeling prostrate before the king or the alternate topos without prostrate figure with the king receiving a processional bearing quantities of recognizable items of value, all we can say within the limits of our knowledge is that this kind of scene in Assyrian art begins and ends with equal abruptness.

## The representational level:  microscopic

> Our basic evidence is sometimes inadequate or untrustworthy.
> Modern drawings of sculptures, when they can be compared with
> the originals..., often omit details; occasionally they re-
> store more than is justified.  Photographs too are not always
> clear.  But far more disturbing are the vagaries of the
> Assyrians themselves.  We have to appreciate that the original
> workmen were not automata, and that great numbers were some-
> times employed at once.  A particular type of dress, for in-
> stance, can be represented in a variety of ways in a single
> palace...  In addition to this, however, the workmen were
> liable not only to leave out details just as modern draftsmen
> have done, but also to make positive mistakes.[42]

The representational level of reality has a second dimension,
which we might call "microscopic," that is, viewed at the level of
specific detail for each figure involved within a total thematic
scene.  While one could describe representational scenes as typical,
because of the presence of focal figures and a small complement of
associates, the fact is that, when viewed in an overall sense, the
nine scenes delineating the topos of the kneeling prostrate figure
and the thirteen scenes of what we have called the alternate topos
display little that can be called typical.  Rather, one might say
each is atypical in the sense that each scene could be thought of as
representing some one real occasion.  This is particularly the case
with respect to the kind of "distances" (measured in terms of number
of figures involved in the processional) from the central focus which,
occur in the bronze gate reliefs of Slm III and the elongated wall
paintings of Tp III.  While there are recurring figures of note
throughout the whole corpus of Assyrian sculptures which have
prompted Reade to make some efforts at specific identification,[43]
when we come to the few examples of our processional theme, there
simply are not any two scenes with exactly the same sequence of
characters, not even those clearly part of the immediate royal en-
tourage.

Nevertheless, a certain cast of characters may be identified
(at least phenomenologically if not by "title") sufficiently clearly
so that we could present in symbolic fashion the order of the two

confronting groups in the immediate vicinity of the king. Though for
the purposes of this paper, a detailed catalogue cannot be given, we
would note that there are certain fixed roles, postures and gestures.
It may be possible to interpret such symbolic images individually but
they need to be viewed in their wholeness and various relationships.

We must understand the significance of the "symbolic gestures"
depicted on the reliefs, particularly that of the prostrate figure
before the king, within the context of the historical development of
the final form of the Assyrian state. But such an understanding leads
on from the representational level of reality to that level in which
verbal form is added.

## The narrative level

Quod non est in verbo, non est in mundo (Proverbial).
The wording has no relevance to the scene in any particular instance. [44]

The interpretation of BO did not begin with any great concern for
what exactly was being said in the lines adjacent to the panels.
Clearly Layard had "seen" first and the deciphered reading which
followed merely bore out the specifics, though it generated some
excitement insofar as a biblical personality was understood to be
named. Otherwise the object list of tributory gifts confirmed the
visual inspection, making possible without doubt some greater degree
of specific identification. All this is clear in Layard[45] and in
Rawlinson's appropriation. [46]

The verbal or narrative level of reality does take us one
step further, by identifying for us specific "personal names" (hereafter PN) and "geographic names" (hereafter GN). Had we not already
had more than a century of efforts to reconstruct the history of
Assyria, it is clear that the representational level of reality represented by the reliefs would not have been sufficient to identify
either the erect king who stands facing the on-coming processional
or the kneeling prostrate figure. But can we in fact identify the
latter? This brings us back to all the evidence which we have

catalogued in the preceding sections. Let us review what we have
discovered, but in the context of some new concerns.

Aside from obelisks, all of which, including fragments, combine
inscriptions with relief panels, we adduced, as appropriate to our
thematic concern, wall and related smaller reliefs, reliefs in
bronze from gate bands, and wall painting. With respect to the
obelisks, aside from the clear epigrams, especially of BO, that
which is readable is annalistic and of no particular relevance to
our processional theme, though it is not without reference to
occasions involving tribute which might have been brought pro-
cessionally. Concerning such a matter annals do not explicitly
speak. We will later note the significance of annalistic inscriptions for assisting our search for that vocabulary which makes
explicit the aforementioned "symbolic gestures," including that of
our kneeling prostrated figure, as well as the king's posture.

Of the relevant catalogued evidence, the wall paintings alone
had no proximate inscriptions. Had they been found first they
would have been unidentifiable in the verbal sense. The identification of those found by the French as belonging to Tp III or his
reign rests upon comparative reference to the wall reliefs and the
archaeological discovery of objects with inscriptions.

The other types of materials adduced combine inscriptions with
relief, though with this distinction: the wall reliefs, whether of
Anp II or of Tp III, show no specific correlation between text and
relief, as the above quotation from S. Smith has reminded us. Anp
II's "Standard Inscription" on larger reliefs simply cut across the
mid-section, including any figures present, royal or otherwise, with
no regard, though not necessarily with unpleasing results.[47] Only
those relatively few slabs from the throneroom of the Northwest
Palace and an occasional other slab or room originally showed the
distinctive feature of separating panels of relief by a band of
text. But in no direct way can the abbreviated "Standard Inscription"
employed thereon be said to provide a narrative for the relief. We
may conclude this from its indiscriminate use and especially its

application to ritual figures who are not referred to in its words.[48]
The panels themselves have no inscriptions.

In the two panel formats which concern us in the wall reliefs of
Tp III, the intervening inscription was annalistic and sequential
rather than abbreviated and repetitive. Only a few larger wall slabs
with single relief figures from the reign of Tp III have survived
(generally in but partial condition; e.g., those of the king and the
"keeper of the bow," respectively BM 118900 and 118899)[49] upon which
an inscription originally went across the center, though pausing to
avoid aspects of the figure. Some few of the panels, especially
those of militaristic topoi, show an isolated name identifying the
city under siege or destruction (the three surviving examples include: BM 115634, BM 118908, and a slab preserved only in drawing).[50]

A closely analogous situation applies when we come to the
bronze gate bands and to the limestone thronebase, both of Slm III.
As to the latter, which overall is a kind of miniature wall relief,
its platform surface inscription is but an abbreviated conglomerate
of annalistic entries down to his thirteenth year but not presented
in strict chronological order.[51] They have no particular relationship to the scenes on the sides, though they incorporate in conclusion a longer three-line statement appropriate to the unique
scene on the front. By way of contrast the inscriptions found above
the reliefs must be defined as epigrams in the manner of those of BO.

With respect to the embronzed gate, its long door-sheathing inscription is selectively annalistic from the first nine years of his
reigh,[52] and can be related to some of the more militaristic bands,
since they cover graphically some of those same years and their
relatively short epigrams are clearly meant to relate to the
particular scene upon which each is inscribed.

Yet not all 32 scenes of the 16 bands have inscriptions. Aside
from the two fragmented bands (XVR; XVIL) of which not enough remains
to reconstruct the scenes totally or to be sure that more than a
single inscription was originally present, 8 of the 28 remaining
scenes have no inscription at all (IIRl; IVRl; VLl; VIIIRl; XLu;

XIR1; XIIIR1). The 22 inscriptions[53] are formulaic, following one
of four verbal patterns, or in a single instance (XL1) combining
two. The largest verbal pattern with nine examples (IR1; VIILu;
VIIIRu; IXLu; IXL1; XL1; XIIIlu; XIIIL1; XIIIRu) belongs to
militaristic topoi, well expressed by its eipgram as "I captured
GN/PN" (GN/PN akšud); five other examples (IIRu; IIIR1; IVRu;
XVR; XVIL) portray "the smiting of PN/GN" (tiduku ša PN/GN).
Twice alone (IRu; XIVL1), and once in combination (XL1) there is
illustrated the setting up of the royal image (salma.../salam
šarrutiia ušaziz). Of the nine processionals of the alternate
topos (without kneeling prostrate figure though with varying
postures of the king) one is described by the epigram tiduku ša
PN/GN (IIIR1), one by GN/PN akšud (IXL1), two are uninscribed
(VL1; VIL1); the other five (IIIRu; VLu; VILu; VIIIL1; XIRu),
plus the incomplete fragments of a similar theme but missing the
king (XIVLu), constitute the fourth formulaic category, which is
defined as "tribute of PN/GN" (madatu ša PN/GN), verbally comparable
to the epigrams of BO or the side inscriptions of the thronebase.
Yet of greater importance to us is the fact that those two scenes
belonging to the topos of the kneeling prostrated figure (XLu;
XIIIR1) show no inscription at all. One could of course relate
each of them to the other scene of its respective band, which in
both cases are GN/PN akšud. But in two (IR; VIIL) of the five
cases where both registers of a band are inscribed, the GN/PN
definitely do not coincide; in two others (IXL; XIIL) the PN is
the same but the GN represents different cities; and in the last
(XIVL) the situation is ambiguous because of fragmentation, but
would not appear to coincide since the geography of Tyre permitted
no image to be set up within. For our purposes lack of inscription
means no guarantee of identification of the kneeling prostrate
figure. But the problem remains until we reach our discussion of
the levels of meaning.

The fragmentary inscription of WO is annalistic of military
operations. To that extent the relief art and the narrative share
thematic concerns. Even so our topos fits neither art nor text.

Considering its shattered condition, very little can be said for
the present concerning the inscription of the Basalt obelisk of Anp
II that was not already said by Gadd.[54] The longest passages he relates to the "Standard Inscription," another to the inscription of
the lamassu.[55] Above one relief he made out the start of the formula
madatu ša, but with PN/GN broken away, by no means unsuitable for the
alternate topos.

The long inscription of BO is annalistic, but abridged by comparison to fuller accounts available for particular years. The
tabular correlations have been given by Schramm.[56] From overall
verbal content one might hazard the guess that BO as monument is
the commemorative piece for Slm III's "jubilee" of his "thirty-
first" year (according to the obelisk, line 174, which counts from
the year of his accession) when he took for a second time the
limmu,[57] since every one of his years receives some entry, however
sparse (several lines) or full (15 or more for the final years
incorporated). But that this text is difficult to correlate with
the five epigram lines (including the two above the panels with the
kneeling prostrate figure), each based upon the formula madatu ša
PN/GN, is best suggested by the simple observation that none of the
4 PN and only two of the 5 GN found in them occur in the 190 lines
of the longer inscription. The onomastic elements of the fourth
epigram ᵈMarduk(AMAR.UD)-apla(A)-uṣur(PAB) ᴷᵁᴿsu-ha-aia(A.A.) do not
occur anywhere in the surviving texts of Slm III, and we have to look
back to inscriptions of the reign of his father Anp III to find the
land and its annexation into Assyria.[58]

Clearly we have exhausted the levels of reality capable of
phenomemological description, and efforts to enter upon levels of
meaning are now required. The proverb at the head of this section
was oft quoted by I. G. Gelb in his historiography seminar also with
the reverse implication that there should be a word for what appears
in the world. To the words we must then turn.

## III. Levels of Meaning

## Vocabulary

ma-da-tu-šá PN/GN "objects" am-hur-šu (BO epigrams).

In contrast to nāmurtu, madattu (Babylonian mandattu) is
applied strictly only to compulsory payments, and not to
gifts freely offered; nadanu is the regular Akkadian word
for to pay..., and madattu could therefore be accurately
translated as 'payment'. In fact, of course, it is generally recognized to be the usual Assyrian word for 'tribute',
by which is meant the payment imposed by his overlord upon
a subject. The majority of references to this institution
are to be found in the Assyrian king's annals, and describe
the imposition (or increasing) of this compulsory payment
on kingdoms which had been subjected in war.[59]

The evidence of the reliefs from the gate bands and the throne-
base, which have the alternative topos and come from the same reign
as BO, is very valuable to us. Since no kneeling prostrate figure i
present, there can be no question of personal identification, even i
the instances in which the formulaic inscription provides PN. It is
noteworthy, on the other hand, that in the two instances in the gate
bands of reliefs of our primary topos, no inscription occurs at all.
We are thus forced to consider the meaning of the words and the
meaning of the scenes as having equal but separate weight, at least
from an analytical perspective.

What was altogether clear to Layard, who could not yet read the
words, was that the scene was a procession concerned with acquisitio
whether they be booty or gifts or something in between. The vocabul
bore that out but made other distinctions, which not only increased
in number with time but showed evolution of meaning reflective of
the passage of time.

In general Postgate's point about madattu is well enough taken,
though his full argument fails to make several matters clear. He
had defined nāmurtu, or its Babylonian form tamartu, as meaning "in
nA times...a subsidiary gift to accompany tribute,"[60] which would
imply that his sharp contrast could have madattu "applied strictly
only to compulsory payments, and not to gifts freely offered."[61]
The assumption is that if there are two words they represent diverger
elements of the same society. While he has discussed middle Assyria

evidence for the background meaning of nāmurtu solely on the basis
of the archive of Ninurta-tukul-Aššur from Aššur,[62] he does not take
into account the usage of the Assyrian royal inscriptions.  From at
least the time of Samsi-Adad I (1813-1781) the basic word for "tribute"
was biltu (CAD, 2.234-6); with the reign of TN I (Tukulti-Ninurta,
1244-1208) one finds biltu u madattu or biltu u tamartu being used
interchangeably.  The former prevails in the annals of Tp I (1115-
1077) and those of Anp II.  On the other hand, nāmurtu appears almost exclusively in the annals of TN II (890-884), quite obviously
with meanings going well beyond "subsidiary gift" to include full
tribute.  It would appear from the more "propagandistic" annals that
either madattu or nāmartu might comprehend both ends of Postgate's
contrasting spectrum, and probably several shades of verbal coloration
in between.

On another kind of historical level, especially pertinent to
the purpose of this study, the trans-Euphratean territories have no
history of incorporation within the Assyrian empire prior to Anp II.
Hence, there is no precedent for the "gift" (madattu, Anp II would
say!) being given in advance of submission under the pressure-fear
of Assur's power.  Admittedly the "gift" on these occasions sets a
precedent tantamount to submission, which the Assyrian thereafter
assumes, so that the act of "giving" must continue or the territorial
ruler will be considered a rebel.  It would therefore seem appropriate
to put together both meanings suggested by Postgate for the period
of Slm III.

Noteworthy in Postgate's study, however, though again dependent
upon documentary materials from the later neo-Assyrian reigns, is
his discussion of the processes of payment, including not only time,
place, and materials, but also the ceremonial occasion and its
accompanying "hospitality."[63]  While we might well see therein the
base for the occasion of the kneeling prostrate figure, it is nevertheless well to recall that the environment being shown in the relief
art of Slm III (especially in the evidence of the bronze gate bands)
includes occasions which clearly took place in the field and not in

the acropolis or arsenal palaces. And that is as much the case of scenes with Slm III seated as with him standing erect. Clearly the Assyrians could transport in a mobile fashion all the symbols and trappings of official government. On the other hand, the reliefs from walls or thronebase might well serve as a permanent reminder of the appropriate postures and gestures to be employed within the roya complex of the capital city.

Schramm identifies for us many of the thematic elements appropriate to the reigns of the individual kings as employed in the surviving inscriptions. Pertaining to the verbal theme "Der König erhält Tribut," he counts about 80 textual instances, which after the elimination of duplicates reduce to about 45 actual instances (though by "actual," we mean only literary, without trying to guarantee "historicity").[64] He does not tell us that in these instances "tribute" is rendered almost without exception by madattu, and never by nāmurtu. Yet clearly the instances cover the variety which Postgate tried to separate. Such annalistic preference is consistent with the evidence from the inscriptions on the reliefs. Only those reliefs from the reign of Slm III have any epigrams, and in those either madattu or no word at all is employed if the matter is one of the reception of a procession bearing "objects" to the king. Moreover, by implication of the consistent verb employed as predicate, of which the noun madattu is accusative, the king simply "received" (am-hur or am-hur-šu from the root maharu, AHw, 577-80). To be sure, this verb had already a history of usage with whatever noun designated the tribute/gift, but that is precisely the point. One cannot make sharp distinctions from the thematic usage alone. Much more rarely at the level of predicate usage, distinct verbs express the more subtle points of the tribute/gift being "imposed" (šakanu, AHw, 1134-9) or "increased" (šuturu, s.v. atāru, CAD, 1/2 487-492).

With the reign of Tp I the inscriptional references to these "gifts," however expressed, whether voluntary or exacted, begin to receive enlargement by a cataloguing of the "objects" which make up this revenue. This cataloguing usually includes the five metals: silver, gold, tin, copper/bronze and more rarely, iron.[65] From the reign of Slm III, aside from the five metals and various containers of gold or copper/bronze, "objects" listed in the annals include: horses broken to the yoke, cattle, sheep, wine, garments of brightly colored wool or of linen, cedar logs and resin, other rare woods, elephant hides, tusks, and ivory. The single instance of a gate band with its own list (XIV) and the two thronebase examples follow these same preferences and emphases. By way of contrast, both the epigrams and reliefs of BO display in addition the exotic, especially in animals. Clearly this is most unusual _madattu_, and we have increasing right to assume that while BO must be "read" with great care, it points us to the exceptional and not to the typical, even though the means of expression, whether text or art, employs common elements.

Themes

> The terrifying _melam_ of Assur, my lord, overwhelmed him
> and he came up to me; my feet he grasped; his obligations
> I took; silver, gold, iron, cattle, sheep -- his "tribute"
> I received. (BO 134-5).

> The sculptures like the annals are propaganda and represent
> only what the rulers of Assyria wished us to remember; the
> subject matter is also affected by stylistic considerations.
> There is nonetheless, at all times, a mass of information
> which must bear some positive relationship to the truth.[66]

While Schramm identifies many of the main thematic elements of the verbiage of the royal inscriptions of Slm III, regrettably he lists them in translation rather than in the original.[67] More problematically, he does not take the trouble to correlate which thematic elements regularly or typically go together, nor does he attempt to identify the verbal theme with its representational equivalent. For example, he does not note that the receipt of "tribute" (_madattu maharu_) occurs only when the "enemy" is not destroyed, never when he is (ak-šud ab-búl aq-qur ina girri áš-ru-up in that marvelous redundancy!). On these latter occasions plunder may be plundered (šallu šalalu). But madattu is the "gift" of those who chose not to fight, though occasionally of those against whose cities siege was laid (lamû) or within whose cities they were shut up (esēru) before "the terrifying melam of Assur overwhelmed" them. The verbiage, because it is so compressed, especially in the more summarizing inscriptions, does not always spell out in full what actually took place. We may not read into a text more than it says, but we may assume, especially from the relief art, that a certain kind of scene ensued: a processional, in some instances with kneeling prostrate figure.

There are special cases. In seven instances reference to madattu is combined with verbiage expressing the theme of grasping the king's feet (šepē-ia sabatu: Mon I 23; II 21, 57, 86; Ann.Cam. III 43; Nim. Stat. E 17, 26), and on two additional occasions Slm III goes even further to note that the setting up of a king followed the former gesture (a-na šarrū-ti ina ili-šunu šakanu: BO 139-40, 154-5); these were persons who had not been among the rebels who withheld madattu but rather who saw that it was "received." Once there is enthronement without reference to the grasping of feet gesture (BO 95). One might also note the occasion involving Marduk-zakir-sumi, wherein Slm III established him on the throne of his father (ina <sup>GIS</sup>kussî abi-šú ú-kin: Thronebase 46), to which we referred before in commenting on the unique symbolic gesture of "shaking hands."

If epigrams are thought to apply to the reliefs with which they are found, what is the correlation of the PN in epigrams with those who are inscriptionally defined as having "grasped the king's feet?" Nil. In fact, none of those so defined in annals are even named in epigrams. By way of contrast and comparison, alternate topoi found in the epigrams produce these connections. For the thronebase both epigrams identify PN from whom the king did receive tribute according to the annals, but with this difference: for the south face the pairing of PN$_1$, Mušallim-Marduk son of Ukani, and PN$_2$, Adini son of Dakuri, ties exclusively into palu 9; moreover the pair recur as pair in scene IXRu of the bronze gate bands and are documented together from the Balawat door-sheathing inscription as well, though in both of these cases without chronological specificity. Evidently, this paired event was somehow unique in the reliefs, though from annalistic notices there are four other occasions when two or more PN are grouped for the receipt of madattu. By contrast the north face's PN Qalparunda of GN P/Ḫattina could fit any one of a variety of occasions and perhaps two or more different persons, on which see the possibilities discussed by Hulin.[68] The epigram of BO panel V is relevant to the text but we have already noted that the processional depicted there is incomplete.

With respect to the bronze gate bands the seven processional instances defined above as having epigrams tie into PN and/or GN found in annals, but are not able in general to be fixed exclusively to one particular year. This is not surprising, considering that on a few occasions, though none related to these epigrams, found in the longer annalistic texts for particular years (e.g. the Monolith's coverage of the first six years), Slm III will specify that he has imposed madattu and that he "yearly received it" (šatti-sam-ma am-da-ḫar, lines II 26-7, 29, 30, once with the specification "in my city Assur" II 24, all from his own limmu year), or at least intended to. Yet even when vague as to occasion, it is clear that the five madattu instances no more imply capture or destruction in the epigrams than would appear from the passivity of the scene. On the other hand, the two processions we have discussed involving tiduku (IIIRl) and akšud (IXLl) portray at least the capture and perhaps burning of a city and the taking of prisoners, if not burning with fire. We come then to the two scenes of primary topos of BO and the implications which arise therefrom.


Identifications

Thus, if the Ancient Mesopotamian historian is to give
any meaningful account of his materials at all he must
of a necessity relax the stringent claim of "what the
evidence obliges us to believe" and substitute for it a
modest "what the evidence makes it reasonable for us to
believe," for it is only by taking account of evidence
which is suggestive, when the suggestion is in itself
reasonable, that he will be able to integrate his data
in a consistent and meaningful presentation.[69]

While from his first palu, Slm III, following his father's
precedent, had crossed the Euphrates and reached "the Sea of the
Setting Sun," his significant involvement west of the Euphrates and
south along the coast began in what he called typically and consistently palu 6, or limmu Daian-Assur (Mon. II 78). Confusion
occurs because the long but compressed inscription of BO distinguished these two years by using the latter mode of reference
as though it dated palu 4 (BO 45), which simply does not square with
the eponym lists. Yet even in BO, consistently the great event of
palu 6 is the battle at the city qar-qa-ra. This event was evidently of such significance that Slm III included it in every summarizing
inscription, including especially the impressive monuments and
statuary of his reign, even when the latter bore no dating notations.
Since $^m$a-ha-ab-bu$^{KUR}$sir-'-la-aia(A.A.) was a participant (named only
Mon. II 91-2), though commemorated under the more typical reference
to the leadership of $^{md}$adad(IM)-id-ri šá$^{KUR}$dimašqi(ANŠE.ŠÚ) and
$^m$ir-hu-li-na$^{KUR}$a-mat-a-a, the event has also served as a point of
reference for much discussion of the history[70] and chronology[71] of
ancient Israel. Slm III remembers, however, incorporating these two
principal PN, the "12 kings" of Hatti and/or the Sea Coast (a-hat-tam
ti; once he states "15" Tgr. II 21),[72] which he comes close to en-
umerating in detail only in the Monolith, though even there he does
not in fact give us a full twelve, but only 7PN and 11 GN! Irhuleni
alone is named three times in the epigrams to the bronze gate bands
in connection with scenes (IXLu, IXLl, and XIIIRu) though on each
occasion a divergent GN(city) is identified as captured (akšud).

But one of these is precisely qa-ar-qa-ra. Adad-idri is not en-
countered beyond the annalistic references.

While the 6th palu, because of "Ahab," has attracted considerable attention, what has received less notice is the meaning
of the same vague general reference to these "12 kings" for palu
10, 11, and 14. In each identifiable instance the leadership
remained the same. Instead, it is the suddenness of the appearance
with palu 18 of two other names, and simultaneously the disappearance
of the two leaders and the rest of the "12," which tells us that
the earlier circumstances confronting Slm III have been altered,
though not entirely improved. While the first of these new names,
ᵐha-za-ᵓ-ili šá^KUR dismašqi, appears to continue the opposition toward Assyria in which his own predecessor had joined, the uniquely
detailed but undated statue inscription (KAH I 30) indicates this
new king is no legitimate successor ("son of a nobody"), but rather
a usurper, perhaps even a regicide.[73] Nevertheless, this throne
change made the opposition of Damascus no less formidable, and Slm
III returns against Hazael in palu 21 as well. It is noteworthy
that in both of these years Slm III records receipt of madattu from
both Tyre and Sidon, which is also illustrated twice in gate bands
(IIIRu and XIV), to which pair in palu 21 Byblos (Gebal) is added,
while with them in palu 18 we meet ᵐia-ú-a DUMU ᵐhu-um-ri-i.

Specifically, the PN appears twice more in the same ortho-
graphy in annalistic texts (IIIR 5; 6: 25-6; Kurbaᵓil Stat. 29-30),
and once written ᵐia-a-ú DUMU ᵐhu-um-ri-i (Ann.FS IV 11), all told
four times, rather than the three cited by P. K. McCarter[74] in his
peculiar effort to revise the history and chronology by having the
Akkadian spelling be hypocoristic for "Jehoram," thus enabling
"Ahab" to live longer than the year of the battle of Qarqar. This
is as problematic methodologically as E. R. Thiele's effort to make
the iron-rigidity of a chronological system finally apply to the
biblical text.[75] Thiele continues to do yeoman service in his
studies of "the mysterious numbers of the Hebrew kings," but his
purpose remains numerologically literalistic. As many important

historiographic studies have attempted to illustrate, it is less than clear what the "historiosophic motivations of the editor(s) of Kings" were when they came to the dynastic houses of Omri/Ahab and of Jehu.[76]

Uninteresting to either McCarter or Thiele, and to most others, is the actual evidence of the scenes on BO, since for them the matter is strictly or finally on the verbal level. McCarter admits "the frequent irregularities in cuneiform representation of foreign names,"[77] at which point it is unclear whether he means in the Assyrian's own divergent orthographies, as noted about re ia-ú-a/iaa-a-ú, or as compared to the same names in their own texts. The latter problem may be the more interesting, if only because so few good examples survive. Of the former, the name in the epigram over the first panel of BO illustrates further the divergence: $^m$su-ú-a$^{KUR}$ gíl-za-na-aia(A.A.) is met with in the madattu listings of Slm III's accession year and his palu 3 under the forms respectively $^m$a-su-ú (Mon. I 28) and $^m$a-sa-a-ú (II 61). This PN does not appear again, though the GN in this gentilic form stands typically in the abridged annals and appears on a bronze gate band (VIILl). J. V. Kinnier-Wilson reviewed the problems and evidence for this location.[78]

PN$_1$ DUMU PN$_2$ does not particularly dominate the lists of madattu providers. But one of the seven PN of the "12 kings" is given in this fashion, and elsewhere the ratio does not exceed one in three or four out of the approximate total of 45. Of petty kings mentioned in the royal inscriptions of Slm III who gave the great king madattu and who might well have been confirmed in, if not installed upon, their respective thrones, only a few examples receive some degree of confirmation by contemporaneous records from their own locality. The early twentieth century excavations at Zinjirli in northwest Syria, ancient Y'dy/SM'l "under Mount Amanus" (šá šep kur ha-ma-ni) as Slm would say, produced a series of four monumental stele and statuary illustrative of both dynastic sequence and relationship to Assyria. The later two, correlated specifically with the reign of Tp III, make explicit the role of the Assyrian. For our purposes on two counts, however, it is the earliest that

deserves attention.[79]   King K̲l̲m̲w̲ claims to have hired the king of
Assyria to assist him against an opponent king (lines 7-8: w̌s̲k̲r̲
ꜣn̲k̲ ꜥl̲y̲ m̲k̲l̲ ꜣš̲r̲), clearly indicative of previous relationship,
borne out at the genealogical level, and the obvious way a vassal
state might express the consequences and expectations of its
(annual) m̲a̲d̲a̲t̲t̲u̲-gift (cf. 2 Kgs 16:5-10).  The king calls himself
k̲l̲m̲w̲ b̲r̲ h̲y̲/h̲y̲ꜣ, the latter (actual father) being him whom Slm III
knows, again with considerable orthographic diversity, as h̲a̲-a̲-n̲i̲-/
h̲a̲-a̲i̲-n̲u̲[KUR]s̲a̲-m̲a̲/a̲m̲-ꜣ-l̲a̲ (Mon. I 42, 53) or h̲a̲-i̲a̲-a̲-n̲u̲/h̲a̲-i̲a̲-n̲i̲
DUMU g̲a̲b̲/g̲a̲-b̲a̲-r̲i̲ (II 24, 83), upon whom tribute was first imposed.
But within K̲l̲m̲w̲'s own text h̲y̲ꜣ does not appear, at least directly,
as son of g̲b̲r̲, is certainly not his immediate successor, and may
not be related (lines 2-3), though equally certainly the latter is
thought of as dynastic founder, as the list of gods with which the
text concludes demonstrates (lines 15-16).  When we add in the
great variety of writings, the parallel to i̲a̲-ú̲-a̲ DUMU h̲u̲-u̲m̲-r̲i̲-i̲
is direct.

  The issue we have proposed throughout can now be stated in its
final form.  It is not, of course, who the men are who are portrayed
in the symbolic gesture of kneeling prostrate before the king at the
head of a processional line bearing m̲a̲d̲a̲t̲t̲u̲.  Rather the key issue
is what they are doing.  Concerning the former matter, we noted much
earlier the impossibility of guaranteeing final correlation of PN
names in a text, even as epigram, with figures shown in the relief,
though the probability may be high.  Certainly the relief created by
the Assyrian propagandist meant to be representative for the kind of
scene necessary to complete the reception of the "gift," and the
m̲a̲d̲a̲t̲t̲u̲ vocabulary of inscription or epigram points to this as well.
Unquestionably an even more impressive scene might have been staged
on the occasions of the receipt of this m̲a̲d̲a̲t̲t̲u̲ within the palace
of the royal city itself, to which an occasional text makes reference
when its annual requirement can be defined.  Perhaps some of the
processional scenes of the alternate t̲o̲p̲o̲s̲ do in fact belong within
the palace rather than without.  We have catalogued detailed

differences. But clearly <u>madattu</u> was also received in the field, as
is evident by appurtenances present in relief. Moreover, on some
fewer occasions it provided the situation in which he who gave
<u>madattu</u> received from the great king his right to sit upon the local
throne. "The evidence makes it reasonable for us" to think that
the symbolic gesture twice recalled on this commemoriative monument
from Slm III's jubilee is in fact a description of such events.

As Elat has observed, there is one more important ingredient in
the epigrams. We have already spoken of the rather unique and exotic
objects which make up <u>madattu</u> in both the epigrams and the relief
panels of BO. There is one textual item, nowhere else included in
an Assyrian royal inscription, that appears among the <u>madattu</u> for
both <sup>m</sup><u>su-ú-a</u> and <sup>m</sup><u>ia-ú-a</u>: for the latter $^{GIS}$<u>hu-tar-tu šá gat šarri</u>
"the staff of the king's hand"; for the former, who was accompanied
by his brothers, when "they came <u>into the presence of</u>" (<u>ina mahri-ia</u>
<u>u-sa-u</u>)[80] Slm III, the expression is made plural, $^{GIS}$<u>hu-tar-a-te</u>(MES)

> The <u>hutartu</u> was not a sceptre, a symbol of royal authority,
> which is designated by <u>hattu</u>. This latter word, as distinct
> from the <u>hutartu</u>, is often mentioned in neo-Assyrian documents,
> but never included in a tribute or handed over by a vassal
> king to his Assyrian overlord. It thus seems to us that the
> <u>hutartu</u> was rather a symbol of protection or ownership of
> property...[81]

Elat sees this borne out by the term's later use as one of the symbol
marked by branding on a slave.

> ...we can assume that in handing over the <u>hutartu</u>...both
> wished to symbolize their kingdoms had been handed over to
> the protection of the king of Assyria.[82]

## IV. Epilegomena

The concept of total or comprehensive reading of the text
must be understood in two ways, both of them equally necessary. The most obvious and simple way is that the document be read <u>in its entirety</u>: a completeness in quantity,

necessary to understand why the text was written. There is, however, a more complex way of understanding the concept of totality: the texts must be read <u>from</u> <u>all possible points of view</u>. This type of completeness, in quality, is necessary to understand why the text was written in that particular way... Naturally, whoever seeks pieces of information is interested in finding the event, and tolerates with annoyance the burden (if felt) of the pattern which "distorts" the event. But whoever (like the ogre of M. Bloch) is seeking man is much more interested in the pattern (which is a product of man) than in the event, which makes up, so to speak, the rough and occasional material for the pattern.[83]

We are left, of course, with the final questions usually asked. Why do the epigrams select as PN for the BO scenes <sup>m</sup><u>su-ú-a</u> <sup>KUR</sup><u>gíl-za-na-aia</u>(A.A.) and <sup>m</sup><u>ia-ú-a</u> DUMU <sup>m</sup><u>hu-um-ri-i</u>? Because, they represent "what actually happened!" But, why only those two, and not the others, some others? That is the pair Slm III and/or his craftsmen chose for BO to remember! Why then do not the annalistic texts say of either of these two the words appropriate to the gesture? Why do not epigrams use words to describe the gesture? It was not necessary! Clearly the relief was far more "readable" to more observers than any text! But would the "reader" know who was meant? If he did, he did; if he did not, why should he? Undoubtedly the relief's function was paradigmatic. Do we? Of course not! Is then the figure on the second panel the biblical Jehu? Clearly these questions and many of the answers proceed from the wrong assumptions, for they are not concerned with history at all, but only with meaning for us!

Historians since G. Rawlinson, whether concerned with Israel or Assyria, or their art, have been divided in their interpretation of the scene on BO or its epigram, but only on the issue of whether the figure represents in fact the Israelite king, or merely the chief of his ambassadors delivering <u>madattu</u>. Each of these historians provided a different explanation of the meaning of Jehu relative to Slm III; none provided a statement on what more the scene adds beyond the simple level of visual reality.

Clearly if Jehu is to be included among those for whom the

scene would fit, though not exclusively, since such is beyond what
can be legitimately "read" from the relief, the matter rests on the
posture of the respective dynastic houses of Israel towards Assyria.
Assuming we can make the correlation, we know where "Ahab" stood;
we cannot answer for his two immediate successors.  But Slm III had
to meet and fight coalitions "in the area" as late as palu 14.  By
palu 18 all was changed.  The lone adversary was "Hazael," again
assuming the correlation, while from "Jehu" madattu was received.
The prophetic action of anointment, according to 1 Kgs 19:15-16
(cf. 2 Kgs 8-9), was for both of these men, but it did not make
them allies.  Rather old allies now became enemies at war with one
another.  It is noteworthy that Tadmor, studying Jehoash the grandson of Jehu in the new texts of Adad-nirari III (810-783), whose
Rimah stele singles out the former's madattu, comments:  "The em-
bassy of Joash emphasized the renewed dependency of Jehu's dynasty
upon the kings of Assyria in his bitter struggle with Aram."[84]

BO may not actually portray Jehu of Israel, but not because he
would not fit.  With this relief as supportive evidence, and "read"
for its own meaningful contribution, the epigram wherein "Jehu" is
written now says much more.  It was madattu to Slm III that bought
for Jehu the throne, and meant the survival of his dynasty over the
next century by continued gifts to the successors of Slm III.  But
as Hall, having observed that it was also Slm's enemies that Jehu
had murdered, aptly put it, for Slm III it meant that "the neutrality
if not the active help, of Israel could therefore be counted on."[85]
For Israel an era of peaceful alliances which in coordination made
difficult the westward expansion of Assyria was over.  Thereafter,
war with her neighbors prevented significant resistance, and the
increasing necessity to call upon Assyrian assistance subverted her
own national life as well.

And yet such a solution is not really any more germaine than
all the others which can be read in the historical treatises of the
past hundred-plus years since this first long Assyrian inscription
was resurrected from the earth and read with renewed excitement.

For any attempted solution lures us back to the unattainable. Our words must reiterate those with which we began, though the reference is now not simply to the impossibility of collecting the materials. Rather, in the words of Liverani, the ultimate matter lies at the base level of reality itself:

> We are not in possession of the historical event, only of some interpretations of it: the views taken by the different actors and witnesses, and the opinions of the historians who reconstruct events through those views. I am afraid that the concept of "historical event" ... is a pure abstraction, which in all cases implies a choice in interpretation, a way of understanding and of presenting. The reconstruction of the most artless and common episode of everyday life is already a simplification in itself: ... We must resign ourselves to recognize that the so-called "event" is, upon objective consideration, so complex as to be impossible to describe and in fact unusable: every use of it implies a drastic simplification which is necessarily biased in one direction.[86]

## Footnotes

1.  F. M. Powicke, *Modern Historians and the Study of History* (London: Odhams, 1955) 104.

2.  Unless otherwise noted, dates follow J. A. Brinkman apud A. L. Oppenheim, *Ancient Mesopotamia* (Chicago: University of Chicago, 1964) 335-347.

3.  Cf. A. H. Layard, *Discoveries in the Ruins of Nineveh and Babylon* (London: J. Murray, 1953) 613.

4.  A. H. Layard, *Nineveh and its Remains* (2 vols.; New York: George P. Putnam, 1849) 1.281-2.

5.  C. J. Gadd, *The Stones of Assyria* (London: Chatto and Windus, 1936) 35, 147-8.

6.  G. Perrot and C. Chipiez, *A History of Art in Chaldaea and Assyria* (trans. W. Armstrong; 2 vols.; London: Chapman and Hall, 1884) 1.257.

7.  *A Guide to the Babylonian and Assyrian Antiquities, British Museum* (London: British Museum, 1900) 19.

8.  Photographs in ANEP, 120-1, figs. 351-354; for bibliography and discussion of the text see R. Borger, *Handbuch der Keilschriftliteratur* (2 vols.; Berlin: W. de Gruyter, 1967, 1975) 1.296, 2.200; W. Schramm, *Einleitung in die assyrischen Königsinschriften* (Leiden: E. J. Brill, 1973) 2.79 [IIIbFl].

9.  Gadd, *Stones of Assyria,* 128 with reference to Original Drawings I xi, xii; his pl. 6 shows one face reconstructed from the shattered fragments in which condition it was found; ANEP, 119 fig. 350 lower, shows in the only other photograph published, part of one other face. Cf. E. Sollberger, "The White Obelisk," *Iraq* 36 (1974) 233 n. 20; Diagrammatic plan in R. D. Barnett and M. Falkner, *The Sculptures of Assur-nasir-apli II (883-859 B.C.) Tiglath-Pileser III (745-727 B.C.) Esarhaddon (681-669 B.C.) from the Southwest Palaces at Nimrud* (London: British Museum, 1962) 2, fig. 3; J. E. Reade, "The Palace of Tiglath-Pileser III," *Iraq* 30 (1968) 69; for bibliography see Borger, *Handbuch,* 1.292 and Schramm, *Einleitung,* 46-7 [II rl].

10. New photographs of the obelisk appear in Sollberger, "White Obelisk," pls. XLI-XLVIII and J. E. Reade, "Assurnasirpal I and the White Obelisk," *Iraq* 37 (1975) pls. XXVIII-XXXI; Reade also provides a diagrammatic sketch of the panel sequence, p. 131 fig. 1, while Sollberger publishes C. D. Hodder's drawings made

in 1853 of each of the four faces (=Original Drawings VI xli, xlii) alongside the new photographs of those respective faces on pls. XLII-XLV.

11. For bibliography see R. Borger, *Einleitung in die assyrischen Königsinschriften* (Erster Teil; Leiden: E. J. Brill, 1961) 135, 138-42 [Xb,e]; Borger, *Handbuch*, 1.218, 2.122; J. A. Brinkman, *A Political History of Post-Kassite Babylonia, 1158-722 B.C.* (Rome: Pontifical Biblical Institute, 1968) 383-6; for photograph, ANEP, 152, fig. 440.

12. See Schramm, *Einleitung*, 48-9.

13. Reade, "Assurnasirpal I," 143.

14. See M.E.L. Mallowan, "The Excavations at Nimrud (Kalhu), 1953," *Iraq* 16 (1954) 119, pl. XXVII, no. 1 = *Nimrud and its Remains* (2 vols.; New York: Dodd, Mead & Co., 1966) 1.183, fig. 118; Schramm, *Einleitung*, 46-7 [IIr].

15. Layard, *Nineveh*, 1.282.

16. *The Art of Ancient Mesopotamia* (London: Phaedon, 1969) 122-125, with special reference to fig. 91 on p. 123; Reade ("Assurnasirpal I," 149) has commented appropriately that it is unwise to rely unduly on this suggested boustrophedon sequence which Moortgat derives from E. Unger's study of 1931.

17. *Art of Ancient Mesopotamia*, 123.

18. Ibid., 126-137; G. Turner, "The State Apartments of Late Assyrian Palaces," *Iraq* 32 (1970) 177-213; J. Meuszyński, "The Throne Room of Assur-nasir-apli II," ZA 64 (1975) 51-73.

19. Gadd does not include this relief in his comprehensive study, but see Layard, *Nineveh*, 1.68-70, and compare Gadd, *Stones of Assyria*, 157-8 with Layard, *Nineveh*, 2.34 as appropriate to wall relief of Tp III no. 2 below. Published in Barnett & Falkner, *Sculptures*, pls. LXXIV-V.

20. Ibid., 27, pls. LXXXI-LXXXIII (=BM 124961+132306).

21. See Gadd, *Stones of Assyria*, 132. Cf. Layard, *Nineveh*, 1.116-133, 271-300. There is a photograph in E.A.W. Budge, *Assyrian Sculptures in the British Museum* (London: British Museum, 1914) pl. XX.1.

22. "The Throne-Room," 68-69.

23. Y. Yadin, *The Art of Warfare in Biblical Lands* (2 vols.; New York: McGraw-Hill, 1963) 2.388-9.

24. Barnett & Falkner, *Sculptures,* pl. XCV, XCVI, LXXXIX and pp. 28-29; Gadd, *Stones of Assyria,* 157-8 refers to a copy in Or. Dr. III S. W. xvii.

25. See H. Tadmor, "Introductory Remarks to a New Edition of the Annals of Tiglath-pileser III," *Proceedings of the Israel Academy of Sciences and Humanities* 2 (1968) 168-187; Schramm, *Einleitung,* 125-131.

26. See Barnett & Falkner, *Sculptures*, pl. LXXXVIII, and XCII-XCIII for lower register alone [BM 118934 + 118931].

27. Gadd, *Stones of Assyria,* 151; Barnett & Falkner, *Sculptures,* pl. XVIII.

28. Ibid., pl. XIX for photograph; cf. Gadd, *Stones of Assyria,* 154.

29. Barnett & Falkner, *Sculptures,* pls. III-IV; for an impression of the total slab and the adjacent continuation, see Gadd, *Stones of Assyria,* pl. 77.

30. Barnett & Falkner, *Sculptures,* pl. LIX.

31. D. Oates, "Balawat (Imgur Enlil): The Site and its Buildings," *Iraq* 36 (1974) 173-178; L. W. King, *Bronze Reliefs from the Gates of Shalmaneser, King of Assyria B.C. 860-825* (London: British Museum, 1915) 5-11; E. Michel, "Die Assur-Texte Shalmanassars III. (858-824), 11," WO 4 (1967) 30-37; Schramm, *Einleitung,* 72-73.

32. Roman numeral gives band number; R(Right) or L(Left) gives side of gate; l(lower)and u(upper) gives register.

33. King, *Bronze Reliefs,* 35-36 and pls. LXXVIII-LXXX, portions of 2 bands apparently in a single register.

34. The re-discovery was stimulated by Mallowan's find of yet another pair belonging to Anp II at Balawat.

35. A. Parrot, *The Arts of Assyria* (New York: Golden Press, 1961) XVI.

36. Ibid., 103-4, fig. 112 & 113.

37. D. Oates "The Excavations at Nimrud (Kalhu), 1962," *Iraq* 25 (1963) 6; cf. Ibid., pls. III-VIII (with labels a and b switched on both plates IV and V); republished with greater photographic detail in Mallowan, *Nimrud,* 2.444-50, figs. 369-371. Also P. Hulin, "The Inscription on the Carved Throne-Base of Shalmaneser III," *Iraq* 25 (1963) 48-69.

38. Summarized in Brinkman, *Political History,* 196, n. 1199.

39. Ibid., pl. II, 192-3, nn. 1179, 1181.

40. See Oates, "Excavations at Nimrud," 20-22; Moortgat, *Art of Ancient Mesopotamia,* 139; A. D. Kilmer, "Symbolic Gestures in Akkadian Contracts from Alalakh and Ugarit," JAOS 94 (1974) 183 n. 24 sub "treaties."

41. Moortgat, *Art of Ancient Mesopotamia;* T. A. Madhloom, *The Chronology of Neo-Assyrian Art* (London: Athlone, 1970); J. E. Reade, "The Neo-Assyrian Court and Army: Evidence from the Sculptures," *Iraq* 34 (1972) 87-112.

42. Reade, "Neo-Assyrian Court," 90.

43. Ibid., 87-108.

44. S. Smith, *Assyrian Sculptures in the British Museum* (London: British Museum, 1938) 7.

45. *Nineveh,* 1.282-3; *Discoveries,* 613, 626.

46. *The Historical Evidences of the Truth of the Scripture Records Stated Anew* (London: Gould and Lincoln, 1860) 324-5 nn. XXV-XXIX; *Monarchies,* 2.106-108.

47. For the "Standard Inscription" of Anp II see L. W. King, *Annals of the King of Assyria* (London: British Museum, 1902) 212-221; Brinkman, *Political History,* 390-394; Schramm, *Einleitung,* 39-42; E. Porada, *The Great King, King of Assyria* (New York: Metropolitan Museum of Art, 1945) and Stearns, *Reliefs.*

48. C. C. Smith, "Some Observations on the Assyrians and History," *Encounter* 30 (1968) 340-353.

49. Barnett & Falkner, *Sculptures,* pls. XCVIII, XCVII.

50. Ibid., pls. XXXVIII and LXX and by drawing only pl. LXII which names Gezer of Palestine, cf. pp. 40-42 for comments.

51. Hulin, "Throne-Base of Shalmaneser III," 49-50.

52. Schramm, *Einleitung,* 72.

53. Michel, "Die Assur-Texte, 11," 34-37.

54. *Stones of Assyria,* 128-9.

55. Cf. L. W. King, *Annals,* 203.

56. *Einleitung,* 87-90.

57. E. R. Thiele, *The Mysterious Numbers of the Hebrew Kings* (Chicago: University of Chicago, 1951) 287-8.

58. M. Elat, "The Campaigns of Shalmaneser III against Aram and Israel," IEJ 25 (1975) 33 n. 31 with reference to texts.

59. J. N. Postgate, *Taxation and Conscription in the Assyrian Empire* (Rome: Biblical Institute Press, 1974) 119.

60. Ibid., 154.

61. Ibid., 119.

62. Ibid., 156-162.

63. Postgate, *Taxation and Conscription,* 121-130.

64. Schramm, *Einleitung,* 100-101.

65. N. B. Jankowska, "Some Problems of the Economy of the Assyrian Empire," *Ancient Mesopotamia: Socio-Economic History* (Moscow: "Nauka" Pub. House, 1969) 253-276.

66. Reade, "Neo-Assyrian Court," 87.

67. *Einleitung,* 100-102.

68. "Throne-Base of Shalmaneser III," 65; and for the GN, including the recent return to older reading with "P" rather than "Ḫ", Hawkins in RLA IV/2-3 (1973) 160-2.

69. Th. Jacobsen, "Early Political Development in Mesopotamia," ZA 52 (1957) 95.

70. W. W. Hallo, "From Qarqar to Carchemish: Assyria and Israel in the Light of New Discoveries," BA 23 (1960) 34-41.

71. Thiele, *Mysterious Numbers,* 42-54.

72. Michel, "Die Assur-Texte Salmanassars III. (858-824) 10," WO 3 (1964) 152-3.

73. Elat, "Campaigns of Shalameser III," 26 n. 5, with reference to the peculiar Akkadian expression šadâsu ēmid "he disappeared forever," CAD, 5.140; cf. 2 Kgs 8:15.

74. "'Yah, Son of ʿOmri': A Philological Note on Israelite Chronology," BASOR 216 (1974) 5 n. 1.

75. "An Additional Chronological Note on 'Yah, Son of ʿOmri'," BASOR 222 (1976) 19-23.

76. See the references cited by Elat, "Campaigns of Shalmaneser III," 30-31 nn. 22-25; to which may be added Tadmor's study of the subsequent Assyrian reigns and the contributing problems relating to the Assyrian-Aramaean-Israelite triangle in "The Historical Inscriptions of Adad-nirar; III," Iraq 35 141-150 with references.

77. "'Yad, Son of ʿOmri'," 5.

78. "The Kurbaʾil Statue of Shalmaneser III," Iraq 24 (1962) 108-111.

79. ANET$^2$, 500-1, for translation and references = ANET$^3$, 654-5; cf. ANEP, 156 fig. 455 especially for costume of this king.

80. Not as Luckenbill, Ancient Records, 1.220, mistranslates "against," Mon. II 61.

81. Elat, "Campaigns of Shalmaneser III," 33-34.

82. Ibid., 34.

83. M. Liverani, "Memorandum on the Approach to Historiographic Texts," Orientalia 42 (1973) 180-181.

84. "Historical Inscriptions," 64.

85. The Ancient History of the Near East (8th rev. ed. by C. J. Gadd; London: Metheun & Co., 1932) 453.

86. "Memorandum," 185.

# ISRAEL'S PROPHETS AS INTERCESSORS

Arnold B. Rhodes

Israel's prophets were intercessors, and a study of their intercessory role leads to the heart of the biblical faith and life.  The
purpose of this paper is to attempt to increase the visibility of
the prophets as intercessors, especially in the American context.
It is intended in no way to minimize the prophet as one called and
endowed by Yahweh to receive and communicate the word, to interpret
God's action in history, to engage in political activity, to counsel
and rebuke political and religious leaders, and to protest against
injustice and other breaches of the covenant.

Of course within the framework of Israel's traditions, the
prophets are not the only persons who engaged in intercession.
Prayer is a distinctively human activity in this world and is bound
up with the creation of humankind in the image of God (Gen 1:26-27).
It therefore highlights the interpersonal relationship between God
and human beings.  Intercession is usually a prayer which by its
very nature dramatizes the horizontal as well as the vertical dimensions of the concept of the *imago Dei*.  Prophetic intercession
is closely related to the living of life as people experience it in
every age.

We pursue our purpose through a presentation of the motivations
undergirding this endeavor, representative evidence for the role of
Israel's prophets as intercessors, and implications derived from
the evidence.


## I.  Motivations

In addition to the fact that the subject of this article fits

107

into the theme and purpose of this volume, there are two less obvious motivations for its selection.  First, I share the long-standing concern of Professor Rylaarsdam "that the scholar of Scripture should be a critic of all versions of religion that appeal to Scripture."  In our time great emphasis is being placed upon what is sometimes called "prophetic ministry."  It is crucial that no aspect of the ministry of Israel's prophets be overlooked in establishing valid criteria for determining the nature of "prophetic ministry" in the present-day covenant community and the contemporary world.  There is a need to appreciate Israel's prophets in the fullness of their faith and life.

The second motivation centers around the comparative neglect of the intercessory role of Israel's prophets, particularly by Americans, and grows out of an experience which is continuing in the form of an investigation.  I was in the process of preparing to teach a course entitled "The Prophets of Israel" when I was confronted as never before by the fact that the prophets were among the greatest, if not the greatest, intercessors in Israel. At once I realized that this aspect of the prophets' activity had not been emphasized in most of the materials I had read on the prophets.  When I came prepared to lecture to my class on the subject, I began by asking each of the thirty persons present if he or she had ever considered intercession as an activity of Israel's prophets, and in every case the answer was an emphatic, "No!"

Then I began to ask theological professors, ministers, and laypersons the same question.  While this part of the investigation is only in its early stages, it is interesting that, out of those asked, only two have answered the question in the affirmative.  The most impressive "no" I received came from a person who is widely recognized as one of the ablest theologians in this country.

My next step was to make a more thorough inquiry into the available literature on the subject.  Obviously those who write commentaries on the relevant biblical books cannot avoid commenting on the passages where intercession is involved.  Beyond this obser-

vation, however, I wanted to know what scholarly books and articles
about the prophets deal in any significant depth with the intercession of the OT prophets.  Therefore, I enlisted the help of an
experienced librarian and a research assistant to work with me in
finding the answer to the question.  By using the multiple resources of two excellent theological libraries, I discovered that
the overwhelming majority of books and articles on the prophets
written by American scholars do not mention intercession in any
depth, if at all.

The case is different among biblical scholars in a number of
other lands.  However, to the best of my knowledge, no biblical
scholar has ever written a book devoted exclusively to Israel's
prophets as intercessors.  Though F. Hesse's dissertation, Die
Fürbitte im Alten Testament,[1] requires updating and critical evaluation, it remains the best resource for studying the intercession
of Israel's prophets as well as the subject of intercession in the
OT as a whole, including the intertestamental literature available
in 1949.  While G. von Rad's writing on prophetic intercession is
not confined to his Old Testament Theology,[2] this work includes
his best on the theme.
     There are only two articles known to me which deal altogether
with the prophets as intercessors.  A. S. Herbert, a British scholar,
has written a very brief article entitled "The Prophet as Intercessor."[3]  H. W. Hertzberg, a German scholar, has raised the question, "Sind die Propheten Fürbitter?"[4]  Though he recognizes that
a goodly number of other scholars disagree with him, his answer to
his question is tantamount to "no."  In a nutshell his "no" means
that intercession is not a part of the prophets' office.
     Among those who differ with Hertzberg is H. Graf Reventlow,
also a German scholar.  But Reventlow's disagreement on this matter
did not originate with the publication of Hertzberg's article.  He
was already acquainted with Hertzberg's basic position from the
latter's earlier works, particularly his Prophet und Gott.[5]  In his

_Liturgie und prophetisches Ich bei Jeremiah_,[6] Reventlow devotes
sixty-five pages to Jeremiah's office of intercession. In doing
this, however, he reveals his opinion about prophetic intercession
in the broader OT context. He agrees with von Rad, as over against
Hertzberg, that the office of intercession is deeply anchored in
the nature of prophecy.[7]


## II. Evidence[8]

The word "prophet" (nābî²) in the OT is first used in Gen 20:1-
18. Abraham is called a prophet there, not because he announces
God's word, but because he has the power of intercession. At the
time of the Elohist, the office of the prophet "was less the proclamation of eschatological messages than of authorized intercession."[9]
Abimelech restores Sarah to Abraham, Abraham intercedes for Abimelech,
Abimelech's life is saved, and the barrenness of his wife and female
slaves is cured. Thus in retrospect Abraham is accorded the status
of a prophet.

But is Abraham regarded as a prophet in the J document? Although Gen 12:1-3 is not exactly like the account of the call of
any biblical character who is usually regarded as a prophet, it ·
certainly brings to mind the calls of such persons.

The source divisions of Gen 15:1-21, which deals with God's
covenant with Abraham, are uncertain. E. A. Speiser recognizes
the problem, and he, as well as others, assigns v. 1 along with
other parts of the passage to the Yahwist.[10] The tetragrammaton
is used in this verse: "After these things the word of Yahweh
(dᵉbar yhwh) came to Abram in a vision (maḥzeh) saying: 'Fear not,
Abram, I am your shield; your reward shall be very great.'" The
language and thought here are definitely prophetic and imply a
prophetic call and the reception of a prophetic message. Such an
unusual statement from the Yahwist should not shock us, for Abraham
was a very special person, and extraordinary things could be said

of him in retrospect and in prospect.

Gen 18:17-33, which is attributed to J, includes Abraham's famous intercession for Sodom. If Gen 15:1 belongs to J, it is even easier to see Abraham as the intercessory prophet in Genesis 18. Yet, even apart from the attribution of Gen 15:1 to J, there are reasons for viewing Abraham's intercession for Sodom as the intercession of a prophet. The dialogical nature of the intercession reminds us of similar dialogues between Yahweh and the later prophets. Abraham is depicted as one who is to "charge his children and his household after him to keep the way of Yahweh by doing righteousness and justice ..." (v. 19). In addition, Yahweh's soliloquizing question, "Am I to hide from Abraham what I am about to do?" (Gen 18:17), has very close affinity to the statement in Amos 3:4, "For the Lord Yahweh does nothing without revealing his counsel to his servants the prophets."[11] As the first Hebrew patriarch, Abraham is viewed as an intercessory prophet plus.

The call of Moses in Exod 3:1-4:17 (JE) is essentially the call to be a prophet, even though the word nābî᾽ is not used in the context. Various factors bear witness to this. The "Here am I" of Moses (3:4) reminds us of the "Here am I" of Isa 6:8. God's sending Moses (3:10, 13-14) is paralleled by God's sending the later prophets (Isa 6:8; Jer 1:7). God promises to be with Moses (3:12) and Jeremiah (1:8). Moses and the later prophets receive and bear God's message to their own people and to others (Exod 7:16; 9:13).[12] B. S. Childs maintains not only that Moses' call in the passage under consideration reflects the understanding of prophecy found in later prophetism, but also that classical prophetism reflects Mosaic prophetism even more.[13] In Deut 18:22, it is crucial that a prophet speak in the name of Yahweh (cf. Deuteronomy 13) and speak the truth in that name. According to the Elohist, "Moses confirms his prophetic office by announcing God's one true name."[14] It is probable that the E source comes "from early prophetic circles."[15] Though Moses may be regarded as per-

forming a variety of functions in J and E, he is clearly presented
in both primarily as Israel's prophet par excellence (Num 12:6-7).
This means that intercession, a major part of Moses' ministry especially in J, must be attributed to him as a prophet. The fact
that the word nābî' is not used of Moses in either E or J is not
a major factor in the light of the evidence already provided and
in the light of the fact that we do not know precisely when the
word came to be used in the Hebrew language.

We now take a brief look at Moses the intercessor in materials
primarily belonging to J and E. The people are suffering under
hard bondage in Egypt, and they turn to Moses in distress (Exod
5:22-6:1). Moses complains to Yahweh, and Yahweh promises deliverance.

After the plagues against the Egyptians are underway, Pharaoh
requests Moses and Aaron to entreat Yahweh on behalf of himself and
his people on four occasions (Exod 8:4-11 = Eng. 8:8-15; 8:21-28 =
Eng. 8:25-32; 9:27-35; 10:16-20). In each case it is Moses who
does the entreating, with positive results.

A series of Moses' intercessions center around the murmuring
traditions.[16] A word must be said about Num 14:11-23. Yahweh
threatens to strike the people with pestilence and disinherit them
and offers to make of Moses "a nation greater and mightier than they."
But Moses intercedes for the people on the following grounds: (1)
such action would bring international dishonor to Yahweh's name;
(2) Yahweh would thereby break his promise to lead the people to
the land of promise; (3) Yahweh's power should be used in harmony
with his nature which is loving and forgiving as well as judging.
In response Yahweh pardons the people, but the rebellious ones
must suffer some of the consequences of their rebellion -- they
cannot enter Canaan.

Exodus 32-34 seems to be a redactional unit centering around
Israel's apostasy related to the golden calf and the renewal of
the covenant, in which Moses' intercession is a significant theme.
There is a connection between this narrative about the calf and

that found in 1 Kgs 12:28-33 concerning the calves set up by
Jeroboam at Bethel and Dan.  Exodus 32 shows Moses as capable of
dealing with the people in judgment and yet pleading with God to
forgive them.  According to Exod 32:7-14, Moses entreats Yahweh
to turn from his wrath toward the people and honor the promise
made to Abraham.  From Moses' perspective, to be a new Abraham
(see Exod 32:10) would not be the fulfillment of the promise.
"And Yahweh repented (nāḥam) concerning the evil which he said
he would do to his people" (v. 14).

In the second passage related to the golden calf episode
(Exod 32:30-34), Moses seeks to make atonement (kāpar) for the sin
of the people through intercession, and in the process of his dialogue with Yahweh says that if Yahweh will not forgive their sin,
"blot me, I pray, out of your book which you have written."  Yahweh
does not grant complete pardon, but does not destroy the people.  A
visitation of judgment lies ahead.

A third intercession is found in Exod 33:12-17.  This intercession must be understood in the light of vv. 1-3, especially
v. 3, in which Yahweh says he will not go to the promised land
among the people.  In response to Moses' plea, Yahweh promises that
his presence will go with Moses.  Moses continues his plea by
appealing to the uniqueness of Israel in Yahweh's purpose.  Then
Yahweh grants Moses' request in full.

The brief intercession in Exod 34:9 appears to be a cultic
confession.  This time Moses identifies with his people in a different way, saying, "and pardon our iniquity and our sin."

Deuteronomy gives the most explicit statements about Moses as
a prophet, though Hosea refers to Moses without naming him as a
nābî᾽ (Hos 12:14 = Eng. 12:13).  As a prophet Moses is in a class
all by himself (34:10-12).  He is indeed the model of the true
prophet (18:15-22).  Yahweh speaks to the people through Moses
(5:25-29), and Moses rehearses some of his activity as intercessor
on behalf of the people in his first "sermon" to them (9:18-29).
A brief intercession is also recorded in 26:15.  Closely related

to Moses' intercession is his vicarious suffering for the people
(cf. Num 11:11-15, JE). He does without food and drink (9:18),
is not permitted to enter the promised land on account of the
people (1:37; 3:23-29; 4:21-22), and dies without crossing the
Jordan. By contrast note how the priestly writers have handled
Moses' inability to enter the promised land (Num 20:10-13; 27:
12-23). According to P, Joshua as Moses' successor does not have
the status of Moses and is subject to the inquiry of Eleazar the
priest (Num 27:12-23).

Whatever may be said about the overall portrait of Moses'
various functions as deliverer, ruler, judge, miracle-worker, and
priest (only so named in Ps 99:6), the overarching portrait is
that of the prophet par excellence, who announces Yahweh's word
to the people and intercedes for the people before Yahweh. It was
as a prophet that he liberated his people (Hos 12:14 = Eng. 12:13),
as a prophet that he prayed and suffered for them, and as a prophet
that he died for them.

I Sam 3:1-4:1 is an account of the call of Samuel to be a
prophet.[17] The Hebrew words for "vision" used in 3:1, 15 tend to
suggest a prophetic experience. The double address, "Samuel,
Samuel" (3:4, 10) calls to mind "Moses, Moses" in Exod 3:4. The
"Here am I" of 3:4-7, 16 reminds one of Exod 3:4 and Isa 6:8. Indeed Moses and Samuel are mentioned together as intercessors in
Jer 15:1. In fact, Samuel is called a nābî᾽ in v. 20. Though 1
Sam 9:9 is an editor's note, it is accurate in relating the prophet to the seer (rō᾽eh). Samuel is viewed in the roles of a judge
(7:16), a man of God (9:6), a seer (9:11), the head of a company
of prophets (19:20), and as a political figure. Yet Samuel is not
explicitly called a priest in the entire OT. The parallelism of
Ps 99:6 may suggest this title. Though Samuel is sometimes said to
offer sacrifice, so are judges, kings, and others in early Israel.
W. F. Albright maintains that "Samuel was the first great religious
reformer after Moses and that he rejected - or diminished - the
spiritual role of priests and Levites at the same time that he

turned to ecstatic prophets and local sanctuaries to replace the Shilonic system ..."[18]

In several passages Samuel is depicted as an intercessor, and, in my opinion, this function is to be related to Samuel primarily as a prophet, According to 1 Sam 7:5-11, he promises to pray for the people as they gather at Mizpah. The people confess their sins, Samuel judges them, and they request Samuel to intercede for them: "Do not cease to cry to Yahweh our God for us, that he may save us from the hand of the Philistines." Samuel offers a burnt offering and prays for the people, and Yahweh saves the people from disaster.

1 Sam 12:18, somewhat similar to the passage just mentioned, is a brief prayer of Samuel for rain at a time of the year when it does not ordinarily rain. The rain comes, and such a miracle makes a tremendous impact on the people. Therefore, in terror they request Samuel to pray to Yahweh his God to save them from death, since they have sinned in asking for a king; and Samuel encourages them, saying: "Moreover as for me, far be it from me to sin against Yahweh by ceasing to intercede on your behalf ..." (1 Sam 12:23).

When Samuel receives Yahweh's word concerning the rejection of Saul, he is angry and cries "to Yahweh all night long" (1 Sam 15:11; cf. 15:35). Such crying is apparently a form of intercession which is based upon the presupposition that Yahweh sometimes changes a decision as an act of compassion.

We continue our study of prophetic intercession in the time of the early monarchy by giving attention to an unnamed man of God from Judah, to Elijah, and to Elisha. 1 Kgs 13:1-32 revolves around the man of God from Judah. The text itself gives evidence that it was written or compiled about 600 B.C. and gives an interpretation of an event from about 900 B.C. This man of God goes to the sanctuary at Bethel and cries out against the altar there. When King Jeroboam stretches out his hand and gives the command to lay hold of the man, his hand dries up and he cannot draw it back. The king requests the man to intercede for him, the man does intercede, and Jeroboam's hand is restored. The story presents a man of God as one empowered to speak the effective word of judgment and to exercise effective intercession. The remainder of the narrative indicates that the man of God and an old prophet from Bethel are both, in some sense, in the category of the nābî'.

In 1 Kgs 17:17-24 (cf. 2 Kgs 4:32-33), Elijah is presented as a man of God who cries to Yahweh to restore the life of the son of the widow of Zarephath and employs restorative action as well. The restoration of the child's life gives the woman real assurance that Elijah is a man of God.

In the account of the famous contest on Mount Carmel, Elijah's prayers involve both petition and intercession (1 Kgs 18:36-42) for the fire and the rain. The pouring of the water on the altar (vv. 30-35) and Elijah's bowed position (vv. 41-42) suggest acted prayer. In the context Elijah is clearly a nābî' (18:22, 36), and his opponents are "prophets" of Baal and Asherah (vv. 19, 25), although sacrifice is essential to the contest.

Elisha as a prophet and a man of God endowed with might prays that his servant may have a vision of Yahweh's transcendent power (2 Kgs 6:17) and also prays a prayer of imprecation upon the threatening Syrian soldiers (v. 18). The imprecation, which is answered by a temporary blinding of the Syrians, is a form of intercession for Elisha's own people (vv. 20-23).

The classical prophets are called by Yahweh, perform miracles infrequently, announce Yahweh's word of judgment and salvation, and intercede for others, though all of these things are not attributed to every one of them. Our 8th century classical representatives are Amos and Isaiah  Amos has left us a brief word about his intercessory ministry in the account of two visions: that of the locusts (7:1-3) and that of the judgment by fire (7:4-6). These two autobiographical accounts are parts of a four-vision series, which is interrupted by a biographical narrative about Amos and Amaziah in which Amos speaks of his prophetic call. The chronology of this section is uncertain. In the first vision Amos asks Yahweh to forgive Jacob because he is so small. In the second vision the prayer is the same, except the word "cease" replaces the word "forgive." In both instances Yahweh changes a previous decision, saying, "It shall not be." This statement is Yahweh's word, not a literary device. In the two later visions of the series (7:7-9; 8:1-3) there is no intercession. Within chronos there are kairoi of possible forgiveness, when intercession to avert destruction is in order. Within chronos there are also kairoi of certain judgment, when some kinds of intercession are inappropriate. But even Amos thinks there is some hope for a repentant remnant (5:6, 14-15). Such a hope suggests a judgment of refining rather than one of absolute destruction.[19]

In the account of Isaiah's call to be a prophet (Isaiah 6), Isaiah so identifies with his people and feels a responsibility for them that he confesses their sinfulness as well as his own (v. 5). When he hears the negative aspects of his commission, he bursts out with a spontaneous, "How long, O Lord?" (6:11). And this outburst comes close to intercession.

The narrative of Hezekiah's appeal to Isaiah at a time Jerusalem was besieged by Sennacherib (2 Kgs 19:1-7 = Isa 37:1-7) throws light on the role of the prophet as intercessor. This narrative is not to be treated as if it were insignificant simply because it was not written by Isaiah himself.[20] Sennacherib's threat is delivered by the Rabshakeh to Hezekiah's officials. In response to the threat Hezekiah rends his clothes, puts on sackcloth, initiates a public fast, goes to the temple, and sends a legation to Isaiah to request the prophet's intercession "for the remnant that is left." According to John Gray, such intercession is a part of the fast.[21] The remnant is composed of the persons in Jerusalem at the time of this event.

For this study the important observation is that Isaiah as prophet is approached by the king through a legation composed of his chief officers, including "the senior priests." Such an appeal recalls the long and continuing tradition of the intercessory role of Israel's earlier prophets. It seems that Isaish has already

received Yahweh's response to the intercession before it is made
or that he has already interceded and received an answer before
the legation arrives.

The prophetic intercessors of the 7th century are Habakkuk
and Jeremiah. The book of Habakkuk is full of seemingly in-
soluble problems. Some understandings of its setting, sources,
forms, and date which differ from the one presupposed here do not
cancel the intercessory elements in the book (1:2-4; 1:12-2:1).
The first intercession is in the form of a lament in which the
prophet is not only concerned about himself but also and primarily
for those of his people who suffer at the hands of their unjust internal neighbors. Yahweh responds by saying he is rousing the
Chaldeans to punish such injustice (1:5-11), which reminds us of
Yahweh's use of Assyria as "the rod of my anger" (Isa 10:5).

The heart of the prophet's second lamenting intercession revolves around the question of Yahweh's own justice in permitting
the Chaldeans to swallow up those Judeans who are more righteous
than the Chaldeans. In essence Yahweh's answer (2:2-5) is: Let
me be God, Habakkuk, and I will take care of the Chaldeans in my
own time and way, "but the righteous shall live in his faith-
faithfulness (ᵉemûnâ)." Habakkuk intercedes as the representative of his people, and Yahweh's answer applies not only to
Habakkuk, but also to all of his people who have faith in Yahweh
and live out that faith in faithfulness.

Jeremiah's emotional battery was highly charged, and this
fact is reflected in the tensions of his prayer life. Since
intercession is mentioned so frequently in connection with his
activities, we approach the subject topically: (1) the negative
evidence for his ministry of intercession and (2) the positive
evidence for this ministry. The negative evidence converges on
the occasions on which Yahweh forbids Jeremiah to intercede for
the people. The first occurrence (7:16) follows the famous temple
sermon and introduces a section on false worship. The second (11:
14) is found in a section in which the people are reminded of the

Exodus and accused of breaking the Sinaitic covenant by going after other gods (11:1-17). The third (14:11) and fourth (15:1) are parts of a long liturgical lament (14:1-15:9). After Yahweh has forbidden Jeremiah to pray for the welfare of the people (14:11), Jeremiah deliberately intercedes for them by passing the responsibility for the people's sins to the (false) prophets (14:13-16). But Yahweh refuses to exempt the people themselves from responsibility. The fourth prohibition of intercession continues this dialogue and includes a reference to Moses and Samuel, great intercessors of the past. The people wanted indulgence, not real forgiveness. So many prohibitions of intercession clearly indicate that Jeremiah was in the habit of interceding for his people.

The positive evidence for Jeremiah's ministry of intercession is even more plentiful. Some of this evidence comes in contexts of expostulation and lament. In 4:9-10, Jeremiah accuses Yahweh of deceiving his people by saying, "It shall be well with you." This appears to be a reference to the message of the false prophets whom Yahweh has permitted to speak. Jeremiah's moving lament in 8:18-23 (Eng. 8:18-9:1) is very close to intercession. In the lament of 10:19-24, whose background is the threat from the north, Jeremiah so identifies with his people that he prays vicariously: "Correct me, Yahweh, in justice; not in anger, lest you bring me to nought." The LXX and VT translators substituted "us" for "me" because the context refers to the land and the people, but they failed to see the vicarious identification of Jeremiah with the land and the people he loved. Jeremiah prays for a judgment of correction, not for one of annihilation.

A second type of positive evidence comes from statements of Jeremiah about his intercessions. In the context of plots against him (18:18-23) he reminds Yahweh of how he has interceded for his enemies (vv. 19-20). Yet, like some of the psalmists, he prays for the most severe vengeance on them and their families. Imprecation is intercession in reverse, and it can be understood (though not recommended) on the lips of one who was being emotionally tor-

tured and who believed that the justice of God was to be worked
out in the here and now.

We find another statement about Jeremiah's intercession in
the account of his encounter with the prophet Hananiah (28:6).
Hananiah gives in oracular fashion the prediction that temple
vessels, Jeconiah, and the people taken to Babylon in 597 will
be returned within two years.[22]   And Jeremiah responds, "Amen!
May Yahweh do so ..." Though Jeremiah does not think that such
a return will take place within two years, he devoutly desires it.

A third type of positive evidence for Jeremiah's intercessory
ministry is derived from the passages which tell of requests for
intercession that are brought to him.  When Pharaoh Hophra sends
soldiers to relieve besieged Jerusalem in 588, hopes are raised
among the people of the city that a deliverance like the one in
the time of Isaiah and Hezekiah will take place again.  Therefore, Zedekiah sends a legation of two officials to request Jeremiah to "pray for us" (see 37:1-17; cf. 21:1-10).  Jeremiah gives
Yahweh's word to the effect that Pharaoh's army will return to
Egypt and the Chaldeans will be in control.  After Jerusalem has
fallen, the leaders and people left in the city request Jeremiah
to pray to Yahweh in order to learn what they should do (42:1-6).
Jeremiah replies, "Behold, I will pray to Yahweh your God according
to your words, and whatever Yahweh answers I will tell you." The
leaders and people agree to act as Yahweh sends them word by Jeremiah.  The sequel to the intercession is found in 42:7-43:13.

A fourth category of witness to Jeremiah's prophetic role as
an intercessor is found in his encouragement of others to intercede.
He warns the priests in Jerusalem (among others) not to accept as
true the words of the prophets who say that "the vessels of Yahweh's
house will now shortly be brought back from Babylon" (see 27:16-22).
The crucial verse is 18: "If they are prophets, and if the word of
Yahweh is with them, then let them intercede with Yahweh of hosts,
that the vessesl which are left in Yahweh's house, in the house of
the king of Judah, and in Jerusalem may not (also) go to Babylon."

The temple vessels were of special importance because they represented the life of the people under Yahweh in their own land. If these persons are really prophets and have Yahweh's word, then they should intercede. Meaningful intercession is in some sense still a possibility. This statement by Jeremiah shows he regarded intercession as an integral responsibility of the prophetic office.

In his letter to the exiles of the 597 captivity, Jeremiah includes these words within one of the oracles from Yahweh: "Seek the welfare of the city where I have sent you into exile, and make intercession for it to Yahweh, because in its welfare will be your welfare" (29:7). The shalom of Yahweh's special people is bound up with the shalom of their captors. Perhaps Jeremiah opens the door slightly to the affirmation that Yahweh's salvation is intended for all people.[23]

Jeremiah was not only a prophet of refining judgment, but also a prophet of hope (31:1-34; 32:1-15) and intercession. The author of 2 Maccabees thought Jeremiah was still interceding even after his death (15:14). Jeremiah was also a human being who said what he thought to other human beings and to Yahweh.

The three prominent passages in Ezekiel that have to do with prophetic intercession fall within the first part of the book (chaps. 1-24), which is dated before 587. The first passage is 9:8. It is found in the context of the departing of the glory of Yahweh by stages from the temple and Jerusalem, a representation of the devastating judgment that is underway. Ezekiel is so impressed by what he sees and hears that he cries out in intercessory anguish, "Ah Lord Yahweh! Are you going to wipe out all that is left of Israel in the outpouring of your wrath upon Jerusalem?"

The second passage is 11:13, which pivots about the death of Pelatiah. Via psychic transit Ezekiel is transported to Jerusalem, where he sees twenty-five participants in a council meeting. In the midst of the vision he receives a message from Yahweh. The council members have caused and will cause death to others and will be judged. Pelatiah, one of the council members, dies suddenly.

Ezekiel is shocked and feels the heavy significance of the event.
"Pelatiah's death is more than a mere judgment upon one individual."
It is a sign of the impending judgment upon the twenty-five and
those ruled by them. The cry of Ezekiel has the force of an almost
hopeless intercession: "Ah Lord Yahweh! Will you make a full end
of the remnant of Israel?"

The third passage is 13:5. Ezekiel seems to associate the
failure of the foolish prophets to go up into the breaches with
their failure to intercede (cf. Ps 106:23; Exodus 32).[25]

Deutero-Isaiah presents us with some very profound material
on prophetic intercession. Isa 51:9-10 begins a lament on an intercessory note, in which Yahweh is called upon to wake up and act
redemptively as in ages past. The prophet is probably speaking as
a representative of the people.

The heart of intercession in this prophet centers around Isa
53:12c, "And as for him, he bore the sin of many, and makes intercession for the rebels." In interpreting this couplet it is important to state my general approach to the four Servant Songs.
While fluidity in the concept of the servant in Deutero-Isaiah as
a whole is admitted, the primary concentration in these songs is
upon the individual servant. In drawing his protrait of the servant, the prophet has used a confluence of figures from Israel's
traditions. The royal motif may be present, but it is hard to
find since the suffering of Israel's kings was not usually hallowed
with vicarious righteousness. The royal motif, however, may be
seen in the court language that is sometimes used in the songs and
in the servant's impact upon the kings of many nations (52:15).
The real king is Yahweh.

The priestly motif is seen particularly in the picture of the
slaughtering of the lamb (53:7) and the reference to the sin offering (53:10). But a priest is not the servant. Priests offered
animal sacrifices. The servant is a human being who puts his own
life on the line in obedience to the will of Yahweh.

In Israel's history it is the prophets primarily who put their

lives on the line for the people. In the OT many persons are called
"the servant of Yahweh" or "the servant of God." However, in Jeremiah we find five occurrences of the expression "my servants the
prophets" and once "his servants the prophets." Jeremiah is not
the servant of the Servant Songs, but he was surely one of the
persons in the mind of Deutero-Isaiah as he drew his portrait of
Yahweh's supreme servant. Like Jeremiah, the servant is called
from the womb (49:1; Jer 1:5). There is no question about Jeremiah's
suffering at the hands of those he served. The hip$^c$il of the verb
pāga$^c$ means "intercede" or "interpose" and is used in Isa 53:12c.
"The word paga$^c$ occurs in the sense of intercede only ten times in
the Bible, and more often in Jeremiah than in any other book."[26]
This fact may well suggest the influence of Jeremiah on Deutero-
Isaiah's picture of the servant.

Another figure in the prophet's mind as he drew the portrait
of the servant was Moses. As we have seen, Moses interceded for
his people, suffered for them, and put his life on the line in
their behalf -- and whatever else Moses may be called, he is called
a prophet and servant of Yahweh.

Verses 6 and 12 speak of the servant's vicarious action in
behalf of sinners, and v. 12c also speaks of intercession, which
is vicarious prayer (note the imperfect in the second stich of
the couplet). Vicarious action to the death and intercessory prayer
are united in an intercessory life-style. The servant has a mission
to Israel and to the nations (49:6), but no one is forced to receive the gift. The fourth song begins and ends with Yahweh's
vindication of the servant.

When Isaish 40-55 is read as a whole, it is plain that Yahweh's
people are to be both a servant people and a prophetic people. The
servant-prophet has a people, just as elsewhere in the OT the Davidic
king has a people, the high priest has a people, and the one like a
son of man has a people.

Trito-Isaiah includes two passages which are to be interpreted as prophetic intercessions, 62:6 and 63:7-64:12. In 62:6 it seems that the prophet has set watchers on the walls of Jerusalem, as it were, to remind Yahweh of the people's plight until Jerusalem is reestablished. The watchers are probably to be viewed as prophets.

Isa 63:7-64:11 (Eng. 63:7-64:12) is one of the longest intercessory prayers in the Bible. It has been dated by J. Muilenburg between 560 and 550,[27] i.e., shortly after the destruction of Jerusalem and the temple, which is a major concern of the prophet. God is appealed to as father, redeemer, and potter. Abraham and Jacob are dead, and hope rests in Yahweh alone.

The precise dating of Joel's ministry is debated, but it is probably accurate to place it in the 4th century B.C. In the tradition of the 8th and 7th century prophets, Joel calls upon his people to repent and hopes Yahweh will relent (2:12-17). A solemn fast is called, and the priests (not the prophets) offer the prayer of intercession in the temple (v. 17). It appears that Joel was a cult prophet, and his book makes a movement in the direction of the priestly and apocalyptic perspectives.

There are intercessory elements in the Psalms, but it is not possible to identify those composed by prophets. Psalm 20, which is an intercession for the victory of a Davidic king, was probably written by a court prophet or cult prophet.


III. Implications

It is not accidental that the first occurrence of the word nābî᾽ in the OT is used in relation to intercession.

Israel's prophets stood at the top of ancient Israel's various types of leaders during most of its history.[28] They had access to the divine council; they spoke with authority to other leaders, to the people of Israel, and to the nations of the world; and they spoke to Yahweh on behalf of others as a part of their official responsibility. Moses as prophet is presented as Yahweh's agent of liberation and as the giver of the Torah itself. Kings, priests, and others sought the counsel and the prayers of the prophets.

The prophets were no dehumanized megaphones operated by a mechanical Glorified Computer. They entered into real dialogue with Yahweh, sometimes even to the point of expostulation and argument. At times their intercessions were the occasion for Yahweh to change plans out of compassion, but this does not mean they controlled Yahweh; God listened and was affected. The data presented underscore the interpersonal relations between Yahweh and the prophets, and the word "anthropomorphic" cannot be waved as a magic wand over these data as if the relationship were unreal. Contingency is a theological reality from the prophetic perspective and essential to the divine-human adventure.

There are both likenesses and differences between Israel's preclassical and classical prophets; but both deserve the title nābî᾿, and both groups practiced intercession. The fact that intercession is not explicitly mentioned in some of the prophetic books of the OT does not necessarily mean that the prophets after whom the books are named did not engage in intercession.

Some intercessions were not and are not appropriate on every occasion, but intercession as such was never forbidden to Jeremiah or to any other prophet on an absolute basis with respect to all occasions. There are kairoi for intercession and kairoi for refraining from intercession. True intercession is not asking for unrighteous indulgence, but for grace.

Prophetic intercession was by no means a failure because the response to it was sometimes negative, just as prophetic proclamation was not a failure because the people often refused to repent upon hearing it. The positive results of both intercession and proclamation are often overlooked, especially in the long perspective of continuing history. Intercession can cross barriers where other kinds of crossing are forbidden, and it may be a means of opening doors to other types of relatedness. Yahweh may use it to generate new situations and set up alternatives that did not exist previously.

The intercessory life-style is a major yardstick of the quality of human life. Intercession is evidence of concern for people and evidence of faith in the God of love and power. One of the most needed elements among ordained personnel and laypersons in various religious bodies is the cultivation of the intercessory life-style as servants of God. Such a style of life broadens perspectives, enlarges horizons, and speaks an authentic word to a disillusioned, sinning, suffering, and dying world. Intercessory prayer is vicarious asking; vicarious service in intercessory acting. As prophetic servants of God, we may unite in one inseparable whole the word and the deed, the word-deed from God and the word-deed to God. When understood deeply, it is recognized that the intercessory life-style comes only through death and may lead to death. Ultimately the vindication of such a life-style is in the hands of God alone.

We are not to idolize Israel's prophets, but we can learn from them. More research needs to be done in the investigation of their ministry of intercession and its present-day significance. How much has the intercessory role of these prophets influenced those who have been regarded by many as "prophetic types" in recent years? Have NT scholars given sufficient attention to the intercessory role of Israel's prophets in interpreting the portraits of Jesus found in the Gospels and in the interpretation of other parts of the NT, particularly the letters of Paul? Why have American biblical scholars and Americans in general tended to neglect Israel's prophets as intercessors?

# FOOTNOTES

1. F. Hesse, *Die Fürbitte im Alten Testament* (Erlangen: Dissertation, 1949; photocopy, 1951).

2. G. von Rad, *Old Testament Theology* (2 vols.; New York: Harper & Row, 1962-65), 1. 97, 292-95, 323; 2. 51-52, 131, 189-90, 210-11, 222, 275-77, 403-04.

3. A. S. Herbert, "The Prophet as Intercessor," *Baptist Quarterly* 13 (1949) 76-80.

4. H. W. Hertzberg, "Sind die Propheten Fürbitter?" *Tradition und situation: Artur Weiser zum 70. Geburtstag* (ed. E. Würthwein and O. Kaiser; Göttingen: Vandenhoeck & Ruprecht, 1963) 63-74.

5. H. W. Hertzberg, *Prophet und Gott* (BFCT 28; Gütersloh: C. Bertelsmann, 1923).

6. H. Graf Reventlow, *Liturgie und prophetisches Ich bei Jeremiah* (Gütersloh: Gerd Mohn, 1963) 140-205.

7. Limitations of space preclude comments on other important books and articles from various lands. E.g., one such article is by S. M. Paul, an Israeli scholar, and others, "Prophets and Prophecy," *Enc Jud* 13 (1971), 1150-81, esp. cols. 1169-71.

8. For rather complete listings of the OT passages pertaining to intercession, see F. Hesse, *Die Fürbitte* 143-47; P. A. H. de Boer, "De voorbede in het Oude Testament," *OTS* 3(1943) 42-120.

9. G. von Rad, *Genesis* (Rev. ed.; Philadelphia: Westminster, 1972) 228. The patriarchs in general are referred to as prophets in Ps 105:15.

10. E. A. Speiser, *Genesis* (AB; Garden City: Doubleday, 1964) 110.

11. This verse from Amos may be a later insertion.

12. On the call of Moses, see J. C. Rylaarsdam, "The Book of Exodus," *IB* 1(1952) 870-80; M. Noth, *Exodus* (OTL; Philadelphia: Westminster, 1962) 38-47; B. S. Childs, *The Book of Exodus* (OTL; Philadelphia: Westminster, 1974) 53-71.

13. Childs, *Exodus* 56.

14. Ibid. 69.

15. von Rad, *Theology*, 1. 293.

16. Exod 15:22-25; 17:1-7; Num 11:1-2; 12:13-16; 14:11-23; 21:1-9.

17. The sources of 1 Samuel are too complex and uncertain to attempt an analysis of them here.

18. W. F. Albright, *Samuel and the Beginnings of the Prophetic Movement* (Cincinnati: Hebrew Union College, 1961) 18.

19. These thoughts were stimulated in part by Hesse, *Die Fürbitte* 121-23.

20. Cf. Reventlow, *Liturgie* 143.

21. Gray, *I & II Kings* (OTL; 2d ed.; Philadelphia: Westminster, 1970) 684.

22. On Hananiah, see T. W. Overholt, *The Threat of Falsehood* (SBT 2/16; Naperville: Allenson, 1970) 37-45.

23. Cf. Hesse, *Die Fürbitte*, 131.

24. W. Eichrodt, *Ezekiel* (OTL; Philadelphia: Westminster, 1970) 141.

25. For an interpretation of Ezekiel's understanding of going up into the breaches, see von Rad, *Theology*, 2. 275-76.

26. S. H. Blank, *Jeremiah: Man and Prophet* (Cincinnati: Hebrew Union College, 1961) 234.

27. J. Muilenburg, "Isaiah, Chapters 40-66," IB 5(1956), 729-30.

28. Cf. K. Baltzer, "Considerations Regarding the Office and Calling of the Prophet," HTR 61(1968) 567-81.

# JEREMIAH AND THE NATURE OF THE PROPHETIC PROCESS

Thomas W. Overholt

I

There has been a tendency in research on OT prophecy to focus
on the content of the prophetic message, and this has had a notice-
able affect on the kinds of problems that have been raised in the
study of this material. For example, since revelation from Yahweh
is taken to be the source of a prophet's message, his utterances
have been examined for what they might show us about the nature of
Yahweh. It is reasoned that Yahweh can be known most concretely
in the relationship he established with Israel. Since the prophets addressed themselves to both the promises and obligations of
that relationship, their proclamations are considered fertile
ground for observations about his character and activity.

Or again, the preoccupation with the content of the prophetic
message has led to discussions of the nature of prophecy itself.
The prophet is seen to be Yahweh's messenger, and there has been
considerable debate over the relative weight to be assigned to
such possible components of prophecy as ecstasy, the rational
construction of the message by the prophet, and possible connections
with the organized cult.

One of the results of this tendency to focus on the content of
the message has been the dominance of a one-way view of the prophetic process: Yahweh revealed his will to the prophet, who in
turn conveyed it to the people. There is little formal consideration
of any reversal of this flow. It has been acknowledged, of course,

that other factors were at work in this one-way informational
chain.  For one thing, it is clear that a prophet's message was
addressed to a particular situation.  Still, one often has the
impression that the dynamics of the historical context are thought
of as providing information and motivation mainly for Yahweh himself, who presumably saw the situation and rendered his judgment
on it.  This minimizes the role of the prophet and his audience
in evaluating the flow of current events and shaping the prophetic word that responded formally to them.  Claus Westermann's
emphasis on the prophet's "alert consciousness" and contribution
to the final shape of the message he proclaimed is a partial break
with this tendency of interpretation.[1]

It is also acknowledged that the prophet's message was meant
to evoke a response from his audience, but neither the dilemma
this caused for his hearers nor the possibility that their response
would in turn affect the prophet is often taken seriously.  Discussions of "false prophecy" are a case in point.  The major dilemma posed by a confrontation between two prophets (e.g., Jer 28)
was that of the hearers, who had to decide how they would respond
to the two conflicting pronouncements.  But instead of recognizing
the dynamics inherent in such a situation, the tendency has been
to attempt to formulate a set of concrete rules capable of being
applied in a rather mechanical way by anyone desiring a way out of
the dilemma.[2]  Yet these conflict situations seem to be one clear
indication that the people had a vital role in the dynamics of the
prophetic process.

In short the dominant emphasis on normative content in the
study of OT prophets has diverted attention from some aspects of
the social process characteristic of the way they and, I would
contend, all prophets exercise their peculiar task.  Opportunities
for using cross-cultural examples to aid in understanding OT prophecy have largely been rejected or ignored.  Doubtless, this has
occurred because a preoccupation with the culturally conditioned
content of, for example, American Indian and OT prophets has

suggested that the two are basically distinct and therefore in-
comparable phenomena.  Such conclusions may also reflect chauvin-
istic theological judgments about the inferiority and inauthen-
ticity of other peoples' gods and revelatory experiences.

In thinking about this problem I have found it useful to em-
ploy a model of the prophetic process that focuses on the reciprocal
interaction and adjustment among three distinct actors or groups of
actors:  the supernatural, the prophet, and the people to whom the
prophet's message is addressed.  This interaction takes place within a concrete historical-cultural situation which affects both the
prophet's message and his auditors' evaluation of it.  I have previously tested this model on an example of American Indian prophecy.[3]
The purpose of the following discussion is to describe it and its
relationship to some of the vast literature on OT prophecy and then
to make a concrete application of it to the prophet Jeremiah.


II


The model of the prophetic process that I am proposing is represented in diagrammatic form in Figure 1.  The two essential components of this model are a set of three actors and a pattern of
interrelationships among them involving revelation ("r"), proclamation ("p"), feedback ("f"; here used in the broad sense of
information returned by the receptor to the sender of a message),
and expectations of confirmation ("e").  When applied to prophetic
materials from the OT, the generic term "supernatural" would be replaced by "Yahweh" and specific prophets and groups named, as appropriate to the context under study.

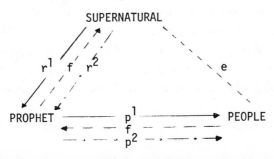

The focus on interrelationships among the actors has some important implications for our conception of the prophet's function and authority. Since the prophet acted as the messenger of Yahweh, we can say that the primary source of his authority lay in the revelation he'received. We can note the claims of the prophet that Yahweh took the initiative in calling him and that he had received such revelations (Amos 7, Isaiah 6), but these experiences constituted an essentially private, theological justification of his activity. Even at this level we must remember that the prophet was a man who lived within a specific cultural and historical context, and that both his perception of the revelatory experience and his later articulation of it were affected by this cultural screen. But there is another more public and, if you will, existential aspect of the prophet's authority, namely his acceptance (or rejection) by the people. This second aspect is necessitated by the private nature of the revelatory experience. It is at once the more tangible and more critical aspect of the prophet's claim to authority, since it was the auditors who had to decide whether or not, and how, they would act in response to his message. In coming to their decision they in effect tested the cultural "competence" of that message by deciding whether or not it was in continuity with their social and theological traditions and relevant to the current socio-political situation.

The auditors were in most cases members of the prophet's own cultural community, but it is important to remember that as individuals they held a wide range of views of that culture. We ought not expect the response to the prophet's message to have been unanimous, or label all those who dissented from it misguided or "false." Such dissent as existed came to the prophet in the form of feedback, an extreme form of which was outright rejection.

This notion of feedback is at the heart of the interrelationships among actors, and arises from the assumption that the act of prophecy is not static, but dynamic. The people whom the prophet addressed had their existence in the midst of a concrete historical

and cultural situation,[4] and one of the consequences of this and
of viewing their acts of acceptance as part of what constituted
the prophet's authority is the possibility that their reactions had
some effect upon his message.[5] In addition the prophet himself had
to test his own message against both the situation and the responses
of his hearers as he perceived them, and so there must also be room
for feedback from the prophet to Yahweh and a renewal of the revelation, either in the same or altered form. The possibilities
for change or alteration of either the revelation or the message
were thus very real.

Operating on the basis of this model, we can now list in a
more systematic way the component elements we would expect to find
in any given example of the prophetic process. The minimum number
of components essential for the operation and identification of the
process are three: 1. the prophet's revelation, 2. a prophetic
message based on that revelation, and 3. feedback from the people.
In general the prophet's message will have the following characteristics: it will stand in continuity and some degree of harmony
with the cultural traditions of the prophet and his audience, it
will take cognizance of (be relevant to) the current historical
situation in which he and they find themselves, and it will take
"adequate" account of relevant factors external to the prophet's
culture.[6] Feedback will take the form of actions and sets of
expectations the tone of which - positive, negative, or neutral -
will be determined in large part by how well the message is perceived as meeting the three criteria of competence outlined above.

In addition five other components are possible, indeed, even
probable, although our ability to discover them will depend largely
on the amount and kind of data extant for any given instance of
prophecy. The five are: 4. prophetic feedback to the source of
revelation, 5. additional revelations, 6. additional messages,
and 7. adjustment of expectations on the part of the hearers.
8. Finally, a fourth actor may be added to the basic model sketched

in Figure 1 due to the presence of disciples, who may on occasion
convey the prophet's message to the people.

A lengthy review of the literature on OT prophecy is neither
possible nor desirable within the scope of this study. However, a
few brief comments seem in order to illustrate the dominance of the
view of prophecy as a one-way process and set the stage for the
analysis of the Jeremiah materials that follows. Since one of the
claims I will be making for the model involves its usefulness in
cross-cultural comparisons of the prophetic process, we can begin
by considering J. Lindblom's magnificent study, Prophecy in Ancient
Israel.[7] It is of special interest that Lindblom assumes prophecy
to be a universal human phenomenon. During the course of a first
chapter devoted to prophets outside Israel, he establishes what he
considers to be the three defining characteristics of prophecy:
the prophet was a person who was conscious of having received a
special call from his god, who had revelatory experiences, and who
proclaimed to the people the message received through revelation.
With respect to the OT materials these characteristics are discussed at length, but it is important to note that this definition
of the prophetic act remains essentially within the one-way informational chain mentioned above. In keeping with this there is
a heavy emphasis on the content of the message. It is in their
message that the main difference between the primitive and classical
prophets in Israel is to be found, and the last third of the book
is devoted to an exposition of the proclamations of the latter
under the rubric "the religion of the prophets."

For all its talk about "Sitz im Leben," form criticism has
tended more to affirm than modify the dominant conception of the
prophetic process. In his Basic Forms of Prophetic Speech, for
example, Claus Westermann argues that the prophets' utterances
were essentially those of messengers and that the formal sequence,
"reason" followed by "announcement of judgment," implies an active
participation of the prophets in shaping the content of their
message. This emphasis on the "alert" consciousness of the prophet

leads him to play down the role of ecstasy in revelation on the basis that "it is impossible for a message to be received in a state of ecstasy."[8] At best we see here a slight modification of the one-way conception of the prophetic act, but significant inter-action between the prophet and people is left entirely out of account and that between Yahweh and the prophet nearly so. The prophet helped shape the content of his message on the basis of the revelation he received and the details of the current situation as he saw them. To accomplish this task he had to be "alert," but there was no apparent necessity for any formal feedback from him to Yahweh.[9]

I mention as a final sample of the consensus in operation R. B. Y. Scott's The Relevance of the Prophets, where the revelation of the divine word is stressed as basic to the prophetic act: "Theirs was a positive and urgent message that was neither derived from tradition (though the tradition was part of it), nor produced by reflection upon an existing body of religious belief. They spoke at an immediate divine command." Yet, although I consider revelation to be of critical importance in the prophetic process, I can only feel that Scott's insistence upon the one-way nature of the proph-etic act raises certain problems and makes consistency difficult. For in other places he speaks of "prophetic insight," of the fact that being a prophet does not necessarily lead to an obliteration of "the human and personal factor," and of the fact that, as a result of his call, the prophet "was not a puppet, but a conscious instrument."[10] If there is no contradiction here, there is at least a serious tension between the more human, self-controlled, and rational aspects of the prophetic existence and the inter-vention of Yahweh's word. My suggestion is that the dynamic model of the prophetic process outlined above will prove useful in deal-ing with that tension.

There has not been a great deal of effort on the part of OT scholars to use anthropological materials to help illuminate the nature of prophecy.[11] The model I am proposing derives from my

study of both the OT and anthropological accounts of prophetic
movements. I have already applied it in a study of the Ghost Dance,
an Indian prophetic movement wide-spread in the American West around
1890, and my contention is that it is useful in studying OT prophecy as well. Its various components are clearly present in the
book of Jeremiah. The objection is conceivable that because of
his relative lateness and distinctive qualities Jeremiah is by far
the most likely OT figure to "fit" the model. To such a suggestion
I would reply that the OT as we have it is, after all, a statement
of Yahwistic orthodoxy and much more interested in theological content than in historical and social processes.

Let it be clear that I am neither arguing that this side of
the prophetic act has been altogether ignored nor proposing that
what is required is that prophetic studies take an entirely new
direction. There has been general recognition of the fact that
the aim of prophecy was to evoke a response from the people. The
intention of the present study is simply to take these factors more
specifically into account. James L. Crenshaw's Prophetic Conflict
seems to me to represent an important step in the same direction,
stressing the active intellectual involvement of the prophet in the
shaping of his message as well as the tensions and conflicts the
prophet experienced within himself and between himself and his
audience.[12]

III

It is now time to turn to a discussion of the prophet Jeremiah
in terms of the proposed model. Jeremiah is particularly suited to
interpretation in these terms, since by comparison with other OT
prophets our information about his activity is exceptionally full.
This is primarily due to the presence in the book of Jeremiah of
two special categories of material. The first of these, the prophet's complaints to Yahweh, has been widely recognized and discussed,

and provides us with several specific instances of feedback, both
from the people to Jeremiah and from the prophet to Yahweh.[13] The
second, a collection of direct quotations from the people, has not
received so much attention, although Crenshaw has pointed the way
toward using them in a more dynamic description of the prophetic
act. In particular he sees mirrored in them a "vox populi" against
which the prophets had to struggle.[14]

This body of direct quotations is remarkable both in size
(nearly 100 instances in Jeremiah as compared to approximately a
dozen each in Amos and Hosea) and in distribution (instances occur
in approximately 80% of the chapters and are scattered fairly evenly
through the book). My own study suggests to me that these quotations
are for the most part products of Jeremiah's rhetorical skill and
not verbatim records of the speech of others. But in any case the
validity of using them to understand the kind of audience feedback
he was receiving does not rest on such verbatim reporting, for
without doubt they accurately reflect his perceptions of how people
were reacting to him, reactions which were sometimes quite tangible
(20:1-6; 26) but other times much less so (11:18-19; 20:7-8).

In applying the model to the interpretation of Jeremiah several
options are open. One might, for example, work systematically through
each of the eight components listed above and discuss all the evidence relevant to each. For the sake of brevity, however, and because the dynamic interaction between the three main actors in the
prophetic process is the feature of most immediate concern here, I
have chosen in what follows to concentrate mainly on the events of
revelation and proclamation and on the implications of the model
for our understanding of prophecy.

The Revelation - Feedback - Revelation Sequence. The conviction that the message of the prophet was based on revelation
received from Yahweh is recurrent in the book of Jeremiah. The
superscription to the book as a whole defines the date and duration
of Jeremiah's ministry in terms of when the word of Yahweh came to
him (1:1-3; cf. 25:1-3), and the very first episode we encounter in

it is an account of the experience by which the prophet understood himself to have been called and commissioned as Yahweh's messenger (1:4-10). Furthermore, it would seem that the call experience was not the only occasion on which the prophet felt he had received a revelation from Yahweh. One gains this impression, for example, from the various conventions by which prophetic utterances are introduced: "And Yahweh said to me ..." (3:6, 11) or "The word of Yahweh came to me saying ..." (2:1). But more importantly, we have recorded for us a number of apparent visionary and/or auditory experiences which, because of their content and context, cannot plausibly be assigned to a single occasion (1:11-12, 13-19; 13:1-11; 18:1-11; 19:1-15; 24:1-10).[15]

The communication that took place in Jeremiah's revelatory experiences was not all one-way. Feedback from the prophet to Yahweh begins in the call experience itself with the protest that because of his youth he was not up to the task that was being imposed upon him (1:6), and each of the six complaints also contains this element. These focus on the problems that Jeremiah had remaining faithful to his prophetic office and give prominent place to feelings of ill-will directed against his personal enemies. The wickedness of the latter was pointed out (12:4; 18:23), as well as the unfairness of their continuing to prosper (12:1-2). The demand was made that they be punished by Yahweh (11:20; 12:3b; 15:15; 17:18; 18:21-23). On the other hand, Jeremiah asserted his own righteousness and faithfulness to his office (12:3a; 15:16-17; 17:16; 18:20), complained bitterly about the burdens of being a prophet (20:7-9, 14-18), and even accused Yahweh of acting unfaithfully (15:18; cf. 20:7-9).

We will be returning to the matter of the people's hostility toward the prophet. What needs to be pointed out here is that one of the factors in all of this mutual hostility was the question of the validity of the prophet's revelation and the message based upon it. Jeremiah had announced that disaster would befall the people, not because he took delight in doing so, but because he understood that to be the content of his revelation (17:16). And the people, who would not have been inclined in any case to accept such a judgment, at some point began to subject him to intense ridicule because what he had threatened had failed to occur (17:15; 20:7-8). It is evident that Jeremiah also had his doubts about the validity of the revelation (15:18; 20:7·), and that these doubts were one of the main elements in his feedback to Yahweh. 5:4-5 may be another indication of this process, by which the prophet reacted to his understanding of his revelatory experience.

Finally, the complaints also contain two examples of Yahweh's rejoinder to the prophetic feedback (12:5-6; 15:19-21). These are clearly to be understood as "additional revelations," the burden of which was to confirm the message that the prophet had been proclaiming all along. By implication, we can assume that a similar feedback-response series lies behind that portion of the Hananiah episode (ch. 28) in which Jeremiah was temporarily unable to dispute the message of his opponent, but "sometime later" returned to condemn him as a liar. Given the nature of prophecy, it seems to me necessary to assume that any alteration in message would be understood by the prophet to be grounded in an additional revelation from the god, and therefore insofar as the announcement of a "new covenant" (31:31-34) and other passages of a more "positive" tone (e.g., 32:1-15) can be taken to reflect a segment of Jeremiah's message, they also imply further revelations.

The Proclamation - Feedback - Proclamation Sequence. It is clear from the passages cited above that in large part Jeremiah considered his task as a prophet to be one of proclaiming to the people a message he understood to be based on a series of revelations from Yahweh. In general his primary message was fairly consistent - that because of their actions and the "falsehood" that pervaded their existence the people were standing on the brink of a great national catastrophe - and well-known, and we need not pause to elaborate on its specific content. We know that it evoked considerable response, and it is to this feedback from the people to the prophet that we now turn.

Jeremiah's message clearly evoked a good deal of hostility. This opposition was sometimes stated in general terms, that the prophets are 'windbags' and their words not those of Yahweh (5: 12-13), but more often as direct personal attacks on Jeremiah. He was derided because of the failure of his proclamation to come to pass (17:15; 20:7-8), and the laments make it clear that this was more than just a casual disagreement, since in some cases it gave rise to threats against his life (11:18-23; 18:18, 22; 20:10). On at least one occasion he was beaten and put into the stocks by a member of the priestly establishment (20:1-6; cf. 29:26-28). Following his "temple sermon," the priests, prophets, and people attempted to engineer a death sentence for him (26:7-9), and on another occasion the princes attempted to dispose of him by throwing him into an abandoned cistern (38:1-6). We also have references to his being pursued by the agents of an angry king (36:26), accused of treason (37:13-14; 38:1-4), and imprisoned (32:2-3; 37:15-16, 20-21).

Even this does not exhaust the negative responses to Jeremiah's proclamation. The book abounds in references to prophets whose message, broadly characterized as one of "peace," stands in flat contradition to that of Jeremiah. The classic example is the conflict with Hananiah described in ch. 28. There are also several instances of persons refusing outright to obey what he conveyed to them as the will of Yahweh (43:1-7; 44:15-19). On the positive side, we have references to individuals and groups who were in support of the prophet (26:16-19, 24; 36:13-19; 39:11-14; 40:1-6), as well as occasions on which he was sought out by someone who wished to learn Yahweh's will for the current situation (21:1-2; 38:14-16; 42:1-3). Many of these passages contain the kind of direct quotations from the people mentioned above.

The fact that the feedback to Jeremiah's proclamation was mixed leads to the question of the criteria by which the people formed their judgment of it. This question has been widely discussed under

the rubric "false prophecy," and this very notion highlights the
problem of the nature of prophetic authority, for how could there
be two conflicting prophets who represent the same God?  The tendency has been to seek more or less absolute criteria, such as the
presence or absence of a prophetic "call," the morals of the prophet, or the fulfillment of his predictions, for distinguishing between true prophets and impostors.  I do not believe such criteria
work very well, since the situations in which the prophets acted
are known to have been fraught with crisis and ambiguity.  I have
suggested above three characteristics of a prophetic message, each
of which contains a kind of standard by which it could be evaluated.
But there is no guarantee that two persons, using these same standards,
would come to equivalent conclusions about what the prophet said.
It is evident that both Jeremiah and Hananiah had a following, and
it seems equally clear that the followers of each could find some
legitimate grounds for believing that their man's message was faithful to the tradition and relevant to the current historical situation.
I have dealt specifically with this problem in another place, and
will not repeat that discussion here.[16]  What is important to notice
is the intensity and significance of the element of feedback in this
segment of the prophetic process.  Whatever else may be said, each
prophet clearly had his own source of authority and moral support
in a group of followers, and each had to defend his claims against
those who would disavow them.

Finally, we must ask whether Jeremiah's message was affected
by the nature of the feedback he received.  Here the data are not
so clear, but some tentative suggestions may be offered.[17]  Recall
again the dispute between Hananiah and Jeremiah.  Contrary to what
Jeremiah had been saying, Hananiah proclaimed that within two years
Yahweh would break the power of the King of Babylon and bring about
the return of the Judean captives from exile (28:2-4).  Jeremiah's
response was that, while it would indeed be gratifying if such were
the case, Hananiah's message had broken with the tradition of proph-
esies of doom and could therefore be judged valid only if it were

actually fulfilled (28:5-9). It appears that a criterion of judgment has been introduced here, but Hananiah apparently was not deterred by it. We also note that when Jeremiah himself later returned to resolve the conflict, this "criterion" played no part in what he said. Hananiah then reasserted his position and emphasized his conviction by breaking the symbolic yoke bars that Jeremiah had been carrying on his neck. At this point Jeremiah "went his way" (v. 11), returning only "sometime after" (v. 12) to reassert his own message and condemn Hananiah.

The striking thing here is the pause. While the message of Jeremiah apparently did not change, he was for a period stymied and forced to retreat for some reconsideration and/or renewal of his conviction. In the discussion of the prophet's feedback to Yahweh we have noted other indications that he resisted the kind of message he felt called upon to proclaim, and it seems reasonable to conclude that the intensity of the negative feedback he experienced causes him to pause and reconsider both the content of what he said and even his own continuance in the prophetic office (cf. 20:9).

Beyond this, there is the question of more substantive changes in Jeremiah's message as the result of feedback. The most obvious instance of such a change is the various prophecies of a hopeful future located in the mid-section of the book, and I have found a recent study by Thomas M. Raitt[18] to be helpful in dealing with these much-debated passages. Raitt isolates six passages which display a shift in content from judgment to a combination of that sentiment with promises of salvation and which he argues are "true to Jeremiah's thought and within the horizons of the situations he felt it was his ministry to interpret."[19] These utterances have in common the fact that they are set in the period between the two Babylonian conquests of Jerusalem and therefore address themselves to a dual audience/situation, viz., exiles who were now in need of comfort and the king, princes, and others who still remained in Judah and who were in need of continued chastisement. That the

exile was a severe blow to the people which demanded and received
immediate interpretive reflection cannot be doubted.  Clearly there
were those who saw the events of 597 as penalty enough for the
nation's transgressions against Yahweh and in their nationalistic
zeal announced that the restoration would come speedily (28:2-4;
29:4-9, 24-28).  Others, we may infer, were inclined much more
toward despair.  In each case the reaction was both to the actual
historical events and to the prophet's (and others') interpretation
of their cause.  And now the prophet began to introduce elements
of hope into his message.  Raitt seeks to differentiate the emphasis of such elements from similar passages coming from later
redactors of the Jeremiah tradition or for the Deuteronomists,
noting that it is his unique prophetic authority which lies behind the combination of judgment and unconditional hope characteristic of these passages.  What I wish to point out is that this
shift in the content of his message followed a significant alteration in socio-political circumstances and thus also in the kinds
of feedback he was receiving from important segments of his audience.  One part of what we mean when we refer to Jeremiah's "authority"
arises as a result of his response to this feedback, of his creative
interpretation of a dual or ambiguous situation.[20]

The final interactive element in the model, which I have labeled "expectations of confirmation," deserves a brief comment.  It is
evident that the Judeans were engaged in other kinds of relationships with Yahweh than those channeled through the prophets.  The
book of Jeremiah itself makes reference to the people's turning to
Yahweh in times of trouble and their expectation of his deliverance
(2:27; 7:10; 14:7-9, 19-22).  While in some cases of prophetic
activity these expectations served to reinforce positively the
prophet's message,[21] here they had the opposite effect, confirming
the people in the very attitudes against which Jeremiah argued.

IV

Let me conclude by suggesting some of the implications of this view of the prophetic process. First, a brief comment on von Rad's suggestion that in Jeremiah we have a prophet who "was no longer at one with his office and his tasks."[22] One factor in this tension was probably Jeremiah's experience of his own powerlessness to effect his desired ends, of the breakdown of his own authority. For him the dialogue inherent in the prophetic process was disrupted in both directions. Both Yahweh and the people were experienced as unyielding.

Next, I call attention to one of the points with which we began: without the god and the people there can be no prophet, and the correlate of this fact is that the source of a prophet's authority is real, arising both from his "call" and the people's response to his message. This is a point which has not gone unnoticed in studies of non-biblical materials. In the course of their discussion of the Mahdiyya movement in the Sudan (1881-99), for example, R. H. Dekmejian and M. J. Wyszomviski discuss the ambiguity in Weber's notion of charisma: charisma is a personal (psychological) gift, but it is insignificant without social acknowledgment. Charismatic authority is in fact characterized by a "highly spiritual relationship" between the leader and his followers in which they become subject to his charisma and find their values transformed.[23] Ann Ruth and Dorothy Willner make a similar point when they suggest that the decisive point in validating charisma is not divine inspiration but rather how the prophet "is regarded by those subject to his authority." The "process" of validation, then, involves "interaction between the leader and his followers."[24] As a final example, I refer to Peter Lawrence, who describes the emergence and development of five successive "cargo beliefs" in New Guinea over the period 1871-1950. These were grounded in a "cargo ideology" which was rooted in the native mythology and displayed a remarkable consistency through time, becoming "an intrinsic part of the culture of the area." The last of the five movements began around the end of World War II. Its leader, Yali, advocated cooperation with the Australian colonial government and a program of "secular" reform, and made no supernatural claims about himself. But his teachings were widely misunderstood. People began to view him as a cargo cult leader, and attributed to him (claimed that he had had) visions and supernatural experiences. As Lawrence points out, it was only by setting Yali in such a framework that his utterances became "intelligible" to the people. Yali's audience attributed prophetic authority to him, in effect making him a prophet even in the absence of any claims to revelatory experience. Without their reaction he would neither have claimed to be nor been a prophet.[25] Since prophecy is always situation-bound and public, private revelation alone is insufficient to establish its authority.

Thirdly, there is the matter of "false prophecy." The heterogeneity of the audience which a prophet addresses suggests that the refusal to believe or follow his teachings cannot automatically be taken as a sign of perversity or cultural "incompetence." We have suggested how complex the matter of evaluating a prophet's proclamation is. We are well aware of the fact that in our own day personal perceptions of the cultural heritage and of the current historical situation can diverge widely and that people of good will can differ profoundly on matters of great importance. We need to assume, I think, that the same was true in other times and cultures. We recall the observation of Crenshaw and others that the impact of the canonical prophets on their contemporaries was comparatively limited.[26] Many in their audience seem not to have wanted to believe them, while on the other hand some did believe (or acted as though they believed) their rivals. To distinguish between rival prophets is rather more easy with benefit of hindsight, and one should guard against self-righteous judgments ("...they should have...") regarding former generations' existential dilemmas. The prophetic process seems to me to be one in which there is a dynamic interaction, struggle, if you will, in quest of the "truth." Further, that "truth" is always culturally defined.

Finally, I would like to point to the potential that this
model has for engaging in comparative studies of prophecy. The
content of a prophet's message is important, of course, when one
is dealing with a specific culture and historical context and
trying to understand the role of a particular prophet within it.
But content can become a stumbling-block in cross-cultural comparisons, for it is difficult to avoid the pitfalls of ethno-
centricity and hindsight. Since it focuses on how the prophetic
process works and not on culturally-conditioned content, the model
utilized here should facilitate the making of cross-cultural comparisons and may be able to contribute to our knowledge of how
cultures change.

FOOTNOTES

1. *Basic Forms of Prophetic Speech* (Philadelphia: Westminster, 1967).

2. Cf. my *The Threat of Falsehood: A Study in the Theology of the Book of Jeremiah* (SBT 2/16; London: SCM Press, 1970), especially 24-48.

3. "The Ghost Dance of 1890 and the Nature of the Prophetic Process," *Ethnohistory* 21 (1974) 37-63.

4. Care should be taken not to distinguish so sharply between the historical situation, viewed as a "constant" factor in the prophet's operation, and the specific reactions of the people to him that the intimate relationship between the two is clouded. For the most part we are dealing not so much with the "objective" situation as with one or another interpretation of current events.

5. In a recent paper Burke O. Long ("The Sitz im Leben for Accounts of Prophetic Vocation," delivered at the SBL Annual Meeting, 1976) has pointed out that to act as a prophet is to make certain transcendent claims, but the social realization of these claims depends on the acceptance of the prophet by his audience. A fuller discussion of this aspect of the prophet's authority appears in IV below.

6. For an example of how criteria like these might be used in distinguishing between conflicting prophetic claims and the views of the covenant on which they were based cf. my *Threat of Falsehood,* 92-104.

7. Oxford: Blackwell, 1962.

8. Philadelphia: Westminster Press, 1967; esp. 62-63, 86-87, 102-103.

9. By contrast, a recent paper by Robert R. Wilson ("Prophecy and Ecstasy: A Re-examination," delivered at the SBL Annual Meeting, 1976) stresses the importance of the social situation in shaping the prophet's activity.

10. Revised edition (New York: Macmillan, 1968), 91-92, 97, 162.

11. Some recent examples of such an effort are the papers of Wilson and Long referred to above. In addition see B. O. Long's "The Social Setting for Prophetic Miracle Stories," *Semeia* 3 (1975) 46-59, and M. J. Buss, *The Prophetic Word of Hosea* (BZAW 111: Berlin: de Gruyter, 1969), esp. chap. VI.

12.  Berlin: de Gruyter, 1971 (BZAW, 124).

13.  The usefulness of the complaints for understanding Jeremiah's feelings and the more individual aspects of his conduct of the prophetic office has been seriously challenged by H. Graf Reventlow (*Liturgie und prophetisches Ich bei Jeremia,* Gütersloh: Mohn, 1963), who insists on the prophet's official cultic function as mediator between Yahweh and the people, and E. Gerstenberger ("Jeremiah's Complaints: Observations on Jer 15:10-20," JBL 82 [1963] 393-408), who attributes the present form and context of one particular complaint to later Deuteronomic reflection. Both of these studies raise interesting and valid points, but I am unable to accept their conclusions as valid for the whole body of Jeremiah's complaints. In fairness it must be said that Gerstenberger does not generalize from his conclusions. Reventlow, however, does, even though the three complaints that are potentially most damaging to his thesis (18:18-23; 20:7-13, 14-18) are omitted from his discussion. John Bright ("Jeremiah's Complaints: Liturgy, or Expressions of Personal Distress?," *Proclamation and Presence: Old Testament Essays in Honor of Gwynne Henton Davies* eds. J. I. Durham and J. R. Porter; [Richmond: John Knox, 1970] 189-214) makes a convincing critique of Reventlow's position. In a recent discussion of the complaints William Holladay has referred to the series of dialogues involving God, Jeremiah, and the people as a "three-way conversation" (*Jeremiah: Spokesman Out of Time* [Philadelphia: Pilgrim Press, 1974] 106). Cf. also John M. Berridge, *Prophet, People, and the Word of Yahweh* (Zurich: EVZ-Verlag, 1970), esp. 114-183.

14.  *Prophetic Conflict,* esp. 23-48.  Cf. also W. H. Horwitz ("Audience Reaction to Jeremiah," CBQ 32 [1970] 555-564), who argues for using these quotations to help establish the historicity of the text.

15.  The relative weight as evidence to be assigned to any of the formulae or passages cited in this paragraph and others that might be added to them will depend in part on one's view of the composition of the book of Jeremiah. The problems here are great, and the literature growing rapidly. Cf. my "Remarks on the Continuity of the Jeremiah Tradition" (JBL 91 [1972] 457-62) and the literature cited there, and more recently William L. Holladay, "A Fresh Look at 'Source B' and 'Source C' in Jeremiah," VT 25 (1975) 394-412.

16.  *The Threat of Falsehood,* especially chs. II and V.  Cf. also Crenshaw, *Prophetic Conflict,* on the ambiguities and tensions built into the prophetic situation (pp. 1-4), the influence of the vox populi on the prophets (pp. 23-38), and the prophets' "desire for success" (pp. 65-66).

17.  It should be pointed out that the possibility that a

prophet's message will undergo certain alterations as a result of feedback from his audience does not create the necessity that such change will in fact occur. Jeremiah's preoccupation with what the people said indicates a certain need on his part to take their responses seriously, though the book yields more evidence for the strength of the effect of such upon him personally (discouragement, doubts about the plausibility of his own message, hopes that the message of his opponents was plausible - 28:6, etc.) than for its causing major changes in his message.

18. "Jeremiah's Deliverance Message to Judah," *Rhetorical Criticism: Essays in Honor of James Muilenburg* (ed. J. J. Jackson and M. Kessler; Pittsburgh: Pickwick Press, 1974) 166-85.

19. Ibid., 167; the passages are 24:4-7; 29:4-7, 10-14; 32:6-15, 42-44; 31:31-34; 32:36-41; 33:6-9.

20. An important study by H. G. Barnett (*Indian Shakers,* Carbondale: Southern Illinois University Press, 1957) allows one to glimpse the dynamics of a prophetic movement in another culture from its inception through its routinization. In its early years the leadership of the Shakers was comparatively fluid, and a number of disciples of the original prophet, John Slocum, and converts, often manifesting prophetic characteristics themselves, were influential. Barnett records several instances in which feedback from the audience apparently resulted in a change in the message and its attendant practice, e.g., abandonment of the doctrine of individual confession of sins (283-4) and the aberrant version of the Shaker message developed by Lans Kapala, presumably under pressure of negative reactions from whites (63-5).

21. As, for example, in the case of reactions to Wovoka, the Ghost Dance prophet; cf. my "Ghost Dance," 47-48.

22. G. von Rad, *Old Testament Theology* (2 vols.; New York: Harper & Ros, 1962-65) 2.205.

23. "Charismatic Leadership in Islam: The Mahdi of the Sudan," *Comparative Studies in Society and History* 14 (1972) 193-214. Cf. also J. Wach ("Master and Disciple: Two Religio-Sociological Studies," JR 42 [1962] 1-21); though he distinguishes between master and (the less decisive) prophet, his sentence describes the process to which I am referring: "The master reads his calling in the eye of his disciple, just as the disciple hears destiny speak in and through the master" (2).

24. "The Rise and Role of Charismatic Leaders," *Annals of the American Academy of Political and Social Science* 348 (1965) 77-88, esp. 79, 81. At a more general level C. Erasmus ("The Leader vs. Tradition: A Case Study," *American Anthropologist* 54 [1952] 168-78) has argued that the leader or innovator must be

150

intelligible to his group, appealing to its situation and interests.
His genius is thus limited by the group's interest and understanding: "To be achieved, 'genius' must also be ascribed" (176).  Peter
Worsley (*The Trumpet Shall Sound* [2 ed.; New York: Schocken, 1968]
xii) has remarked, "Charisma is thus a function of recognition:
the prophet without honor cannot be a charismatic prophet."  Cf.
also S. C. Kincheloe, "The Prophet as a Leader," *Sociology and
Social Research* 12 (1928) 461-68.

25.  *Road Belong Cargo: A Study of the Cargo Movement in the
Southern Madang District New Guinea* (Manchester: Manchester University Press, 1964), esp. 255-56, 269.

26.  *Prophetic Conflict*, esp. chap. V; also I. Engnell, *A Rigid
Scrutiny* (Nashville: Vanderbilt University Press, 1969), 140, 142.

# THE POLITICAL BACKGROUND OF JEREMIAH'S TEMPLE SERMON

Jay A. Wilcoxen

When the career of ancient Israel is seen in terms of the recurrent tension and struggle between the two great themes of divine promise and call to obedience, together with their respective covenant traditions, the period of the late monarchy in Judah assumes special importance. In the time of King Josiah and the prophet Jeremiah the effort to hold those themes together came to a climax and was given literary expression in ways that have had far-reaching consequences for later ages. Within that important period a particularly critical moment was the delivery by Jeremiah of his famous temple sermon. For later times that sermon was significant chiefly for the timeless character of its religious and ethical import. In its own time, however, it was part of a life-and-death struggle for the survival and correct understanding of the kingdom of Judah as the covenant people of the God of Israel. The purpose of the present essay is to review the nature of that struggle, and especially its political aspects.[1]

## I. The Occasion of the Sermon

The temple sermon of Jeremiah is that speech in which the prophet is reported to have threatened the temple of Jerusalem with the fate of the old sanctuary of Shiloh. It is reported twice in the book of Jeremiah, once in the sermonic style often found in that book (7:1-15) and once in a biographical passage that goes on to tell what happened to Jeremiah after the sermon was delivered (26:1-19).[2] The biographical passage indicates that the occasion of the sermon was "the beginning of the reign of

151

Jehoiakim, son of Josiah, king of Judah" (26:1). The phrase "the beginning of the reign" was evidently a technical expression designating that portion of the year that remained after a new king came to the throne until the next official new year. In the case of King Jehoiakim this is known to have been either late in the year 609 or early in the year 608.[3] Jeremiah's temple sermon was delivered, then, during those weeks or months in which Jehoiakim was organizing his administration and setting the religious and political policies that he would pursue during his reign. That new reign was the most prominent political fact about the background of the sermon. Jehoiakim had come to the throne under some rather unusual circumstances, however, and these need to be examined fairly closely to appreciate the full import of the sermon.

The foremost political fact about Jehoiakim's kingship was that he had gained the throne through the intervention of the Egyptian Pharaoh, Necho II (610-594). The imperial activities of Necho had thrown Judah into crisis early in 609. Necho was marching to upper Mesopotamia to assist the Assyrian king, Assuruballit II, in his last ditch stand against the rising power of the Medes and the Babylonians. The Judean king Josiah, Jehoiakim's father, opposed Necho and as a consequence met his death at Megiddo sometime in June of 609. For three months thereafter, while Necho was engaged in an unsuccessful attack on the Babylonians at Haran, Judah was ruled by another son of Josiah, Jehoahaz. When Necho returned from the north, however, he imposed a new political arrangement on the kingdom of Judah which included the removal of the new king Jehoahaz and the installation of Jehoiakim in his place. This occurred around September of 609. Why Necho rejected Jehoahaz and preferred Jehoiakim is an important question bearing on the background of Jeremiah's sermon.

One fact relevant to the question is that Jehoiakim, not Jehoahaz, was Josiah's eldest son. According to the book of Kings, Jehoahaz was twenty-three years old when he succeeded Josiah in

June of 609 (2 Kgs 23:31). Jehoiakim, on the other hand, was
twenty-five years old when he came to the throne three months
later (2 Kgs 23:36). As far as is known the succession in the
kingdom of Judah was normally through the eldest surviving son.
(The special case of Solomon is sufficiently explained in 1 Kings
1-2.) Thus, when Necho returned from the north he found a rather
unusual situation in Judah. While a son of Josiah occupied the
throne, it was not the son one would expect. Therefore, from one
viewpoint all Necho did in his political arrangement was to restore legitimacy in the succession to the Judean kingship. He
replaced a younger son of Josiah with the rightful eldest son.
One may suspect, of course, that this restoration of legitimacy
fit very nicely into Necho's purposes anyway, and to see why that
may have been so requires a further consideration of the family
situation of Jehoiakim and his brother.

## II.  The Politics of Josiah's Marriages

The book of Kings supplies enough information about the kings
of Judah to say something about the politics of the royal family,
especially in the period of Josiah and his sons.  This information
includes the ages of the kings at their accessions, the lengths of
their reigns, and who their mothers were.  Josiah's father Amon
reigned for two years before he was assassinated in a palace coup.
At his death he was twenty-four years old (2 Kgs 21:19) and was
succeeded by Josiah who was then eight years old (2 Kgs 22:1).
Josiah was born, then, when Amon was only sixteen years old.  This
suggests that those in power were concerned to secure a natural
heir to the throne as early as possible.  The same concern is
strongly in evidence in the reign of Josiah, for Josiah was only
fourteen years old when his first son Jehoiakim was born and
sixteen years old when his second son Jehoahaz was born.

Apart from the youthful parentage expected of the prince,

two things of political importance are reflected here. One is
the marriage arrangement from which the heir to the throne was expected. The choice of the first wife for the young prince or king
was a weighty matter, as is indicated by the attention given to
the mothers of the kings of Judah in the book of Kings. The women
selected as the first wife would eventually become the queen mother,
a position of no little power in the kingdom of Judah, as is known
from the cases of Bathsheba, Maʿachah, and Athaliah (1 Kgs 2:12-20;
15:9-13; 2 Kgs 11). The second point is that such a state marriage
cannot have been left to the whims of a teenage boy not yet old
enough to rule in his own right. These were arranged marriages,
and the arrangements were made by grandfathers, fathers, and powerful advisers, and in Josiah's case presumably by regents who exercised authority in his name. It is evident, then, that in the
early years of the reign of Josiah one of the leading political
questions would have been the marriages of the boy king. Indeed,
in the complications of Josiah's marriages there may lie the
answer to the question why Jehoiakim, the eldest son, was passed
over for the kingship after Josiah's death.

The three sons of Josiah who subsequently became kings of
Judah derived from two different mothers. Jehoiakim was born to
Zebidah, daughter of Pedaiah of Rumah (2 Kgs 23:36), while Jehoahaz and Zedekiah, the two younger sons, were born to Hamutal,
daughter of Jeremiah of Libnah (2 Kgs 23:31, spelled Hamital at
24:18). The chronology of these marriages seems particularly
significant, but before considering that, a set of circumstances
surrounding the first wife, Zebidah, warrants a digression.

Zebidah's native town is said to have been Rumah, which is
most likely the town in central Galilee later referred to by
Josephus.[4] The book of Kings does not give the native towns of
all the queen mothers of Judah, but those that are given indicate
only two non-Judean queen mothers after the time of Queen Athaliah
in the mid-ninth century. One of these was Josiah's first wife

and the other was his grandmother, Meshullemeth, "daughter of Haruz from Jotbah" and mother of Amon (2 Kgs 21:19). There are three points concerning this Meshullemeth, none of which can be answered with certainty but which, when taken together, are of great interest for the politics of Josiah's marriages.

The first is the location of Meshullemeth's native town, Jotbah. One possible location is in the far south near Ezion-geber, where one of the campsites of the Israelites during their wilderness wanderings is called Jotbathah (Num 33:33-35). The other possible location is in central Galilee, frequently referred to by Josephus as Jotapata (e.g., *J.W.* 2. 20, 6:573. While both locations are outside the probable boundaries of Judah in Manasseh's time, the possibility that Meshullemeth came from central Gailiee is of particular interest, since that was the region from which Josiah's first wife, Zebidah, also came.

The second point concerns Meshullemeth's relationship to King Manasseh. At first sight this seems clear; she was the mother of Amon who in turn is called the son of Manasseh (2 Kgs 21:18). In Biblical Hebrew, however, the term son can also be applied to a grandson (e.g., Gen 31:43), and this possibility needs to be con-sidered in the case of Amon. Manasseh began his long reign of fifty-five years when he was twelve years old (2 Kgs 21:1), which makes him about sixty-seven at his death. Amon, however, was only twenty-two years old at that time, making Manasseh forty-five at Amon's birth. These ages make it quite possible that Manasseh had produced an heir to the throne at the usual early age, but that that son did not survive Manasseh. (One may recall here the unpleasant accusation made against Manasseh in Kings, that he caused his son to pass through the fire, 2 Kgs 21:6.) Manasseh, then, would have been succeeded by his grandson, the son of the former crown prince. The significance of this possibility is that Meshullemeth would then have been Manasseh's daughter-in-law rather than his wife. Her marriage to Manasseh's son would have been arranged by Manasseh, not by Hezekiah before him. The political implications of the choice of Meshullemeth would have been a part of Manasseh's policies in the early and middle periods of his reign.

The third point of interest concerns the political situation in Judah at the time Meshullemeth gave birth to Amon. That was around the year 664.[5] At that time the Assyrian empire was at its zenith and had recently conquered Egypt. Around 667, the young Assyrian king Asshurbanipal took a group of Egyptian princes as prisoners to Assyria, where he executed all of them except one. The one who was spared was also sent back to Egypt as a vassal ruler. His name was Necho, and he was the grandfather of the Necho who would later kill Josiah and place Jehoiakim on the throne of Judah. What is to be noticed here is the similar political situation in which the two vassals of Assyria, Manasseh of Judah and Necho of Egypt, found themselves. The birth of Amon to Meshullemeth took place approximately three years after Necho was restored to rule in Egypt. If the marriage of Meshullemeth to a son of Manasseh at about this time had political implications, those implications are very likely to have included a covert or overt alliance between Judah and Egypt. If this was so, it is possible to trace a continuity in Judean royal policy that begins at least in the middle of Manasseh's reign and extends through the first marriage of the young Josiah. That Judean policy of Manasseh was then resumed in 609 when Jehoiakim, son of that first marriage of Josiah, was placed on the throne by Necho II of Egypt.

The second clue to the political significance of Josiah's two marriages has to do with the chronology of events during his reign. The book of Kings somewhat artificially compresses the events of Josiah's reign into the one great moment in his eighteenth year when he carried out his famous reform (2 Kgs 22:3-23:23). Historical probability suggests, however, that this stage of the reform was the culmination of a step-by-step process that involved the gradual assertion of independence from Assyria as well as whatever internal religious changes were made. Such a view of

Josiah's reign is in fact given in the book of Chronicles, though what independent sources that writer had is unknown. The Chronicles account gives the following sequence of events. Josiah became king when he was eight years old. In his eighth year, while he was still a youth of sixteen, "he began to seek the God of David his father" (2 Chr 34:3), and in his twelfth year he began an extensive cultic purification of Judah and Jerusalem (34:3-7). Then in the eighteenth year the temple was repaired, the scroll found, a covenant made, and a great Passover observance held (34:8-35:19). What is significant about these references in Chronicles is the indication of some change in the religious policy of the king in Josiah's eighth year, for that is the same year in which Josiah's second wife, Hamutal, from the Judean city of Libnah, gave birth to Jehoahaz, the son who would first succeed Josiah. Very possibly the marriage to Hamutal had also been arranged within that year. Thus, the new marriage and some change in the religious policy of the monarchy seem to coincide in Josiah's eighth year, when he was sixteen. And if a new policy for the kingdom was initiated at that time, the likelihood is that it was this same policy that was carried even further in the later stages of Josiah's reform program. That is to say, from one viewpoint, Josiah's reform really began in his eighth year and was carried to completion over a period of ten years. In that case, Josiah's second marriage was one political aspect of his overall reform program.

These clues from Josiah's early marriages permit a clearer view of the relation between Jehoahaz and Jehoiakim, the eldest sons of the two marriages. If the second marriage was peculiarly associated with the policies of the reform program, the first marriage apparently had political implications of an opposite tendency, more in line with the older policies of Manasseh. If Jehoahaz and his mother became identified with the reform party, Jehoiakim and his mother must have been viewed with suspicion by that party. If, finally, at Josiah's death the question was how to continue and safeguard his program, the answer was to make

Jehoahaz king rather than his older brother Jehoiakim.  When, therefore, Pharaoh Necho wished to reverse the policies of Josiah in
Judah, he found a ready ally in Jehoiakim and his supporters.

The household of Josiah appears to have been divided, therefore, over the issue of his reform program.  How did other forces
within the kingdom stand on this issue, and in particular how did
Jeremiah stand on it?


## III.   The Conflicting Parties in Judah


First is the question of the source of support for each side
in the political struggle.  In the case of Jehoahaz, it seems evident that behind him stood the group called "the people of the
land."  Two reports in the book of Kings indicate this.
The first is:

> And [Josiah's] servants carried him dead by chariot from
> Megiddo and brought him to Jerusalem where they buried
> him in his grave.  And the people of the land took Jehoahaz,
> son of Josiah, anointed him, and caused him to reign in
> place of his father.            (2 Kgs 23:30)

The second report comes later, after Necho had replaced Jehoahaz
with Jehoiakim and imposed a heavy fine upon the land.  The payment of this fine is reported as follows:

> And Jehoiakim gave the silver and gold to Pharaoh.  He
> assessed the land to give the silver according to the
> command of Pharaoh; from each man according to his assess-
> ment he exacted the silver and the gold from the people
> of the land to give to Pharaoh Necho.  (2 Kgs 23:35)

Thus, the same people who made Jehoahaz king had the penalty laid
upon them after Jehoiakim became king, and that was apparently at
the explicit command of Pharaoh.  This report permits the further
inference that the fine laid upon the people of the land did not
cause the royal household of Jehoiakim to suffer greatly.  There
is no mention of emptying the royal treasuries, much less of strip-
ping gold from the temple or the palace as had sometimes been done

by conquerors in the past (1 Kgs 14:25-26; 2 Kgs 18:14-16). In
fact, there is evidence that before long Jehoiakim began an ex-
pensive program of rebuilding the royal palace in a rather luxu-
rious style, a building program for which Jeremiah heartily condemned him (Jer 22:13-15). Part of Jeremiah's indictment is that
Jehoiakim employed forced labor in this project (Jer 22:13), which
could have been yet another penalty imposed by Jehoiakim on his
political opponents.

Jehoiakim's source of support was ultimately the Egyptian
king and his army, though a number of princes of Judah appear also
to have been sympathetic to his position (Jer 36:20-26). The continuance of this Egyptian support is seen in the case of the prophet Uriah, who is said to have spoken critically of Jehoiakim in the
same terms as did Jeremiah. Unlike Jeremiah, Uriah feared for his
life and fled to Egypt, where, however, he was simply extradited
back to Judah and executed (Jer 26:20-23).

The political background of Jeremiah's sermon is also illuminated by a consideration of the issues of foreign policy that
faced the kingdom of Judah in its last years. Through the early
reign of Josiah Judah was moving towards independence from Assyria.
As in the time of Hezekiah almost a century earlier, common opposition to Assyrian dominance would lead to cooperation, if not
active alliance, with Babylon (see 2 Kgs 20:12-13). Babylon se-
cured its independence from Assyria in 626, two years after the
beginning of Josiah's cultic reform, according to the sequence of
events given in Chronicles. In the later years of Josiah's reign,
Egypt came on the scene in support of Assyria against Babylon. In
that context, Joshia's opposition to Necho can only have been of
assistance to the Babylonians, whether there was an overt coordination of military actions or not. Thus, in the summer of 609
the choice in foreign policy for Judah was between a pro-Babylonian
and a pro-Egyptian position.

Jehoiakim's choice is clear. He was pro-Egyptian, and even
when Egypt had been driven out of Syria-Palestine, after the battle

of Carchemish in 605, Jehoiakim took the first opportunity to rebel against the new Babylonian suzerain (2 Kgs 24:1-2). The attitude of Jeremiah, on the other hand, while it may have been colored by non-political factors, was consistently pro-Babylonian in its political consequences. He exulted in the Babylonian triumph over the Egyptians in 605 (Jer 46:2-12) and took that occasion to create one of his most provocative demonstrations against Jehoiakim's policies, the famous scroll-reading episode (Jeremiah 36; cp. 46:2 and 25:1). In later years, when Zedekiah had been made king by Nebuchadnezzar, Jeremiah consistently opposed rebellion against Babylon (e.g., Jeremiah 27-28) or counseled surrender to besieging Babylonian forces (e.g., 38:14-28). For this, of course, he suffered from the pro-Egyptian party (e.g., 38:1-6) and was accused of treason (37:11-16). On the other hand, Nebuchadnezzar was not unaware of his friends in the embattled remnant of Judah, and after the capture of Jerusalem Jeremiah was singled out and offered protection and special privileges by the officials of the Babylonian king (39:11-14; 40:2-6).

Further evidence that the advocates of Josiah's reform were pro-Babylonian in their foreigh policy is seen from the role played in this period by the household of Shaphan. Shaphan himself was the "scribe" of Josiah's court, perhaps the king's highest secular adviser (2 Kgs 22:3-10). That he was much older than Josiah is indicated by the presence of one of his sons as a responsible member of the court when Josiah himself was only twenty-six years old (2 Kgs 22:12). Indeed, Shaphan was old enough to have been one of those advisers or regents responsible for the political decisions that led to Josiah's second marriage and the beginning of the reform program. In any case, Shaphan was at the center of those events by which Josiah's reform was given its claim to authority from the God of Israel. It was he who was said to have delivered the newly-discovered torah scroll to Josiah to have read it to him (2 Kgs 22: 9-10).

While Shaphan himself does not appear after the death of Josiah, two of his sons and two of his grandsons appear to support Jeremiah in his opposition to Jehoiakim and to represent a pro-Babylonian position in the foreign policy of Judah. First is Ahikam, the son who was already an official at the time of Josiah's reform covenant. He is credited with saving Jeremiah from the death penalty after the prophet delivered the temple sermon (Jer 26:24). Five years later, when Jeremiah sent Baruch to read the provocative scroll in the temple, it was to the chamber of another son of Shaphan, Gemariah, that Baruch went to find a favorable hearing. There Gemariah's son Michaiah understood the importance of the scroll and notified his father and a group of other sympathetic princes who in turn saw to Baruch's safety and took the scroll to the king (Jer 36:11-19). That scroll event, it may be recalled, took place just after Nebuchadnezzar had driven Necho out of Syria-Palestine, portending doom for Jehoiakim's pro-Egyptian policy. Then, still later, it was a grandson of Shaphan, Gedeliah, son of that Ahikam who had saved Jeremiah's life, whom Nebuchadnezzar chose to be governor of the cities of Judah after the destruction of Jerusalem (Jer 40:5). This choice certainly reflected the Babylonian king's knowledge of how that family had long stood on Judah's foreign policy. Finally, when Jeremiah was given the privilege of settling anywhere he wished after the fall of Jerusalem, he chose to remain with this grandson of Shaphan who had been entrusted with the governorship by the Babylonian king.

The political situation at the time of Jeremiah's temple sermon, then, can be summarized as follows. Two forces were at work within the kingdom of Judah, one favoring the continuance of Josiah's policies and one opposing them. Each of these forces had aligned itself behind a son of Josiah as the champion of its interests. One of these forces was identified as, or included, "the people of the land"; it supported the reform program and favored the twenty-three-year-old Jehoahaz and his mother Hamutal of Libnah.

This party was in a position to impose its will immediately after
Josiah's death, and Jehoahaz became the new king. In the great
international struggle of the time, this party hoped for a Babylonian defeat of Egypt, presumably to preserve room for Judean
independence in line with the policies of Josiah. The other
force was aligned behind the twenty-five-year-old Jehoiakim and
his mother Zebidah of Rumah in Galilee. This force opposed the
policies of the Josianic program and favored alliance with Egypt
in the international conflict. When Pharaoh Necho returned from
his Mesopotamian campaign in September of 609, he deposed Jehoahaz,
laid an apparently crippling financial penalty upon those who had
supported him, and imposed a new regime upon Judah, a regime headed
by Jehoiakim and backed by the Egyptian army. Shortly thereafter
Jeremiah delivered his temple sermon.


IV. The Implications of the Sermon

Given this political situation, the question remains why it
was precisely this sermon by which Jeremiah took his public stand
against Jehoiakim's policies. While the exact wording of the sermon
is not a matter of certainty,[6] two things about its content seem
clear: it attacked the Judeans for placing an inordinate confidence
in the Jerusalem temple, and it threatened that Yahweh himself would
destroy that temple as he had formerly destroyed his own sanctuary
at Shiloh. What was the meaning of this attack and this threat in
the political context in which Jeremiah spoke?

The political background indicates that this content of the
sermon was not an attack on the Josianic program. On the contrary,
it was an attack on a reversal of the Josianic program. Jehoahaz
had just been carried away; the party that supported him was being
deprived of much of its financial resources; and Jehoiakim was in-
augurating a new regime under the auspices of the same foreign king

who had killed Josiah. This new regime would include a building
program to enhance the glory and luxury of the palace complex, of
which the temple, it should be recalled, was a part. This building
program apparently stood in contrast to the policies followed by
Josiah, even at the peak of his power, or so at least Jeremiah
understood it (Jer 22:13-17). What Jehoiakim stood for, then,
was antithetical to what Josiah had represented. Therefore, the
content of the temple sermon may be read as an attack on an anti-
Josianic program.

Read in this way, the sermon implies that the promise of
Jehoiakim's policy was that the Judeans could place unqualified
trust in the Jerusalem sanctuary. Apparently Jehoiakim intended
to renew the claims of that sanctuary to inviolability against
all threats and dangers. Safety was to be found in the temple;
matters of ethics could be inquired into later (Jer 7:9-10). All
that had been heard long before about Zion as the impregnable city
of God was now to be reaffirmed, at the instigation of Jehoiakim
and his supporters. This was apparently the positive side of
Jehoiakim's program, to emphasize the glory and sacred status of
Jerusalem as the city chosen and protected by the God of Israel.
Such a policy on Jehoiakim's part would explain why, just at this
moment, Jeremiah attacked so strenously the old tradition of the
inviolability of Zion.

The second point of the sermon's content, that Yahweh would
do to Jerusalem as he had done to Shiloh, points in the same direction. Why especially the reference to Shiloh? Whatever other
connotations Shiloh had for Jeremiah's hearers, it must have
called to mind the old story of the ark, now preserved in 1 Samuel
4-6 and 2 Samuel 6. In that narrative Shiloh was Yahweh's special
sanctuary, that is, the dwelling place of the ark. The narrative
goes on to recount, however, how the ark departed from Shiloh, resided for some time among the Philistines (to their regret), and
finally came, through the special attentions of King David, to

rest in Jerusalem. From a Jerusalemite viewpoint, this narrative demonstrates how the God of the exodus, for so the God of the ark is referred to in this narrative (1 Sam 4:8; 6:6) moved, by his own choice, from Shiloh to Jerusalem. That is to say, this ark narrative was a cult legend of Yahweh's choice of Jerusalem. It told how Yahweh, who had brought Israel out of Egypt, had finally chosen Jerusalem as his dwelling place. When, therefore, Jeremiah threatened that Jerusalem could become another Shiloh, many hearers must have heard Jerusalem's own sacred story being used against it. Jeremiah's reference to Shiloh, therefore, was yet another attack upon the special status of Jerusalem as the city of God.

That it was against the policies of Jehoiakim especially that this attack was delivered is indicated by its timing. The sermon was not delivered during the reign of Josiah. That in itself may seem surprising, for, as commonly understood, the reform of Josiah had elevated the sanctuary in Jerusalem to a lofty centrality that even that royal chapel had never previously enjoyed, or had enjoyed only briefly during the reign of Hezekiah (2 Kgs 18:4). Josiah did indeed eliminate all other legitimate sanctuaries in Judah and presumable enforced that policy for more than a decade. The only place of proper sacrifice to Yahweh in the Josianic program was the Jerusalem temple. But if it was this exclusive status of the Jerusalem temple that troubled Jeremiah, why did it take him thirteen years to get around to attacking it, and why then just at the time Jehoiakim was beginning a new regime? The occasion of the sermon, and therefore the situation to which its content was addressed, was Jehoiakim's accession, not Josiah's reform.

The content of Jeremiah's sermon indicates, then, that it was an attack on the old tradition of the special sanctity of Zion. The political background indicates that that was an attack upon the new policies of Jehoiakim, not the older policies of the Josianic reform. This conclusion is both important and some-what surprising, for it indicates that Josiah's reform did not in-volve an unqualified assertion of the inviolability of Zion. On

the contrary, it was an anti-Josianic program that involved the
reassertion of this old claim for the city of David. The reform
of Josiah, therefore, gave great centrality and religious importance to the city of Jerusalem, but at the same time also
compromised in some fashion the older sacred traditions about the
city's holiness and centrality. In some manner, the Josianic
program had held together the old promise of Yahweh concerning
David and his great city with other traditions that must have
placed certain qualifications upon that promise. The policies represented by Jehoiakim, on the other hand, apparently dissolved
the tension between that promise and its qualifications. The
special status of the Jerusalem temple was the result of a divine
promise; therefore it was not subject to qualifications from the
side of man. When the representative of this viewpoint came to
the throne of Judah, Jeremiah entered the temple court and delivered a sermon.

FOOTNOTES

1.  What is attempted here is a synthetic essay pulling together many topics that are quite complicated in their own right.
In order to present as complete an argument as possible within
the available space, all discussion and documentation not indispensible to the text is omitted.  What is offered is a reinterpretation of certain data already familiar from the Biblical texts
and from general discussions of the history of the period.  The
text presupposes throughout such general discussions as that of
John Bright, *A History of Israel* (2d ed.; Philadelphia: Westminster,
1972), esp. ch. 8, 309-39, and such treatments of the texts cited
as those in John Gray, *I & II Kings* (2d ed.; Philadelphia: Westminster, 1970).  Even where positions are taken that differ from
those presented in these works, however, no discussion of the
differences, for its own sake, is entered into here.

2.  On the general question of the types of literature in
Jeremiah, see Wilhelm Rudolph, *Jeremiah* (HAT, 12; Tübingen: J.
C. B. Mohr, 1958), xiii-xxi; John Bright *Jeremiah* (AB 21; Garden
City: Doubleday, 1965) lv-lxxxv; and W. L. Holladay, "Jeremiah
the Prophet," IDB Sup 470-472.

3.  On the technical expression, Rudolph, p. 155.  The dates
can be reasonably precise in this period because of the availability
of tablets from the Babylonian Chronicle; D. J. Wiseman, *Chronicles
of Chaldean Kings (626-556 B.C.)* (London: The British Museum, 1956),
esp. 13-32.  See the further literature cited in Bright, *History*,
323, n. 40.  The discussion in the text will refer to Josiah's two
older sons by their throne names, Jehoiakim and Jehoahaz, ignoring
their private names, Eliakim and Shallum.

4.  Josephus, *J.W.* 3. 7,21:233.  Gray, *I & II Kings*, 755.

5.  For this discussion see especially Bright, *History*, 309-
13, and the texts cited in J. B. Pritchard, ANET, 297-301.

6.  The view is increasingly held that the sermonic passages
of Jeremiah often reflect actual sayings and deeds of Jeremiah
which were written out with the situations and concerns of later
audiences in mind.  See, e.g., E. W. Nicholson, *Preaching to the
Exiles* (Oxford: Blackwell, 1970) and specifically on the temple
sermon, W. L. Holladay, *Jeremiah: Spokesman Out of Time* (Philadelphia: Pilgrim Press, 1974), 62-68.

# CAKES FOR THE QUEEN OF HEAVEN

Walter E. Rast

Among the items which brought the inhabitants of Judah into
serious violation of their relationship with Yahweh, and which
prepared the way for the disaster of the early sixth century B.C.,
were the rites devoted to the "queen of heaven." Mention of these
activities is found in two places in the Jeremiah corpus, in 7:18
as part of the divine response to the prophet following the Temple
Sermon, and in 44:19 among the oracles and discourses collected
from the Egypt period. These two passages are critical for understanding the nature of part of Judah's apostasy in the thought of
the prophet. Yet as with so many brief allusions in the biblical
texts, little explanation is given. Apparently the details of
the actions would have been understood at once by contemporaries
of the prophet and thus were only hinted at. But later interpreters and translators were left with having to make the best out
of a text that had become obscure in its meaning.[1] Although these
two verses have been amply commented on, the justification for
considering them anew lies in the opportunity to introduce material
which may illuminate several of the opaque details concerning an
involvement which was seen to be such a threat to Judah's future.

The most difficult textual decisions concern the words kawwānîm,
"cakes," in both verses, and the infinitive form lĕhaᶜăṣibāh, "to
portray her," in 44:19 only. There is a consensus that the word
kawwānîm is best explained as a loan word from Akkadian kamānu and
that it refers to a baked loaf or cake.[2] The more commonly used
words for bread loaves would be ᶜugāh as in Exod 12:39, kikkār for
a particular kind of flat, round loaf as in 1 Sam 2:36, or ḥallāh

as the bread referred to in the rubrics of Leviticus (e.g., Lev
2:4). The fact that this form, otherwise unknown in the Old Testament, is used would favor viewing it as an import. More specifically the word may differentiate a specific type of baked loaf,
a sweetened cake, distinguishing it from the other types mentioned.[3]

With regard to the second problem, the meaning of lĕhaᶜăsibāh in
44:19, this verb (ᶜāsab I) is found only twice in the Old Testament,
once in Job 10:8 where it appears in a Piel form, and in the present
passage as a Hiphil infinitive construct. The form is no doubt related to a common designation for idols in the Old Testament (ᶜāsāb;
cf. ᶜōseb), and it may be a denominative of the latter.[4] The absence of mappîq in the he of the suffix is unusual, but other
instances of this rare phenomenon can be found, and thus it should
be read as a third feminine objective suffix.[5] In this case, then,
ᶜāsab would express the activity of making an object in some way
resembling an ᶜāsāb in that it would have contained the image of
the goddess. The modern translations have followed this clue and
tend to translate similarly: "bearing her image" (RSV), "marked
with her image" (NEB), "with her features on them" (JB), and
"stamped with her image" (Smith-Goodspeed). Bright in the Anchor
Bible translates "depicting her," while Rudolph has "to portray
her" (um sie abzubilden).[6] In reality the noun ᶜāsāb places
particular stress on the physiological features of the deity as
portrayed in an image. For example, in Ps 135:15-17 it is noted
that idols (ᶜăsabbîm) have mouths, eyes and ears but they do not
speak, see or hear. The description in 44:19 is thus clearly one
in which a cake or loaf was made containing the image of the deity.[7]

Besides these two problems, the only other difficult textual
feature is the vocalization of the feminine construct mĕleket,
"queen," in both verses. Following the versions the form should
probably be read as malkat.[8] The two verses may then be translated
as follows:

> The children gather wood, the fathers prepare the fire,
>   and the women knead dough to make sweetened cakes for the

queen of heaven, and pour out libations to other gods in order to provoke me (Jer 7:18).

(And the women said):[9] And when we were burning incense to the queen of heaven and pouring out libations for her, was it without her husbands' approval that we made sweetened cakes for her to mold her figure (Jer 44:19)?

Although full agreement is not to be found on this matter, there are good reasons for interpreting features referred to in these verses as stemming from Mesopotamia, and in particular from the popular cult of Ishtar. This does not mean that practices deriving from Mesopotamia became established in their original form in Judah during the century in which Jeremiah lived.[10] Rather it would seem that elements from Mesopotamian religion, such as those reflected in these verses, became intermixed with the native Palestinian versions of the fertility cult during a century when there was much contact with Assyria, so that a process of syncretism was at work. Thus the title, "queen of heaven," could well have been referred to Astarte or one of the other Palestinian deities, but it is doubtful that the strong associations of that title with Ishtar would have been absent.[11]

Along similar lines the offering of cakes or loaves was a ubiquitous practice associated with the devotion to many different deities, and it constituted an important part of the care and feeding of the gods.[12] Thus it is correct to emphasize that such offerings in themselves are not a distinguishing feature of the cult of Ishtar.[13] This having been said, it is also true that the goddess Ishtar from early times had a special relation to the planting and harvesting of cereal crops in Mesopotamia. Her union with Tammuz, the grain deity, formed the basis for one of the influential myths stressing fertility and prosperity.[14] The offering of bread loaves for Ishtar may thus have had a special kind of significance. A number of references speak of cakes as having been offered to her. One of the illuminating examples is in the sixth tablet of the Epic of Gilgamesh. It appears in the section in which Gilgamesh

responds to Ishtar's efforts to woo him following his successful
battle with the monster Huwawa.  The entire passage presents Gilgamesh's satirical response to the goddess's efforts, of which
Gilgamesh is not a little suspicious.  He says to Ishtar:

> What lover did you ever love constantly? . . .
> Come I will ennumerate your lovers . . .
> For Tammuz, the lover of your youth,
> You have brought about repeated weeping year upon year;
> . . . . . . . . . . . . . . . . . . . . . . . . . . . .
> You used to love the herdsman,
> Who regularly heaped up tumri-cakes for you.[15]

The distinctive type of tumri-cake mentioned in this text is
worthy of attention and will be considered below.  Commentators have
cited other notations about cakes for Ishtar in the Mesopotamian
literature.[16]  In addition to these documented instances, however,
there is a unique terracotta group which has recently been published by Culican.[17]  This object found off the coast near Tyre has
been interpreted by Culican as portraying a ceremonial baking scene,
in which a priest functions to bless the bread being baked in a
beehive oven in the center of the group.  The loaves taken from
the oven are assumed to have been presented as votive offerings to
the goddess, who is prominent among the figures, and whom Culican
takes to be Astarte.[18]  Although this interesting model dates to
the Hellenistic period, it may well reflect an activity not greatly
different from that addressed by the prophet several centuries
earlier.[19]

In order to put the descriptions of Jer 7:18 and 44:19 into
a clearer light, therefore, it is necessary to see them as reflecting practices rather widely disseminated, originating probably very
early in Mesopotamia and eventually being assimilated to the popular devotion to Astarte in the Palestinian region.  Although again
explicit information is lacking, the reference to the women as
"kneading the dough" (lāšôt bāšēq) would suggest that wheat, not
barley, was the cereal involved.  Wheat flour, derived from "bread
wheat" (triticum aestivum) or "club wheat" (triticum compactum)
would have been usable for either bread which was leavened and knead-

able, or for sweetmeats or pastries which, as we have seen, is probably the meaning of kawwānîm.[20]

The detail which attracts attention, however, is the verb lĕhaʿăsibāh translated above as "to mold her figure." If, as has been suggested, this statement may be taken as referring to sweetened cakes which were fashioned to reflect the goddess's image, we might ask what sort of cake preparation and baking lay behind this description. Two possibilities suggest themselves. One is that the bakers could have formed the dough by hand into a figure or shape of the goddess, or of some accepted symbolic form representing her, such as a star or crescent. A second possibility is that they could have used a preformed mold made of wood, stone or clay as a negative from which the positive image produced on the dough could have been made. The latter explanation seems worthy of serious consideration, and in such a case the root ʿāsab in 44:19 would carry the connotation of "to mold."

Archaeologically some evidence is available which can be introduced in regard to this problem. In the first place examples of ceramic dishes which were apparently used for cultic purposes have begun to appear at a number of sites. There is, for example, the disc-shaped platter discovered leaning against the corner of the room with other vessels in Structure I at Lachish. This building was dated to the Late Bronze Age and was interpreted by the excavators as a cultic complex. The flasks found with the platter were probably used for libations while the pan was used for making a flat, unleavened cake, mixed with oil as in the description in Lev 2:5.[21] The importance of this find is that it illustrates a particular kind of pantry vessel evidently used for making special loaves for the cult. Baking dishes have appeared at various sites, but a detailed study of their function is yet to be undertaken. This is especially the case for such vessels as may have been used for specifically cultic acts of baking and offering.[22]

More important for their bearing on the Jeremiah verses, however, is the hoard of decorated, clay molds discovered at

Mari, among which was one which has special relevance. At Mari 47 molds were recovered in Chamber 77 of the palace.[23] These molds were of different shapes, including round, platter-like vessels, square and rectangular molds, and molds in the shape of fish. The rectangular and square forms were sometimes elaborated with geometric patterns, while others contained realistic depictions of animals such as stags (Molds 1032, 1037). The one with special importance for the present study is a rectangular mold (Mold 1044), portraying a nude female.[24] The depiction of the female is realistic, with eyes and facial features appearing as in a normal human being. A heavy gathering of hair, suggestive of a turban, is found on the head. That it is hair is indicated by what appear to be cross-braided locks. The neck is covered with a broad necklace five rings wide. There appear to be bracelets on the wrists. The figure is in a seated position facing frontally. Buttocks are heavy with knees and feet held closely together.

Among features which suggest that this figure is a goddess are the cupped hands underneath the breasts. This motif is known on a prominent type of terracotta figurine, and while the identification cannot be proven for certain, it appears that the example may reflect the goddess Ishtar, otherwise well-attested at Mari, and known farther to the west in the form of Astarte.[25] Parrot has discussed this mold several times and seems to favor its attribution to a goddess.[26]

The key problem, however, concerns the way the mold may have been used. The fact that Mold 1044 was part of a large group of terracotta molds of different sizes, shapes and types precludes almost any other context than that of food preparation. In an early treatment of the group Parrot suggested that the molds would probably have been used to make pastries or cakes, dairy products or cheese, and that they were designed to provide aesthetic delight for the royal table.[27] Pritchard placed this mold under one of his categories for early figurines in Mesopotamia, and thus he

simply assumed its usage in the production of terracotta forms.[28]
However, both the assemblage in which it was found and its dish-
like, rectangular form speak against its use for making the common
figurine types. It seems more likely that Parrot's original suggestion is the correct one, and in this case we would have an
interesting correlation with the description in Jer 44:19. As
for the presence of a mold representing the form of a goddess among
other forms which were secular or commonplace, it would not be surprising to find in the royal quarters vessels containing a depiction of the goddess among others with no apparent religious
meaning. This mixture could simply stress the fact that much of
the popular worship of Ishtar, even in royal circles, was non-
formalized and out of the bounds of the official cultus. Certainly the indications are that the activities in the Jeremiah passages
were of this non-organized sort.

Had the Mari molds functioned in this manner, it is an in-
triguing question to ask whether any molds known from Palestine
might have served a similar purpose. We have already noted a number of vessels apparently used for producing baked goods used for
offerings. Thus far the few vessels which have been assigned to
this kind of activity have been plain vessels. The figured molds
found in Palestine have usually been attributed to the production
of terracotta forms. Most of the examples which have come to light
have been smaller fragments of a mold.[29] However, during the 1963
season at Taanach an intact, well-preserved mold was discovered in
a building designated the Cultic Structure.[30] The goddess portrayed
on this mold, probably Astarte, has two horizontal braids of hair
across the forehead. The eyes are prominent and staring.[31] The
hands hold a disc object over the left breast which has been interpreted variously as a tambourine, bread loaf or sun disc.[32] That
terracotta positives were made from a mold of this type is indicated by the half of a figurine from Stratum VIII at Hazor, which
has some similarities in detail to the Taanach mold although they
do not conform exactly.[33] It is curious, however, that none of the

figurines themselves found at Taanach were made from this mold.[34]

Molds were also evidently used in the production of the "plaque figurines" which are commonly rectangular or oval in form and which have a light impression on the flattened surface, made no doubt by a mold.[35] Thus the evidence in Palestine at present largely illuminates figurine impressions of the terracotta types. However, as in the case of baking dishes, it must be noted that a systematic study of molds and their uses still awaits doing, including the large cache from Mari.[36] The conclusion that molds which appear in excavations were used exclusively for the production of ceramic positives is based more on assumption and intuition than on detailed study. It is at least a question worth asking whether perishable food items used as offerings may not also have played a role in the function of some of these vessels.

The fact is that when we engage the world of ancient Near Eastern image making, we meet a realm of complexity and heterogeneity. Ucko's detailed study of terracotta figurines of the Near East has shown that the reasons for the manufacture of groups of figurines could be varied. Their use as children's dolls, initiation figures, or vehicles for sympathetic magic are all possible explanations.[37] Within this diverse activity of depicting a god or goddess, it may be that we also have to reckon with the use of food materials such as we have seen, but in their case the intention behind the act would be somewhat different since they would be placed before the god or goddess as offerings.

One further feature in the Jeremiah texts may also receive some illumination. Commentators have tended to pass over the detail in Jer 7:18 that the children gathered wood (habbānîm mĕlaqqĕtîm) and the fathers prepared the fire (hā'ābôt mĕbaᶜărîm et hā'ēš). It is possible that this is a simple detail with no significance. On the other hand, if it had some specific intention it might be possible to explain it in the light of some of the comparative date introduced above.

A characteristic of the kamānu cake discussed previously is

that it was apparently baked directly on the ashes or embers of a
fire, and to bring out this aspect the word tumri was used as a
modifier (e.g., kamān tumri).[38] This description distinguished
this kind of loaf or cake from others which were made differently.
During the Iron Age in Palestine the common way of making bread,
even in a cultic context, would have been in an oven (tannûr)
such as we find in Lev 2:4. The group discussed by Culican referred to above would fit this procedure.[39] Were people for one
reason or another to deviate from this normal procedure, it would
be expected that there might be some reference to this fact. It
may not be without significance, therefore, that in a text where
the unusual form kawwānîm occurs we should find a reference to the
preparation of a special kind of open fire. Presumably the meaning
in Jer 7:18 is that the kawwānîm were placed directly on the embers
of the fire since no mention is made of an oven.[40]

The kamānu cake is also cited as having been a special dish of
the shepherd in Mesopotamia.[41] The text in the Gilgamesh Epic referred to above is an example of this. Thus such cakes, if they
were used for offerings, would not have derived from the temple cult
but rather belonged to the more mundane sector of life. Although
the times of Jeremiah are much later and in a different setting, it
may be indicative of something similar that the activities were
carried on by men, women and children, and that they were held in
the "cities of Judah and the streets of Jerusalem" (Jer 7:17; 44:
17).

As far as the people of Judah were concerned, their justification for these popular practices is expressed in Jer 44:17-18. The
Judahites claim that the cessation of their offerings and libations,
perhaps due to an enforcement during Josiah's reign, has been directly responsible for the evil which has come upon them.[42] In
this way they give voice to what must have been a prevalent view
of the time, that the goddess, whether Ishtar in Mesopotamia or
Astarte in Palestine, possessed a unique capacity to ensure protection and prosperity. On the other hand, no discernible way

out of the terrors of the moment seemed to be present in the silence
and apparent inactivity of Yahweh.  The tradition describes the
prophet as hard put to say it just the opposite way.  According
to him their activities were not the way toward a better future,
but a desperate act leading to the waste and desolation (Jer 44:
20-23).

In offering this study in honor of a greatly admired teacher
of the exegesis and theology of the Old Testament, I am conscious
of the interest he has long had in the use of earlier texts and
practices in later Judaism and Christianity.  In this regard it
is interesting to note how impressed bread has continued to be
used up to the present in the Christian eucharist.  Galavaris
has collected much of the historical material, especially on the
bread stamps used for the production of communion bread in various
forms through the history of this feast.[43]  Although a direct evo-
lutionary line ought not be assumed, the procedure of making impressed bread, and most recently wafers, perhaps contains some
elements which are continuous with what was happening in the age
of the prophet.  One wonders whether he would be content with the
practice in its new form.

FOOTNOTES

1. Cf. the LXX's bewilderment in simply transliterating chauōnas for kawwānîm in Jer 51:19.

2. W. Rudolph, *Jeremia* (HAT 12; 3d ed.; Tübingen: J.C.B. Mohr [Paul Siebeck], 1968) 52; A. Condamin, *Le Livre de Jérémie* (E. Bib. Paris: Gabalda, 1936) 69-70.

3. *CAD*, 8.110-11.

4. F. Brown, S.R. Driver, C.A. Briggs, *A Hebrew and English lexicon of the Old Testament* (Oxford: Clarendon, 1962) 781.

5. E. Kautzsch, A.E. Cowley, *Gesenius' Hebrew Grammar* (2d ed.; Oxford: Clarendon, 1910) 58g, 91e.

6. J. Bright, *Jeremiah* (AB 21; Garden City: Doubleday & Co., 1965) 261; Rudolph, *Jeremia,* 260; Luther's "to grieve her" (sie zu bekümmern), following a II form of *ʿāsab* is hardly likely, as is also the KJV's "to worship her."

7. Building on the astral imagery associated with the goddess some have proposed loaves or cakes in the form of a star, Rudolph, *Jeremia,* 55.

8. Ibid., 52.

9. For this addition with support from the versions see Bright, *Jeremiah,* 261.

10. J. W. McKay, *Religion in Judah under the Assyrians* (SBT 2/26; London: SCM, 1973) 45-59.

11. Rudolph, *Jeremia,* 55; cf. for the title "queen of heaven" as applied to the Sumerian Inanna, equated with the Semites' Ishtar, S. N. Kramer, *The Sumerians: Their History, Culture, and Character* (Chicago: University of Chicago, 1963) 153; G. Widengren (*Sakrales Königtum im Alten Testament und in Judentum* [Stuttgart: W. Kohl-hammer] 12) has proposed the goddess Anat, while M.J. Dahood ("La Regina del Cielo in Geremia," *RivB* 8 [1960] 166-68) has identified the goddess with the Canaanite Shapash seeking grounds for this in Ugaritic kn[m] in UT 52, 54; cf. McKay, *Religion in Judah,* 46-7, and W. Culican, "A Votive Model from the Sea," *PEQ* (July-Dec. 1976) 121.

12. A.L. Oppenheim, *Ancient Mesopotamia: Portrait of a Dead Civilization* (Chicago: University of Chicago, 1964) 183-98; H.W.F. Saggs, *The Greatness that was Babylon* (New York: New American Library, 1962) 335-38.

13.  McKay, *Religion in Judah,* 110, n. 18.

14.  Cf. again the Sumerian form of the union of this god and goddess in Kramer, *The Sumerians,* 140-41.

15.  Translation is that of Saggs, *The Greatness that was Babylon,* 374; E.A. Speiser translates the crucial phrase in Tablet VI: 59 as "ash-cakes," <u>ANET</u>, 84, while A. Heidel (*The Gilgamesh Epic and Old Testament Parallels* [Chicago: University of Chicago, 1946] 51) simply has "charcoals."

16.  B.N. Wambacq, *Jeremias* (De Boeken van het oude Testament 10; Roermond en Maaseik: J.J. Romen, 1957) 73.

17.  Culican, "A Votive Model," 119-23.

18.  Ibid., 121.

19.  Ibid., 123.

20.  Oppenheim, *Ancient Mesopotamia,* 44.

21.  O. Tufnell, and others, *Lachish II: The Fosse Temple* (London: Oxford University, 1940) 39 and pl. 54A, no. 338.

22.  For ordinary baking vessels see R.A.S. Macalister, *The Excavation of Gezer II* (London: John Murray, 1912) 43, fig. 238, A. Rowe, *The Topography and History of Beth-shan I* (Philadelphia: University Press, 1930) 18, and Y. Yadin, and others, *Hazor II* (Jerusalem: Magnes, 1960) pl. 74:11; caches of pantry vessels such as those in L. 2081 at Megiddo and the Cultic Structure at Taanach need careful attention in the lifht of their possible cultic use, see W.E. Rast, *Taanach I: Studies in the Iron Age Pottery* (in press).

23.  First discussed by A. Parrot in the preliminary report in *Syria* 18 (1937) 75-77; cf. also A. Parrot, *Mission Archéologique de Mari I: Le Palais* (Institut Francais d'Archéologie de Beyrouth. Bibliothèque archéologique et historique 70; Paris: Paul Guethner, 1959) 33-55.

24.  Parrott in *Syria* 18 (1937) 77 and fig. 13, where Parrot also mentions two other examples from the same site, Molds 1121 and 1122.

25.  J.B. Pritchard, *Palestinian Figurines in relation to certain Goddesses known through Literature* (Philadelphia: University of Pennsylvania, 1943) 42-49. The type with cupped hands under the breasts is Pritchard's Type II. Pritchard leaves the question of the identity of the goddess open, cf. 85-87.

26. *Mission Archéologique de Mari I*, 37 and n. 2; see also A. Parrot, *Mari: Une Ville Perdue* (Paris: Société Commerciale d'Edition et de Librairie, 1936) 169.

27. *Syria* 18 (1937) 76.

28. Pritchard, *Palestinian Figurines*, 47, puts this mold with the figurine type of a goddess with cupped hands under the breasts, but in other details the form here is quite different.

29. O. Tufnell, *Lachish IV: The Bronze Age* (2 vols., Text and Plates; London: Oxford University, 1958) 90 and pls. 47:6, 48:1, 49:2.

30. P.W. Lapp, "The 1963 Excavation at Taᶜannek," BASOR 173 (1964) 39 and fig. 21.

31. Cf. Oppenheim, *Ancient Mesopotamia*, 184.

32. H.G. May, *Material Remains of the Megiddo Cult* (OIP 26; Chicago: University of Chicago) 30; R. Amiran, "A Note on Figurines with 'Discs'," *Eretz-Israel* 8 (1967) 99 and pl. 12; A.D. Tushingham, "A Royal Israelite Seal (?) and the Royal Jar Handle Stamps (Part Two," BASOR 201 (1971) 31.

33. Yadin and others, *Hazor II*, pls. 76:12, 163:2.

34. See those illustrated in Lapp, BASOR 173 (1964) 42, fig. 22.

35. Pritchard, *Palestinian Figurines*, 47; for examples see W.F. Albright, *The Excavation of Tell Beit Mirsim, Vol. II: The Bronze Age* (AASOR 17; New Haven: American Schools of Oriental Research, 1938) pls. 26-27.

36. A well-preserved mold dated to the 15-13th centuries B.C. was discovered recently by the German Institute for Study of the Middle East at Mumbaqa near the Euphrates, east of Aleppo. It is on display in the Aleppo Museum.

37. P.J. Ucko, *Figurines, Anthropomorphic Figurines* (Royal Anthropological Institute Occasional Papers No. 24; London: Andrew Szmilda, 1968) 444.

38. CAD. 8. 110.

39. Culican, "A Votive Model," 120-21.

40. G. Dalman, *Arbeit und Sitte in Palästina* (Gütersloh: C. Bertelsmann, 1935) 4. 35.

41. <u>CAD</u>, 8. 111.

42. Rudolph, *Jeremia,* 261.

43. G. Galavaris, *Bread and the Liturgy: The Symbolism of Early Christian and Byzantine Bread Stamps* (Madison: University of Wisconsin, 1970); for a striking illustration of bread stamped with the Virgin's form, made by monks at St. Catherine's in the Sinai today, see *National Geographic* 125.1 (January, 1964) 89.

# A MEDITATION ON THE WRATH OF GOD:  PSALM 90*

## Walter Harrelson

Within the Psalter there is a small number of psalms that seem
to fit any one of the formal features of the psalms -- hymn, individual or communal lament, psalm of thanksgiving, blessing, wisdom
psalm, Torah psalm, etc.  Rather, they stand out as reflections on
some basic feature of life -- the created world and its workings
(Psalm 104), how religiously to understand the injustices of life
(Psalm 73), how to deal with the glory and the threat of a pervasive divine Presence (Psalm 139), how to confront life's course
in face of the divine wrath (Psalm 90).  Some of the psalm-forms
are found in these, but the formal characteristics seem not greatly to contribute to an understanding either of the setting of such
psalms or of their basic content.  The psalms just listed are in
some respects the jewels of the Psalter.  They provide perspectives
on Israelite religious thought that are distinctive if not unique.
I have come to designate these psalms as meditations or reflections,
the product of individual searching and struggling, available to
the community for such uses in the regular cult as may be made of

*I am grateful to the officers of the Samuel Robinson Lectureship,
Wake Forest University, Winston-Salem, North Carolina, for their
permission to use one of my lectures on the Robinson Lectureship
as a contribution to the volume honoring my colleague and friend
Coert Rylaarsdam.

them, but designed precisely to assist in the meditations of other individuals or of groups who are wrestling with the issues of life explored in them.

This brief study of Psalm 90 aims to show that the author offe just such an act of meditation. He does have a religious "message" for his hearers and readers: that they learn from God to take seriously the swift flow of life and, on life's course, pursue wisdor The author also vividly presents a petition to God, a plea for God to render life meaningful, to give it stability, to make it worth the while. But beyond any particular petition or any effort to offer warning or guidance to others, the author wishes to share the fruits of his meditation on God's character, God's relation to human beings, God's apparent unwillingness to provide to his creatures a substantive, enduring, dependable, and fundamentally meaningful life.

I

The text offers serious difficulties to the translator. The following translation is a slight modification of the text found in the Revised Standard Version.

## Invocation

1 A prayer of Moses, the man of God.
  O Lord, you have been a hiding-place[1] for us,
      generation after generation.
2 Before the mountains were midwifed,
      before you brought forth earth and inhabited land,
      indeed, from everlasting to everlasting,
      you are -- God!

## God the Destroyer

3 You return humankind to dust, yet you summon:
   "Return, children of men!"
4 For a thousand years in your eyes
      are like yesterday as it passes by;
      like a watch of the night.
5 You sweep away the years!$^2$
      In the morning, like grass they grow up;
6      In the morning they bloom and shoot up;
      In the evening they fade and wither.
7 For we come to an end in your anger,
      we are destroyed by your wrath.

## God Marks Iniquities

8 You have set our iniquities before you,
      Our secret acts in the light of your face.
9 For all our days pass by in your wrath;
      We complete our years like a murmur.$^3$
10 Our life-span is seventy years,
      or if we are strong, eighty years.
   Yet, their pride is only trouble and sorrow;
   They swiftly pass, and we fly away.
11 Who weighs$^4$ the strength of your anger
      Or your wrath, according to our fear of you?

## Prayer for Aid

12 So make us know how to count our days,
      that we may bring forward a heart of wisdom.

13 Return, O Lord!  How long?
        Have compassion on your servants!
14 Satisfy us in the morning with your mercy,
        And we will exult and rejoice all of our days.
15 Make us glad for as many days as you have afflicted us,
        for as many years as we have seen adversity.
16 Let your work be manifest to your servants;
        your glory to their children.
17 Let the favor of the Lord our God be upon us,
        and establish the work of our hands upon us;
        the work of our hands -- establish it!

## II

As to form, Hans-Joachim Kraus maintains that this psalm is a
communal lament, one prompted by some long-lasting calamity that is
not identified but must be presupposed.[5]  It contains hymnic element
in the early verses, shows influence from the wisdom tradition, but
is basically a lament of the community, cultic in setting, and expressing the hope of the community for help "in the morning."

There is no doubt that the psalm does have formal similarities
with the communal lament.  It is also true that such laments often
do not identify the particular calamity that evoked them, either
because in the course of time the particularities have been eliminat
or because such laments characteristically sought to leave open the
occasions for lamentation, given the variety of reactions present
within the worshipping community when such laments were employed.
Even so, I am convinced that the poem, although couched in first
person plural language, is intended as a meditation for individuals
and small groups rather than for public lamentation.  I doubt that
it has behind it any particular calamity that befell the people of
Israel.  The theme is not that of how one can confront particular

public perils but how one can confront the God who appears largely
as the wielder of the scythe of death and destruction.

The structure of the poem is not easy to identify. The first
two lines (following the superscription, v. 1a, which apparently
was added by the editors of the Psalter) may be called an Invocation. Hymnic elements are there, but the poet's chief concern
is at the outset to identify the character of God's dealings with
humankind that prompt his meditation. Such a thematic statement
of the poet in the opening line or lines is found frequently in
the Psalter.

After the invocation there comes a section that may divide
into two parts, but the division is not a sharp one. We have noted
in the translation above that vv. 3-7 and 8-11 provide the body of
the poem's identification of the plight of humankind in face of
God's wrath. The first section, vv. 3-7, is the more general, stressing the sweeping, destructive power of God that rolls over all of
human life, making long life of little more significance than a
short span of years, since in the divine perspective, life flour-
ishes and disappears in a twinkling. That same point is developed
in the next section, 8-11, but in that section, a new element appears: God's disclosing the sin of humankind, exposing iniquity
on the way of life, revealing not only the transience of existence
but its features that, to some extent, warrant the divine wrath.

The closing section is in form a communal petition, a prayer
that God be merciful and compassionate, that he assist the community to find wisdom, that he grant the gift of meaning in the midst
of life's apparent meaninglessness.


III


When we examine the text in detail, we are struck by what I
take to be a deliberate ambituity in the poet's presentation of

God's relation to the human community, to the author of the psalm.
God is a hiding-place and thus a refuge from the storms and ravagings
of life (v. 1). But God is also one who hides in his lair as does
the lion or the jackal, ready to come forth in wrath, to spring upon
the defenseless and unsuspecting victim. The Hebrew term maᶜon in
v. 1 is, I believe, deliberately chosen to reflect this ambiguity
and to express the poet's religious ambivalence towards God. The
term is used frequently in the psalter in a positive sense, but its
several other usages include a number that are threatening and omi-
nous.

The same ambiguity is found in the whole of v. 3. God returns
humankind to dust, makes their life no more than the dust from which
it once was taken (Gen 2:7; 3:19), indicates that he will have nothing to do with a human community with permanent human meaning. Yet
the same God who turns all life to dust is the one who keeps summoning the community to "turn," to "return" to him repentant, ready to
make amends, bent upon doing the will of God. This use of the Hebrew
term shuv to express the return of life to dust and also the return
of the community in faith to God is perhaps the most bitter of the
poet's ironies in the psalm.

The ambiguity is continued in this section by reference to
grass (hasir) that quickly grows up and quickly fades, dries up,
and dies. From dust comes the human race; to dust it returns. And
as grass grows from the earth, the dust, so does human life burst
forth in strength and vigor, only ever so quickly to blanch, fade,
dry up, and return to that from which it came.

The poem uses several of the terms to express God's wrath:
ᵓaph, hemah, ᶜebrah, and verbal expressions that also reveal the
destructive power of God turned against the creature. Indeed, it
is precisely this unrelenting anger of God against human beings
that seems to be at the heart of the poem. How is God's wrath to
be understood? How is it to be endured?

The answers traditionally found in the closing prayer seem to me not to exhaust the poet's thought. Merely to learn to count the days as they pass, pass so fleetingly and without recall, and thereby to acquire a wise heart, does not appear to constitute a significant gain. What can the wisdom consist of except the recognition that indeed life is fleeting, is marked by God's wrath, and that one must therefore walk carefully, seeking to avoid the outbursts of anger and rage that come from God, find some modest place for oneself in an essentially meaningless world? The other petition, that God at the least make the number of days of happiness no fewer than the number of those weighted down by affliction and trouble, also seems modest indeed. Such days would constitute perhaps some demonstration of the divine mercy, but mercy, on this view, would seem largely to consist of the absence of divine wrath! God's mercy is God's forbearance, God's decision not to take action in wrath against sinful humankind, God's overlooking sin, God's not springing out from his lair to do damage to those who live their lives in terror.

No, the poet wants more than that. The petition includes the familiar prayer of the individual or communal lament that God return to the community, the individual. The traditional "How long?" also is found. The poet prays for God to bring the satiation of the heart and life, the fulfillment of life in terms of which one then can rejoice, and rejoice all one's days. He wants not merely a wise heart to discern the grim feature of life, so that one not expect too much; and not merely a fair sample of days marked by God's mercy. He prays for that which he lacks: a recognition that in face of the divine wrath that is indeed unrelenting, there is yet meaning in life, tasks that human beings do that have weight, work that stands and abides.

And how is that discovery of meaning to come? It is to come only as the veil is penetrated that reveals nothing but wrath, a veil that makes it impossible to discover God's own work (poʿal) and the purposiveness of God's work. What is God at work in the world to do? Is God's work, God's glory (hadar), discernible?

Can human beings find purpose in their own lives, in their own work, unless they can come to understand what God is doing in and through them, in the world that was itself brought forth by a God who was El from the "time" before there was anything created at all?

And it is here, I believe, that the poet reveals another ambiguity: the ambiguity of the divine wrath. It is the wrath of God that, finally, constitutes his hope. God does not leave human beings alone. He will not leave this worshipper alone, but keeps coming into the poet's life, disclosing all that is hidden there, leaving nothing unrevealed to him. God insists that the life human beings live, fleeting and apparently pointless though it be, be understood to be a responsible life, a life marked by God's constant entering of it. God's being there from everlasting to everlasting, God's being ready to spring out and "get" the sinner, God's being in position to offer the days of joy and rejoicing even when they seem rarely or never to come.

The heart of wisdom for which the poet prays, then, is more than the gift of discernment that life's course sweeps by fleetingly and that one must take advantage of such good as may come along the way. To number the days is to note that each of them, as it passes, is also a potentiality, a day that God has given, one on which God's glory may be revealed, God's work identifiable as purposive and enduring. God was there before the beginning and God is there at the end of human life. God therefore is doing something in the world. What is that something that God is doing? Presumably, God is establishing justice, warning sinners to mend their ways, calling upon his people to practice mercy and lovingkindness, finding persons in their sin and need and both hiding them from trouble and exposing them to God's wrath against all injustice.

The poet thus brings his thought to a close with the prayer that God's pleasant dealings, God's favor (no$^c$am), be extended now and again along the course of life. He prays that as God's work is

disclosed in the world, so also may the meaningfulness of human work
be disclosed. He closes his poem with the terror of the transiency
of human life constrained, diminished, perhaps even muted. No longer
is his eye focused upon that dimension of God's wrath: the wrath
of one who has decreed that the Holy One shall abide for ever but
that all of human and animal life shall be only for a season and then
return to dust and oblivion. No, the eye is focused now upon God's
wrath in direct dealings with historical existence, with the work
of God and of man, with the deeds that appear in the round of historical trafficking. There, wrath still appears, for God marks the
course of human deeds and misdeeds. The poet prays that there may
be disclosed to him what God is fundamentally doing in this world,
so that his own deeds will be illuminated by a recognition of how
they relate to the workings of God. Some recognition of the pro-
vidential and purposive work of God the Creator and Sustainer and
Director of the human pilgrimage is what is prayed for, and we have
no reason to doubt that the meditation disclosed something of what
was so earnestly sought in prayer.


IV


We now can understand one of the strange facts of spiritual
and devotional life: how a psalm that seems so bitterly to assail
God for his wrath and anger and hounding of humankind should turn
up in the funeral services and at the bedsides of those facing desperate trials, illnesses, and death. Psalm 90, precisely as a
meditation on the wrath of God, shows us a God who does come through
as fearsom and fear-inducing, as one who couches in his lair ready
to spring out and seize the worshipper, as one who has decreed that
life shall be but a sigh, a murmur, a passing thing that leads to
nowhere, to a cipher. It also shows us a God who is known to come
in wrath for good reason against those whose secret sins need to be
exposed to the light of day; as one who may strip back the veil that

hides life's fundamental purposes, and bring satisfaction and delight to the life of the worshipper. It shows us a God who in
wrath remembers mercy.

And beyond that, the wrath of God is the clearest sign to a
faithful and struggling community that there is purpose in life.
God's wrath is not a designation for purposeless hostility in the
world. It represents not some dark and nameless Power, some dimension of evil in the world against which the Good must do battle.
It is the Lord who was from the beginning, who acted in the mid-
wifing of the heavens and the bringing forth of earth and inhabited world, and who brings humankind from dust to life, who
watches over the flourishing of life before it returns to dust,
who is the one of wrath. God cares enough for humankind to be
wrathful. God's wrath is a constant and relentless pressure felt
by the faithful in their lives, a presence that warns and admon-
ishes and requires the securing of wisdom that it may be detected
the better. God's wrath is the wrath of the one who will never
be content until there is a just and a fair world, a world in
which human life does indeed flourish, where the days will be
marked by recognition of the divine mercy and grace and kindness,
and where the work of humankind will be established because it is
good work, work done justly and with honor, work that has reason
to be established by a God whose every deed is good.

FOOTNOTES

1. The Hebrew term ma‘on has both positive and negative
connotations. As God's dwelling place (Deut 26:15; Jer 25:30;
and Ps 68:6 [Eng. 68:5]), it is usually a term with positive
significance (but see Jer 25:30). In several other references,
the term is the lair of wild beasts (Nah 2:12; Jer 9:10, etc.).
There is no reason change the text to ma‘oz, which has some
textual support and often has been proposed.

2. The text is clearly corrupt. I have read for shenah
the often-suggested correction shanah, have dropped the verb
yiheyu, and have understood the term shanah as a collective:
you sweep them away -- namely, the years. It might be better to
read the plural, shanim.

3. The term hegeh is difficult. A sigh, a murmur, a rum-
bling of thunder would seem to be the set of associations called
up by the word (see Ezek 2:10; Job 37:2).

4. Literally, "who knows?" The context seems to require a
knowing that deliberates, takes into account, weighs.

5. H.-J. Kraus, *Psalmen* (BKAT 15; Neukirchen Kreis Moers:
Neukirchener Verlag, 1958-60) 629.

# THE HISTORICAL BACKGROUND OF EARLY APOCALYPTIC THOUGHT

Grace Edwards

The interaction between event and the interpretation of event, between history in its long course and developed theology, lies behind all Hebrew scripture. From their earliest consciousness of identity as the people of one God, sustained and admonished by proclamations of the prophets, to the "people of the Book" who ordered their lives in later Jewish history according to Talmudic directions, the Jewish people have maintained this dialectic of history. Theirs has always been a history-making scripture, as well as a scripture-making history.

Apocalyptic literature, whether Jewish or Christian, is a prime example of such interaction, arising in times of oppression to deliver a message of faith and direction to the listener-readers. The basic question has been: Out of what circumstances did this form of thought originate, and why? Later steps can be accounted for in the development of that extravagant, many-faceted complex of symbolisms generally associated with "apocalyptic," but somewhere there was a first step.

What we believe to be the identification of this birth of apocalyptic emerged from a study of the so-called spurious additions to the oracles of the Old Testament prophets, incorporated as a part of the editing of the oracles to form books.[1] This study consisted of two parts: 1. the nature of the materials added, and 2. the intention of the editing. The primary result of the examination of the additions is the conviction that these reveal the rise and earliest evolution of apocalyptic thought in the exilic and early post-exilic periods. Thus the origins of apocalyptic, at the point of transition from prophecy are, we

believe, to be found in the prophetic books, serving to complement
the prophetic message and confirm its fulfillment in history.  The
intention of the editing is to present apocalyptic books.

Our argument is as follows:  that the origins of the apocalyptic pattern are to be found in the historical reactions to the
Babylonian Exile, growing out of all the circumstances succeeding
upon the fall of Jerusalem.

The Sixth Century,B.C., possibly the most decisive period,
world-wide, in all ancient history, marks the transition from
Hebraism to Judaism and the end of prophecy as known before the
fall of Judah as a nation.  However, there has remained a void
in Hebrew literature from ca. 584-538.  The prophets Jeremiah and
Ezekiel and the Book of Lamentations document the fall of Jerusalem
and the beginning of exile.  Approximately fifty years then inter-
vene with no dateable words until the emergence of the nameless
Second Isaiah, known only through his writings.

A portion of the Hebrew population went into exile in Babylonia.  They lived there without nation, king, temple or homeland,
but with their traditions.  And with a question, the Question of
the Exile:  Why has Yahweh destroyed and dispersed his chosen
people, the bearers of his Name?  Faced with this question, and
with the assistance of only a strong and immediate prophetic tradition, what did they make of their situation?

The earliest reactions are of a piece with the laments found
in the Book of Lamentations, outbursts of feeling which voice no
questions, supply no answers, simply describe the land of Palestine in its ruined state and the despair of the people whether
there or in Babylonia.  Disorganization and low morale, lawless-
ness and a form of chaos in Palestine; discouragement, shock,
bewilderment and despair in Babylonia.  The exiles are described
as afflicted, wounded, scattered, blind, in darkness, in the pit,
in the dust.  They voice appeals to Yahweh to forgive and show
mercy, an early understanding of the disaster as an act of judg-

ment upon them for unrighteousness. Here we see the beginning of interpretation of events and the earliest basis for the development of the apocalyptic answer.

Next, we find assurances of divine forgiveness, confidence that punishment will not continue forever, a certainty based on the covenant promises of the past. Isaiah's warning concept of the remnant becomes a basis for hope. The prophetic message is accepted as the foundation for interpretation, except for that which proclaims unqualified total destruction.

The first positive step is a review of Israel's past history in a search for explanations, with strong emphasis on Yahweh's Exodus activity. The pre-exilic life of the people of Yahweh is treated selectively with an eye to what is relevant to the present need. Preoccupied with their new situation, they turned to the prophetic message, in particular to that of Jeremiah, as the most proximate, acknowledging its validity, apparent first of all in fulfillment of the predictive aspect. It had come to pass. Prophecy, of all their traditions, carried the strongest impact, both because of its nearness in time and its relevance. In neo-prophetic writings found among the additions, prophetic warnings of the breakdown of the covenant relationship because of apostasy are continued, and the Exile is set within the context of the broken covenant, as a result of the need to find meaning in events. However, the prophetic message did not reassure, in and of itself. Thus the prophets are constantly reinterpreted in relation to the times. History had overtaken and confirmed prophecy, and the principles needed application to changed conditions.

The review of prophetic proclamation, combined with despair, issues in a piety which we have termed hasidic thought. Falling back on Ezekiel, this faith incorporates acknowledgement of Israel's guilt and need for punishment, but combines this with an emerging faith that when judgment has been fulfilled through suffering, Yahweh will act again to renew the covenant. He will not hold his hand forever against his people. (cf. Isa 28:23-28) This produces a neb-

ulous, indefinite hope of return to Palestine and to Yahweh, more
longing than expectation and set in a remote future. The prophetic message becomes directed to individuals since it was impossible,
in the Exile, to apply it to the nation, and the prophetic emphasis
on the conflict between righteousness and wickedness becomes abso-
lutized.

The hope, which emerges slowly over the years, formulated and
doubtless propagated by those who were giving form to a new prophecy,
begins as a message to the exiles of release, return, and rehabil-
itation of the land and of renewed relationship with Yahweh (cf.
Isa 61:1-9). In the vocabulary of the Exile, "resurrection," far
from referring to individual resurrection, denotes the nation (cf.
Isa 26:19). The only hope visible lies in divine intervention, to
which appeals are made. The logic in theology guarantees that the
vindication of Yahweh's sovereignty must be his deliverance of his
people.

Thus hasidism merges into the beginnings of the apocalyptic
vision. The connections between yearnings and apocalyptic idealization are everywhere apparent. The Hebrew longing, in a land of
strange tongues and customs, for Jerusalem leads inevitably to a
glorified picture, including the elements of early apocalyptic expectation: revenge, a new covenant, leadership of Israel in the
world, etc. Here the prophetic view of history blends with the
apocalyptic view of final history, in stages and by degrees. The
historical judgment, the Exile, becomes the prelude to the cosmic
judgment. According to hasidic standards, the Kingdom is for those
who have not forgotten Jerusalem during exile, a strong element in
the hasidic definition of faithfulness seen by its emphasis in the
resulting apocalyptic hope (cf. Isa 62:1-12). Exhortations to
patience and endurance eventually become an expectation of historical realization of the hope, first defined simply as deliverance
from Babylonia, return to Palestine and rehabitation of the land.

The second determinative event in the development of apocalyptic thinking, the fall of Babylon, gives body to the developing hope. Around the days and events preceding the fall there cluster a number of passages vividly depicting eyewitness accounts of the conditions which look forward (cf. Jer 51:1-14; Isa 13:2-22).

With the fall of Babylon and rejoicing over it, we find the summons to Israel to rise up and return to her land, the necessary condition for the fulfillment of promises for the future. Here Second Isaiah enters the picture of the unknown new prophets. A dream of future conditions upon return begins to be constructed, with emphasis on the restoration of the covenant, the accompanying joy, confidence of future prosperity, large population and fruitfulness of the land.

The earliest approximation to the full apocalyptic drama is found in the visions of the fall of Babylon, with the first scenes of the eschatological slaughter and promises to Israel of the Kingdom. These form a combination of realistic and visionary accounts of Babylon's fall, balancing those of the fall of Jerusalem, reminders of the centrality of Jerusalem in the vision of the future.

The so-called oracles against the foreign nations form the earliest stage in the first part of the two-fold apocalyptic drama, the slaughter of the nations (cf. Joel 4:1-3; Zeph 2:8-9, 10-11; Isa 13:2-22). In most of these oracles the historical and superhistorical are intermingled. Zech 9:1-8 clearly links the oracles against the foreign nations with the eschatological event.

A variety of views is presented of the part Israel is to play in the slaughter. According to one, Yahweh himself will bring judgment on Israel's enemies, who are his enemies, as retribution for sins against Israel, and thereby against him. In a second, Israel is the instrument of Yahweh and will do to her enemies as they have done to her. In a third, the destruction is of all evil, whether Israel or foreign, and her escape from the slaughter will depend on her righteousness. And finally, Israel is one with the nations of the slaughter as purification for the Kingdom (rare).

Three forms of the slaughter are also envisioned: 1. the slaughter of all nations; 2. their choice of subservience or slaughter; 3. their conversion and equal standing with Israel.

From the judgment of the nations, the upheaval is extended to the earth itself (cf. Jer 50:46). Suggested by the fall of Babylon, as well as past violent events, this introduction to the new era represents a return to primeval conditions, the disruption of the structure of the world, in preparation for a new creation. Feelings which were hoarded up during the Exile find expression in a form consistent with the ancient myth of creation. The function of the slaugh ter is to purge the world of all evil, in preparation for the reign of righteousness.

Descriptions of the Kingdom of God, the second half of the apocalyptic drama, are present before the appearance of the apocalyptic form, in the pre-apocalyptic historical passages. The Kingdom is the result of exilic longings, primarily for independence, peace and security. In the beginning, the picture is simply that of an idealized life in which a totally purified people shall reclaim their own soil forever, in restored relations with their God, thus glorifying him who has glorified them. Simple ideals are set forth: inhabiting the land, living in their own homes, eating the produce of their vineyards and enjoying the fruit of their labors guarantees against separation of families, the end of all tyranny; all that they had been denied.

As this exilic longing moves on into apocalyptic dimensions, we find the earth rejoicing over the restoration of Israel (cf. Isaiah 35) as it quaked at the judgment of Babylon. A review of Israel's history such as is found in Isa 65:1-25, culminates in an outline of the features of the Kingdom, which include, here or elsewhere: a new heaven and new earth, with Yahweh dwelling in the midst of his people in Jerusalem, a purified and totally righteous people; miraculous fertility; all-inclusive peace, affecting nature as well as man, and security; celebration and praise of Yahweh and rejoicing; a new covenant; slaughter or conversion of the nations;

and finally righteous leaders, culminating in the concept of the
Messiah.

The prototype of the Messiah is to be found in the figure of
the one who will lead the Israelites back from exile and rule over
the re-established kingdom. This figure accords with the apocalyptic vision of a totally righteous people requiring a totally
righteous ruler. The development proceeds from desire for good
leaders, to one, completely righteous, ruler, finally to one king
who is faithful, righteous, and just, a guarantor of unbroken continuity and peace - Messiah. From visions of a restored kingship
to assurances of its continuing, unbroken and redeemed character.
In some versions of this dream, Yahweh is the sole ruler; in others,
righteous leaders; others, Yahweh's kingship represented by the
Messiah. Thus, we find the movement from longing and need, to
apocalyptic.

To summarize, on the historical plane we find that disaster
produced despair and in time the acceptance of the prophetic message
as applicable to the situation, the Exile as Yahweh's direct act.
Acknowledgements of guilt and repentance, encouragements to patience and faith lead to piety and trust and confidence of vindication in a long view of the future. In the approximately forty
years intervening before the rise of Cyrus, there took place adap-
tation to the new location, including some submissions to the pressures of a polytheism stronger than that in Canaan, calling forth
a new prophetic proclamation. As international events impinge, we
find an expression of hope and confidence of divine intervention
which becomes lively as the fall of Babylon nears. Apathy and resistance to another uprooting and return to a homeland which some
never knew and others barely remembered accounts for the urgency in
exhortations to return, in which Second Isaiah played the major
role. Prophecy has come into its own again, but this time accompanied by comfort and encouragement. On the part of others, the
hope of return includes a desire for revenge on enemy nations which

have been the instruments of Israel's sufferings. Finally, celebrations of the fall of Babylon bring us to the end of the materials on the historical level, combining past and future into a confident and expectant present. No more than this on the historical level, and no apocalyptic here.

However, these reactions have counterparts, certainly from the period of genuine expectation of the fall of Babylon, a confirmation of the hope, in apocalyptic formulations. Thus longing becomes confidence, desire for revenge turns into a vision of divine cosmic slaughter of all unrighteous nations, hope of restoration to the homeland and vindication by Yahweh becomes the proclamation of the Kingdom, prophetic reminders of the necessity for righteousness become a vision of a purified people who shall finally partake of the nature of their God. Encouragement to return is reduplication of Yahweh's Exodus activity on behalf of his people, this time the final deliverance. Resting back on both the myth of creation and the historical myth of the Exodus, the new prophecy is to be the final one. The way to this new vision, prepared by the historical events, leads to a double eschatology of cosmic upheaval, slaughter of all evil and a Kingdom of the purified. The end of the world as it had been known is to be succeeded by life on a super-historical level.

Viewed as reactions to the experience of destruction and exile, these developments follow a plausible psychological pattern, including vengeance on the enemies and comfort in the form of remote hopes, fixed first on a far-distant day which, with the support of historical events, becomes more imminent. Such hopes would naturally concentrate on the return to Jerusalem and restoration of what had been lost. The exiles were impressed with their scattered condition; thus the hope concentrates on re-union. Second Isaiah comes as a member of this new company of prophets, inheriting and building on a developing tradition, and thus fits into the emergency of early apocalyptic.

The Exile is, in part, the period of chaos which is to precede the act of salvation. It provides the conditions for this
first appearance of fully developed eschatology in Hebrew thought.
From the historical day of the destruction of Jerusalem come the
major features of the future Day (cf. Zech 12:1-10). At the other
end of the historical experience, hope becomes more than hope of
the fall of Babylon and return to Palestine; it becomes a theological necessity to envision a world-wide transformation of Yahweh's
creation. Apocalyptic thought had its inception even before the
certainty of change in political powers. The deliverance from
exile is the basis of the hope of salvation, and often (cf. Jer 30:
7-11) the apocalyptic Day is identified with the day of release from
exile.

It has been generally assumed that the contribution of the
Babylonian Exile to Jewish religion was the collecting and codi-
fying by the priests, the conservers, of such ritual materials
as concerned them, as well as some editing of historical and prophetic traditions, but lacking in innovations or forward thrusts.
However, we have seen here, related to the events which produced
it, the emergence of the "new prophecy" which was to sustain not
only the exiles but, in its more elaborated form, Jews and Christians alike in the succeeding centuries and become a permanent
feature of the theology of both. We have no first-hand history of
the Hebrews in exile, but proclamation of this new assurance became the vital lifeline to those concerned with their identity.
Here we discover what is truly a record of the history of the
Exile, a reflection of the thoughts which sustained and gave hope
to existence in an alien land.

This early form shows apocalyptic before its development into
fully structured apocalypse, although such oracles as the "Little
Apocalypse" of Isaiah contain many of the elements of the later
form. As always, the purest form is to be found in the inception
of an idea. So it is here. Where later apocalyptic becomes clut-

tered with scenery of angels, heavens, dates, cryptic historical allusions, making their reading a chore of decipherment and often ambiguous meaning, here the message is unmistakable. All the essentials are present, and there is no question as to intent.

The essence of apocalyptic is a total transformation of former existence as we normally know it. It represents a breaking into history which Jewish life and thought were ready to accept. It was born, as we have seen, slowly, in a period of subjugation, between two violent and determinative events and continued and flowered in succeeding times of crisis. As prophecy is to complacency, apathy and apostasy, so apocalyptic is to times of destruction, despair and helplessness. Both forms of thought are inconceivable in the opposite environment. Every feature of apocalyptic relates directly to its origin. Thus it becomes essential to clarify the message of the prophets and to cease attributing to them concepts which are out of character, out of consistency, and out of their time. The result of such a clarification is a stronger and clearer prophetic message; and the books, rather than becoming atomized are more closely unified. It has been said that the prophet spoke to his own age, the apocalyptist to the future. On the contrary, both spoke of the future; one as retribution, the other as ultimate vindication of Yahweh's nature, and both spoke to their own age.

What, then, marks the transition from prophecy to apocalyptic? As we see, it is the combination of spiritual readiness and historical events. So the visions of the prophets become extended, elaborate and literary, as their symbolic acts are turned into symbols.

The close relationship of these writers to history is seen in their concentration on the two focal points of their time: the historical event of the fall of Jerusalem and the despair it brought; the historical event of the fall of Babylon and the hope it brought. And between, the picture of the reactions of a displaced people. Apocalyptic is thus, in its inception, a pattern of death and resurrection.

FOOTNOTE

1. Grace Edwards, "The Editing of the Old Testament Prophetic Books: a Chapter in the History of Hebrew Religion." Unpublished Ph.D. Dissertation, University of Chicago, 1955.

# THE EXILE IN JEWISH APOCALYPTIC

Donald E. Gowan

The profound influence which the _experience_ of the exile had
on the Jewish religion is well-known and needs no demonstration.
But much less attention has been paid to the influence which the
_idea_ of exile had on the works of Jewish writers of the post-exilic
period.[1] I have drawn some preliminary conclusions about the matter
as a part of a larger study of the theology of exile and restoration
in the OT and subsequent Jewish literature down to the NT period,
and intend to present here some thoughts about the theological
significance of the exile for the writers of apocalyptic literature.
Since two of J. Coert Rylaarsdam's interests during the years I
studied with him were eschatology and the relationship between
faith and history, this paper is dedicated to him with thanks for
all his contributions to my preparation for a life of scholarship
and with the hope that he may find it to be of interest.

Judaism in the post-exilic period continued to appeal to its
history as a way of accounting for its present existence and as an
expression of hope for the future. In its uses of history the
exile tends to play a central role, and this paper will attempt
to provide some of the documentation of that and to suggest some
reasons for it.[2] A thorough coverage of the subject would include
a much broader range of literature than will be surveyed here.
Later efforts at history-writing would have to be examined: of
greater importance would be the "diaspora-novella" such as Daniel
1-6, Tobit and Esther,[3] and the midrashic materials centering
around Jeremiah, Baruch, Nehemiah, Ezra and Zerubbabel.[4] But we

must confine ourselves to two types of literature here:  liturgical
writings, i.e. laments and prayers, and apocalyptic literature.
The two need to be discussed together because of the frequent use
of laments and prayers in apocalyptic and because the occurrence
of these liturgical types in a broader spectrum of Jewish life provides a useful background against which to view the special features
of apocalyptic thought.


## I.  Laments and Prayers


The continuing use of the exile theme in a wide variety of
literary types in post-exilic Judaism shows that, despite the
occurrence of a restoration in Jewish history, with a re-estab-
lishment of a people in the homeland and the rebuilding of the
Temple, the fall of Jerusalem and the exile remained a continuing
problem for Judaism.[5]  The communal lament, with its setting in a
time of national disaster, was a genre which could readily be taken
up by post-587 Jews and filled with specific content drawn from
the experience of the fall of Jerusalem.  The Book of Lamentations
and an undetermined number of Psalms are the immediate results of
the events of 587, and we know from Zechariah 7 and from later synagogue practice that the effects of the fall were profound enough
to call for commemoration in the cult for many years.  Certainly
the fall of Jerusalem continued to be commemorated because the
subsequent history of the Jews constantly recalled to them a tragedy which had produced both the cultic and literary forms through
which they could bewail each new calamity which befell them, and
a historical pattern--sin, destruction of Temple and Jerusalem,
dispersion--by which the meaning of their new experience could be
interpreted.  We encounter the forms and the pattern again and
again in post-exilic literature, and find them used for more than
one purpose.  Nehemiah 9 sets the tone which prevails in later works

there has been a restoration, but the problems created by the fall of Jerusalem and the exile remain unsolved. In this prayer the plight of the Jews in the early post-exilic period becomes the climax of a confession of the community in which the history of Israel's sins and God's mercies is recited in a manner reminiscent of Psalm 106. The traditional pattern is extended to include a specific description of the new predicament. Although some post-exilic literature will follow a similar pattern in continuing to add to Israel's history additional examples of sin and grace (as in the apocalyptic surveys of history, especially), the tendency for prayers of confession and lament is to bring the history to an end with the exile or, as in Nehemiah 9, the early restoration period, and to make of 587 the archetype for all subsequent catastrophes.

That does not yet appear in the prayer for mercy in Sirach 36:1-17, which is written in such traditional psalmic language that only the plea for the gathering of the diaspora in v. 11 makes its post-exilic setting obvious. In this text the unsatisfactory nature of the restoration of Jerusalem and the continuing problem of the dispersion is made clear, but without using materials which have been peculiarly shaped by the experiences of 587. The way in which that event did provide the language for lamenting subsequent tragedies is shown by the lament of Mattathias in 1 Macc 2:7-13, however. The description of the calamity might have originated in 587 or in A.D. 70, but was felt by a second century B.C. author to be fully appropriate to describe the atrocities committed by Antiochus Epiphanes. The poetic description of the desolation of Jerusalem in 3:45 appears to preserve more specific details from the period, but also cannot fail to recall the earlier tragedy to one who reads it, as does I Macc 1:36-40. A comparable lament was also found in Cave 4 at Qumran (4 Q 179).[6]

The date and place of other, similar passages are more difficult to establish, but it is unlikely that any of them is to be under-

stood as merely a fictional effort to recreate the spirit of the
exilic age. The Prayer of Azariah, for example, is in form a
communal lament, the subject of which is the plight of the Jews
brought about by the fall of Jerusalem. It could have been used
in its present form during any number of calamities subsequent to
that, and probably was; one can only say that the peculiarities of
its contents (especially vv. 9, 14-15) are reflections of 587, so
that when added to an OT book it was logical to place it in an
exilic setting.[7] The Prayer of Esther in the LXX additions to
that book (14:3-19) is likely to be the free composition of the
author or translator, unlike Azariah's prayer, which could have
been used communally, but although it does not pray for return from
exile (like Daniel it presupposes the flourishing of Judaism in the
diaspora), when it does appeal to tradition it is to that of election (v. 5), national sin and disgrace before their enemies (vv.
6-10, including slavery) and the debasing of the temple. In a
fragmentary way, then, this lament over the predicament of the Jews
under Ahasuerus makes use of the theology of laments over the fall
of Jerusalem.

The way in which that event became a center around which could
be ranged many literary types and theological concerns is suggested
by 1 Baruch, which brings together a lengthy communal prayer of
confession, a wisdom passage and some orables of consolation, all
under a heading containing some rather cryptic historical notes
about the exile. Only the prayer can be dealt with here. It is
full of reminiscences of earlier biblical language and, in particular, seems to have taken the prayer in Daniel 9 as its model.[8] It
is a fine example of the continuing tradition of producing community laments on the old patterns. Clearly the chief concern is
the continuance of the exile and the disgrace of Jerusalem (2:26),
yet what is not clear, either from the text of the prayer or from
its introduction (1:1-14) is the occasion for which it was intended.
We shall not enter into the debate over the date of 1 Baruch, for

our point is based precisely on the difficulty of dating; this book
is an example of the fact that whether one lived in the time of
Antiochus IV or Pompey or Titus he spoke of his plight in the forms
and terms resulting from the activities of Nebuchadnezzar. Not
only forms and terms but also personages remain constant, as we
see here in our first of many examples. A book which deals with
the plight of exile appropriately comes from the pen of one of
the archetypal exiles, Baruch.[9] The fact that according to Jeremiah's book Baruch remained in Palestine after 587 until forced
to migrate to Egypt must be altered under these necessities, for
the Exile was in Babylonia, and for post-exilic Palestinian Judaism
only those who went into exile in Babylonia were considered to be
true Jews.[10] So a way was found to get Baruch to Babylonia and,
in later texts, even to connect him with Ezra.

The prayer of Tobit in chapter 13 is likewise composed in
traditional moulds which were probably used in the worship of the
post-exilic period to express the problems of exile. The first
part (vv. 1b-7) takes the form of a hymn of thanksgiving set in
the dispersion; the second part (vv. 8-18) is a Song of Zion.
Whether composed for the book or taken from already existing songs
(and remarkably few scholars have questioned the former assumption),
they remain as testimonies to the production, in the exile (vv. 3,
5, 6), of liturgical poems in the traditional Jewish modes expressing the deepest hopes of the pious members of the dispersion and,
as is characteristic of liturgical pieces, timeless in their ap-
plicability, at least so long as the dispersion continues and the
ideal Jerusalem remains unbuilt.

Some of the Psalms of Solomon also show us that new disasters
were inevitably described in the familiar way, although this time
the specific occasion, Pompey's capture of Jerusalem, is relatively
easy to recognize. The second Psalm is a mixture of lament and
thanksgiving, strongly reminiscent of Lamentations and making use
of many phrases and ideas from prophetic denunciations of Jerusalem.

The extent of Jerusalem's sufferings and the intensity with which her sins are condemned are both echoes of 587, and only the description of the conqueror's fate in vv. 30-35 makes it clear that another event has been the occasion for this psalm. The ninth Psalm is a confession of national sin and an appeal for mercy set in a context of exile and probably referring immediately to the captivity of 63 B.C., although only the more explicit historical references in other psalms of the collection enable us to make that judgment. The seventeenth Psalm is also patterned on the national psalm of lamentation and supplication, bewailing the pitiful fate of those dispersed by an alien conqueror (vv. 14, 17, 19-20), but adding an element which is new to the type of literature we have been discussing in this section; a prediction of the coming son of David who will, among other things, "gather together a holy people" (v. 28, cf. v. 50). We have seen prayers for the ingathering elsewhere, the promise of it in the form of a prediction is a standard element, not in the liturgical types of material discussed in this section, but in apocalyptic-style surveys of history.

The prayer of Daniel in chapter 9 is a good example of the way an apocalyptic writer uses traditional liturgical forms and the theme of the archetypal calamity in order to deal with new disasters. Although the author of the book knows four centuries of history since the fall of Jerusalem and outlines much of it in chap. 11, and although he records briefly the restoration of Jerusalem in 9:25, he does not believe that Jeremiah's prediction of a 70-year exile has been fulfilled (cf. 9:2 and 9:24ff.), so that the prayer of a Daniel located in the sixth century need in no way be different from the prayer of the second century author. In one respect, however, the two prayers (if there had been two) should have been different. The exilic Daniel ought to lament the fate of the diaspora and to pray for the return (as often happens, Sir 36:11, etc.) but there is no such emphasis, either in the prayer or in the rest of the book. (The diaspora is just alluded to in

v. 7.) The explanation of this, in a book <u>about</u> exiles, must be that the real problem which was responsible for the final form of the book (Antiochus' persecution) was so peculiarly Palestinian that for once the desolation of Jerusalem could be lamented without complaints about exile and prayers for return. Yet despite this preoccupation with the Palestinian problem (at least in chaps. 8-12), the book which was produced to deal with it has for its setting the classical situation, the exile, and the prayer ostensibly concerns the results of the fall of Jerusalem in 587.

Related in some respects to Daniel are two works which deal with the problems raised by the fall of Jerusalem in A.D. 70: 2 Esdras (4 Ezra) and the Syriac Apocalypse of Baruch (2 Baruch). Since the latter will be considered again, in the section on apocalyptic, the discussion at this point will confine itself to the use of laments which appear in each of these books. In 2 Esdras 3:4-36 the seer raises a complaint concerning the fate of God's people which reminds us of some of the psalms of lamentation and of Hab 1:2-2:4, and the dialogue form by which the complaint is answered reminds us also of Habakkuk.[11] Here the fall of Jerusalem in 587 B.C. (= A.D. 70) is made the occasion for raising a problem of universal scope, that of theodicy, but it is put in a distinctively Jewish form, asking why God has given up his chosen people to those who are no better than they (3:29-36; 4:23-25; 5:23-30). Later in the book a very familiar sounding lament over Jerusalem appears (10:21-22), reminding us of 1 Macc 2:7-13 as of earlier passages.

The laments in 2 Baruch are farther removed from the biblical tradition than most of the others in that they were clearly composed to fit the author's purpose and refer to post-biblical traditions, but they are still redolent of OT language and the author has set them firmly in the context of 587. The brief lament in 5:1 is very familiar in its wording, but its use is new, for in response to it the Lord assured Baruch that the enemy would not overthrow Zion, but God himself would do it. The lament in 10:6-12:4 contains

much familiar language, but introduces legendary material about
the fall in 587 (10:18-19) and expresses a jealousy of Babylon's
prowess which is more characteristic of 2 Esdras than of comparable
OT materials (11:1-2). Another brief lament in wholly traditional
language appears in chap. 35.

In these last two books the distance between the songs of
lament, confession and complaint and the actual worshipping language of the community has increased over what it was for the
earlier examples we have discussed. Yet the lamentation over the
fall of Jerusalem did not disappear from Jewish worship; on the
contrary there was all the more reason for it after 70, and certain
related fast days still appear in the cultic calendar.[12] To a
great extent it would appear that the fall of the second temple
replaced 587 as the archetypal calamity, in that it was in no way
redressed, and it might be an interesting undertaking (although
one which cannot be begun here) to study the extent to which the
falls of the first and second temples have been combined in Jewish
prayer.

## II. Apocalyptic Literature

In addition to the use of laments over the fall of Jerusalem
in Daniel, 2 Esdras and 2 Baruch, there are two other prominent ways
in which the apocalyptic writers use the exile theme: in their
choice of pseudonyms and in the surveys of history which tend to
be typical of their work.

Pseudonyms. Most of the names which were chosen by apocalyptic
writers came from the Pentateuch and range from Adam to Moses, but
there is one group of books noted for the relatively late dates
claimed for their authors. These are Daniel, 2 Esdras and 2 Baruch,
books which are set in the exilic period and which take the fall of
Jerusalem and the exile as their principle concern.[13] While the
actual dates of 2 Esdras and 2 Baruch might seem an adequate ex-

planation of the choice of author and setting for these books,[14]
since they are responses to the fall of Jerusalem in A.D. 70, this
will not account for Daniel, for this earliest of the apocalypses
takes a Jew of the diaspora as its supposed author, confines its
attention to history subsequent to the fall of Jerusalem (chaps.
2, 7-9, 11), and deals explicitly with the problem of its non-res-
toration in chap. 9. The concerns which were expressed so poignant-
ly by Ezra and Baruch were thus not the immediate result of A.D.
70 but had long been a part of the apocalyptic tradition. And
although the works which came between Daniel and these two late
books were given different settings, it can be seen from other
evidence that the exile is one of the preoccupations of the writers
of apocalyptic throughout its history.

Surveys of History. The greatest amount of material relevant
to our concern is to be found within the surveys of Israel's history
which are frequently recounted by apocalyptic writers. These surveys have been the object of a great deal of attention recently but
the questions asked of them have been different from those which are
of concern here.[15] My approach will be to ask two questions of the
texts in order to attempt to learn more about what exile and restoration meant to their authors: 1) What use do they make of the
history of the pre-exilic period? 2) How do they treat the events
of the restoration period and after?

The materials I shall examine include all the surveys of history which lead into predictions of the eschaton, whether or not
they appear in books generally acknowledged to be "apocalyptic."
My reasons are as follows: a) there is as yet no general agreement
on what is and what is not an apocalyptic book; b) however, the
surveys of history are generally accepted as a characteristic
apocalyptic feature; and, c) there is enough similarity in the
pattern followed by all of them that they ought to be considered
together, no matter where they appear.[16]

1) The Pre-Exilic Period in Apocalyptic Surveys of History.
Since the history of Israel, with its great themes--the promise to

the patriarchs, the Exodus, Sinai, the Settlement and the covenant
with David--dominates the greater part of the OT, it should be
instructive to compare the use which apocalyptic writers make of
that same material. For convenience, they may be put into four
groups: a) those who completely ignore the pre-exilic period,
b) those who mention it only as a time of sin, c) those who select
a few details as worthy of mention, and d) those who provide a
fairly extensive survey.

a) The book of Daniel shows no interest in pre-exilic history
save in the prayer in 9:1-19.[17] The surveys of world history in
chaps. 2, 7, 8 and 11 and of Israel's history in 9:24-27 begin at
the time of the exile. This may be explained as due to the author's
use of an exilic figure as his seer, but the same characteristic
also appears in Testament of Joseph 19 and Tob 14:4-7, which begin
with the exile of the northern kingdom. The dominant place played
by the exile in the thinking of these authors is obvious since it
is here that the history which is meaningful for them begins.

b) The pattern, "Sin-Exile-Restoration" which has been identified and discussed by several writers on the Testaments of the
Twelve Patriarchs,[18] typically describes the pre-exilic period by
a series of general references to sin without mentioning any specific
historical details. There are ten such passages in that work and
the most explicit historical reference in any of them is in T.
Zeb. 9:5: "Ye shall be divided in Israel, And ye shall follow two
kings." Others have pointed out that here the Deuteronomistic explanation of the reasons for the exile together with its basis for
a hope of restoration has become a standard pattern for brief eschatological passages which bear some relationship to the full-
fledged apocalyptic uses of history which appear elsewhere.[19]

c) Three texts include a few details from the pre-exilic
period. Jub. 1:7-18 mentions the fulfillment of the promise to
the patriarchs and the persecution of the prophets, but devotes
most of its attention to a catalogue of sins similar to the passages just mentioned. Adam and Eve 29 mentions Sinai and the

building of the temple before introducing a brief form of the Sin-
Exile-Restoration pattern. Apocalypse of Abraham 21-27 describes
the Primordial Era (chaps. 21-24), then skips to the Temple with
its "idol of jealousy" and child sacrifice (25), then to the destruction of the Temple (27). These three passages do not differ
significantly from the Sin-Exile-Restoration group in that for all
of them the exile is the key event in history which calls for an
explanation, and that is provided by citing a list of pre-exilic
Israel's sins.

d) Greater care is obviously called for in estimating the
significance of the exile for authors who provide reasonably extensive surveys of Israel's history. The survey in the Assumption
of Moses begins with the settlement, the earliest event which would
be "future" from Moses' point of view, and briefly alludes to the
period of the judges, the building of the Temple and the divided
monarchy, which is depicted in the familiar way--as a time of sin.
Pre-exilic history in this work does little more than connect the
time of Moses with the time which really interests the author, the
exile and subsequent events.

Three surveys tend to follow the Deuteronomistic schema of
telling history in terms of alternating times of grace and of sin.
The Apocalypse of Weeks in 1 Enoch 93 and 91:12-17 begins with
Enoch and presents a very sketchy treatment of Noah, Abraham, Sinai,
the Temple, Elijah, then the destruction of the Temple and the
exile, covering six weeks of its ten-week time span.[20] The other
two are much more thorough. The Animal Vision in 1 Enoch 85-90
follows OT history rather closely, but shows clearly that the
exile marks a turning point by introducing a new pattern of recitation just before the fall of Jerusalem; the description of
the rule of the 70 shepherds which provides the structure for the
second portion of the vision. The structure of the Vision of Black
and Bright Waters in 2 Baruch 53-74 provides for a strict pattern
of alternating weal and woe. Israel's history is covered from the

first, dark era--Adam's sin--to the twelfth, bright era--the restoration, then two additional eras are added which have to do with the eschaton. The significance of the exile and restoration for this author differs from that of many of the others we are discussing in that for him history ends at that point.

All three of these surveys, which extend from the primordial era to the eschaton, make use in their own ways of the Deuteronomistic interpretation of Israel's history, seem to have thought pre-exilic history important because of their emphasis on the Law and the Temple (which tend to appear prominently both before and after the exile), and for each of them the exile marks a break with the past and the beginning of a radically new situation.

2) The Restoration Period and Beyond. Since the apocalyptic writer used history as a way of leading into eschatology, as well as to make statements about the present, we come to the heart of the meaning of the exile for these authors when we ask how they present the period subsequent to the exile. There are two ways of handling the subject: a) the historical restoration was either imperfect in itself or was followed by new tribulation, so that another, final restoration is expected, or b) the historical restoration is not mentioned at all and one moves directly from the exile to the eschaton. Within these options we can detect a spectrum of opinions concerning the validity of Palestinian Jewish life during the post-exilic period, from positive to negative.

a) In Dan 9:24-27 there is a restoration of city and cult, followed by a period of increasing tribulation from which salvation is promised. There is no negative judgment of the cult, but the whole period is described as one which leads to the end of transgression and sin. Adam and Eve 29:6ff. describes the restoration in more positive terms; indeed, it is said that "the house of God will be exalted greater than of old," but this will be followed by the reappearance of iniquity, to be brought to an end by the eschaton. Two of the short texts in Testaments of the Twelve Patri-

archs also feature this extended pattern. In <u>T</u>. <u>Zeb</u>. 9:5-9 and
Testament of Naphtali 4 the Sin-Exile-Restoration pattern is applied to Israel's past history and then is repeated as the pattern
which will be followed in the time following the restoration.[21]
This extension of the Deuteronomistic schema is, of course, already
to be found in Ezekiel 38-39.

The vision in Testament of Joseph 19 represents a partial use
of the exile materials which is strongly reminiscent of the other
passages dealt with, but which is remarkably positive in its outlook. Nothing is said about sin before the exiling of the nine
tribes and then the three, then all twelve tribes are restored to
a situation of peace and prosperity. Perhaps the whole restoration
is in the author's future, which could account for this, although
R. H. Charles thought otherwise and interpreted the savior-figures
in it as Hasmoneans.

Other texts are less positive about the validity of the restoration itself. Tobit acknowledges that the second temple will
be "not as it was before, not until the time of fulfillment comes"
(14:5). The same kind of mild reservation is expressed in 2 <u>Apoc</u>.
<u>Bar</u>. 68:4,5: "...Zion will again be builded, and its offerings
will again be restored and the priests will return to their ministry, and also the Gentiles will come to glorify it. Nevertheless
not fully as in the beginning."

A more negative opinion was expressed in the Animal Vision,
which says that a "high tower" (the Temple) was built, but that
the bread placed on the table before it was "polluted and not
pure." (1 <u>Enoch</u> 89:73) This text has been cited as an example of
the anti-temple bias of the apocalyptic wing of Judaism,[22] but it
should be noted that it represents only one of several opinions to
be found in the literature. A stranger statement appears in <u>As</u>.
<u>Mos</u>. 4:7-8, which says that the two tribes shall return and rebuild
Jerusalem and "continue in their prescribed faith, sad and lamenting
because they will not be able to offer sacrifices to the Lord of

their fathers." The assumption of a strictly sectarian origin for this text may be one way of accounting for such an opinion.[23]

In each of these passages the restoration which actually occurred in the 6th-5th centuries is included as a part of the recital of history, sometimes simply as an act of mercy, the result of repentance, but on other occasions with reservations expressed about its validity. In either case, a new episode of tribulation must follow in order to bring the reader to the real present tense.

b)  A second group of passages seems to skip from the exile to the eschaton without any acknowledgement of a historical restoration. There may be more than one reason for this; e.g., the texts in the Testaments of the Twelve Patriarchs which have not already been discussed are so brief that it is usually not possible to be certain whether they allude to the restoration or not (Testament of Levi 16-18; Testament of Daniel 5; Testament of Benjamin 9; Testament of Issachar 6; Testament of Asher 7; Testament of Judah 23-25). But the Apocalypse of Weeks clearly moves from the exile in week six to the rise of an apostate generation followed by the election of the righteous, both in the seventh week. Since the elect group must be the sect to which the author belongs, it is evident that the temple which is built in week eight still lies in the future for him and that he found nothing worth recording in the restoration which had already occurred.

It is not quite so clear whether Jubilees refers to a historical restoration or not, but its description of the new era is so enthusiastic ("And I will build my sanctuary in their midst," (1: 17) that it seems likely to be a reference to the eschaton only.[24] The Apocalypse of Abraham clearly skips immediately from the destruction of the Temple to a calculation of the time of the end (chaps. 27-29). It is probably correct to say that these authors considered themselves still to be living in the exile and to have found nothing in the historical restoration worth mentioning as having mitigated that condition.

## III.  Conclusions

Apocalyptic literature begins with the conviction that things are very wrong in this world and seeks to explain why and how that could be, but more important, seeks to assure its readers that the future will make things right.  One explanation of why things have gone wrong was offered by the Deuteronomistic History, which made it the result of Israel's continual sin, and apocalyptic could make some use of that history for its purpose.  But the time when the wrongness of Israel's situation had become undeniable was the exile, and so this event became the archetype of all that was wrong for the Jews throughout their subsequent history.  For some of the writers of apocalyptic the fall of Jerusalem and the exile was taken as the setting for their entire work (Daniel, 2 Esdras, 2 Baruch).  When the seer was a figure from Genesis or Exodus instead, predicting Israel's whole history, the exile marks a turning point in his survey, no matter what other emphases it may contain.

The main themes of the canonical OT history--the promise, the Exodus, the occupation of the land, the monarchy--were of no help in coping with the problems the apocalyptic writers faced.  But the exile was not only actually responsible, historically, for some of them, it was also the kind of history that made sense theologically to people without security, living in an alien world, even though it was their own country.  This was not an outlook which was peculiar to the apocalyptic mentality, for the exile appears prominently, and for similar reasons, in the laments and in other types of literature which were produced throughout this period. There are reflections of party-spirit in apocalyptic, to be sure, but not every unenthusiastic reference to the restoration or to the Second Temple need be accounted for in that way.  The laments provide ample evidence for the existence in Judaism of a general conviction that the restoration experienced so far is by no means the fulfillment of God's intentions for Israel, so that the problems of the exile still remain unsolved. Against this background, apocalyptic may be seen as one type of effort to resolve a problem acknowledged by all.

# FOOTNOTES

1. The importance of this area of study was first emphasized by P. R. Ackroyd, *Exile and Restoration* (Philadelphia: Westminster, 1968) 237-256. In this paper "exile" will frequently be used as a brief way of referring to the whole series of events from the fall of Jerusalem to the rebuilding of the temple.

2. The only similar study which I know of was recently published by Michael Knibb, "The Exile in the Literature of the Intertestamental Period," *Heythrop Journal* 17 (1976) 253-272. His is a helpful work, but the materials used and the approach taken differ from the present paper. He looks at four groups of texts: 1) those which carry on in their own way the Jeremiah tradition of a 70-year exile, 2) one passage which uses Ezekiel's 390-year exile, 3) those which are based on the "Sin-Exile-Restoration" pattern, and 4) those which assume that Israel is still in exile.

3. W. L. Humphreys, "A Life-style for Diaspora: A Study of the Tales of Esther and Daniel," *JBL* 92 (1973) 211-223; A. Meinhold, "Die Gattung der Josephgeschichte und des Estherbuches: Diaspora-novelle I," *ZAW* 87 (1975) 306-324.

4. Jeremiah and Baruch: 2 Macc 2:1-8; 1 *Apoc. Bar.* 1:1-14; 2 *Apoc. Bar.* passim; *Paraleipomena Jeremiou; Lives of the Prophets;* and compare also the late *Jeremiah Apocryphon*. Nehemiah: 2 Macc 1:18-36. Ezra: 2 Esdras passim. Zerubbabel: 1 Esdras 3-4. Cf. C. Wolff, *Jeremiah im Frühjudentum und Urchristentum* (TU 119; Berlin, Akademie Verlag, 1976).

5. W. Harrelson, "Guilt and Rites of Purification related to the Fall of Jerusalem in 587 B.C.," *Numen* 15 (1968) 218-221.

6. M. P. Horgan, "A Lament over Jerusalem (4 Q 179)," *JSS* 18 (1973) 222-234.

7. C. Kuhl, *Die drei Männer im Feuer (Daniel Kapitel 3 und seine Zusätze* (BZAW 55: Giessen: Töpelmann, 1930) 100-103.

8. B. N. Wambacq, "Les prières de Baruch (1,15-2,19) et de Daniel (9,5-19)," *Biblica* 40 (1959) 463-475; cf. H. St. John Thackeray, *The Septuagint and Jewish Worship: A Study in Origins* (London: Oxford University Press, 1923) 80-111.

9. See the section on Pseudonyms, pp. 212-13.

10. Cf. P. R. Ackroyd's point that in the restored community only those who had gone through the experience of exile could be thought of as belonging; *Exile and Restoration,* 243-4.

11.  E. Breech, "These Fragments I Have Shored Against My Ruins: The Form and Function of 4 Ezra," *JBL* 92 (1973) 267-274, interprets the structure of the whole book as based on the lament.

12.  On the Midrash on Lamentations, see Ch. Raphael, *The Walls of Jerusalem* (New York:  Knopf, 1968).

13.  F. C. Burkitt (*Jewish and Christian Apocalypses* [Oxford: Oxford University Press, 1914] 18-19) suggested that the choice of pseudonym was governed by the subject-matter.  Another apocalypse, 3 Baruch, is of no importance here, since despite its ostensible setting it displays no interest in history.

14.  Cf. P.-M. Bogaert, "Le nom de Baruch dans la littérature pseudépigraphique: l'apocalypse syriaque et le livre deutérocanonique," in *La Littérature juive entre Tenach et Mischna*, ed. W. C. van Unnik (RechBib 9; Leiden:  Brill, 1974) 56-72; A. P. Hayman, "The Problem of Pseudonymity in the Ezra Apocalypse," *JSJ* 6 (1975) 47-56.

15.  E. Janssen, *Das Gottesvolk und seine Geschichte* (Neukirchen-Vluyn:  Neukirchener Verlag, 1971); K.-H. Müller, "Geschichte, Heilsgeschichte und Gesetz," in *Literatur und Religion des Frühjudentums* (Würzburg:  Echter Verlag, 1973) 73-105; B. Noack, *Spätjudentum und Heilsgeschichte* (Stüttgart:  Kohlhammer, 1971); D. Rössler, *Gesetz und Geschichte:  Untersuchungen zur Theologie der jüdischen Apokalyptik und der pharisäischen Orthodoxie* (WMANT 3; 1962).

16.  Cf. P. Vielhauer, "Apocalyptic," in *New Testament Apocrypha*, ed. E. Hennecke, W. Schneemelcher, R. McL. Wilson (Philadelphia:  Westminster, 1965) 2. 582-600.

17.  Janssen, *Das Gottesvolk und seine Geschichte*, 51f.

18.  M. de Jonge, *The Testaments of the Twelve Patriarchs:  A Study of their Text, Composition and Origin* (Assen:  Van Gorcum, 1953) 83-86; J. Becker, *Untersuchungen zur Entstehungsgeschichte der Testamente der Zwölf Patriarchen* (AGJU 8; Leiden:  Brill, 1970).

19.  Becker, *Untersuchungen*, 172-177; O. H. Steck, *Israel und das gewaltsame Geschick der Propheten* (WMANT 23; Neukirchen-Vluyn: Neukirchener Verlag, 1967) 152f.

20.  The text is interpreted as a symbolic history of the Qumran community by J. P. Thorndike, "The Apocalypse of Weeks and the Qumran Sect," *RQ* 3 (1961) 163-184.

21.  Becker, *Untersuchungen*, 218, considers the repetition of the pattern in Testament of Naphtali 4 to be the result of later editing.

223

22. R. G. Hamerton-Kelly, "The Temple and the Origins of Jewish Apocalyptic," *VT* 20 (1970) 1-15.

23. Janssen, *Das Gottesvolk und seine Geschichte,* 105-108. For a variant opinion, cf. J. A. Goldstein, "The Testament of Moses: Its Content, Its Origin, and Its Attestation in Josephus," in *Studies on the Testament of Moses* (ed. G. W. E. Nickelsburg, Jr.; SBLSCS 4; 1973) 49f.

24. G. L. Davenport, *The Eschatology of the Book of Jubilees* (SPB 20; Leiden: Brill, 1971) 25, 28 n.1; a contrary opinion by M. Testuz, *Les Idées Religieuses du Livre Jubilés* (Geneve: Droz, 1960) 166.

# N ALLEGORY CONCERNING THE MONARCHY:    ZECH 11:4-17; 13:7-9

Lester V. Meyer

In Matt 27:9, the words of Zech 11:12-13 concerning the thirty
pieces of silver paid out to the shepherd as wages are attributed
to Jeremiah.  If this is not a simple lapse of memory, brought about,
perhaps, by recollections of Jer 32:6-25 and 18:2-12, it may indicate
some "early uncertainty of tradition"[1] about the authorship of the
latter chapters of Zechariah.  But until modern times the unity of
the book was taken for granted.  When Joseph Mede[2] asserted in the
seventeenth century that Matthew's statement was a true indication
from the Holy Spirit regarding authorship, and that these chapters
fit better into Jeremiah's time than into Zechariah's, his opinion
was at first ignored.  But eventually Zechariah 9-14 came to be regarded as a collection of pre-exilic oracles appended to the post-
exilic book of Zechariah, and this view prevailed until nearly the
end of the nineteenth century.[3]

It was Bernhard Stade who, in an article[4] which became the
basis of all subsequent discussion of the question, demonstrated
to the satisfaction of the majority of scholars that Zechariah 9-
14 not only is not by the author of Zechariah 1-8, but is post-
exilic in date.  The question of the date of these chapters is, of
course, closely related to that of their literary unity or disunity.
Stade held that Zechariah 9-14 is a literary unity, and presented
a detailed argument for dating it in Hellenistic times (c. 280 B.C.).
But the view that one author is responsible for all six chapters
has been for the most part rejected.[5]  It can still be said that
"the general tendency of present-day scholarship is to regard
Zech 9-14 as a collection of oracles by two or more different

writers and to connect these oracles with different situations in the life of the nation during the late Persian or Greek periods."[6]

This paper is a study of one passage in the collection, Zech 11:4-17, to which, for reasons to be explained, 13:7-9 is appended. It does not address itself to questions of date of authorship, but maintains that the passage constitutes a three-part allegory depicting the history of Israel, and especially the role of the monarchy in that history.

That Zech 11:4-17 is an allegory is not immediately apparent. In a first-person narrative, the shepherd describes himself as having played the part of a shepherd by taking two staffs and naming them, then breaking them and disposing of his wages, and subsequently becoming a shepherd once again. This might well lead to the supposition that the passage is an example of what Westermann calls an "account," as distinguished from a "prophetic speech" or a "prayer."[7] If it is an account, then it is an account of a symbolic action performed by the prophet.[8]

More careful consideration makes it apparent, however, that Zech 11:4-17 is in fact not an account of a symbolic action at all, simply because what is described was not (and could not possibly have been) actually performed by the prophet in response to his perception of the divine word. For him to have done so would require that he supplanted the existing "shepherds," by which quite clearly is meant the rulers of the people (vv. 5-6); that he himself became the "shepherd," taking two staffs as his badge of office (v. 7); that he later destroyed three existing "shepherds" (v. 8); that he then abdicated his office and received termination pay (vv. 9-12);[9] and that he later took office once again, this time with "the implements of a worthless shepherd" (v. 15).

The fact that the various elements of the passage are conventional literary images also weighs against viewing it as an account of a symbolic action. Other passages portray shepherds who devour and destroy and scatter the sheep and so arouse Yahweh's

indignation (Jer 23:1-2; Ezek 34:1-10; cf. Zech 11:5, 16-17); sheep
that are themselves not blameless (Ezek 34:17-22; 37:23; cf. Zech
11:8-9); shepherds sent by Yahweh (Jer 23:4; Ezek 34:23; 37:24; cf.
Zech 11:4,7,15); and even the two sticks representing the union between Israel and Judah (Ezek 37:15-22; cf. Zech 11:7,10,14).

Furthermore, the passage intermixes action and meaning, event
and what is symbolized by the event, in a manner uncharacteristic
of the undisputed accounts of symbolic actions. This is reflected
in the very phraseology: "shepherd of the flock doomed to slaughter"
(v. 4); "the implements of a worthless shepherd" (v. 15).[10]

Another passage which, like Zech 11:4-17, resembles an account
of a symbolic action but in fact is not, is Jer 25:15-29. Yahweh
commands the prophet, "Take from my hand this cup of the wine of
wrath, and make all the nations to whom I send you drink it." The
cup, which is to be forced upon those who refuse it, is the fore-
runner of the sword which Yahweh is summoning against all the inhabitants of the earth. Here too there is obviously no possibility
of actual performance by the prophet; the cup is a conventional literary image for divine judgment (Isa 51:17, 22; Jer 51:7; Ps 75:8);
and there is an intermixing of action and meaning (e.g., the phrase
"wine of wrath" in v. 15).

Zech 11:4-17 is not, then, an account of a symbolic action; it
is, rather, a "parabolic narrative"[11] a "literary vision of a pronounced allegorical nature,"[12] or, more simply, an allegory.[13] Although allegories are to be found elsewhere in the Old Testament
(e.g., Proverbs 8; Eccl 12:1-7), most of them occur in the prophetic literature. Ezekiel, in particular, is a rich source (15:1-8;
16:1-63; 17:1-24; 19:1-14; 21:1-32; 23:1-49; 24:3-14); it is with
good reason that that prophet complained to Yahweh, who had just
commanded him to preach to the forest of the Negeb, "Ah Lord God!
they are saying of me, 'Is he not a mĕmaššēl mĕšālîm?'" (21:5).
Especially noteworthy are those passages which, like Zech 11:4-17,
depict historical events in allegorical form. Thus in Isa 5:1-7

Judah is depicted as a vineyard, planted and tended by Yahweh, but
producing only wild grapes, and so about to be destroyed by Yahweh.
In Ezekiel 16 Jerusalem is depicted as the unwanted daughter of
pagan parents who expose her to die. She is rescued by and subsequently betrothed to Yahweh, who lavishes gifts on her, but she
proves extravagantly unfaithful to him. Ezekiel 23 depicts Samaria
and Jerusalem in similar terms.

The most prominent term in Zech 11:4-17 is, of course, rō‘eh.
"Shepherd" was a common royal title in the kingdoms from which Israel derived its kingship.[14] The king was considered to have been
appointed shepherd by the gods. Thus Gudea of Lagash calls himself
"Shepherd envisaged by Ningirsu in his heart;" Hammurabi of Babylon
says, "When Shamash . . . with radiant face had joyfully looked
upon me--me, his favorite shepherd, Hammurabi;" and Assurnasirpal
II of Assyria addresses himself to Ishtar, "Thou didst single me
out with the glance of thine eyes; thou didst desire to see me
rule; thou didst take me from among the mountains; thou didst call
me to be a shepherd of men."[15] Therefore it is to be expected that
the term rō‘eh is also applied frequently in the Old Testament to
the king or his equivalent, and that he is described as having been
made shepherd by Yahweh. Yahweh appoints "a man over the congregation" that the people may not be "as sheep which have no shepherd"
(Num 27:15-23); he takes David from following the sheep, that he
and his house may shepherd Israel (2 Sam 5:2; 7:8-16; Jer 23:4-5;
Ezek 34:23-24; 37:24; Mic 5:1-3; Ps 78:70-72); he can even say of
Cyrus, "He is my shepherd, and he shall fulfill all my purpose"
(Isa 44:28).

It is the responsibility of the shepherds to preserve the people
in safety in the land. Those who do not do so are subject to punishment and removal by Yahweh:

"Woe to the shepherds who destroy and scatter the sheep of
my pasture!" says Yahweh. Therefore thus says Yahweh, the
God of Israel, concerning the shepherds who care for my

people: "You have scattered my flock, and have driven them
away, and you have not attended to them. Behold, I will
attend to you for your evil doings," says Yahweh (Jer 23:1-2;
cf. 1 Kgs 22:17-23; Jer 10:21; Ezek 34:1-10).

When the shepherds are described as good, it is most often in retrospect, as an idealization of David's rule, or in prospect, as
a promise for the future:

He chose David to be his servant, and took him from the sheep-
folds; from tending the ewes that had young he brought him to
be the shepherd of Jacob his people, of Israel his inheritance.
With upright heart he tended them, and guided them with skillful hand (Ps 78:70-72). And I will give you shepherds after
my own heart, who will feed you with knowledge and understanding (Jer 3:15).

Shepherds are said to have been present at the deliverance from
Egypt (Num 27:15-17; Isa 63:11); while the most lamented result of
the rule of bad shepherds was the scattering of the flock, there
will be shepherds who will gather it again in a new and greater exodus:

"Then I will gather the remnant of my flock out of all the
countries where I have driven them, and I will bring them
back to their fold, and they shall be fruitful and multiply.
I will set shepherds over them who will care for them, and
they shall fear no more, nor be dismayed, neither shall any
be missing," says Yahweh (Jer 23:3-4).

It is significant that this passage continues:

"Behold, the days are coming," says Yahweh, "when I will
raise up for David a righteous Branch, and he shall reign
as king and deal wisely, and shall execute justice and
righteousness in the land" (Jer 23:5; cf. Ezek 34:11-17,
23-24; Mic 5:1-3).

Ro⁽eh is, then a royal title. In this allegory the shepherds represent the monarchy in Israel.

That the shepherd is depicted in Zech 11:4-17 as speaking in the first person singular can lead to a confusion of the figure of the shepherd and that of the prophet. Thus Dentan, for example, even though he does not think of the passage as an account of symbolic actions which actually were performed, goes so far as to suggest that "It is not impossible that the prophet who speaks these words may himself have once occupied for a brief period the position of governor under the Ptolemies."[16] While "not impossible," it is also not at all required; the passage is an allegory, in which the speaker is the representative of the monarchy.

The other prominent element of the allegory in Zech 11:4-17 is the maqlôt. The significance attached to these staffs in vv. 7,10,14 indicates a relationship between this passage and Ezek 37: 15-28, in which one stick is labeled "Judah" and another "Joseph," and the two are joined in the prophet's hand as a symbol of the reunification of Israel. The term used in Ezekiel, however, is ʿēṣîm, a word of very general meaning which is perhaps best translated "wooden sticks" in this context. It is possible that the use of the term maqlôt in Zechariah 11 is intended to convey a more specific meaning, but the variety of ways in which it is used elsewhere in the OT makes it difficult to determine what that meaning might be. Maqqēl is used of the shoot of a tree (Gen 30:37-43; Jer 1:11), the staff carried by a traveler (Gen 32:11; Exod 12:11; Num 22:27), a weapon (Ezek 39:9 and perhaps 1 Sam 17:40), a staff from which oracles may be sought (Hos 4:12 and perhaps Num 22:27), and a scepter (Jer 48:17). The fact that it is a shepherd who handles the maqlôt in the allegory in Zechariah 11 leads to the expectation that the term is used because it means a shepherd's staff, but that is nowhere else the case in the OT (with the possible exception of 1 Sam 17:40). The usual word for a shepherd's staff is šēbet (Lev 27:32; Mic 7:14; Ps 23:4), but that term also carries a wide variety of other meanings.

The meaning of the term maqlôt, then, is not distinctive enough to attach any significance to the fact that it, rather than one of

the possible alternatives, is used in Zech 11:4-17. However, the
context in which it appears indicates that these staffs are considered to be appropriate for the shepherd's use:  he takes them
up when he assumes responsibility for the sheep (v. 7); the breaking of them seems to symbolize the relinquishment of that responsibility (vv. 10-14); and, while it is difficult to imagine what
is meant by "the implements of a worthless shepherd" (v. 15), the
use of the word ʿôd implies that the earlier role of shepherd required implements too, presumably, that is, the staffs.  The use
to which they are put is perhaps more what might be expected of
a ruler's scepter than a shepherd's staff; gestures suitable to
the accession and abdication of a king seem rather extravagant in
a shepherd who takes a position and then leaves it.  But of course,
if the shepherd is understood to be a royal figure, it is not necessary to distinguish between his staff and a scepter.  Commenting
on Mic 7:14a ("Shepherd thy people with thy staff, the flock of
thy inheritance"), Pedersen remarks that here "a prophet designates
the ruler's scepter as a shepherd's crook."[17]

In the related passage, Ezek 37:15-28, one wooden stick sym-
bolizes Judah, the other Joseph or Ephraim (v. 16).  The imagery
in the allegory in Zechariah is more involved.  Here the two staffs
are named nōʿam and hōbĕlîm (v. 7); the breaking of the first of
these is said to result in annulment of the covenant made by the
shepherd with all the peoples (v. 10), and the breaking of the
second in annulment of the brotherhood between Judah and Israel
(v. 14).  In the case of the first staff, the major difficulty is
presented by the word hāʿammîm.  If it is conjectured that the
original reading was singular rather than plural,[18] or if the plural is translated as "tribes" rather than "peoples,"[19] then this
staff signifies the covenant between Yahweh and Israel.  This is
the case whether the speaker at this point is considered to be
Yahweh or the shepherd, since the shepherd is acting as Yahweh's
agent.  If, on the other hand, hāʿammîm is read as "peoples,"
then the staff signifies the restraint under which the nations

(presumably hostile to Israel) are kept by Yahweh.[20] The former
of these views derives some support from the Targums, which relate the breaking of this staff to the deportation of the Israelite
king by the king of Assyria, thus referring the covenant to Israel
only. Such an interpretation is not reflected in the LXX or Peshitta,
both of which support the MT.[21]

In the case of the second staff, it may be held to signify,
quite literally, the union between north and south; but this could
refer either to the political union between the two kingdoms (cf.
Ezek 37:22)[22] or to the religious union between post-exilic Samaria
and Judea.[23] The Lucianic recension and the Ethiopic translation
have "Jerusalem" in place of "Israel;" this may preserve an old
variant of interest for the history of the text, though of course
not well-enough attested to take precedence over the MT.[24] On the
other hand, if "Judah and Israel" is taken as a conventional expression for "the whole nation," then this staff may simply signify
brotherhood and unity among the covenant people.[25]

In Ezek 37:15-28 the two ʿēsim are used to convey a promise
of blessing to Israel. The staff, however, sometimes occurs in
the OT as a symbol for the judgment of Yahweh on the people (Jer
1:11-12; Num 17:25; Ezek 7:10; Eccl 12:5).[26] That is also the
case here, where the two maqlōt are broken as a sign of judgment.

The discussion has so far dealt largely with Zech 11:4-14,
which constitutes the first part of the allegory. The shepherd
is a royal figure; his two staffs signify the benefits of his
rule; the breaking of these staffs represents judgment on Israel,
the flock over which he was appointed by Yahweh. All of this is
in the past; it has already taken place. It is not unlikely that
the allegory refers to specific historical events and persons. To
attempt an identification is, however, unrealistic. It is notorious
that even straightforward historical narratives can be invested by
an imaginative interpreter with an amazing variety of "meanings"
simply by allegorizing them, and apparently the reverse process--

the historicizing of allegorical passages--offers similar possibilities. At any rate, the numerous attempts to do this with these verses have resulted in a veritable thicket of speculation; for example, thirty proposed identifications of the three shepherds (v. 8a) were enumerated by Kremer as long ago as 1929,[27] and the speculation still goes on.[28] But the allusions are too cryptic and our knowledge of the history too limited to yield any firm results. What is clear is that the monarchy, intended to bring the benefits of the covenant to Israel, is pronounced a failure.

Zech 11:15-17 constitutes the second part of the allegory. The nucleus of this part is the cry of woe in v. 17. Such woe-sayings, which usually occur in series (e.g., Isa 5:8-23; Hab 6:6-19), are a variant form of the prophetic judgment-speech and resemble judgment-speeches to individuals, except that the introductory word hôy already implies judgment.[29] In v. 17 the accusation is directed against the shepherd, described as hāʾĕlîl, because he deserts the flock; this is reminiscent of similar complaints in Jer 10:21; 23:1-2; Ezek 34:1-10.

Vv. 15-16 provide an introduction to this cry of woe; this is shown by the correspondence between the phrases rōʿeh ʾĕwilî (v.15) and rōʿî hāʾĕlîl (v. 17).[30] V. 16 also serves the purpose of widening the judgment to include not only the shepherd but also the flock. Furthermore, vv. 15-16 provide a link with vv. 4-14; the command of v. 15 is described as a sequel to that of v. 4 (ʿōd), and the plight of the "flock doomed to slaughter," described in vv. 5-6,9, is taken up in v. 16 in an echo of Ezek 34:3-4. Thus vv. 15-16 are a continuation of the allegory of vv. 4-14; the first part of the allegory describes events which have already transpired, while the second part introduces a judgment the fulfillment of which lies in the future.

In this respect, too, Zech 11:4-17 resembles such passages as Isa 5:1-7; Ezekiel 16 and Ezekiel 23. The same two-part structure is evident in each of these. It is somewhat obscured in the Isaiah passage by the rhetorical appeal to the listeners (vv. 3-4) and the explanation of the terms of the allegory (v. 7); nevertheless, vv.

1-2 are clearly an allegorical description of Judah's sinful past
and vv. 5-6 of the divine judgment her future holds. Even more
clearly, the first 34 verses of Ezekiel 16 are an allegorical presentation of Jerusalem's sinful past; beginning at v. 35 the allegory describes the divine judgment Jerusalem's future holds (vv. 44-
63 are most likely not part of the original[31]). In Ezekiel 23 the
transition from past to future, so far as Jerusalem is concerned,
comes at v. 22. These lengthy allegories are thus greatly-expanded
examples of the prophetic judgment-speech: first the accusation
which provides the reason for judgment (here the whole history of
the nation's unfaithfulness); then the announcement of the judgment
which is to come.[32] In the same way, Zech 11:4-14 describes Israel's
past as displeasing to Yahweh, while vv. 15-17 turn to the future
and depict harsh action on Yahweh's part. It is true that the
element of judgment is not restricted to vv. 15-17 but, especially
in the breaking of the staffs, already appears in vv. 4-14, where
only accusation might be expected. However, such expanded accu-
sations characteristically portray God's earlier saving actions as
background, including earlier deeds of punishment which should have
provided warning to the people to turn from their sins before Yahweh's
wrath expressed itself more severely.[33] The same feature appears
in the Ezekiel allegories (16:27; 23:9-10) and elsewhere (e.g., Amos
4:6-12).

The suggestion by Heinrich Ewald[34] that Zech 13:7-9 belongs
after 11:4-17 has been accepted by some more recent scholars[35] and
rejected by others.[36] It is accepted here because of the evidence
that Zech 13:7-9 continues the allegory of 11:4-17. This is indicated not only by the reappearance of the shepherd, but also by his
designation as rōᶜî in both passages and by the threat of a sword
directed against him (11:17; 13:7). It is true that the shepherd
of 11:15-17 is said to be ʾĕwilî and ʾĕlîl, while the shepherd of
13:7-9 is called geber ʿămîtî. This might suggest that the latter
is a "good" shepherd; on the basis of the use of the term geber in

passages like Dan 8:16; 9:21, Elliger sees in him an exalted figure of the time of salvation.[37] However, nothing is said here about the way in which the shepherd carries out his office. Neither rōʿî (which is used in 11:17 and of Cyrus in Isa 44:28) nor geber ʿămîtî implies goodness in the sense of a benevolent concern for the flock, Israel, but only the direction and control of Yahweh, who uses such a shepherd to accomplish his purposes with his people.[38]

13:7 is a "sword-saying" like those in Jer 47:6-7 (against the Philistines); Jer 50:35-38 (against Babylon); and Ezek 21:33-37 (against the Ammonites). Similar imagery occurs in Ezek 30:21-26, where a sword is directed against Egypt, and in Jer 25:34-38, where it is against all shepherds and "lords of the flock" in the sense of the kings of all the nations (cf. vv. 17-26). But the closest parallel is Ezek 21:13, a "sword-saying" in which the sword is directed against Israel (cf. vv. 6-12) and its rulers (cf. v. 17). In this last reference, the sword is said to be in the hand of the king of Babylon (Ezek 21:23-37); in any case, the "sword-saying" is war poetry and implies destruction in battle.

In 13:7, as in 11:17, the sword is directed against the shepherd. The main concern of these verses, however, is with the sheep that are scattered by the loss of their shepherd (cf. 1 Kgs 22:17). Of them it is said waḥăsibōtî yādî ʿal-haṣṣōʿărîm. If haṣṣōʿărîm are the whole flock, then the gesture is a threatening one; that is certainly the force of the preposition ʿal in the first part of v. 7. If, however, haṣṣōʿărîm are the third part that will be left, the gesture may be intended to indicate protection. The ambiguity may even be intentional, since the remnant must survive a difficult purification.[39] The same ambiguity characterizes a similar image in Isa 1:25.

V. 8 depicts the destruction of a large portion of the people. It may be that the use of the verb kārat, with its basic meaning of "cut off," relates this destruction to the sword of v. 7 and again implies destruction in battle; however, the verb is frequently used

in a more general or metaphorical sense (e.g., Isa 48:19; 55:13;
56:5; Jer 7:28; 33:17; Joel 1:5,16; Zeph 3:7). According to v. 9,
even those who escape will be subjected to fire. Fire as the agent
of Yahweh's judgment on Israel appears elsewhere (e.g., Amos 7:4;
Ezek 15:1-8; 22:17-22); but this passage is most closely related
to Ezek 5:1-12, a symbolic action in which both a sword and fire
are used to depict Yahweh's judgment on the populace of Jerusalem
divided into three parts. All of these passages apparently envision a complete destruction; the last of them, however, is
followed by the promise of a remnant that will survive and turn
to Yahweh:

> Yet I will leave some of you alive. When you have among
> the nations some who escape the sword, and when you are
> scattered through the countries, then those of you who
> escape will remember me among the nations where they are
> carried captive, when I have broken their wanton heart
> which has departed from me, and blinded their eyes which
> turn wantonly after their idols; and they will be loath-
> some in their own sight for the evils which they have
> committed, for all their abominations. And they shall
> know that I am Yahweh; I have not said in vain that I
> would do this evil to them (Ezek 6:8-10).

This is not far from the thought of Isa 1:25 ("I will turn my
hand against you and will smelt away your dross as with lye and
remove all your alloy.") and of Zech 13:7-9; where destruction
is a means of purification.[40]

The purpose of this purification is the preservation of a
faithful community. The language of v. 9b is reminiscent of the
description of the day of Yahweh in Joel 3:5:

> And it shall come to pass that all who call upon the name
> of Yahweh shall be delivered; for in Mount Zion and in
> Jerusalem there shall be those who escape, as Yahweh has
> said, and among the survivors shall be those whom Yahweh
> calls.

It also echoes the language of Hos 2:25 ("I will say to Not-my-people, 'You are my people;' and he shall say, 'You are my God'.") But it is more significant that these same phrases recur in Ezek 37:23,27, where they provide the sequel to the episode with the two sticks symbolizing the reunification of Israel. This provides additional evidence that Zech 13:7-9 is related to 11:4-17, and that what is described in the former is the restoration of the relationship symbolized by the two staffs of 11:4-14. In the process, the focus of attention shifts from the monarchy to the people, more specifically, to the purified remnant that Yahweh will restore to relationship with himself.[41]

Thus Zech 11:4-17 and 13:7-9 are, together, an allegory in which the monarchy has the central role. Vv. 4-14 summarize Israel's past. That past is seen as displeasing to Yahweh; it featured a monarchy that failed to bring blessing to Israel. Vv. 15-17 portray Israel's future. It is to be the time of Yahweh's judgment; the monarchy still has a part to play both as agent and as victim of that judgment. 13:7-9 continues the portrayal of Israel's future, but the concern is with the purpose and outcome of Yahweh's judgment. The movement of the entire allegory is from past failure through imminent judgment to ultimate blessing.

238

FOOTNOTES

1.  A. Bentzen, *Introduction to the Old Testament* (2 vols. in 1; Copenhagen:  G. E. C. Gad, 1959) 2. 158.

2.  *Dissertationem Ecclesiasticarum Triga:*  . . . *Quibus accedunt Fragmenta Sacra,* a Josepho Medo, Anglo, London, 1653; cited by B. Otzen, *Studien über Deuterosacharja* (Copenhagen:  Munksgaard, 1964) 11.

3.  R. C. Dentan, "The Book of Zechariah, Chapters 9-14:  Introduction and Exegesis," IB 6. 1089.

4.  "Deuterosacharja," ZAW 1 (1881) 1-96.

5.  An exception is provided by P. Lamarche, who has attempted, in *Zacharie IX-XIV:  Structure Littéraire et Messianisme* (EBib; Paris:  Librairie Lecoffre, 1961), to demonstrate through analysis of the literary structure that the six chapters were written by a single author who made use of older materials.

6.  Dentan, "Zechariah, Chapters 9-14," 1090.

7.  C. Westermann, *Basic Forms of Prophetic Speech* (Philadelphia:  Westminster, 1967) 90.

8.  Among such accounts of symbolic actions are 1 Kgs 22:11; 2 Kgs 13:14-19; Isaiah 20; Jeremiah 19; 27-28; Ezekiel 4; 5; 12; etc.

9.  Although frequently explained as the equivalent of the price of a slave, it is more likely that "thirty pieces of silver" signifies simply an insultingly low price (E. Reiner, "Thirty Pieces of Silver," *Essays in Memory of E. A. Speiser* [AOS 53=JAOS 88/1; New Haven:  Yale, 1968] 186-90; E. Lipiński, "Recherche sur le livre de Zacharie," VT 20 [1970] 53-55).

10.  K. Elliger, *Das Buch der zwölf kleinen Propheten II* (ATD 25; Göttingen:  Vandenhoeck & Ruprecht, 1959) 160-61.

11.  O. Eissfeldt, *The Old Testament:  An Introduction* (New York:  Harper & Row, 1965) 438.

12.  J. Lindblom, *Prophecy in Ancient Israel* (Philadelphia:  Fortress, 1962) 146.

13.  Bentzen, *Introduction,* 1. 180.  Bentzen distinguishes between the parable, which "generally has only one point of comparison," and the allegory, which "has a series of metaphors, all with their meaning."

239

14. L. Dürr, *Ursprung und Ausbau der israelitisch-jüdischen Heilandserwartung* (Berlin: C. A. Schwetschke & Sohn, 1925) 116-24.

15. H. Frankfort, *Kingship and the Gods: A Study of Ancient Near Eastern Religion as the Integration of Society and Nature* (Chicago: University of Chicago, 1948) 238-39.

16. Dentan, "Zechariah, Chapters 9-14," 1103.

17. J. Pedersen, *Israel: Its Life and Culture* (4 vols. in 2; London: Geoffrey Cumberlege, Oxford University, 1926) 3-4. 79.

18. Elliger, *Propheten*, 161-62.

19. Otzen, *Studien*, 154.

20. Dentan, "Zechariah, Chapters 9-14," 1104; F. Horst, "Nahum bis Maleachi," *Die zwölf kleinen Propheten* (ed. T. H. Robinson and F. Horst; HAT 14/1; Tübingen: J. C. B. Mohr, 1954) 252.

21. M. Saebø, *Sacharja 9-14* (WMANT 34; Neukirchen-Vluyn: Neukirchener, 1969) 77.

22. Otzen, *Studien*, 154, 156.

23. Elliger, *Propheten*, 164; A. Gelin, *Aggée, Zacharie, Malachie* (SBJ; Paris: Les Editions du Cerf, 1960) 51.

24. Otzen, *Studien*, 257; Saebø, *Sacharja 9-14*, 83-84.

25. H. G. Mitchell, J. M. P. Smith, and J. A. Bewer, *A Critical and Exegetical Commentary on Haggai, Zechariah, Malachi and Jonah* (ICC; Edinburgh: T. & T. Clark, 1912) 310; Denten, "Zechariah, Chapters 9-14," 1105.

26. Otzen, *Studien*, 154-55; cf. P. Wood, "Jeremiah's Figure of the Almond Rod," *JBL* 61 (1942) 99-103.

27. J. Kremer, *Die Hirtenallegorie im Buche Zacharias auf ihre Messianität hin untersucht* (Münster i. Westf.: Aschendorffsche Buchdruckerei, 1929) 83-85.

28. E.g., R. Tournay, "Zacharie XII-XIV et l'histoire de'Israël," *RB* 81/3 (July 1974) 357. I did not have access to Tournay's earlier article, "Zacarias 9-11 e a Historia de Israel," *Atualidades biblicas* (Petropolis, 1971) 331-49.

29. Westermann, *Basic Forms*, 137.

30. Elliger, *Propheten*, 166.

31. Eissfeldt, *Introduction*, 380.

32. Westermann, *Basic Forms*, 92-136.

33. Ibid., 131-32.

34. *Die Propheten des Alten Bundes* (2 vols.; Stuttgart: A. Krabbe, 1840) 1. 308-24.

35. E.g., Bentzen, *Introduction*, 2. 158; A. Weiser, *The Old Testament: Its Formation and Development* (New York: Association, 1961) 468.

36. E.g., Eissfeldt, *Introduction*, 438; G. Fohrer, *Introduction to the Old Testament* (Nashville: Abingdon, 1968) 468.

37. Elliger, *Propheten*, 175-76.

38. R. A. Mason, "The Relation of Zech 9-14 to Proto-Zechariah," ZAW 88/2 (1976) 237.

39. Lamarche, *Zacharie IX-XIV*, 92.

40. H. Gese, "Anfang und Ende der Apokalyptik, dargestellt am Sacharjabuch," ZTK 70/1 (March 1973) 47.

41. Mason, "The Relation," 238.

PART THREE


INTERPRETING SCRIPTURE

# THE 'NAVEL OF THE EARTH' AND THE COMPARATIVE METHOD*

Shemaryahu Talmon

## I

The comparative method, which has carved itself a secure niche
in modern biblical research, significantly broadened the field of
discussion of those social phenomena and principles of thought that
distinguished the culture of Israel. This method of study removed
biblical Israel from the isolationist ideology which characterizes
generally the biblical and particularly the prophetic outlook. Careful observation disclosed an elaborate network of channels linking
Israelite society with the nations in whose proximity, indeed midst,
she dwelt; from Egypt in the south, through the Canaanite expanse
on both sides of the Jordan, and on to Mesopotamia in the northeast.
In the two millennia before the common era the nations of the ancient
Near East existed in a state of geographic-territorial continuity,
which in that period of limited means of communication was a <u>sine
qua non</u> for close and constant "give and take" on the social and
intellectual plane.

Even those scholars who dispute the far-reaching assumption
of a "Pattern of Culture," which presumably served as a foundation
for all the ethnic-national cultures which took root between Mesopotamia and Egypt, surely cannot ignore the multiplicity of facts
pointing toward the interweaving of Israel in the fabric of mutual
relations in the realm of thought and action that involved the
majority of the peoples of the area. The sheer abundance of parallels drawn from various aspects of life, language, literary forms
and conventions, articles of belief and of ritual, methods of social

243

and political organization, bases of social thought, brought on a
wave of publications that wrenched Israelite society of the biblical
period from its ideological position as "a people dwelling alone
and not reckoning itself among the nations" (Num 23:9).[1]

Comparative research has not limited its compass to contemporaneous cultural systems, i.e., to the discernment of similarities between the linguistic, literary, and intellectual values of biblical
Israel and those of the other nations of the ancient Near East.
Rather the comparative method widened its scope of inquiry and included as well cultures that from the standpoint of chronology and
geography were far removed from ancient Israel:  the Arabic society
of the pre-Islamic period,[2] and the culture of classical Greece and
its later Hellenistic development.

The comparison with extra-biblical materials, culled from contemporaneous literature of the ancient Near East or from post-biblical
writings, recommends itself when one examines a term or concept that
occurs but once in the Bible, and cannot be satisfactorily explained
either from context or through etymological derivation.  An extra-
biblical source in which the subject matter is sufficiently clear,
can sometimes offer an analogy by which a biblical crux can be
satisfactorily solved.

There can be no quarrel with the comparative method as long
as it is employed within the bounds of reason, i.e., as long as it
does not divorce the item under discussion from its proper context
in the compared culture (with the exception of phenomenological aspects and theoretical models that apply to many cultural systems
but are distinctive features of no one in particular).  However,
this required methodological ground rule is not always observed.
Sometimes, the researcher seems to permit his penchant for resemblances and parallels to run wild, and the great expanse of ancient
Near Eastern literature is relentlessly searched for every possible
similarity or likeness, with biblical counterparts.  Drawn by these
parallels and similarities which emerge from a given body of literature, the researcher is disposed to close an eye to factors

which differentiate one cultural system from another; he will bring
close items which, in fact, are quite disparate and will join what
should be kept separate.  It seems that these shortcomings result
from insufficient attention to the need for establishing basic
guidelines for comparative research and from a disregard of rules
which govern other disciplines which focus on comparison of cultures and societies and the concomitant processes of acculturation.
Comparative biblical study yet lacks proven fundamentals of method
by which the process of research can be subjected to objective
criteria, and the reliance upon subjective intuition limited.

It is possible that despite the wide and varied ramification
of comparative research the time is not yet ripe for drawing general conclusions from unconnected facts which have been assembled
piecemeal.  The formulation of a methodology of comparative research demands a synoptic, inter-disciplinary comprehension and
requires the participation of experts from distinct fields of
research:  language, literature, sociology, and intellectual history.  Such a concerted effort has yet to see the light of day.
The issue is in need of a comprehensive discussion which goes beyond the limits of our present concern.  It would, nevertheless,
appear that we can define a basic principle by which any comparison
of an item from the Bible with its counterpart in other cultures
should be guided:  before positing the resemblance of a biblical
phenomenon with a contemporaneous or a pre-biblical counterpart,
it is imperative to examine first the biblical literature itself
for possible parallels, foremost the immediate context under discussion.  This rule is especially important when one deals with a
literary motif or with bases of biblical thought which embody in-
cipient religious concepts destined to come to full flower in the
Jewish or non-Jewish literature of the post-biblical period.

## II

We shall exemplify the approach outlined by examining the
connotation of the term tabbûr, found only twice in the Bible, in
Judg 9:36-37: "And when Gaal saw the men, he said to Zebul, 'Look,
men are coming down from the mountain tops.' ... and he said, 'Look,
men are coming down from the centre of the land (tabbûr hā'āres)
...';" and in Ezek 38:11-12: "I will go up against the land of the
unwalled villages; I will fall upon the quiet people who dwell securely ... who dwell at the centre of the earth (tabbûr hā'āres)."

The meaning of tabbûr has not been etymologically ascertained.[3]
J. Boehmer sought to link the term with Aramaic, Syriac, and Arabic
tur; and tibbûr and also Tabor with the Akkadian noun duppuru and
the Ethiopic dābär, all of which share the common meaning "mountain."
Albright connected tabbûr with Ugaritic tbrrt meaning "brightness,"
"splendour," or "purity."[5] D. Winton Thomas suggested deriving
tabbûr from nbr and conjectured that it approximates Ethiopic henbert
and Amharic enbert whose meaning is identical with rabbinic tabbûr -
tibbûr and biblical šr(r).[6] This suggestion is undoubtedly intended
to support the hypothesis that in the two above-mentioned biblical
occurrences of tabbûr the term is equivalent to tibbûr in Mishnaic
Hebrew. Indeed, it was so understood in the LXX which rendered it
in both instances omphalos, and in the Vulgate where it is rendered
umbilicus. As a result of the identification of tabbûr -- isolated
from its biblical context -- with tabbûr/tibbûr of rabbinic usage
and the rendering omphalos in the Septuagint, the mythical idea of
the "centre of the earth" marked by a major sanctuary was introduced
into biblical thought. It is claimed that according to the Book of
Ezekiel, Jerusalem and her Temple are regarded as the focus of the
world, whereas the Book of Judges conceived of Mt. Gerizim as the
"navel of the earth," thus reflecting the central role which that
site was to play in the faith of the Samaritans as a competitor
with Mt. Zion and Jerusalem. The representation of the world in

the form of a human body, a disc or a square,[7] whose centre is
marked by a tall mountain, representing its navel, is prevalent
in the mythical traditions of many cultures. Just as the embryo
is bound at the navel to the mother's body, so the world of man,
as well as the underworld, is linked with the higher spheres, the
world of the gods, by the central mountain, the likeness of the
umbilical cord (vinculum). From this image sprang the identification of a sanctuary erected atop an imposing mountain, or the
tallest mountain (though this need not be the geographic reality),
with the "navel of the earth."

The currency of the conception of the sanctuary as tabbûr
hāʾāres in Greek mythology was proven by Roscher, who may be
considered the innovator of modern omphalos research.[8] In the
Odyssey (1,50) Homer describes the geographical centre of the sea
as its navel: "the sea-washed island, the navel (omphalos) of all
the waters." Roscher speculated that this image had its place even
in the most ancient representations of the world as a whole, though
the first explicit occurrence is with Epimenides (Plutarch, Moralia,
409E): "nor was the centre of the earth a navel." Roscher also
demonstrated that the principal sanctuaries of Greece, Delos, Epi-
daurus, Paphos, Branchidae, Miletus, and especially Delphi, were
imagined by their respective adherents to be the centre of the
earth, i.e., its navel. He further entertained the hypothesis that
the image of a mountain as the centre of the earth was already current among the nations of the ancient Near East. On a Babylonian
map of the heavens and the earth, for example, the city Babel is
presented as the centre of the world. More than once a temple standing on the height of a mountain is spoken of as the "link between
the heavens and the earth;" the heavens have their foundation in
the mountains which serve them as supporting pillars. In none of
these instances, however, do we find this world centre designated
by an equivalent of the term tabbûr.

Roscher's hypothesis underwent a further development at the

hands of Wensinck, who determined that the idea of the 'navel' in
the ancient world (and in Jewish thought as well) was expressed in
five sub-images: (1) the centre of the earth, (2) the highest
elevation in the surrounding area, (3) the meeting-point of the
upper and the lower world, (4) the matrix of the created world,
and (5) the source of nourishment for the world and its inhabitants.
Such images are indeed found in Jewish-Hellenistic literature; they
represent there the city of Jerusalem and the Temple which is regarded as the heart of the city. This description is also found
in ancient maps of the Land of Israel; once again, more as a concept than as a reflection of geographic reality.

The idea emerges in the Letter of Aristeas (83) in the portrayal of Jerusalem as viewed by a Diaspora Jew who made a pilgrimage to the Holy City: "When we arrived (in the land of the
Jews) we saw the city situated in the middle (or in the centre) of
the whole of Judaea on the top of a mountain of considerable alti-
tude" (Charles, II,103). A similar description comes in the Ethiopic
Book of Enoch (26:1-6) in the course of the narrative of Enoch's
journey through the universe: "And I went from there to the middle
of the earth, and I saw a blessed place in which there were trees
with branches abiding and blooming of a dismembered tree. And I
saw a holy mountain, and underneath the mountain to the east there
was a stream and it flowed to the south. And I saw towards the east
another mountain higher than this, and between them a deep and narrow ravine: in it also ran a stream underneath the mountain,"
(Charles, II, 205). The author resorts to similar language in
his description of the site of Gehinnom (90:26): "a like abyss
was opened in the midst of the earth, full of fire" (Charles, II,
259). Likewise, Philo of Alexandria pictures Jerusalem as being
in the centre of the world (Legatio ad Gaium 37,294). The identical
conception, though focused on the Temple rather than on the city,
is employed by Hectaeus of Abdera (c. 300 B.C.E.), as cited by
Josephus Flavius (Contra Apionem, I, 197 ff.). In his description
of the Jews and their land, Hectaeus notes that in addition to

many fortresses and villages in different parts of the country there is one fortified city called Jerusalem, and "nearly in the centre of the city" stands the Temple, (LCL I,243).

The term tabbūr hā'āres, i.e., omphalos, is found in Josephus's own description of Judaea on the eve of the rebellion against the Romans (J.W. 3. 3, 5:51-52): "In breadth it stretches from the river Jordan to Joppa. The city of Jerusalem lies at its very centre, for which reason the town has sometimes, not inaptly, been called the 'navel' of the country" (LCL, II, 591). It is impossible to determine with precision whether the word "country" (chōra) signifies here Judaea or the world as a whole. It appears that Josephus fused two conceptions. One of these is already apparent in the Book of Jubilees (8:19) as an early midrash on Gen 10:25: "for in his days the earth was divided ..." In the division of the world among the sons of Noah, the central expanse falls to the lot of Shem, who "knew that the Garden of Eden is the holy of holies, and the dwelling of the Lord, and Mt. Sinai the centre of the desert, and Mt. Zion the centre of the navel of the earth: these three were created as holy places facing one another." (Charles, I,26).

The identification of the central portion of the world as its "navel" is often found in rabbinic literature, occasionally with an abstraction of its primary meaning. In a midrash on the various names of the city Tiberias, a connection is struck with the term tibbūr: "And why is it called Tiberias? Because it is situated in the very centre (tibbūr) of the land of Israel" (Bab. Tal. Meg. 6a). In Sanhedrin 37a (Cant 7:3) "Your navel is a rounded bowl..." is expounded as follows: "'Thy navel' -- that is the Sanhedrin. Why was it called 'navel'? -- Because it sat at the navel (tibbūr) of the world." Rabbi Shelomo Yitzhaki (Rashi) ad loc. explains "the Temple is in the centre of the world." According to Jellinek, the Hellenistic basis of the image of the navel is evident in a late midrash which reads: "'In wisdom God founded the earth ...' The Holy One Blessed Be He created the world like the infant of a

woman.  In the beginning a new-born develops from the navel and
extends from there.  What is the earth's navel?  This is Jerusalem.
And its central point is the altar.  And why was it called the
foundation stone?  Because from it the entire world was established."  (Bet HaMidrash, V,63)  This midrash is certainly tied to a
similar one found in the Tanhuma (ed. Buber, p.78):  "Just as the
navel is placed in the centre of the man, so the land of Israel is
the navel of the world, as it is written 'who dwell at the centre
(tabbûr) of the earth' (Ezek 38:12).  The Land of Israel is at
the mid-point of the world, and Jerusalem in the middle of the
Land of Israel, and the Temple in the middle of Jerusalem, and
the Sanctuary in the middle of the Temple, and the Ark in the middle of the Sanctuary, and before the Sanctuary is the foundation
stone from which the world was established."[10]  This midrash implies
that already in those days the accepted interpretation of tabbûr
in the text of Ezekiel was as corresponding to Jerusalem, the
centre of the Land of Israel.  Wensinck's claim that the idea of
the "navel" is as widespread in Jewish tradition as in the traditions
of other peoples is based largely upon evidence of this sort.[11]
But since he bases his assumption solely on post-biblical witnesses,
no support can be derived from them for the interpretation of the
term tabbûr in the biblical literature.  Seeligmann was undoubtedly
correct in observing "that the concept of the 'navel of the earth'
in later Judaism originated in Greek mythography which characterizes
the centre of the world by the term omphalos.  Jewish-Hellenistic
diaspora literature, conferred upon the mythographic motif a rationalistic dimension so as to present Jerusalem as the centre of the
world, at a time when the city served as a pilgrimage centre for
Jews from all over the world."[12]

The foregoing discussion makes clear that the biblical term
tabbûr is to be explained neither through conjectured mythic parallels from cultures of the ancient Near East, which themselves
are not above doubt,[13] nor through derivation from rabbinic tabbûr/

t̲i̲b̲b̲û̲r̲ or the LXX rendering o̲m̲p̲h̲a̲l̲o̲s̲.  In order to establish the
term's actual meaning we must turn to motifs in biblical literature
which resemble those present in the relevant passages from the
Books of Judges and Ezekiel and to expressions synonymous with
the images found there.


III


It is desirable that we open the comparative inner-biblical
discussion with the passage from the Book of Ezekiel, reasoning a̲
m̲a̲i̲o̲r̲i̲ a̲d̲ m̲i̲n̲u̲s̲, for even those who hesitate to establish a mythological association of the term t̲a̲b̲b̲û̲r̲ h̲ā̲ʾā̲r̲e̲s̲ in the Abimelech episode (Judg 9:37) cast little doubt upon its presence in Ezekiel 38
where the futuristic assault of Gog on Israel and Jerusalem is related.  The passage reads as follows:

10. "Thus says the Lord God:  On that day thoughts will
come into your mind, and you will devise an evil scheme

11. and say, 'I will go up against the land of unwalled
villages; and I will fall upon the quiet people who
dwell securely, all of them dwelling without walls,
and having no bars or gates';

12. to seize spoil and carry off plunder; to assail the
waste places now inhabited, and the people who were
gathered from the nations, who have gotten cattle and
goods, who dwell at t̲a̲b̲b̲û̲r̲ h̲ā̲ʾā̲r̲e̲s̲.

The Jerusalem Targum translates t̲a̲b̲b̲û̲r̲ as t̲o̲k̲p̲a̲, and the Peschitta
renders s̲u̲p̲r̲a̲; these renderings seem close to the meaning at hand.
As against this, the LXX translates the term - o̲m̲p̲h̲a̲l̲o̲s̲, and the
Vulgate - u̲m̲b̲i̲l̲i̲c̲u̲s̲ t̲e̲r̲r̲a̲e̲.  The medieval commentators explain
the phrase similarly, without doubt in the wake of its rabbinic
usage.  Thus R. David Kimhi (and other traditional commentaries):
"The Land of Israel is called t̲a̲b̲b̲û̲r̲ h̲ā̲ʾā̲r̲e̲s̲ for it is in the mid-

dle of the world, just as the navel is in the middle of the body."
Rashi combined this interpretation with that of the Targum; "on
the height and strength of the land as the navel is in the middle
of the man and slopes down on all sides."

The LXX (and the Vulgate) are responsible for the tendency of
most modern commentators to perceive in the text an expression of
the mythic belief that Mt. Zion and the city of Jerusalem stand in
the centre of the Land of Israel and of the world as a whole.  The
most recent commentator on the Book of Ezekiel, W. Zimmerli, adopts
a cautious stance on the matter, observing that in the book generally
and in the Vision of the Temple (chaps. 40-48), indeed, throughout
the Bible, Jerusalem is not presented as the heart of either Israel
or the world.  He sides, nevertheless, with the opinion that the
passage before us does not speak of a war like any other, but of
the war to be waged "am Ort der Mitte der Welt."[14]  This explanation
remains unsubstantiated by the text, as a rigorous inquiry will
demonstrate.

Since we were aided neither by the etymological investigation
nor by comparative research in explicating tabbûr hā'āres (Ezek
38:12), let us now turn to an examination of the problem from the
standpoint of the context and the structure of the passage.  Zimmerli defines the unit Ezek 38:10-13 as an expansion of the basic
speech concerning Gog (vv. 1-9) and sees in the remaining text of
the chapter three interpretative additions appended in the course
of time, vv. 14-16; v. 17; vv. 18-23.  The principal prophecy is
continued in chap. 39:1-5.  Ezek 38:10-13 is therefore perceived
as an independent unit.  I accept this argument with two reservations:  (1) vv. 14-16 are not an independent unit but must be
discussed in connection with vv. 8-9, which are related to them
by content and language;  (2) the basic address ends with v. 7
and not v. 9 (against the Massoretic division).  These suggestions
are strenghtened by a structural examination of the passage, which
reveals several literary-technical means employed by the editor
in his redaction of the Gog episode:  summary line, inversion,

conflated phrases in which each of the components is derived from a different constituent sub-unit, and the <u>inclusio</u> pattern.[15]

Summary Line: This method of signifying the close of a unit in a sequence of passages which were combined to form a comprehensive complex is applied here to the passage as a whole as well as to constituent components. The Vision of the Dry Bones (chap. 37), which directly precedes the complex of prophecies concerning Gog, ends with the closing formula: "Then the nations will know that I the Lord sanctify (m$^e$qadeš) Israel, when my sanctuary (miqdašî) is in the midst of them for evermore" (37:28). An almost identical formula is found at the conclusion of the prophecies concerning Gog: "...and through them I have vindicated my holiness (w$^e$niqdaštî) in the sight of many nations. Then they shall know that I am the Lord their God ..." (39:27-28). This very closing formula further serves within the complex to distinguish secondary units whose definition will be discussed below: "...that the nations may know me, when through you, O Gog, I vindicate my holiness (b$^e$hiqadšî) before their eyes" (38:16); "So I will show my greatness and my holiness (w$^e$hitqadištî) and make myself known in the eyes of many nations" (38:23); "... and the nations shall know that I am the Lord, the Holy One (qādôs) in Israel" (39:7).

Inclusio Pattern: The sequence of this method lies in the author's (or editor's) taking up at the end of a passage in similar terms what had been stated in its beginning, so much so that the two elements enclose the text between them in the manner of brackets. Thus the opening and closing formulae delineate the extent of a literary unit as conceived by the author or of a self-contained passage which an editor inserted secondarily into a given literary complex. By the discernment of this method, the passage 38:10-14 emerges as an originally independent unit whose extent is marked by the closing formula 38:15-16, which employs terms nearly identical with those found in the opening formula 38:8-9.

Opening Formula (38:8-9)

    (A)  After many days you will be mustered:
          in the latter years you will go against the land
          that is restored from war, the land where people
             were gathered from many nations
          upon the mountains of Israel, which had been a
             continual waste;
          its people were brought out from the nations and
             now dwell securely, all of them.

    (B)  You will advance, coming on like a storm, you will
          be like a cloud covering the land.

    (C)  you and all your hordes, and many people with you.

Closing Formula (38:15-16)

          and come from your place out of the uttermost parts
             of the north,

    (C)  you and many peoples with you,
          all of them riding on horses, a great host, a mighty
             army;

    (B)  you will come up against my people Israel, like a
          cloud covering the land.

    (A)  In the latter days
          I will bring you against my land ...

The principal elements of the closing formula are presented in a precisely chiastic order in relation to their parallels in the opening formula, to the exclusion of v. 8, which will be discussed below, thereby illustrating the technique of inversion.

    The parallelism of the opening and closing formulae, with slight lexical alterations, is likely to play a major role in the mutual clarification of exegetically difficult expressions. In the present instance it can be shown by the parallelism that the phrase "in the latter years" (v. 8) is synonymous with "in the latter days"

(v. 16) and that both connote "after many days" (v. 8). Likewise, the idiom "my land" (v. 16) illumines the phrase "the land that is restored from war ..." (v. 8). This important interpretative principle shall figure prominently in our discussion of the meaning of the term tabbûr.

Inclusio patterning is also present within the unit circumscribed by the bracketing vv. 8-9 and vv. 15-16. This technique allows us to recognize 38:12-13 as a secondary unit whose unique vocabulary sets it apart from the immediate context:

    12. "to seize spoil
        and carry off plunder ...
        who have gotten cattle and goods ..."
    13. "(Have you come) to seize spoil ...
        to carry off plunder ...
        to take away cattle and goods ...?"

In view of the foregoing analysis, we discern the following structure in the unit 38:10-14, bracketed by the opening (vv. 8-9) and closing (vv. 15-16) formulae:

Opening Formula

    8. After many days you will be mustered; in the latter years
        you will go against the land that is restored from war,
        the land where people were gathered from many nations
        upon the mountains of Israel, which had been a continual
        waste;
        its people were brought from the nations and now dwell
        securely, all of them.
    9. You will advance, coming on like a storm, you will be
        like a cloud covering the land,
        you and all your hordes, and many people with you.

Introduction

    10. Thus says the Lord God:
        On that day thoughts will come into your mind,
        and you will device an evil scheme

Strophe A
> 11. and say, 'I will go up against the land of unwalled villages;
> I will come upon the quiet people who dwell securely,
> all of them dwelling without walls, and having no
> bars or gates;'

Strophe B$^1$
> 12. to seize spoil and carry off plunder;
> to assail the waste places which are now inhabited, and
> the people who were gathered from the nations,
> who have gotten cattle and goods,
> who dwell at tabbûr hā ares.

Strophe B$^2$
> 13. Sheba and Dedan and the merchants of Tarshish and all its
> villages will say to you,
> 'Have you come to seize spoil?
> Have you assembled your hosts to carry off plunder, to
> carry away silver and gold,
> to take away cattle and goods, to seize great spoil?'

Conclusion
> 14. Therefore, son of man, prophesy, and say to Gog,
> Thus says the Lord God:
> On that day when my people Israel are dwelling securely,
> you will know

Closing Formula
> 15. and come from your place out of the uttermost parts of
> the north, you and many peoples with you,
> all of them riding on horses, a great host, a mighty army;
> 16. you will go up against my people Israel, like a cloud
> covering the land.
> In the latter days I will bring you against my land,
> that the nations may know me, when through you I vindicate
> my holiness before their eyes, O Gog.

This schema reveals four distinct elements that compose the
complex 38:10-14: (1) Introduction, v. 10; (2) Strophe A, the

speech of Gog, v. 11; (3) Strophes $B^{1,2}$, encompassing a dual interpretation of Gog's evil intentions: in the words of the Lord
or his prophet, V. 12, and in the words of Sheba and Dedan, etc.,
v. 13; (4) Conclusion, which completes the introduction, v. 14.
The passage as a whole is bracketed by the opening (vv. 8-9) and
the closing (vv. 15-16) formulae.

The author-editor emphasizes the contextual continuity of
these distinct elements through conflated phrases each of whose
components comprises a different constituent subunit: The parallels between the opening and closing formulae have already been
observed, as have the resemblances between the beginning and end
of Strophes $B^1$ and $B^2$. The introduction and conclusion, moreover,
are linked through the formula "Thus says the Lord God: on that
day ..." (vv. 10,14); whereas the word tēda$^c$ ("you will know,"
v. 14) both stands in opposition to and completes the text "thoughts
will come into your mind, and you will devise an evil scheme" (v.
10). Common to Strophe A and to the closing formula are the
phrases "I will go up against the land" (v. 11) and "you will go
up against my people" (v. 16), as well as the terms "I will come"
(v. 11), "and (you will) come" (v. 15), "I will bring you against
my land" (v. 16). The connection between Strophe A and the Conclusion will be discussed below.

It is noteworthy that Strophes $B^{1,2}$ share no linguistic resemblance with either the introduction or the conclusion; nor,
for that matter, with Strophe A, thus signifying the distinctiveness of vv. 12-13 ($B^{1,2}$) within the complex 38:10-14. On the other
hand, the phrase "the waste places which are now inhabited, and
the people who were gathered from the nations," which sets off v.
12 from v. 13, indicates the relation between Strophe $B^1$ and the
opening formula: "the land where the people were gathered from
many nations upon the mountains of Israel, which had been a continual waste; its people were brought out from the nations ..."
(v. 8). At the same time, the phrase hiqhaltā q$^e$hālekā ("Have you

assembled your hosts"), whereby v. 13 is set off from v. 12, echoes
the expressions qāhāl rāb (v. 4) and qᵉhālekā haniqhālîm (v. 7) of
the basic speech concerning Gog, as well as qāhāl gādôl of the
closing formula (v. 15). It follows that the opening stich of
v. 13 ("Sheba and Dedan and the merchants of Tarshish and all its
villages"), which has no parallel in v. 12, must be seen as an
allusion to the similar expression in the basic speech: "Persia,
Cush, and Put are with them ... Gomer and all his hordes ..." (vv.
5-6).


IV


More crucial to our concern, viz. the clarification of the
term tabbûr, are those phrases which give expression to a central
and recurring theme in the prophecies concerning Gog, the security
of Israel on returning to her land. This idea receives added emphasis in the appendices of chapter 38 to the basic speech. It
might be said that the phrase "the people Israel dwelt securely
in its land," with such linguistics variations as will be discussed, is the leitmotif that characterizes most of the units con-
stituting the complex 38:8-16: opening formula, "(its people were
brought out from the nations) and now dwell securely, all of them"
(v. 8); Strophe A, "(I will come upon) the quiet people who dwell
securely" and the accompanying "all of them dwelling without walls,
and having no bars or gates" (v. 11); "(on that day) when my people
Israel are dwelling securely" (v. 14). An echo of this phrase is
heard as well in the close of the Prophecy of Return (39:25-26)
which concludes the complex of prophecies concerning Gog: "when
they dwell securely in their land with none to make them afraid"
(v. 26). This expression is retained yet once more, by principle
of opposition, at the end of the basic speech: "I will send fire on
Magog and on those who dwell securely in the coastlands" (39:6).

We have before us a description of a tranquil settlement that
is not dependent upon fortifications to ensure its security, because
it is defended by the Lord.  This settlement stands "upon the mountains of Israel" (38:8, 21; 39:2,4,17) or "on the Land of Israel"
(38:8,9,16,18,19; 39:12,14,16,26,28), which is the land sanctified
by the God of Israel and not to be polluted (38:12-16).  It is
worthy of note that in all of this we have found no allusion to
the idea that this land is the centre of the world or that Jerusalem
is the heart of the land.

Due to the wide currency of the theme of "the security of Israel" in the different components of the complex of prophecies concerning Gog, it is surprising that the idea does not find expression
in Strophes B[1,2]; at least not in the sort of explicit language cited
above.  For although these strophes are distinguished from the other
components of the complex, the editor sought to fasten them in the
literary continuum by means of conflated phrases, similar to those
which appear in other units.  This leads us to examine the phrase
"who dwell at tabbûr hā̄āres," the root of the problem reviewed
here.  The other phrases connected with the verb "to dwell" (yšb),
as discussed above, are all concerned with the secure dwelling of
the people Israel in their land or on the mountains of Israel.  It
may be conjectured, therefore, that the unexplained tabbûr also par-
takes of this sense, whether being truly synonymous with the notion
of security (bth) or signifying an area of land regarded as more
secure than others in the face of the attacks of an enemy.  The term
tabbûr is clarified through the adjacent description of the people
dwelling there as those "who have gotten cattle and goods."  For
tabbûr bears upon that phrase just as in v. 11 the expression "all
of them dwelling without walls, and having no bars or gates" serves
to interpret "the land of unwalled villages" and "the quiet people
who dwell securely."

In the description one hears an echo of a similar image in Ezek
28:25-26, couched in almost identical language:

> Thus says the Lord God:  When I gather the house of Israel
> from the peoples among whom they are scattered, and manifest
> my holiness in them in the sight of the nations, then they
> shall dwell in their own land ...  And they shall dwell
> securely in it, and they shall build houses and plant vine-
> yards.  They shall dwell securely ...

It appears that these phrases are formulaic expressions in biblical
literature, and not only in the Book of Ezekiel, which express the
idea of an open and secure settlement in a spacious location that
lives at peace with its neighbours and fears not for its future--
until destruction suddenly descends upon it.  In Jeremiah's prophecies against the nations, the campaign of Nebuchadnezzar king of
Babylon against Kedar and the kingdoms of Hazor is described in
similar images:  "Rise up, advance against a nation at ease, that
dwells securely, says the Lord, that has no gates or bars, that
dwells alone.  Their camels shall become booty, their herds of
cattle a spoil" (Jer 49:31-32).  We may also compare the ancient
tradition concerning the inhabitants of the entrance of Gedor, who
were conquered by the Simeonites seeking pasture for their flocks,
as related in the lists of genealogists in the Book of Chronicles:
"there they found rich, good pasture, and the land was very broad,
quiet, and peaceful" (1 Chr 4:40).  The author then proceeds to explain that "the former inhabitants there belonged to Ham," implying
that they were not from the autochthonous population and did not
mingle with their neighbours.  Likewise, the tradition concerning
the conquest of Laish by the Danites in the Book of Judges exhibits
both contextual and linguistic similarities, to the point of employing phrases like those found in Ezekiel and in the above-mentioned parallels:  "(they) saw the people who were there, how they dwelt
in security ... quiet and secure ... and how they were far from the
Sidonians and had no dealings with anyone"[17] (Judg 18:7, 27-28);
and again:  "When you go, you will come to a secure people.  The
land is broad ... a place where there is no lack of anything that
is in the earth" (Judg 18:10).

It becomes apparent that the term tabbûr hā'āres in Ezek 38:
12 is simply one other expression which defines the condition of
the people that returns to its land, "the waste places which are
now inhabited," and occupies itself with the raising of livestock
on sites needing neither fortifications nor systems of defence,
certain in their security. This vision contains nothing of the
idea of the "centre of the earth" or "the centre of the land of
Israel." It is even doubtful whether there is any suggestion that
this settlement stands on a high mountain. Au contraire, for a
settlement "on the mountains of Israel," mentioned intermittently
in the Gog passage, certainly does not refer to the peaks of the
mountains, but to settlements on the terraces or hollows between
them. This claim is strengthened by the parallelism between tabbûr
hā'āres and 'eres p'rāzôt ("the land of unwalled villages," v. 11).
In the two latest appearances of the term p'rāzôt in the Bible,
the same characteristics and traits are prominent as in Ezekiel.
In Zech 2:8 the sense is of a comfortable expanse for the raising
of cattle: "Jerusalem will be inhabited as villages without walls,
because of the multitude of men and cattle in it," and in Esth 9:19
"the Jews of the villages, who live in the open towns" are mentioned
as a type of community different from those of the fortified towns
like Susa the capital (v. 18). It is possible that we should consider as well the term p'rāzôn in the Song of Deborah (Judg 5:7)
in this light. Although the etymological derivation of prz has not
been sufficiently clarified, the most likely suggestion is that its
meaning corresponds to Arabic farez which denotes a hollow between
mountains,[18] i.e., sheltered valleys[19] well-suited for the raising
of livestock, whose location may evoke a comparison with the navel
in the human body.[20]

In summary, the phrase tabbûr hā'āres in Ezek 38:12 is not to
be explained by extra-biblical parallels indicating an elevated
site, a mountain peak that is the centre of the surrounding expanse,
be it the Land of Israel or the entire earth; nor is it to be bur-
dened with mythic ideas concerning the centrality of Jerusalem and

the Temple in the universe. Similar expressions in the immediate
literary context are in parallel biblical texts not only serve to
blunt the purported mythological point of the term; they actually
bring us to a realistic topographic-ecological interpretation of
it.

The meaning of the term tabbûr hā᾽āres which emerges from the
analysis of Ezek 38:12 is applicable also to the other occurrence
of the phrase in the Book of Judges:

> And when Gaal saw the men, he said to Zebul, 'Look, men
> are coming down from the mountain tops!' And Zebul said
> to him, 'You see the shadow of the mountains as if they
> were men.' Gaal spoke again and said, 'Look, men are
> coming down from tabbûr hā᾽āres, and one company is coming
> from the direction of the Diviners' Oak.' (9:36-37)

This text describes the descent of Abimelech's army from the mountain tops, and the division of that army into three companies upon
reaching a sort of plateau in order to attack the city below. Thus
explained Rabbi Isaiah of Trani, "a place evenly between the cities
from which one could head to this city and one to that, like a
cross-roads."[21] N.H. Tur-Sinai[22] justifiably suggested that we
understand tabbûr hā᾽āres here in the sense of plateau, i.e., the
level land at the midway point of a mountain.[23]

The trend to discover in the Bible vestiges of the omphalos
myth in connection with Jerusalem is not limited to occurrences of
the word tabbûr. Texts which speak of Jerusalem as standing b$^e$tôk/
b$^e$qereb the nations or the land also have been interpreted like
tabbûr hā᾽āres in Ezek 38:12. Principal among them is Ezek 5:5:
"This is Jerusalem; I have set her in the centre (b$^e$tôk) of the
nations, with countries round about her." Zimmerli, ad loc, with
many others, discerns in the verse once again in the theme of the
omphalos. In his opinion, Ezekiel employs here parallelismus mem-
brorum in order to emphasize the distinction of Jerusalem as the
centre of the world of nations. He is then drawn into exaggerated

conjectures, all dependent upon that same text: just as in the Roman Empire all of the roads came together in the Forum of the capital city, and as the kingdom of China perceived itself as the "Middle Kingdom," so did the prophet envision Jerusalem as the focus of the world. This status did not come to the city in any natural manner, but through the choice of God: "I have set her in the centre of the nations."[24] In order to refute this argument, it suffices to point out passages in the Book of Ezekiel in which tôk / b$^e$tôk are employed without implying in any way the meaning of "centre:" "They also shall go down to Sheol with it, to those who are slain by the sword; yea, those who dwelt under its shadow among (b$^e$tôk) the nations" (38:17); and its parallel "You shall be brought down with the trees of Eden to the nether world; you shall lie among (b$^e$tôk) the uncircumcised, with those who are slain by the sword" (38:18); cf. 5:2; 20:8; 43:7; Isa 24:13, et al.

V

Despite the weakness of the proofs adduced in support of the conjectured identification of tabbûr hā'āres with the Greek omphalos, and the accompanying mythic implications, this supposition has become a tenet of modern biblical study, especially in commentaries to the Books of Judges and Ezekiel.[25] With the emergence of comparative research this emphasis has grown even more pronounced. Motifs assuredly drawn from the intellectual orbit of the Canaanites or the Jebusites, were discovered in the biblical description of Jerusalem, without any decisive demonstration. In his work, Myth and Reality in the Old Testament, B.Childs states that the Israelites perceived in Mt. Zion the foundation stone of the world; the umbilical cord connecting the heavens, the earth, and the underworld; the centre of the earth, which is likened to a disk; the cosmic tree

as well as the new Garden of Eden.[26]  S. Terrien went one step further, claiming: "In all probability, the myth of the navel of the
earth, far from being an incidental aspect of worship at the temple
of Jerusalem, constitutes in effect the determining factor which
links together a number of its cultic practices and beliefs that
otherwise appear to be unrelated."[27]  Terrien envisions the myth
of the navel (tabbûr) as the vital common denominator of biblical
thought and ritual.  In its light all becomes explicable:  the cult
of the serpent and of the Underworld in the temple in Jerusalem;
sun-worship; androgynous cultic practices and the institution of
male prostitutes.  Their parallels are widespread, encompassing,
for example, the temple in Delphi.  In Terrien's opinion there
simply can be no overstatement of the influence which this mythic
belief exercised on the faith of Israel in the biblical period and
thereafter.  The idea of omphalos certainly underwent novel interpretation within Israel's intellectual universe.  Through this very
interpretation a mythical view of space was absorbed into a dynamic
theology of time, and the resultant combination became a mainstay
of the ideological principles attached to Mt. Zion and the Temple.[28]

Terrien is forced to admit that "these beliefs do not receive
an explicit formulation in the early traditions concerning the building of the temple."  He nevertheless surmises that "the illusions
found in the pre-exilic psalms and prophets, Ezekiel, and his post-
exilic successors clearly indicate that the acceptance of the omphalos myth, in a modified form, antedates by centuries the testimony of the Chronicler, the post-canonical Jewish literature, the
New Testament, and Christian folklore."[29]

Childs, Terrien, and others have devised motifs, phraseology,
and ideational complexes in abundance as proof of the existence of
the idea of a "world mountain" (Weltberg) identical with the "navel
of the world" in biblical thought.  An examination of the assumed
parallels presented in order to bolster this conjecture, however,
reveal a castle built on sand.  Uncertain terms such as tabbûr and

general idioms like tôk or kereb are the objects of tendentious interpretation based wholly upon the assumption that Israel absorbed
into the very warp and woof of her culture the mythic ideas of other
cultures of the ancient Near East. It is imperative to note that
even the vestiges of Canaanite or Jebusite mythic principles which
took hold in the popular beliefs of various groups and factions
within Israel, or which were received from Mesopotamian religions,
cannot be construed to have served as the basis of Israel's spiritual world or of the belief in the holiness of Jerusalem and Mt.
Zion. This is not to deny that the biblical authors occasionally
historicized mythic elements known from ancient Near Eastern cultures. It is totally unacceptable, though, to hypothesize cultural
transfers except in those instances that can be founded sufficiently
clear literary resemblances. When the linguistic aspect provides
nought but unclear and difficult hints, one cannot depend upon forced
testimony from external sources in order to explain cruxes in the
Bible.

FOOTNOTES

*Translated from the Hebrew by David Satran.

1.  All biblical quotations, with minor variations, are ac-
cording to the Revised Standard Version.  Quotations from the
Apocrypha and Pseudepigrapha follow *The Apocrypha and Pseudepi-
grapha of the Old Testament* (2 vols.; ed. R. H. Charles; Oxford:
Clarendon, 1913).  Citations from Josephus Flavius follow the
Loeb Classical Library edition.

2.  J. Wellhausen, *Reste arabischen Heidentums* (Berlin:  G.
Reimer, 1885) remains the fundamental work in this area.  Cf. M.
Buber, *Königtum Gottes* (Berlin:  Schocken Verlag, 1932).

3.  No etymological derivation of tabbūr is given in W.
Gesenius and F. Buhl, *Hebraeisches und Aramaeisches Handwoerter-
buch ueber das Alte Testament* (17th ed.; Berlin:  Springer Verlag,
1949); L. Koehler and W. Baumgartner, *Lexicon in Veteris Testa-
menti Libros* (Leiden:  E.J.Brill, 1953-58).  A. Kohut, *Aruch Com-
pletum*, seeks to derive the noun "from the Samaritan word t$^e$bar =
Hockpunkt, i.e., an elevated point on the human body" (vol. 4, 13).

4.  J. Boehmer, "Der Gottesberg Tabor," <u>BZ</u> 23 (1935) 33-41;
<u>Idem</u>, <u>ZS</u> 7 (1929) 161-69.

5.  "The Role of the Canaanites in the History of Civilization,"
*The Bible and the Ancient Near East* (ed. G.E. Wright; Garden City,
N.Y.:  Doubleday, 1961) 252 n.7.

6.  D. Winton Thomas, "Mount Tabor, the Meaning of the Name,"
<u>VT</u> 1 (1951) 229-30.

7.  W. Roscher, *Omphalos* (Abh. d. Königl.-Sächs. Gesellsch. d.
Wissenschaften, Phil.-Hist. Klasse, Bd. 29,9; Leipzig:  B. G. Tuebner, 1913) 20.

8.  Cf. *Neue Omphalosstudien*, (Ibid.Bd. 31,1; Leipzig:  B. G.
Tuebner, 1915); *Der Omphalosgedanke bei verschiedenen Volkern, be-
sonders den semitischen* (Sitz. Ber. d. Sächs. Akad. d. Wissensch.,
Bd. 70,2; Leipzig B.G. Teubner, 1918).  Cf. N. V. Herrman, *Omphalos*
(Orbis antiquus 13; Muenster:  Aschendorff, 1959); S. Thompson,
*Motif Index in Folk Literature* (Copenhagen:  Rosenkilde and Bagger,
1955-58) A 875.1, 151,1.

9.  A. J. Wensinck, *The Ideas of the Western Semites Concerning
the Navel of the Earth* (Amsterdam:  Johannes Müller, 1916) xi.

10. M. Gruenbaum, ZDMG 31 (1887) 199; H. Z. Hirschberg, "The Temple Mount in the Arabic Period (638-1099)," *Jerusalem Through the Ages* (ed. J. Aviram; Jerusalem: Israel Exploration Society, 1968) 110 (Hebrew).

11. *Navel of the Earth,* chap. 1.

12. I. L. Seeligmann, "Jerusalem in Jewish-Hellenistic Thought," *Judaea and Jerusalem* (Jerusalem: Israel Exploration Society, 1957) 192-208, esp. 200ff. (Hebrew).

13. R. J. Clifford, *The Cosmic Mountain in Canaan and the Old Testament* (HSM 4; Cambridge, Mass.: Harvard University, 1972) 135, 183.

14. W. Zimmerli, *Ezechiel* (2 vols.; BKAT 13; Neukirchen-Vluyn: Neukirchener Verlag, 1969) 2. 955-57. Zimmerli depends upon the opinions of Roscher, Wensinck, H. Schmidt, *Der heilige Fels in Jerusalem* (Tübingen: J.C.B. Mohn, 1933), and W. Caspari, "tabur-Nabel," ZDMG N.F. 11 (1933) 49ff.

15. These methods of *literary compostion* will be treated in a comprehensive work under preparation. For the present, see S. Talmon and M. Fishbane, "The Structuring of Biblical Books - Studies in the Book of Ezekiel," ASTI 10 (1976) 129-153.

16. Duplication of the combination "to seize spoil ... to carry off plunder" also occurs in Ezek 29:19 and 39:10, and with some variation in 26:12. We might perhaps discern the source of this usage in Isa 10:6. The simple combination "spoil ... plunder" is more common, *vide* Isa 8:1-3; Jer 49:23; Ezek 7:21; Dan 11:24, and cf. Deut 3:7; 20:14; Josh 8:2; Esth 3:13; 8:11; 2 Chr 20:25; 28:8.

17. In the opinion of many critics ꜣaram should be read here, according to context and several ancient versions.

18. Cf. the dictionaries of Brown-Driver-Briggs and Koehler-Baumgartner, s.v. prz.

19. Perhaps we should similarly interpret the expression "Flee, wander far away, dwell in the depths, O inhabitants of Hazor" (Jer 49:30, cf. v. 8).

20. Cf. Maimonides, *Mishneh Torah, Book of Knowledge,* Fundamental Principles of the Torah 4,2: "The nature of fire and air is to ascend from below; that is, from tabbûr hāꜣāreṣ upward towards the sky." Tabbûr hāꜣāreṣ, therefore is a depression, and not an elevated site.

21. *Commentary on the Prophets and Hagiographa of Rabbi Isaiah of Trani, the Elder* (ed. A.J. Werthheimer; Jerusalem: Katav wᵉSepher, 1959) 16.

22. N. H. Tur-Sinai, "Tabbûr and Bāmāh," *The Language and the Book* (Jerusalem: Bialik Institute, 1955) 233ff. (Hebrew).

23. J. M. Wilkie ("The Peshitta Translation of Tabbûr Hāʾāres in Judges IX 37," VT 1 [1951] 144) suggests the Syriac reading tuwnh instead of dʾrsʿ which appears but once in Judg 14:18 and which C.F. Burney also emends to tuwnh. Wilkie translates the phrase "the inner chamber of the land."

24. Zimmerli, *Ezechiel*, 1.133.

25. E.g. M Dahood, *Psalms 101-150* (AB 17a; Garden City, N.Y.: Doubleday, 1970) 142; W. D. Davies, *The Gospel and the Land* (Berkeley: University of California, 1973) 6ff.; T. H. Gaster, *Thespis* (Garden City, N.Y.: Doubleday, 1961) 183. A notable exception to this rule is the careful entry by D. Sperling ("Navel of the Earth," IDBSup [1976] 621-23) which came to my attention only after the completion of this article.

26. B. S. Childs, *Myth and Reality in the Old Testament* (SBT 27; London: SCM Press, 1960) 83-93.

27. S. Terrien, "The Omphalos Myth and Hebrew Religion," VT 20 (1970) 317-38.

28. Ibid., 338.

29. Ibid., 319-20.

# GNOSTICS AND THE INSPIRATION OF THE OLD TESTAMENT

Robert M. Grant

Early in the Christian era many Gnostics treated the OT much
as Hellenized Jews and Christians treated it. That is to say,
they took literally what they thought was clear and in agreement
with their religious outlook and they took allegorically what was
obscure and not in agreement. For such persons the inspiration of
the OT books was rarely a problem; more often, it was a basic assumption. Debates were carried on over the extent of the canon,
i.e. over what books were inspired and what books were not. But
this debate usually concerned only books relatively peripheral,
not the primary writings such as the Pentateuch or the major and
minor prophets.

The idea of discontinuity between the OT and some later revelation does not seem to have troubled many Christians. It is implicit, however, in the Gospel of Matthew, composed after the destruction of the temple in Jerusalem, in such sayings of Jesus as
"I came not to destroy but to complete" and those in the form "it
was said...but I say." Such sayings (along with "Moses for the
hardness of your hearts...") were taken with full seriousness by
Christian Gnostics after the second Jewish war of 132-135, and two
main conclusions were drawn. First, there were those who had come
to believe that the world was created by the devil and that he was
the author of the OT. Creation by the devil was upheld by the Car-
pocratians and legislation by him, by unnamed Gnostics mentioned
by the Valentinian teacher Ptolemaeus.[1] Ptolemaeus, on the other
hand, placed the creator or demiurge, who also gave the law, between
the good Father and his adversary the devil. He ascribed three

levels of the law. It consisted of the law of God the creator himself, the law given by Moses, and the additions made by the elders.[2]
Obviously the three are related to Valentinian theology, but they
also have a more objective basis in what Jesus taught according to
Matthew. Ptolemaeus' older contemporary, Marcion, who like Ptolemaeus taught at Rome, did not investigate such subtle points but
simply wrote a book of Antitheses to show that the creator-god of
the OT was merely just, while the Father of Jesus was the only good
God. This distinction, as I have suggested, was based on the rabbinic and Philonic explanation of the use of the names Yahweh (read
as Adonai and translated as kyrios) and Elohim (God, theos) in the
OT.[3] Jewish exegetes of the Bible did not, of course, suppose that
there were two gods. This is the Gnostic contribution.

Many Gnostic groups held that the world had been created not
by one demiurge but by a group of six or seven spirits acting in
concert. They believed, accordingly, that the prophets and their
prophecies had been inspired by these spirits. Such a doctrine is
ascribed by Irenaeus--apparently in reliance on an earlier, though
not necessarily more reliable, source--to the followers of Simon
Magus, Saturninus of Antioch, and Basilides of Alexandria.[4] Further
details are given for the views of Saturninus and Basilides. Saturninus held that some prophecies were inspired by Satan, while
Basilides taught that the basic law was given by the prince of the
powers, the one who led the people out of the land of Egypt (as Exodus indicates).[5] Presumably such attributions were based, at least
in part on the divine names in the OT, as we shall see in certain
other cases.

In the Apocryphon of John, a Gnostic book now known from four
Coptic versions and used in another form by Irenaeus, we find criticism of "Moses." Was the Spirit of God (the Mother) "agitated
over the waters" (Gen 1:2)? No, she went to and fro in the darkness
of ignorance. In the case of Adam, it was "not as Moses said, 'He
caused him to fall asleep' (Gen 2:21), but he covered his perception

with a veil." Moses' story about Adam's rib is also wrong, literally; so is the notion that Noah "hid himself in an ark."[6] These
passages in Moses (and others) had already aroused the curiosity
and the allegorizing skill of people like Philo.[7] They were re-
jecting the literal meaning but they did not call Moses wrong.
The new Gnostic boldness may be Christian in origin. Of course
when Isa 6:10 is ascribed to Ialdabaoth in the Apocryphon this goes
beyond Christianity.[8]

Marcion's discipline Apelles also criticized Moses and en-
deavored to give mathematical and philosophical proofs that he was
wrong. The ark was too small for the animals that went into it.
The creation narrative in Genesis is full of philosophical-theo-
logical absurdities and contradictions. Because of these, he tri-
umphantly ended each discussion with the claim that the theological
idea or the story "is false; therefore the writing is not from God."[9]

Such criticisms were picked up in the Clementine homilies, where
we read that Moses himself certainly did not write Genesis because
it describes his death. Actually "the law of God through Moses was
given to seventy wise men to be handed down orally." It was written
down about 500 years later and burned under Nebuchadnezzar. In fact,
it was lost many times. That is why it is full of interpolations.[10]
This relatively rational theory is combined with the polemical view
that the one who interpolated was "the evil one," i.e. the devil.[11]
It should be noted that just as Ptolemaeus relied on the teaching
of Jesus for his theory of levels, so the Clementine author relies
on Jesus for a test of what has been interpolated and what has not.[12]

The teaching of Jesus contradicts much of the OT picture of
God, and indeed he said that "many prophets and kings desired to
see what you see and hear what you hear."[13] Epiphanius wrongly
claims that (Pseudo-) Clement praises the OT prophets. In his
view the Clementine literature had nothing to do with the Ebionites. He was wrong.[14] But he does give information about the
Ebionite view of the OT. The Ebionites recognized Abraham, Isaac,
and Jacob, also Moses and Aaron, and Joshua just as Moses' suc-

cessor.[15] (This looks much like the Samaritan canon, but doubtless the Ebionites could refer to Exod 3:15 for the God of Abraham, Isaac, Jacob, and Moses, to Exod 4:15 for Moses and Aaron, and to Deut 31:23 for Joshua.) On the other hand, they firmly rejected Samson, David and Solomon (and, a fortiori, Samuel, who anointed David), Elijah, and Elisha. More than that, they explicitly anathematized the major prophets: Isaiah, Jeremiah, Ezekiel, and Daniel. Indeed, we are told that they condemned all the prophets, i.e. the minor ones as well as the majors.[16] According to Epiphanius, if you asked one of them a question as to how he knew his own ideas were right he would say, "Christ revealed it to me."[17] This could mean either that he was getting personal revelations or, more probably in the light of Ebionitism, that he had studied the teaching of Christ in the gospels.

The Ebionites were not the only critics of the prophets. The Gnostic--specifically, Naassene--teacher Justin wrote a book called Baruch in which he explained that the hostile serpent Naas had kept the message of Moses and the other prophets from getting through, and indeed their source of revelation, Elohim and his servant Baruch, had been obscured by the serpent and its allies. The prophets were able to express hints about the true gospel but the hints could be understood by Gnostics only, people who could understand what Isaiah meant when he said, "Hear, heaven, and give ear, earth; the Lord has spoken," or "Israel did not know me" (Isa 1:2-3), or Hosea in the words, "Take for yourself a wife of fornication, for the earth has fornicated in fornication from behind the Lord" (Hos 1:2). According to Hippolytus, these Gnostics had many books in which they went through all the prophetic writings.[18]

Perhaps the most interesting example of Gnostic criticism of the inspiration of the Old Testament is to be found in a relatively early system related to the Apocryphon of John and described by Irenaeus. As in the Apocryphon, there are six or seven planetary spirits.[19] Irenaeus assigns names and effects as follows:

(1)  Ialdabaoth:   Moses, Joshua, Amos, Habakkuk
(2)  Iao:          Samuel, Nathan, Jonah, "Michaeas"
(3)  Sabaoth:      Elijah, Joel, Zechariah
(4)  Adonai:       Isaiah, Ezekiel, Jeremiah, Daniel
(5)  "Eloeus":     Tobias, Haggai
(6)  "Horeus":     "Michaeas," Nahum
(7)  Astaphaeus:   Ezra, Zephaniah

(1)  Obviously the Pentateuch or, indeed, the Hexateuch has to be
assigned to the prince of the spirits.  In the Apocryphon and elsewhere he is the creator-god, the guide of the Israelites at the
Exodus, and the legislator.  In addition, according to Irenaeus'
source, Ialdabaoth chose Abraham and gave him a covenant and a
promise.  There was a good reason for assigning the inspiration of
Amos to the same deity:  Amos refers to Yahweh's creating the world
(5:8), his guidance at the Exodus (2:10), and his giving the law
(2:4).  It is hard to see, however, why Habakkuk was assigned to
the same inspirer.  Was it because both Amos (4:2) and Habakkuk
(1:15) compared the fate of men to their being caught with fish-
hooks?
(2)  Samuel and Nathan, both associated with King David, spoke of
Yahweh--as did other prophets!  But the Gnostic exegete is trying
to create a grid of inspiration, so to speak.  There is some point
in including Jonah here, for in Jonah 1-3 non-Hebrews use the name
Elohim, while the prophet Jonah knows that God is Yahweh (the text
of chapter 4 is corrupt).  But then we are given the name Michaeas.
If this means Micah, there is nothing distinctive about the choice.
(3)  The name Sabaoth is absent from the books Genesis through
Judges.  On the other hand, it is clear that Elijah referred on
special occasions to Yahweh Sabaoth (1 Kgs 18:15; 19:10, 14).  (A
fortiori Sabaoth spoke through Elisha, Elijah's successor.)  Yahweh
Sabaoth is notably named in Zechariah 1 and 14, and hosts occur in
Joel 2:2-11 and 4:14.

(4)  The instruments of Adonai were Isaiah, Jeremiah, Ezekiel, and Daniel, i.e. the major prophets.  Key passages "prove" the point. Isaiah 6:1 tells us that "in the year of King Uzziah's death I saw Adonai Yahweh," while Jeremiah addresses God as "Adonai Yahweh" (1:6) and the spirit that inspired Ezekiel told him to speak for "Adonai Yahweh" (2:4, etc.).  In Dan 1:2 the "read" name of God, Adonai, has come into the written text--as Gnostics noticed.

(5)  Something seems to have gone wrong in regard to Eloeus or Eloah.  Certainly the assignation of Tobit to his spirit (Elohim) is right, but then Haggai is wrong, for the name frequently used by Haggai is Yahweh Sabaoth.  Perhaps the error arose when Job was dropped.  In Job the name Eloah is frequent.

(6) and (7)  Here, it must be confessed, it is hard to find any sense at all.  As for Horeus, Nahum describes Yahweh as jealous and vengeful, but that does little good in our effort to correlate. The fact that "Michaeas" occurs for the second time may suggest that another Michaeas from Micah is meant; if so, he is probably the Micaiah of 1 Kings 22 who was apparently given a true spirit, not a lying spirit, by Yahweh.  And as for Astaphaeus, whoever he is, a spirit who inspires both Ezra and Zephaniah is hard to understand.  Perhaps Zephaniah has wrongly taken the place of Haggai. Both Ezra (-Nehemiah) and Haggai are concerned with rebuilding the temple.

What about all the Old Testament writings that are omitted? What we have consists of the Hexateuch prophets mentioned in 1-2 Samuel and 1 Kings, the major literary prophets, 9/12 of the minor prophets, Ezra, and Tobit.  Judges (with Samson) and Ruth are left out, as are the books of Chronicles.  Job was not a prophet.  Neither David (traditional author of the Psalms) nor Solomon (traditional author of wisdom-literature, etc.) required consideration. Probably the omission of Hosea, Obadiah, and Malachi was accidental, unless the Gnostics found Hosea's behavior too much to take.

The analyses of all these Gnostic teachers deserve attention, for they are based not only on Gnostic theory but on real exegetical problems within the Old Testament books. Surely the Gnostics went beyond what we find in the opening verse of Hebrews, with its reference to God's speech through the prophets "in many and various ways." But they were aware of the differences not only between the OT books and the gospel but even among the various OT books. As they made their analysis they dealt not merely with the divine names, which provided an occasion for claiming that there were differences, but especially with the theological content of the books.

A significant point of departure must have been the fact that the census ascribed to the inspiration of Yahweh in 2 Sam 24:1 is assigned to Satan in 1 Chr 21:1. A simple correlation could allow a Gnostic exegete to view Yahweh as Satan.[20] Vigorous orthodox teachers could promote synthesis in the face of such analysis and insist--as Irenaeus insisted in Christian circles--upon the inspiration of the whole Bible by the one Holy Spirit. Without such leadership, religious communities are likely to sink in the quicksand of obscure exegetical questions. To combine analysis with synthesis is the task of the theological exegete, as Coert Rylaarsdam has demonstrated throughout his significant career.

276

FOOTNOTES

1. Irenaeus, *Adv. haer.* 1. 25. 4; Epiphanius, *Haer.* 33. 3. 2.

2. Epiphanius, *Haer.* 33. 4-5.

3. *Vigiliae Christianae* 11 (1957) 145-47.

4. Irenaeus, *Adv. haer.* 1. 23. 3; 24. 2; 24. 5.

5. Cf. Hippolytus, *Ref.* 5. 25. 4-5 (rather different).

6. *Ap. John,* pp. 45, 8; 58, 16; 59, 17; 73, 4 Till (W. Till, *Die gnostischen Schriften des koptischen Papyrus Berolinensis* 8502 [Berlin: Academie, 1955]; translation in W. Foerster, *Gnosis I* [Oxford: Clarendon, 1972]).

7. Philo, *Opif.* 30; *Leg. all.* 2.19; *Quod det.* 170.

8. *Ap. John,* p. 59, 1-5.

9. A. v. Harnack, *Marcion* (ed. 2; Leipzig: Hinrichs, 1924) 413*-416*.

10. *Clem. hom.* 3. 47.

11. Ibid., 2. 38. 1. According to the anti-Marcionite, Rhodo, Apelles ascribed "the prophecies" to an adversary spirit (Eusebius, *H.E.* 5. 13. 2).

12. Ibid., 3. 49. 2; cf. G. Quispel, *Ptolémée: Lettre à Flora* (Paris: Cerf, 1949) 78.

13. Ibid., 53. 2 (synthesized from Luke 10:24 and Matt 13:17).

14. Cf. H.J. Schoeps, *Theologie und Geschichte des Judenchristentums* (Tübingen: Mohr, 1949) 159, 466-67.

15. But they rejected some expressions within the Pentateuch (Epiphanius, *Haer.* 30. 18. 7).

16. Epiphanius, *Haer.* 30. 18. 4; cf. 15. 2.

17. Ibid., 30. 18. 9.

18. Hippolytus, *Ref.* 5. 26. 24-26, 36; 27. 4-5.

19. *Ap. John,* pp. 41-42; roughly the same names in two of the three other versions (cf. M. Krause--P. Labib, *Sie drei Versionen*

*des Apokryphon des Johannes im Koptischen Museum* [Wiesbaden:   Harrassowitz, 1962]).   Text in Irenaeus, *Adv. haer.* 1. 30. 11.

20.   See my *Gnosticism and Early Christianity* (ed. 2, New York:
Columbia, 1966) 56-61.

# ORIGEN'S INTERPRETATION OF THE OLD TESTAMENT AND LÉVI-STRAUSS' INTERPRETATION OF MYTH

Raymond B. Williams

Origen's method of biblical interpretation has been a mystery and enigma to many scholars; R.P.C. Hanson called it "theological fantasy."[1] The foremost critic of Lévi-Strauss' structuralist interpretation of myth has written, what could just as well have been written of Origen, that his methods "lead into a world where all things are possible and nothing sure."[2] Yet both Origen and Lévi-Strauss claim that there is a logic which governs their hermeneutic, a logic separate from other logics. For Origen it is the logic of the spiritual level; for Lévi-Strauss it is the logic of the deep structure. Lévi-Strauss is concerned with the logic of myth (mythologique); Origen is concerned with the logic of the Word.

The thesis of this paper is that there are parallels between the allegorical interpretation of scripture of Origen and the structural study of myth of Lévi-Strauss. Each believed that the test before him represented a context of meaning at another level of abstraction from the surface meaning. They relied upon similar associations of various elements of the text to point to the deeper, spiritual meaning. This is not an attempt to argue that Origen was a structuralist before Lévi-Strauss. Origen cannot be called a structuralist; indeed, nothing would be gained by the designation. Still, a comparison of his method with that of Lévi-Strauss can provide new insights to Origen's work and provide another element in the present discussion of the structural interpretation of scripture.

There is presently a wave of interest in the application of structuralist methods of interpretation to scripture.[3] It is only a matter of time before the Bible becomes the grist for every new

hermeneutical mill. The methods used and results attained display
marked differences from the results of recent historical-critical
research. Yet there are similarities between the kind of interpretations coming from contemporary structuralist interpreters and
Origen's commentaries and homilies. The insights gained from the
study of Lévi-Strauss may provide us with a new appreciation of
Origen's work. Because structuralist interpretations share many
of the characteristics of Origen's interpretations, we may also
learn to anticipate some of the strengths and weaknesses of this
approach to the text.

Lévi-Strauss wrote that "myth grows spiral-wise until the
intellectual impulse which has produced it is exhausted."[4] There
is no particular meaning in myth; rather, myths generate myths.
There is a continual immanation of myths in succession each of
which reveals a meaning in another one. Thus, as Paz summarizes
the process, "Myths communicate with each other by means of men
without men knowing it."[5] Hence, Lévi-Strauss would undoubtedly
view Origen's interpretation of scripture as he did Freud's interpretation of the Oedipus myth, as another mythic transformation.[6]
He wrote concerning Mythologiques I that "this book on myths is itself a kind of myth."[7] Origen's interpretation is a mythic transformation growing spiral-wise out of the texts with which he was
working.

Three aspects of Origen's interpretation relate to Lévi-
Strauss' interpretation. He sought to elaborate two homologous
levels of meaning -- the literal and the spiritual. He postulated
a unity of scripture not related to historical development which
allowed him to see the elements of the New Testament as transformation of the Jewish scriptures. He searched the texts for grammatical, etymological, or geographical details which could provide
the key to the spiritual level of meaning. These aspects are illustrated in his interpretation of one portion of the Gospel of
John which concerns the Jordan River (John 1:28). A review of

these aspects will make clear the similarities between the hermeneutics of Origen and Lévi-Strauss.

## I.  Two Levels of Meaning

Two important influences on Lévi-Strauss were his study of
geology and his study of Freud.  He learned that beneath the surface structure of the earth or of a mental process, e.g., a dream,
there is a deep structure.  Beyond the rational surface structure
there is "a category at once more important and more valid:  that
of the meaningful."[8]  The geological surface is a bewildering puz-
zle of jumbled rocks and features.  Yet a cross-section shows that
what is hidden, the invisible strata, is a structure which determines and gives meaning to that which is above it.  There space and
time commingle.  Thus, he concludes,

> Unlike the history of the historians, history as the geol-
> ogists and the psychoanalysts see it is intended to body
> forth in time -- rather in the matter of a tableau vivant
> -- certain fundamental properties of the physical or
> psychical universe.[9]

These disciplines taught him to explain the visible by the hidden.

Lévi-Strauss applied this lesson to his understanding of myth.
Various myths present a complex mass of data -- trivial incidents,
contradictions, confusions of sequence, time and space.  The task
of the interpreter of the myth is to get beneath the manifest sense
of the myth to the deep structure.  There are elements in the story
which are indicators to point the interpreter to the deeper level,
and this in turn will illumine the text.  Lévi-Strauss confesses
that the interpreter will need "a fundamental delicacy of perception -- sensibility, flair, taste:  all are involved -- if he
is to detail and assess the complexities of the situation."[10]

Origen's understanding of the logic of the Word is that there are two levels of scripture, the literal and the spiritual. In Peri-Archon, Book IV, he briefly outlined a three-fold interpretation of Scripture. In a homily on Leviticus he wrote, "The divine scriptures have three senses: historical, moral and mystical; that is to say that they have a body, soul and spirit."[11] This three-fold division is, however, rarely found in his interpretation. What in the theoretic formulation was a trichotomy became in practice a dichotomy. In practice Origen stressed the literal level and the spiritual level.

In an interesting parallel to Lévi-Strauss' reference to geological landscape, Origen pictured the scripture as a field containing a well-hidden treasure.[12] The surface meaning corresponds to the field as a whole full of all kinds of plants, whereas the truths which are stored away and not seen by all lie as if buried beneath the visible plants. These are the hidden treasures of wisdom and knowledge -- the spiritual meaning. Origen gave a summary of his position in the preface of Peri Archon:

> Then there is the doctrine that the scriptures were composed through the spirit of God and that they have not only that meaning which is obvious, but also another which is hidden from the majority of readers. For the contents of scripture are the outward forms of certain mysteries and the images of divine things. On this point the entire Church is unanimous, that while the whole law is spiritual, the inspired meaning is not recognized by all, but only by those who are gifted with the grace of the Holy Spirit in the word of wisdom and knowledge.[13]

Origen moved from the anthropological trichotomy (body, soul, spirit) to a literal-spiritual dichotomy because his system was governed by the ontological structure of the visible world and the eternal word or reason. We are concerned here with the embodiment of the Word at three levels -- creation, incarnation, and inspiration

| A | | B | | C |
|---|---|---|---|---|
| The Word | _in_ | Creation | _is_ _to_ | Reasonable World<br>Rational Beings |
| as The Word | _in_ | Incarnation | _is_ _to_ | Jesus Christ |
| as The Word | _in_ | Inspiration | _is_ _to_ | Scripture |

There are two manifestations of the embodiment of the Word in creation. The world is reasonable and ordered, and this points to the rational principle which is operative in creation. There is also the embodiment of the Word in all rational creatures. The incarnation is a transformation of creation so that the Word is embodied in the human form of Jesus. The Word which is the rational principle of all creation was hidden in the flesh of Jesus. In a sense, the Word is not revealed in human flesh; he is hidden in it. Origen stressed the hidden, secret character of the Word become flesh. His advent was a symbol;[14] his body was a type and a sign;[15] and his deeds were symbols and signs of the spiritual Word and his spiritual works.[16] The end result is that **for** Origen the whole life and ministry of Jesus became a shadow and a symbol of a higher reality. The gospel of the words and deeds of Jesus of Nazareth is a sensible gospel which points beyond itself to the spiritual gospel.

The Word in the incarnation presents himself to different reasonable beings in different forms (_epinoiai_).[17] In the listing of the various titles for Christ Origen came very close to saying that the Word presents different forms to men of different levels of understanding'. For some he is light, life, and truth, and for others lamb of God and suffering servant. Because Christ embraces the whole reason of all things, he communicates this truth to every creature in proportion to its worthiness.[18] Some believers know Christ only after the flesh. It is the task of the spiritually minded man, however, to reach behind the earthly, visible, material flesh to the Word.

The same structure is present in Origen's interpretation of the inspiration of Scripture. The presence of the Word in the

letter of scripture extends the incarnation.  The literal level of
the texts conceals the spiritual meaning.  The Holy Spirit has so
guided the writing of scripture that it is profitable for man at
whatever level of spiritual advancement he has attained.  The outer
covering is so adapted to men that it is profitable for the improve-
ment of the multitude.  The literal stories and laws are transparen†
so that those who are capable of understanding deeper mysteries
find concealed in them those deeper truths.[19]

The imperfections of scripture are evidence for Origen which
points to the existence of a spiritual level of meaning.  The Holy
Spirit arranged for certain stumbling-blocks, hindrances, and im-
possibilities to be placed in the midst of the laws and narratives
of scripture as sign posts pointing the reader to the hidden spiritual truths.  Origen viewed this world, the life of Jesus, and
the scripture as physical symbols which point to the true realities
of the spiritual world.  It is the task of the perfect Christian
and especially of the interpreter of scripture to transform the
sensible gospel into a spiritual gospel.[20]

Thus Origen's interpretation is governed by a basic binary
opposition.  It is not the opposition between nature and culture
so prominent in Lévi-Strauss' work, but that between earth and
heaven, human and divine.  Origen suggested that this basic opposition is transformed into homologous pairs in many texts.  The
relation of two items in one sphere corresponds to the relation of
two items in another sphere.

Origen found a perfect illustration of this basic binary opposition as well as an explanation of the transformations mentioned
above in Jesus' act of making medicinal salve from spittle and dirt
(John 9:6).

dirt : spittle :: outside : inside :: letter : spirit

:: human : divine :: below : above :: earthly : heavenly
Origen indicated that the Word of God does not come to man devoid
of matter and bodily expression because the pure essence of the

Word is greater than human nature can now grasp. Thus, the spittle of Jesus represents the Word and divine thoughts. The soil of the earth is related to the spittle as all that relates to the announcement of the Word in human events and history relates to the Word. This is a figure for the incarnation, but Origen immediately applied it to scripture. The letter of scripture is its earthiness which was combined with the heavenly Word.[21] In myth the antitheses are mediated in a way impossible in other logics. So the simple union of dirt and spittle in a medicinal salve represents the healing union of the divine and human in Jesus as well as the union of the earthly and heavenly in scripture.

Lévi-Strauss looked beyond the surface structure of a myth to the concealed deep structures which determine "how the myths operate in men's minds without their being aware of the fact."[22] Ultimately this leads the investigator to the innate structuring capacity of the human mind and reveals something fundamental about man. Origen moved rapidly behind the literal story to the spiritual meaning which had been clothed in the literal text. The interpreter seeks always to discover the spiritual truths hidden by the Holy Spirit in the letter. The spiritual interpreter will discover the reality of the Word in scripture, and this reality of the Word will be seen to be homologous with the reality of the Word concealed in the incarnation and in creation.


## II.  Unity of Scripture:  Transformation of The Old In The New

Lévi-Strauss suggests that one characteristic of myths is that they do not end; they, like rites, are interminable.[23] Myths generate myths in a conical spiral so that the same themes go through numerous permutations. The meaning of the story is not complete in itself, but is discovered only in the relationship of the story with alternate forms and presentations of the myth. Even Freud's inter-

pretation of the Oedipus myth becomes an authentic alternate form
of the story. Lévi-Strauss does not study the various myths in
sequence (diachronically), but all together (synchronically). The
myths are read as an orchestra score with full attention to the
harmony. What is unfinished in one part is supplied in another.
The full meaning appears only behind or beyond the text and becomes
a reality in the mind of the hearer or reader.[24] What becomes clear
is the logic of myth.

So Lévi-Strauss argues that some elements of a myth or story
are incomprehensible and become clear to the reader only when seen
in other contexts. Thus he argues that some elements of a Tukuna
myth which are impossible to interpret in the native context becomes clear when brought into association with myths from another
culture.[25] This is the critical point at which many are led to
reject his approach. He suggests how one might read a myth once
it has been divided into its basis units and arranged in columns.

> Were we to tell the myth, we would disregard the columns
> and read the rows from left to right and from top to
> bottom. But if we want to understand the myth, then we
> will have to disregard one half of the diachronic dimension
> (top to bottom) and read from left to right, column after
> column, each one being considered a unit.[26]

When he has placed the several transformations of myth or elements
of myths in these new relationships, the deep structures of the
various myths present the same image.

The structuralist approach to the relation of various myths
and alternate forms of the same myth has suggested to some scholars
a way of viewing the relation of the Jewish scriptures to the New
Testament. Dan Via contends that structural analysis has shown
that Paul understood some aspects of the Jewish tradition "uncon-
sciously" because his thought and Deuteronomy belong to what Michel
Foucault calls the same epistemological field. This is that uncon-

scious order, arrangement, or configuration of ideas and discourse in which a culture feels at home, that kind of rationality by which a culture seeks to constitute the knowledge of something as knowledge. Thus, Paul works with a meaning-system, a structure, within which Deuteronomy is also a transformation.[27] Edmund Leach has made brief reference to the relation of the Jewish myth of the Passover and the Christian myth of the Last Supper; "Thus, the Christian story is, in a quite explicit sense, a new version of the much earlier Jewish story but generalized on a more metaphysical plane with certain key elements reversed."[28]

One of Origen's oft repeated principles is that scripture must be explained by scripture. He quoted a saying of a Jew of his acquaintance to the effect that scripture, because of its obscurity, is like many locked rooms in one house. Before each room he supposed a key to be placed, but not the one belonging to it; the key in each door will not open the door it is in but will open one of the others, and each key has on it signs indicating to the experienced reader which door it will open.[29] Even a casual reading of his commentaries and homilies will suffice to show how Origen ranged from one end of the Bible to the other for associations which would help to explain the text he was considering. These are not, however, simply random and arbitrary associations.

Two considerations supported Origen's practice of interpreting scripture by scripture: the uniform inspiration of scripture and the resulting harmony of scripture on the spiritual level. Concerning the first he spoke of the unity of inspiration with reference to the Word that was in the beginning. He explained that the Word of God which was in the beginning was not words, for the Word is one, being composed of many speculations, each of which is part of the Word in its entirety. He indicated that one can conclude that all the sacred books are one book; they speak one Word.[30] While they do not always appear to be speaking one Word at the literal level, the harmony is found at the spiritual level. When

scripture is understood spiritually, each part fits in its place
to complement and explain the other. Only the interpreter who is
able to read correctly the signs on the different keys is able to
open the door to the true harmony of scripture on the spiritual
level.

Origen had a strong apologetic purpose in maintaining the unity
of scripture. The theological foundation of orthodoxy -- that God
the creator and God the redeemer are one -- had in hermeneutics its
equivalent in the postulate that the Old and New Testaments are
equal in their inspiration, their worth, and their holiness. The
Christian doctrine of God was at stake in the desire for a proper
understanding of the unity of scripture.

This harmony and the true meaning of scripture are not to be
found on the level of the spiritual meaning hidden within the historical situations. Thus, Origen's interpretation of the relation
of elements of the Old Testament story and the New Testament story
was not diachronic, i.e., the Old as preparation or prefigurement,
but synchronic, i.e., elements of the Old related to the New by
anagogē. René Cadiou referred to this fact when he said that
"what Origen and his fellow workers did was to place the two testaments one on top of the other instead of placing them side by
side."[31]

Henri-Charles Puech points to a serious conflict in early
Christianity over the interpretation of time.[32] On the one hand
there was the horizontal interpretation of segments of time through
one another in which the earlier events are types or prefigurations
of the subsequent events and are related to them as the shadow is
related to the full, authentic reality. On the other hand there
was the vertical interpretation of temporal events through the
fixed and atemporal, archetypal realities of the upper intelligible world. In one the image anticipates the model, while in the
other the transcendent model is for all eternity prior to the image.
Origen occasionally referred to the law and prophets as prefigure-

ments of the gospel.  Usually, however, he sought to find in both
testaments structures of transcendent, unchanging, and atemporal
truths.

Lévi-Strauss reads myths as orchestra scores.  Each myth provides some elements of the total pattern.  The myths or stories are
reduced to separate elements and organized as follows:

| 1 | 2 | | 4 | | 6 | |
|---|---|---|---|---|---|---|
| | 2 | | | 5 | | |
| | | | | | | 7 |
| 1 | | 3 | 4 | | 6 | 7 |

He interprets the myths synchronically rather than diachronically.
Origen reads the spiritual meaning of scripture in the same way.  He
places the various passages from the gospels and from the Jewish
scriptures "on top of one another" and ranges up and down the score
pointing out connections and relationships between the various
stories.  This leads to what often seems to be fanciful analogies,
verbal slights of hand, and mind-bending associations.  They are,
however, no less controlled than those of Lévi-Strauss.  The goal
is to reveal the spiritual meaning that lies behind the surface
structure of scripture, the logic of the Word.


## III.  Keys to "Deep" or "Spiritual" Structures


According to Origen, all Christian theology is Biblical theology.  There is no secret or esoteric doctrine independent of scripture, every doctrine was derived from the text.  Moreover, there
is a fundamental unity of text and meaning.  All secret, spiritual
truths are clothed in the form of what he called the bodily part.
Therefore, the truth can only be attained by means of a minute study
of the text.  Although he scorned those whose concern was with the
bare letter alone, Origen was more concerned with the letter than
most because only through the letter could he reach the heights of

spiritual interpretation. Thus, quaintly enough, the spiritual
exegesis of Origen was in a way the most crassly literal in application for it accepted the principle that there is no detail of
the text that is without spiritual significance. Not even the
smallest detail was accidental. In many instances his whole interpretation rested upon the careful observation of such detail.

One is reminded that according to Lévi-Strauss the changes
or transformations in myths are not accidental, but follow the
unconscious logic of myth. One of the reasons he avoided the
edited, published myths of modern men is that the conscious intention of the editors may have "accidentally" destroyed the logic
of myth preserved by la Pensée sauvage. Origen held that none of
the details of Biblical stories, especially of those in the gospels,
are accidental. Even the inconsistencies and contradictions are
deliberate and important. They represent different transformations
of the logic of the Word. Thus Origen wrote:

> I do not condemn them [the Evangelists] if they sometimes
> transform an episode to serve their mystical aim, so as to
> speak of a thing which happened in a certain place as if it
> had happened in another, or of what took place at a certain
> time as if it had taken place at another time, and to in-
> troduce into what was spoken in a certain way some changes
> of their own. They proposed to speak the truth when it
> was possible both materially and spiritually, and where
> this was not possible, it was their intention to prefer
> the spiritual to the material. The spiritual truth was
> often preserved as one might say in the material lie.[33]

Lévi-Strauss presents an interesting and somewhat amusing
picture of the mechanics or organizing the elements of a variant
of a myth under study before computers were available to him.[34]
Each variant of the myth was divided into its basic functions,
each of which was placed on a card. A variant of average length
required several hundred cards. To discover the pattern of rows
and columns for the cards, he constructed vertical boards about
six feet long and four and a half high where cards could be pigeon-

holed and moved at will. When the cards, and thereby the elements
of the myth, were reorganized in this manner, the various relationships within the myth and with other myths became evident. With
the use of computers, the frame of reference became multi-dimensional
and much more complex as evidenced in his Mythologique.

We do not know the mechanism by which Origen organized the mass
of material he used in his commentaries and homilies, but there are
some similarities in the result. Origen was one of the first Christian writers to present commentaries on books of the Bible with detailed comments on the text phrase by phrase. Each passage was
divided into its smallest unit. The commentary then set out the
relation of elements of the text with other elements from both
Jewish and Christian stories that were in any way related. Origen
interpreted the newly organized elements of the story synchronically,
up and down the columns, because the truth of the passage was not
to be discovered in the diachronic sequence of the story, but in
the synchronic relationship which became clear in association with
other texts. Origen's reorganization of the material is as minute
and detailed as Lévi-Strauss', and often just as difficult to follow.
Note as an example Origen's interpretation of John 2:13, "And the
passover of the Jews was at hand."[35]

| | | |
|---|---|---|
| Passover of the Jews | Christ | RITUAL |
| Your Passover | Passover of the Lord (Exod 12:48) | |
| Human Passover | True Passover | |
| Regulations of the Law concerning sacrifice (Exod 12:8) | | ANIMAL |
| Sheep sacrificed | Lamb of God | |
| Sheep killed by those keeping the Law | Christ killed by those transgressing the Law | |
| No bone broken | Christ's bone not broken (John 19:32) | |
| Flesh eaten | Christ's flesh and blood eaten | FOOD |
| Lamb not eaten raw (roasted) | Word eaten cooked | |

Raw (literal interpretation)        Cooked (spiritual)
Words burn within us like fire (Jer 5:14)
Hearts burn within us by the way when he opened
    the Scriptures (Luke 24:32)

Regulations of the Sacrifice - Lamb must be cooked whole
        Head = principle and essential doctrines
        Feet = last branches of learning
        Entrails = that which is hidden within
One must not break the unity of the scripture which is
    the Word of God

This is a bewildering association of passages. Origen has moved from the contrast between the Passover of the Jews and the Passover of the Lord through the correspondences between the sacrificial regulations and the death of Christ to contrast between the literal interpretation of the Word (ingestion of that which is raw) and the spiritual interpretation of the Word (ingestion of that which is cooked). He is searching for a logic and structure that is present at a level separate from the diachronic. The attempt becomes understandable, if not convincing, even though he concludes his treatment with the charming confession, "We have already spoken of these things to a greater extent than the passage demands."[36]

What resulted from the application of this "method" was a minutely detailed study of the text for any indication of spiritual meaning. Origen's comments provide a wealth of detail concerning the text and various related passages. While he undoubtedly created mysteries and perplexities out of insignificant verbal distinctions, this was, as Charles Bigg suggested, "a fault on the right side."[37] The detailed study of the text, the relation of texts and images on the basis of association schemes foreign to historical-critical study, and the audacity of some of the resulting comments parallel the work of Lévi-Strauss on myth.

## IV. Origen's Interpretation of Jesus and John at the Jordan

An example of Origen's detailed interpretation is found in his commentary on the meaning of the word "Jordan" in John 1:28 which leads him to a discussion of synchronically related passages in the Book of Enoch 37:1; Gen 6:2; John 1:14; 1 John 5:8; Josh 3:14-17; 2 Kgs 2:8,9; 2 Kgs 5:1-19; Ezek 29:3-5 and other intermediate points. Each of these passages is in some way a transformation of the elements of part of the other passages. The first three are related in the following manner.

| | | | | |
|---|---|---|---|---|
| Jordan | = | their going down | = | Jared |
| Jared | = | father of Enoch | = | Time of Enoch |
| Sons of God | | descend | | to daughters of men |
| souls | | descend | | to bodies |
| River | | descends | | to which one must come (purification) (salvation) |
| Jesus (Joshua) | | descending | | Makes glad city of God (the church) |
| Word of God | | becomes flesh | | and dwelt among us |

The interpretation starts with the fact that Jordan and Jared came from the same root (yrd ) which means "go down" or "descend." Jared, in both the Book of Enoch and Genesis, was the father of Enoch, and this reminded Origen that the sons of God descended to the daughters of men during the time of Enoch. The word "descends" also refers to the descending of souls to tabernacle in bodies. The name of the Jordan River means "to descend" and the river descends; at the same time people go down to the river to be purified. This reminded Origen of the reference to the river which flows to make glad the city of God which is clearly a transformation of the descent of Jesus to bring purification and healing to the church as in John 1:14, "The Word became flesh and dwelt among us."

In the Incarnation the Word takes on different aspects:

| Drink | Water | Wine | Blood |
|-------|-------|------|-------|
| Food | | Bread | Flesh |
| Baptism | Water | Holy Spirit | Blood |

According to Origen, the Word is sometimes referred to under one
aspect, again in another aspect.  Food and drink are transformations of the form of the incarnation and of the sacraments as well.
When properly understood, these transformations agree, as 1 John
records, "There are three witnesses: the Spirit, the water and the
Blood; and these three agree."

Jesus' baptism in the Jordan is a transformation of Joshua's
passage through the Jordan.  The etymology of the names is the
significant key.

| Joshua | crosses sweet water (Jordan) | Moses crosses salt water (Red Sea) |
|--------|------|------|
| Joshua's baptism | sweeter than ( $\neq$ ) | Moses' law |
| Jesus' law | sweeter than ( $\neq$ ) | Moses' law |
| Joshua's ark | $=$ | Presence of God |
| Christian Baptism | $=$ | Presence of God |

Origen implied that Paul should have referred to Joshua's crossing
over the Jordan as the true type of Christian baptism.  The logic
of the Word suggests it.  Joshua's crossing of the Jordan superseded
Moses' crossing of the Red Sea just as Christian baptism superseded
the old law of Moses.  In the same way as the ark of the covenant
represented God's presence with Israel (Josh 3:10), so Jesus is
God's presence to those who are baptized.

Elijah and Elisha were involved in an incident which is related to the presence of Jesus and John at the Jordan (2 Kgs 2:8-
12).  Elijah crossed the Jordan in a kind of baptism as a preparation
for his ascension.  Elisha, however, passed through the Jordan twice
which enabled him to receive a double gift of the spirit.  Clearly,
Origen's understanding of Jesus' baptism in the Jordan caused him
to see meaning in all other events related to the Jordan.  The reference to Elisha caused him to move to a consideration of the cure

of Naaman by washing in the Jordan.

| Naaman | goes to Jordan | cleansed of leprosy |
|---|---|---|
| Leper | goes to Jesus | cleansed of sin |
| Elisha (prophet) | points Naaman to | Jordan (healing agent) |
| John (prophet) | points Sinner to | Jesus (healing agent) |

This portion of the interpretation is straight forward, and not foreign to much Christian exposition and preaching. Such synchronic transformations have become a part of our mental picture of the biblical record. Origen continued, however, to relate the rivers of religion to the enemies of Israel through a reference to Ezek 29:3-5.

| Naaman | = | enemy Syrian | Rivers of Babylon |
|---|---|---|---|
| Pharaoh | = | enemy Egyptian | Rivers of the Nile |

| Rivers of Enemy | inferior to | Jordan |
|---|---|---|
| Jews | wept by | Waters of Babylon |
| Jeremiah | rebuked those | wishing water from rivers of Egypt |

| Enemy (Dragon) | in | River of Egypt |
|---|---|---|
| God | in | River of Zion |
| Father | in | Son |

| Those washed in Jordan | put away | Reproach of Egypt |
|---|---|---|
| Washing | cleanses | Leprosy |
| Baptism | removes | Sin |

Origen concluded that just as the waters of the Jordan are superior to the rivers of all the enemies of Israel, so the Christian baptism prefigured by the baptism of Jesus by John is superior to all other means of salvation. All of this is found by the skillful interpreter in the reference in the Gospel of John to Jesus and John at the Jordan.

Origen related the various stories and texts from the Bible as transformations of each other. The Christian story has grown "spiral-wise" and the meaning of each portion of the story can be discovered only when it is related to the other transformations in such a way as to bring out the logic of the Word. No telling of the story is final or more true than the other because, as Origen held, the spiritual meaning is found in every transformation of the story. Because they agree on these points, the synchronic interpretations of Origen and Lévi-Strauss bear many structural similarities.

Both Origen and Lévi-Strauss have a theoretical structure, one the logic of myth and the other the logic of the Word, within which their interpretation takes place. Origen's hermeneutic is an integral part of his theology. This is shown by the interweaving of his doctrines of creation, anthropology, and incarnation with his doctrine of inspiration. Therefore, his interpretation has a structure of meaning which can be understood, if not universally accepted. Much of what is currently being done by structuralist interpreters of scripture seems to come forth from a hermeneutic in search of a theology or philosophy.

A theological or philosophical basis for hermeneutics is necessary if only to provide the limitations for what is valid interpretation. The grounds for invalidating an interpretation must come from the theological or philosophical system of which the hermeneutic is a part. How is one able to say that a particular portion of allegorization or structuralist interpretation is invalid? If one cannot make such a judgment then we are indeed led into a world where all things are possible and nothing sure.

Antiochian interpreters attacked Origen and the Alexandrians because they neglected the historical reality of the Christian faith in order to concentrate on the eternal, spiritual meaning. The thrust of their argument was that the allegorical interpretation could not do justice to the ideas of a community that was as self-consciously historical in orientation as Judaism and Christianity. Current structuralist interpretation of the Bible raises this question anew.

Lévi-Strauss' interpretation suggests that myths are related to the natural structures which are inherent to the way man thinks. Man may not consciously understand the ways in which this natural structure is present in the myth, but it is difficult to understand how a man could be alienated from this natural structure. The Biblical materials deal primarily with belief structures, not natural structures. The Biblical writers themselves understood that one could become alienated from these structures by the act of unbelief. Origen understood that correct interpretation comes as the result of a gift of the Spirit and this is dependent upon an act of commitment.

No claim is made that Origen was a structuralist. Rather, it is the case that a reading of Lévi-Strauss' work causes one to view Origen's interpretation in a new light. The associations and transformations in Origen's interpretation can be seen to follow a careful logic which Origen believed to be the logic of the Word. A study of Origen also provided a wealth of material for those who are engaged in the application of the structuralist method to Biblical material. Origen attempted a similar interpretation centuries ago, and his interpretation is, if one accepts Lévi-Strauss' view, a transformation within the Christian community of the basic Christian story.

298

# FOOTNOTES

1. R.P.C. Hanson, *Allegory and Event* (London: S.C.M. Press, 1959) 283.

2. E. Leach, *Lévi-Strauss* (London: Fontana, 1970) 82.

3. Cf., *Interpretation* 28 (1974), *Semeia* 1 and 2 (1975), and *Soundings* 58 (1975).

4. C. Lévi-Strauss, "The Structural Study of Myth" in *Structural Anthropology* (Harmondsworth, Eng.: Penguin Books, 1972) 229.

5. O. Paz, *Claude Lévi-Strauss: An Introduction* (New York: Dell Publishing Co., 1970) 39.

6. Lévi-Strauss, *Structural Anthropology,* 217.

7. C. Lévi-Strauss, *The Raw and the Cooked: Introduction to a Science of Mythology: I* (New York: Harper Torchbooks, 1969) 6.

8. C. Lévi-Strauss, *Tristes Tropiques* (New York: Atheneum, 1974) 55.

9. Ibid., 57.

10. Ibid..

11. Origen, *Lev. h.*, v. 5.

12. Origen, *Peri Archon* iv.3.11, ed. P. Koetschau ("Die griechischen christlichen Schriftsteller der ersten drie Jahrhunderts," Vol. 22), 339, line 1, to 340, line 9. References to this work will be abbreviated *P.A.* and will be to this edition.

13. *P.A.* i.pref.8 (14, lines 6-13).

14. Origen, *Commentary on the Gospel of John xiii.56=390,* ed. E. Preuschen ("Die griechischen christlichen Schriststeller der ersten drie Jahrhunderte," Vol. 21), 287, lines 20-24. References to this work will be abbreviated *Co.Jn.* and will be to this edition.

15. *Co.Jn.* x.35(20)=228 (209, lines 16-21).

16. *Co.Jn.* i.7=40 (12, line 16).

17. *Co.Jn.* ii.18(12)=128 (75, line 27 - 76, line 8).

18. *Co.Jn.* i.27=186 (34, lines 19-21).

19. *P.A.* iv.2.8 (320, line 10 - 321, line 2).

20. *Co.Jn.* i.8(10)=44 (13, lines 11-13).

21. *Co.Jn.* Frag. 63 (534, lines 4-16).

22. Lévi-Strauss, *Raw and the Cooked,* 12.

23. Ibid., 6.

24. Ibid..

25. C. Lévi-Strauss, *Mythologiques---l'origine des manières de table* (Paris: Librairie Plon, 1968) 11, 12.

26. Lévi-Strauss, *Structural Anthropology,* 214.

27. D. O. Via, Jr., *Kerygma and Comedy in the New Testament: A Structuralist Approach to Hermeneutic* (Philadelphia: Fortress Press, 1975) 63, 64.

28. E. Leach, "Structuralism in Social Anthropology" in *Structuralism: An Introduction* ed. David Robey (Oxford: Clarendon Press, 1973) 54.

29. Origen, *Philocalia: Co.Ps.i* in J. Armitage Robinson (ed.), *The Philocalia of Origen: The Text Revised with a Critical Introduction and Indices* (Cambridge: The University Press, 1893) 38.

30. *Co.Jn.* v.5 (102, line 24 - 103, line 8).

31. R. Cadiou, *La jeunesse d'Origène: histoire de l'école d'Alexandrie au début du III$^e$ siecle* (Paris: Etudes de théologie historique, 1936) 55.

32. H.-C. Puech, "Gnosis and Time," *Man and Time: Papers from the Eranos Yearbook* ("Bollingen Series," Vol. 3, No. 3; New York: Pantheon Books, 1957) 47 and 52.

33. *Co.Jn.* x.5(4)=19,20 (175, lines 11-21).

34. Lévi-Strauss, *Structural Anthropology,* 229.

35. *Co.Jn.* x.16(13)=88-107 (pp. 186-189).

36. Ibid., 189.

37. C. Bigg, *The Christian Platonists of Alexandria* (Oxford: Clarendon Press, 1886) 131, n. 2.

RUCTURALISM AND HISTORY:   THE STRUCTURE OF THE NARRATIVE
IN MYTH, FOLKTALE, AND THE SYNOPTIC GOSPELS

Glendon E. Bryce


The importance of history for the Judaeo-Christian tradition
is underscored by the mutual affirmation of both Jew and Christian
that the divine self-disclosure occurred "in, through, and by means
of history." If the phrase "Judaeo-Christian" is an ambiguous one,
it does at least point to a common denominator that links the two
religious communities genetically.[1] Sharing as a common heritage
the history recorded in the Hebrew Bible, the predication of both
Judaism and Christianity is an historical one, a present existence
which is grounded in past events. Whether their subsequent histories diverge from the intention disclosed in the event and its
interpretation in the Old Testament or bring it to a fuller development, they define themselves in the present in terms of what they
conceive to be the meaning and goal of this history. Whereas
Judaism has sought to realize its existence in terms of the meaning of history, Christianity may be said to have developed its
self-understanding more directly in relation to the goal of this
history.[2] Although the two faiths differ sharply at this point,
both of them ground their existence in a divine revelation that is
linked to history and historical process.


I.  History and Structure


The distinction between history and the goal of history is a
question that addresses itself to the so-called "scientific" historian in quite a different way.[3] It involves two different con-

ceptions of the task of the historian. Even if the interpreter
of history conceives his function rather narrowly by analogy to
that of the physical scientist, seeking to discover immanent laws
of cause and effect, he may venture beyond this purely descriptive
task and seek to discover dimensions of the historical process that
transcend the multiplicity and variety of its immanental forms.
As a result of what he perceives to be emergent patterns of meaning, he may propose a telos of history, a goal that shapes, for-
mulates, and interprets the movement of history. Whether he believes that it has emerged at some distinct point in time, as
though history is its own self-interpreter, or whether it is a
creative reinterpretation based upon particular configurations of
interrelated historical data, as a more subjective construction,
he attempts to discern some pattern of meaning within history that
discloses its aim or purpose.

Those who have rejected or qualified a "scientific" approach
to history have often done so in the context of this second perspective, perhaps to preserve residual pockets of human freedom or
even to place some understanding of the meaning of human existence
at the center of history.[4] Unfortunately, although historians
assert that the meaning of the past, whether of a dead or living
culture, can best be apprehended if it is understood historically,
an assumption that has only recently been challenged by the French
anthropologist Claude Lévi-Strauss, the term "history" has dissolved into one or another of these two different perspectives and
has become a word laden with ambiguities. In order to bring these
two approaches into some relation to each other, it is evident that
some model is needed that permits the distinction to be maintained
and yet is flexible enough to allow for the development of significant correlations between them.

The problem of history, then, must be faced on two fronts, as
a question of events and their relations and as a question of meaning. Unfortunately, the positivistic predisposition toward the fir

concern has led historians into a cul-de-sac that has obscured the larger interpretative task. Conceived scientifically, the function of the historian has been understood too narrowly as the reconstruction of the past in a genetic, chronological, and contextual sense. Of course, this task in itself is a difficult one. It is complicated by the fact that the historian encounters the past, not by direct experience, but as it is mediated through linguistic and extra-linguistic sources. Provisionally, he accepts these direct and indirect witnesses as attesting past events, as references to and projections of reality. Then, utilizing his own criteria of what constitutes an historical event, he proceeds to authenticate the events attested and to reconstruct them and their relations within the context of their spatial and temporal coordinates.

What is often overlooked is that this process presupposes the establishment of selective and interpretative criteria that determine what will be called "history." Moreover, they confer upon this term an elevated rank that also bestows upon the events that are designated by it and upon the interpretative criteria employed a special status that is by implication denied to other phenomena. What is conceived to be historical, then, is a reality that has been subject to a dual screening process which, from the perspective controlling the conception of history, filters out impurities and eliminates unacceptable coloration. If the historian of our time has the right to question the historiographer of the past about his ideological interests and those of his audience, he too must be asked not only to identify the audience for whom his account is meaningful but also to be willing to disclose the perspectives that he has utilized to convert a limited account of the phenomena of the past into the status of learned historical discourse.

The critical task of the historian, then, is one that is fraught with dangers. Where he has available sources and where they are reliable, he must distinguish between what belongs to

the category of micro-histories, the innumerable phenomena that
appear within a limited scope of time, and macro-history or history as event. Out of the multiplicity of events and states, both
public and private, he must select some and assign to them a special
significance. Otherwise, his account of what is historical would
dissolve into a series of unrelated private experiences, anecdotes,
and trivial occurrences. One of the enigmas of historical research,
of course, is the precise connection between micro-histories and
macro-history. From the point of view of the Egyptian or Roman
historiographers, the escape of the Hebrews from Egypt or the
birth of a child to Mary and Joseph in Bethlehem of Judea were
micro-histories. At the time that they occurred and even for some
years to follow, they were not events whose immediate effects were
to change the destiny of nations or societies. Whether they were
unknown or ignored, their precise relation to macro-history was
not evident. In order to clarify this relationship, some criteria
are needed by which the historian can identify events as macro-
history.

Furthermore, where sources are limited and where the historian must make a decision about the relative merit of the few
documents available, a priori decisions may surrender to adverse
judgment testimonies that attest important dimensions of the meaning of the past for those who experienced it. When the account of
David's kingship in Israel, subsequently limited to the Succession
Narrative in 2 Samuel, is exalted to the place of temporal primacy
in the historiography of the ancient Near East, this is a judgment
rendered by modern interpreters who prefer histories that are more
humanistic, or rationalistic, and that are based upon a purely
immamental understanding of history.[5] This reveals the way in
which underlying presuppositions control a particular historical
perspective, not simply as philosophical predispositions but as
personal affinities toward certain types of phenomena. It is obvious that the court chronicle of David gives less attention to
the way in which the transcendent dimension impinges upon history

than the book of Exodus does. It does not develop the relations
between religio-cultic factors and historical events as the book
of Ezra and Nehemiah do, nor, for that matter, does it probe the
deep religio-psychological motivations bearing on human actions as
the book of Jeremiah does. This is an example of how the selective process that separates between micro-histories and macro-
history can make distinctions one-sidedly and thus eliminate from
view perspectives that in themselves constitute perhaps important
motivational linkages explaining the relation between events. Perhaps from a broad perspective that utilizes criteria relating to
the significance of the event on a quantitative scale, one can assert that the court chronicle of David represents a unique historiographical perspective. However, since an immanental understanding of events is already present in other ancient Near Eastern
literature, its uniqueness cannot be attributed solely to this
factor.[6]

Moreover, because modern historians have concentrated upon
the reconstruction of the past as history, this has led into the
dead-end of "historicality," the reduction of history to historicity. Naturally, it is incumbent upon the historian who seeks
to discover and interpret events to determine with as much precision as possible what actually occurred and its effects within
a given context. However, when history and historicity are equated,
they focus the perspective of the historian too narrowly and lead
to a distorted conception of the role of the historiographer. On
this premise the Greek historians may be judged superior to the
Israelite chroniclers because they supply a greater number of
factual data and a wider variety of historical coordinates.

Such a quantitative conception of history, linked to the
selective perspective that gives a superior place to non-religious
accounts of events, has led archaeologists and historians of the
Bible to seek to recover its historicity. In this procedure little
or no distinction was made between history as event and history

understood in terms of its extra-linguistic coordinates such as topography, geography, monuments, etc. Within the context of biblical history this has led to premature identifications of the rubble of the ruined cities of the past with the events narrated in the Old Testament, such as the equation of storehouses at Megiddo with the stables of Solomon or the premature belief that the burned timbers of thirteenth century Palestinian towns are evidence of the Hebrew conquest.[7] Nevertheless, events cannot be disqualified from the arena of history because of arbitrary standards of verification that derive from an obsession with historicity.

Unfortunately, the failure to distinguish between history and the spatial and temporal coordinates within which events have taken place, has led to a confusion of elements that ought to be kept distinct. Time and space are in reality only the conditions of history, not history itself. Although the temporal dimension is more abstract, both time and space may be conceived as the coordinates by which history as event receives its anchorage in historicity. Often, however, temporal data may be absent or imprecise and geographical fixation only very vague. This does not, however, deny the event as such. Even though precise temporal and geographical data are lacking, the Exodus may be regarded as an event. Of course, these coordinates also play a role in helping to establish the meaning of an event. Isolated skirmishes in a battle may seem insignificant until they are set in relation to a total plan of attack. Thus, historicity as such leads beyond itself to geographical and temporal factors that involve social, cultural, and economic determinants.

When explored fully, these geographical coordinates establish an important distinction that differentiates between event and state. Such elements are more than mere toponyms without relevance to history as such or with a meaning that is limited to territorial contours and distance. Villages, towns, cities, provinces and countries attest a sociological dimension and call into existence

the human societies that inhabit them and give to them their par-
ticularity.  Although a topographical designation may seem to be
a mere cipher, this is only an appearance due to knowledge that is
presupposed or to historical condensation attributable to historiographic economy.  What is evident, however, is that when these
coordinates can be filled out, the historian becomes aware that
events may occur in the context of relatively stable social structures.  The event may merely be the recurrence of certain self-
contained functions of a specific social order, such as tribal wars
or feudalistic jousts.  But they may also profoundly affect and
change societies, destroying an old order and bringing a new social
order into existence.  Thus, the interrelationship between event
and state develops the meaning of the term "historical event" in
a more complex way, reflecting another important dimension of history, the dynamic interplay between the two.

The use of the term "structures" in relation to events introduces a deeper dimension of historical study.  It has been said
that the more history is different, the more it is the same.  This
axiom reflects another approach to history, equally as "ideological"
as more traditional historiography, that seeks to discover beneath
the temporal fluctuations of history certain profound structures
that are not affected by but can account for historical events.[8]
These fundamental structures of history, which are cultural, social,
and economic, are subject to structural transformations representing
the operations of immanent laws.  They may be set over and against
the multiplicity of micro-histories and history as event.  They are
organized in a hierarchy as a system, having groups of related categories and laws or rules by which they function.  They account
for a great number of changes which, in one sense, are not historical as events that suddenly and decisively affect or change history.
For example, a structure of kinship involving exogamic marital
practices can account for a multiplicity of micro-histories which
occur within a particular system of exchange.  Such structures are

existing states that may continue during periods of history, even during periods of upheaval, relatively unchanged. They may, of course, gradually change or be suddenly modified by the intrusion of external events.

The relation between this more fundamental history and historical events is a complicated one that both allows for and inhibits human freedom. Compatibilities among diverse structures leave room for human freedom to exercise its impact. Economic power and military leadership come together at unique moments in history to bring nations into power. The unique combination of social factors in Israel and political factors in the ancient Near East at the time of the military leadership of Saul provided the occasion for David to assert his drive toward kingship, to establish himself on the throne, and to subdue the small states of the Syro-Palestinian era. Historical events are subject to the interplay of various deep structures, and these structures are themselves brought into new configurations by historical events. Such structures, however, may operate at the collective level rather independently, having their own existence, inter-locked in self-contained overlapping systems that produce a multiplicity of interrelated micro-histories. Demographic expansion or economic growth or recession are historical undercurrents involving structures that operate relatively autonomously on the basis of systems of self-enclosed internal relations. When such structures become embodied in collectivities that seem to operate independently, as when international agencies control the economy by withholding the grain supply or super-powers dominate the territorial relations of countries, ancient historians and religious interpreters, such as the Jewish apocalypticists, view them as transcendent cosmic forces of good and evil.

Thus, the search for economic, social, and cultural structures and the internal systems of operations that they involve is a quest for the deeper foundations of history. The unity and autonomy of

these structures is never absolute because they are themselves in
flux, hybrid creations combining both past and present. Their
synchronic realization is constantly subject to the pressure of
diachrony in the form of minute changes or major modifications
that will give them a different form in the future. Nevertheless,
the context within which human freedom takes on meaning and human
destiny can be understood is this deeper synchronic level which
sets in opposition states and events.

History, then, may be conceived as three dimensional, consisting of the following levels:

1. Surface:    Micro-histories.
2. Medial:     Macro-history.
3. Profound:   Foundational history.

At the phenomenological level it appears as an infinite chronological succession of events in time and space. At the level of
event, it consists of a succession of significant functions that
are diachronic, i.e., related by implication in the temporal sequence. At its deepest level, however, it is synchronic, comprised
of a series of interlocking and interrelated structures, some more
fundamental than others.[9] This model has the advantage of avoiding
an oversimplification of history and of allowing for the complex
interplay of economic, social, and cultural structures that operate by immanent laws. The relation between these deep structures,
which have been investigated with respect to primitive cultures by
Lévi-Strauss, and historical events, is a complex one, as the configuration of terms freedom, destiny, and constraint indicates.
At the same time each level has a certain autonomy that allows the
interpreter to focus upon history as event or as structure without
insisting that a precise correlation be made. Ideally, of course,
this correlation is in one sense the axis of history, but it cannot rule out other ways of looking at events, since the precise
nature of the access from one level to another is extremely complicated.

Already, however, it has been observed that between the contemporary historian and past history are the historiographic traditions of the past. The recovery of history, then, depends in large part upon these traditions, particularly where ancillary evidence is scarce. Yet history, as a totalising discipline, deals with all of reality, not just a part of it. As such, history-writing is more than just a reification of a certain content that assures its transmission. The historian must also formulate and organize this content in particular ways to bring out its significance for his own time and for posterity. History is also mediated through literature, and this means that not only particular literary forms but also literary structures at the deepest level become extremely important for the understanding of history. Reflections upon diverse literary forms, whether myth, legends, or historical narrative, make us aware that the problem of history involves more than just content. It also includes in its purview the significance of specific literary forms. Moreover, if history is mediated through language, linguistic structures also assume a role of fundamental importance in the recovery and interpretation of the past.

With the development of textual semiotics as a discipline that deals with logico-linguistic structures, the question of the structure of the narrative, as it appears and has been studied in literary and historical materials, becomes paramount in the quest to discover how linguistic structure and semantic content are interrelated. Although it would be possible to investigate historical traditions by a typological study of their narrative form, using this term in the traditional sense, the pervasiveness of the narrative suggests that it would be fruitful to investigate a series of diverse traditions by a study of the structure of the narrative. By an analysis of their "form," i.e., linguistic structure, using the term as developed and employed by the Danish linguist Louis Hjelmslev, the similarities and differences between historical, quasi-historical, and non-historical literary materials can be com-

pared, apart from specific presuppositions about the content of
each or judgments about their relative values or merits in relation
to literature or history as such.[10]  At the same time traditions
that are more historical or less historical, using the term in the
narrow sense of historicity, can be probed without prejudice to
determine whether significant distinctions can be made at the level
of the deep structure of language.

## II.  History and the Structure of Myth

The problem of history confronts the anthropologist in a way
different from the historian.[11]  Whereas the historian may have in
his possession documentary evidence of a past that may not reach
into the present directly, the anthropologist may encounter a primitive society and discover that he has no evidence that will give
him direct access to its remote past.  Therefore, lacking temporal
coordinates by which to reconstruct tribal histories out of the
multiplicity of phenomena that exist in the present, he cannot
study the past as an historian, who seeks to interrelate individual
events localized in time and space.  On the other hand, if he tries
to focus upon the temporal order of events and ideas, not only is
he forced to choose a temporal "frequency," whether days, years,
or centuries, by which to relate them consistently, but he is also
required to give up the comparative task, which to some degree com-
pensates for the lack of documents, by which to understand the
institutions and techniques that implement social life.  Moreover,
the rigorous criteria that are needed to establish historical
stages or even cycles, evidence of priority, interrelationship,
and centrifugal development of phenomena, makes the reconstruction
and interpretation of the traditions of primitive tribes an ex-
ceedingly difficult task.  In some cases all that the anthropologist
can say is that earlier historical stages do exist, but their development cannot be traced.  Therefore, it is not at all surprising

that some anthropologists have shifted from a diachronic to a synchronic approach that seeks to understand phenomena, not in terms of how they have developed, but as relations of constituent elements that exist as structures at one time.

It is this approach that Lévi-Strauss has adopted in order to understand the function of myth in primitive societies. Although he admits that all societies are involved in history and change and that the development of myth in primitive societies can be interpreted, where sufficient records exist, by means of an historical approach, he chooses to approach this specific subject synchronically for two reasons. First, he believes that anthropology ought to conceive its task as distinct from that of the history. Whereas "history organizes its data in relation to conscious expressions of social life...anthropology proceeds by examining its unconscious foundations."[12] In response to certain assumptions that are implicit in a purely historical approach, his own critique of it is premised upon the following series of questions. Why should mythical beliefs relating to animal or plant species be regarded as vestiges of earlier stages when other causes, perhaps equally as cogent, are rejected as explanations of them? Why should unconscious factors, which the historian must call to his aid from time to time, not be given full consideration in the study of systems of belief and action? Moreover, if the unconscious includes linguistic structures that provide conceptual schemes by which mental phenomena are organized, why should "the logico-aesthetic tendency of the human mind to classify into categories the physical, biological, and social entities which constitute its universe" be dismissed as insufficiently objective?[13] To rest content, as the historian often does, with conscious expressions of social life, may simply decorate rationalizations and secondary elaborations with the designation of history.

The second reason for the selection of a synchronic approach by Lévi-Strauss was his attempt to understand primitive societies from within. From his field investigations he concluded that al-

313

though both primitive or "cold" societies and modern or "hot" societies continually experience history, primitive human groups
seek to deny diachrony and maintain their primeval state as an
ever-present synchronic realization of the timeless reality of
mythical antiquity. Their synchronic perspective continually
tries to assimilate contingency and duration by means of commemorative rites that recreate the sacred atmosphere of mythical
times and with the aid of mourning rites that conjoin the dead of
present time with their ancestors.

> The commemorative and funeral rites postulate that the
> passage between past and present is possible in both
> directions. They do not furnish the proof of it. They
> pronounce on diachrony but they still do so in terms of
> synchrony since the very fact of celebrating them is
> tantamount to changing past into present. It is there-
> fore understandable that some groups should have sought
> to give tangible confirmation of the diachronic essence
> of diachrony at the very heart of synchrony.[14]

Thus a tension exists in primitive thought between the diachronic
intrusions that weaken the realization of the synchronic state and
that insert contingency into the mythical structure. However, with
varying degrees of tension mythical thought succeeds in incorporating
history into its system.

In his synchronic approach to the mythology of the Indians of
the Americas, Lévi-Strauss sought to discover how the massive body
of mythological stories grew, what its function in primitive society
was, and what specific kind of thought-process it represented. In
order to account for the conceptual process involved, he formulated
a structural law, an equation that represented the interrelations
between the elements.[15] This equation of proportion, the simple
formula

$$A : B :: C : D$$

(A is to B as C is to D) not only explained the function of myth but also accounted for its growth. In general, he concluded that primitive men conceive religious roles by a mental process that unites form and substance in a generative system of binary logic. In this system various possibilities are realized by a system of inversions and substitutions of roles.

Three specific roles, represented in the structural law of myth, may be extrapolated, the substitutionary role, the mediatorial role, and the inversional role. When an irresolvable contradiction exists, such as that between life and death, the substitutionary role involves the reduction of the tension by transmuting the con- stituent elements of the elementary structure of meaning represented. For example, in Zuni myths the opposition between the farmer and the warrior is a transmutation of a more fundamental tension be- tween life and death, now embodied in the two professions, one that produces life and the other that causes death. This sharp tension is then further reduced by the substitution of the second pair, the predator and the herbivore. In this way irresolvable tensions are reduced through a progressive substitution of related pairs that refocus the question posed in the original contradiction. Having begun, of course, the process continues until the original impulse that gave rise to it is exhausted. The conceptual process that appears in myth also occurs in ritual, where primitive man seeks to integrate a whole series of related tensions by acting them out dramatically.

This process of commutation is effected in each case by the introduction of the mediatorial role represented in the third term. Thus the predator, which eats what it kills, emerges as the mediator between the agriculturalist, who eats but does not kill, and the warrior, who kills but does not eat what he has destroyed. The mediator between the second pair, the predator and the herbivore, is the scavenger. Like the predator, the scavenger eats meat even though, like the herbivore, it does not hunt. Thus, in Indian my- thology the religious mediator referred to by anthropologists as the trickster, is associated with the carrion eaters such as the buzzard or raven. While there are mediators of the first order and of the second order, involving roles that are complex and ambiguous, the fundamental discovery emerging from this structural study relates to the function of myth. Stated in the words of Lévi-Strauss himself, "mythical thought always progresses from the awareness of oppositions toward their resolution."[16]

It is the inversional role, however, that accounts for the growth of myth. Myths grow by the addition of a supplemental content. Although this introduces a disjunction into the structure, it also adds a different element that permits a new mediation to develop at another level. The disjunction itself involves an inversion or permutation of the last element of the law of proportion. As a formula it may be written in symbols that distinguish between the action or function (F x/y) and the term value (a/b) as follows:

$$Fx \ (a) \ : \ Fy \ (b) \ \backsim \ Fx \ (b) \ : \ Fa\text{-}1 \ (y)^{17}$$

The two halves of the formula are structurally homologous, the two pairs of oppositions representing two sets of contradictory functions. As illustrated in the Zuni myth, the correlation is based upon a structural equivalence, not upon identical contents.

| A | Consumer (Fx) Farmer (a) | | C | Consumer (Fx) Predator (b) |
|---|---|---|---|---|
| B | Non-Consumer (Fy) Warrior (b) | $\backsim$ | D | Consumed Herbivore (y) |

The function of the farmer, the cultivator of plants that sustain life, is to consume the food that he produces. The function of the warrior, who causes death by killing others, is not one of consumption; he does not eat what he kills. This relationship is equivalent structurally to that which exists between the predator and the herbivore. The carnivore hunts, killing animals and consuming their flesh as food. The herbivore, on the other hand, is an animal that does not hunt but itself is killed and eaten as food. Food producers (A, C) sustain life as against death (B, D).

The opposition between the predator and herbivore is not premised, however, upon their dissimilarity, as though it was the content that determined the structural law. It is premised upon the function of the predator. For this reason the function of the third element, the predator, becomes the term value of the last element of the formula, in this case on the basis of the opposition between the verb "consumes" and its counterpart in the passive, "consumed." It is this relation that is fundamental to the structural law of myth, and it is this contradiction that permits it to function as such. The presence of the herbivore, representing this function as a term value, is not essential as such, since in another culture it could be represented by some other species, e.g., a bird or reptile. But the herbivore does embody the function which has become the term value of the last element. The predator eats, and what is consumed is the herbivore.

The addition of this new element, however, breaks the continuity of the structure itself. If it were not for this element, the formula would simply continue with its series of structural correlations. The herbivore introduces into the infrastructure an element that negates the farmer. The farmer cultivates and produces food, sustaining life. But in the order of nature the herbivore also produces food for the carnivore. The role of the herbivore in nature, being consumed as food, represents a negation of what the farmer represents, food production and life. Thus, the herbivore has as its function the negation of the vocation of the farmer. What is consumed as food brings death, denying the association of food-production with life. This is represented graphically in the formula by the inversion of the function (y) and the term value (a-1) in the last element of the structural law.

C   Consumer (Fx)       Predator (b)
D   Farmer Negated (Fa-1)   Consumed Herbivore (y)

The two variants at each end of the formula (A, D) are in a symmetrical, though inverted, relationship (a versus a-1). In this way the structure of myth folds back into itself, death at the end negating life at the beginning, thus restoring the tension with which the process began. However, although the oppositions are not overcome, they are reduced by the progressive substitution of elements.

If the structure is discontinuous, however, the addition of new content at the end adds a supplemental element by which the structure can be moved to a new level and begin all over again. The new structure begins with the opposition between the last two elements, what in the original formula represented a substitution of new but related elements. In the Zuni myth the new opposition is between the predator and the herbivore.

Flesh Consumer (Fx) Predator (a)
Plant Consumer (Fy) Herbivore (b)

Following the formulaic program, the mediator would be an animal that consumed flesh but did not hunt, the scavenger. As we have already observed, the carrion-eater, such as the coyote, does play a mediatorial role in Zuni mythology. Of course, various mediatorical possibilities arise according to the combinations of animal roles. The herbivore may also be a mediator of the human order because of its similarity to both the agriculturalist and the hunter, while the scavenger is a mediator of the second or animal order, being related to the food-producer and the predator. What is essential to observe at this point is the way in which the new content generates new possibilities of opposition and mediation. Like a rope that folds back into itself as it piles up, the structure of mythology is discontinuous, but its content moves it to a new level. Also, the correlations between the two parts of the structural law of myth are not purely arbitrary because the mediations themselves provide transitions from the first element to the last.

Careful scrutiny of the actual procedure of Lévi-Strauss reveals that his discovery of oppositional elements is firmly based upon categorical generalizations of content. Studying a series of myths synchronically presupposes a collection of a wide variety of interrelated mythical stories that can be correlated and set in opposition according to their semantic investment. For example, in the Oedipus myth different kinship relations that are related in the unfolding of the story from beginning to end are brought into relation to each other by the semic category of proximity.[18] When Cadmos seeks his sister, who has been ravished by Zeus, the relations between the two are obviously close. Oedipus' murder of his father is an aggression that expresses the alienation or distance between them. The orientation of the contents yields an immanent infrastructure based upon an elementary structure of meaning, a simple binary opposition. Being close and being distant signify the overrating and the underrating of blood relations. Although the bundles of mythemes are conceived as functions, the actions of different subjects, they are related by their similarity of content within the narrative structure as a whole.

Aside from a series of related problems concerning the determination of the meaning of the various and disparate contents, the choice of a category by which to relate them, and the particular level at which the category becomes operative, the critical issue is whether the synchronic approach to myth, as suggested in the programmatic study of Lévi-Strauss, really embodies a structure of meaning at the most profound level. As we proceed, it will become clear that Lévi-Strauss is dealing with only one aspect of myth as narrative, the structure of its content. Of course, this is a fundamental consideration, and the method that is proposed is one way of penetrating beneath the apparent array of unrelated elements of content to an infrastructure that may exhibit the fundamental tensions of a society. What is even more important, however, is the fact that this understanding of the synchronic dimensions of mythology may bring into sharper focus those elements in the narrative structure that are truly diachronic.

Although this part of the study has moved from the question of history to that of myth, the importance of the approach of Lévi-Strauss is related to the work of the historian of religion. First, it raises the question of the degree to which the lack of the actual living cultural context vitiates the reconstructive effort of the religious interpreter.[19] With respect to biblical studies, Lévi-Strauss asserted that it is the historian of tradition, equipped to analyse and assess the impact of the redactional process, who can better recover mythological residues in the OT than the scholar armed with inapt methods and ready to play a structuralist "game."[20] Second, if the meaning of mythology is derived from an immanent infrastructure of interrelated elements, any approach that interprets religious symbols according to their overt content is severely limited. This is what Lévi-Strauss meant when he asserted in his dialogue with Paul Ricoeur that meaning was determined "by position."[21] Although Mircea Eliade has attempted to avoid falling into the trap that is baited with content by including function within its scope, the fact that two disparate elements may have the same function within two different mythological or ritual systems undercuts the substantialistism implicit in Eliade's morphological studies. In the final analysis the morphology of a symbol refers primarily to its content, not to its function. Yet function and structure are fundamental dimensions of the meaning of religious symbols for the interpreter who seeks to understand them from within their own social and cultural context.

## III.  History and the Structure of the Narrative

The discovery of the mythical structure by Lévi-Strauss came more than two decades after the original publication of Vladimir Propp's foundational study on the morphology of the folktale.[22] In the same year that the French anthropologist launched his proposal for the synchronic study of mythology in his programmatic essay in English, the work of the Russian folklorist on the structure of the folktale appeared in English translation. Whereas

Lévi-Strauss approached mythology paradigmatically, Propp had studied the folktale syntagmatically. The paradigmatic approach conceived myth as an elementary structure of meaning consisting of at
least two sets of contradictory functions. These functions, including their subjects and objects, what Lévi-Strauss designated
mythemes, formed a paradigm of binary oppositions representing the
infrastructure of the myth. In his syntagmatic analysis of the
corpus of Russian folktales, Propp concentrated upon the series of
functions that followed one another in the temporal sequence. He
discovered that within certain limits the series of relations embodied in the functions appeared in a fixed order. These functions
comprised the set of relations or the grammar of the narrative,
what assigned the variable content its place and meaning within
the narrative structure. It was the narrative syntax or "form,"
that actually produced the meaning of the story by determing the
functional relations of the semantic contents.

The distinction between the narrative syntax and the variable
contents or the substance may be illustrated at the level of the
sentence. The fundamental set of relations that is the elementary
basis of meaning is the grammar of the sentence. This grammar or
"form" may be distinguished, however, from the substance. The substance of a language is comprised of all of the words including the
total number of their meanings that are recorded in the dictionary.
The "form" of a language is the syntactical system that structures
the words into sets of relations that makes them intelligible as
sentences. "Form," then, is the structuring set of relations that
exists before the sentence but appears in it; it is the grammatical
system that "makes sense."

Applied at a level superior to that of the sentence, "form"
is the immanent system articulated in the narrative that produces
meaning by setting the substance or narrative components in a coherent relation to each other. In contrast to the definition of
form utilized in biblical studies, where it is a specific and con-

tingent configuration of content determined by a variety of historical and cultural factors, the Sitz im Leben as Hermann Gunkel defined it, the semiotician who analyzes the structure of the narrative understands the term "form" to refer to the system that organizes and shapes the substance of language at its narrative and discursive levels.[23] The narrative, then, is made up of two distinct linguistic components: its discursive component is the substance with its semantic content; its narrative element is comprised of the "form" or syntax.

The discovery of the structure of the narrative came as a result of Vladimir Propp's search for the invariant elements in the folktale that embody its structuring system. In his archaeological investigation of the narrative, the corpus of Russian folktales that Propp excavated was like a series of proximate but different tells that provided an adequate yet not too heterogeneous cross-section of its terrain. Using the corpus of folktales, he discovered that what had traditionally been regarded as the invariable element in the tales, the actors allegedly endowed with fixed traits and roles as "ontological subjects," were in reality an unstable element, varying from one tale to another. What all of the tales had in common and what was pertinent to them was the invariable functions that were embodied in the different elements making up a story. Maximally, each tale consisted of thirty-one functions or narrative components, what may be called "morphologues," and the investment of these "morphologues" with an order, variable within limits, produced the story as it unfolded from beginning to end. Likewise, he defined the actors by their functions, using the designation dramatis personnae in a sense quite different than the traditional usage. Dramatis personnae were spheres defined by functions, and all of the actors in the folktales could be reduced to seven roles, each embodying a particular function.

Adopting Hjelmslev's distinction between "form" and substance, Greimas reformulated the thirty-one functions discovered by Propp in more logical terms, showing how they could be combined in pairs

that were related by implication.[24]  Besides reducing the number
of functions to twenty and explicating the way in which the actants
were related on their separate axes, he also explored several dimensions of the narrative structure that Propp had ignored, such
as the modalites and the canon of the tests.  Focusing upon the
functions in the correlated content of the narrative, i.e., the
introduction and the conclusion, and the status of the principal
test in the topical content, i.e., the transformational action in
the story, he raised two fundamental questions growing out of his
study of the structure of the folktale.  Why does the Russian folktale begin with the violation of an interdiction?  What is the relation of the principal test, the struggle and victory of the hero,
to the rest of the functions?  The answer to the first question is
based upon a synchronic interpretation of the narrative as an elementary structure of meaning, i.e., two contrary terms.  The
second problem and its solution springs from the diachronic reading of the narrative as a transformation of the structure, i.e.,
an inversion of terms.  The resolution of these two problems yielded
significant results related to the understanding of the transformational function of the folktale and the historical dimension implied by the transformation.

By categorizing and homologizing the functions appearing in
the related content of the narrative structure, Greimas was able
to correlate the categories paradigmatically and in this way interpret the narrative as an achronic structure.  In the following di-
agram the first function, the rupture of the contract (No. 1), and
the last one (No. 11), the establishment of the contract, are related inversely according to their position in the narrative structure.  (The "morphologues" may be read diachronically by the numbers
or synchronically by the grouping of the functions under the positive and negative signs).

CORRELATED CONTENT

| INVERSED CONTENT (−) | STRUCTURAL ELEMENTS | POSED CONTENT (+) |
|---|---|---|

### Functions — Modalities — Functions

1. Rupture of Contract (Prohibition and Violation)

11. Establishment of Contract (Injunction and Fulfillment)

2. Reconnoitering of Villain (Information Extorted)

a) Cognition (Object-message)

[8. Manifestation of Hero (Information Revealed)]

3. Deception of Villain (Submission of Hero)

b) Power (Object-force)

9. Revelation of Villain (Submission of Villain)

4. Crime of Villain (Creation of Lack)

c) Volition (Object-good)

10. Punishment of Villain (Liquidation of Lack)

TOPICAL CONTENT

Canon of Tests

5. Mandating of Hero (Contract and Acceptance)

d) Contract (Mandate-Acceptance)

6. Qualifying Test (Reception of Helper)

8. Glorifying Test (Recognition of Hero)

7. Principal Test (Defeat of Villain, Objects Regained, Demand for Recognition)

e) Struggle (Confrontation-Success)

f) Result (Attribution)

Likewise, the reconnoitering, deception, and crime (Nos. 2, 3, 4) can be combined into one category, crime and lack, and related inversely by position to the vindication of the crime and restoration, a combination of the functions, manifestation, revelation, and punishment (Nos. 8, 9, 10).

1. Prohibition and Violation (−)  ≈  2-4. Crime and Lack (−)
11. Injunction and Fulfillment (+)     8-10. Vindication and Restoration (+)

These elements may be correlated paradigmatically, i.e., vertically, yielding the following equation: the existence of a contract is to the absence of a contract as the situation of lack is to the full enjoyment of powers.

This correlation enables one not only to understand the folktale as an elementary structure of signification represented in two contrary terms, restriction versus freedom, but also brings into relation the two different domains that reveal the significance of the initial prohibition and its violation. Given the fact that the folktale is one place where the collective value system of the society is manifest, this appears in the initial prohibition. The negation of this prohibition, however, viewed strictly as the inversion of a function, is the negation of a negation, an ambiguous function at least, if not a positive one. It brings into conflict the social order, the restriction of powers, and individual liberty, the free play of powers, as a result of which the prohibition is violated. If the establishment of a social contract is opposed to its violation, the rupture of the contract is an affirmation of the freedom of the individual. Therefore, the folktale poses two choices equally impossible and unsatisfying, social restriction or individual liberty. This explains the appearance of the prohibition and violation at the beginning of the tale and that serves as a spring releasing the narrative action. It also provides a basis for understanding the transformational functions appearing in the topical content.

This paradigmatic analysis of the folktale raises the question of the diachronic status of the narrative. In Greimas' analysis of the functions, he discovered that most of them can be related either by implication, or by contiguity, or by their reversibility, as appearing under the positive and negative sign. The one group of functions, however, that cannot be related this way are the tests appearing in the topical content, particularly the principal test. These three tests are comprised of the qualifying test in which the hero receives the power to defeat the enemy, the prin-

:ipal test, in which he defeats the villain, and the glorifying
:est, in which he is recognized by society as the hero. The prin-
:ipal test, in particular, is comprised of a canonical schema of
:hree functions, the contract and its acceptance (d), the struggle
(e) involving confrontation and success, and the result, the at-
:ribution (f), whether virtual or real, of the object desired.
The contract and the struggle, however, are not related by implication, for the contract may be followed simply by the assignment of a difficult task, as in the glorifying test. The two are
not contiguous; the mandate may be separated from the struggle by
other functions. Also, they cannot be reversed; the struggle must
follow the contract, whether explicit or implicit. In fact, the
principal test does not stand under the negative sign; it is only
related to what precedes and what follows as a metalinguistic
activity, negating the negative sign. It appears as a frozen sequence only because of the redundance of its form but not because
of any internal relations of causality. Thus, it manifests the
two elements that define history, choice and irreversibility. The
hero is free to accept or reject the contract, but having accepted
it, his action is irreversible; the struggle must always follow
the contract. It is the principal test, then, that introduces the
diachronic, i.e., "historical" aspect into the narrative structure.

The transformation of the paradigmatic opposition is contained
in the second correlation, which, interpreting the same categories
diachronically, i.e., reading horizontally, focuses upon their relation by implication: In a world without law (prohibition and
violation) the values are overturned (villainy and lack); the restoration of these values (vindication and restoration) makes possible a return to law (injunction and fulfillment).[25] The opposition between the prohibition and the injunction of the synchronic
correlation is replaced by the diachronic relation of implication
between the prohibition and its violation and the crime. Similarly, by implication the vindication or defeat of the villain

makes possible the injunction, the positive command that represents
the full enjoyment of the powers regained, which replaces the prohibition. Since these oppositions are not apparent, the story appears as a state of equilibrium ensuing the principal test that
neutralises the original contradiction. From this perspective it
mediates between structure and action, permanence and history, and
society and the individual, containing in itself both the synchroni
and diachronic aspects.

Generalizing on the basis of these two models, Greimas suggest
that perhaps it is possible to divide narratives according to their
function into two classes: stories that speak of an order accepted
and tales that tell of an order that has been rejected. In the
first type man confronts the existing order and is faced with the
need to explain and justify it. In this case, as anthropomorphized
the existence of day and night, men and women, or agriculturalists
and hunters, would be explicated as a result of the quest of man
or his struggles that have installed this order. The mediation
would signify the humanisation of the world, giving it an individual and historical dimension. In the second type, the existing
order is regarded as imperfect, and the cosmos is one from which
man is alienated. For this reason man must take the reins of the
fate of the world in his hands and give it a new direction. As an
archetype of mediation involving a promise of salvation, this model
gives an account of the diverse forms of soteriology relating to
the cosmos and the social order. What must be stressed, of course,
is that this model is a structural one and resides in the interrelation between the paradigmatic and syntagmatic dimensions of
the literature, not simply in a superficial classification based
upon a manifest content, which in some cases might be misleading.

As the study of the structure of the narrative, centered
around the corpus of Russian folktales, has shown, this approach
to literature has important ramifications bearing upon the work
of the historian. Although it does not utilize the traditional

ategory of cause-effect that is so pervasive in historical studies,
t also avoids certain ambiguities and pitfalls associated with its
se.[26] All sorts of relations, defined rather loosely, causality,
robability, likelihood, and even belief, are included in the cat-
gory of cause and effect for which a typology has never been es-
ablished. Moreover, where spatial and temporal coordinates are
acking, causes cannot be established with any real certainty. This
eans the historian must either give up the historical quest or
urrender effects to conjectural causes based upon hypothetical
econstructions that are external to the historical sources. The
aucity of social, cultural, and economic data does not necessarily
ean, for instance, that all of the Russian folktales are unhis-
orical. An interesting parallel bearing on the question of his-
oricity is found in the case of the Egyptian story of the journey
f Wen-Amon to Syria. When it was published in a collection of
exts by the Egyptologist Alan Gardiner, it was placed with a group
f Egyptian myths and legends.[27] Subsequently, it was realized
hat this story was not a folktale at all but an actual report,
nd it was suddenly elevated to the rank of an historical text.
his re-evaluation of the text came not just as a result of the
iscovery of new data bearing on the question of its historicity
ut also as a result of a comparison of this tale with the other
yths and legends with which it had been associated.

Although Greimas admitted that the lack of knowledge of the
ystem of values underlying the Russian folktales was a serious
acuna, he maintained that structural interpretation could artic-
late pertinent formal categories and show how the organization
f contradictory values is mediated.[28] Within a literary corpus,
r even an individual text, as we have already perceived, these
ormal categories are also the means by which diachrony can be
stablished. If the perspective is shifted for the moment from
ets of values to states, it becomes evident that the determination
f the principal test, what changes a situation from one state to

another, is decisive in the evaluation of the significance of event
Of course, there may be a series of interlocking events that lead
to the moment when the struggle is resolved, but once this is discovered, it enables the historian to work backwards through the
series of events that precede and that represent the power or
competence needed to change the state. Of course, if the state
is one of evil or lack, the historian may attempt to reconstruct
the events that created it. If this resides in certain social ills
he may be required to move to the level of foundational history
and study the relevant social, cultural, or economic structures
that can elucidate the nature of the social problem or the reasons
why the social injustices became acute. This does not mean that
the historical task is thereby simplified, but it does point toward
the need for historians, who deal with all of reality, to define
their object of investigation more precisely. Therefore, what
Greimas has asserted about values with reference to the folktale
can be enlarged to cover the relationship between events and states
a subject to which the last section of this study will be devoted.

## IV. History and the Passion Narrative

Since the subject of history is an especially acute one when
it is raised in the context of theological interpretation, the
question of the meaning of the life of Jesus as presented in the
Gospels may be approached through the study of the structure of
the narrative. Of course, a study of the life of Jesus as reported in the Gospels is beyond the scope of this brief study.
Rather, I will focus on Louis Marin's study of the Passion narrative.[29]

In his interpretation of the Passion narrative, Marin has
combined the equation utilized by Lévi-Strauss and the analysis
of the function of the principal test made by Greimas. At the

outset he poses the thesis that 'the original tension between the eternal and the mortal, has been transmuted in the Gospels into the antinomy between life and death. By this process of commutation the fundamental opposition between life and death is brought into relation to Jesus, the mediatorial figure. However, it is in Jesus himself that it originates and is resolved, and it is "the structure of the mediatorial person" that reveals what the structure of the Gospel is. Thus, as an ambiguous figure occupying a mediatorial role, the structural relations linked in Jesus are revealed in the Gospels through the series of struggles that he undergoes. All of these find their linkage in the Passion narrative, the principal struggle that is not correlated in the narrative structure with any other element. In it all of the other elements are condensed and resolved by the way in which the passion manifests the structural relations linked in the person of Jesus.

In his utilization of the formula of Lévi-Strauss, Marin insists that it is not a question of merely projecting the structural law upon Jesus but rather of seeing the way in which the unique element, the Passion, which may be interpreted as a metalinguistic action, manifests the transformation of the contradiction between life and death. Schematically, it may be represented as follows:

Death (Man) : Life (God) ⌣ Death (God) : NON-man (Life)[30]

Death, which is the function of man, is to life, which is the function of God, as the death of Jesus, which is the function of God, is to the eternal life that negates man. The third element, of course, mediates between the first two, and the last element includes the inversion of the function and the term that introduces the dissymmetry into the equation. It is the negation of man that is the function of life. The last element, then, does not raise the question of the ontological status of Jesus as the primary focus but rather by introducing a new element moves the structure to a new level.

The inclusion of supplementary content related to the negation

of man, although not essential as such to the structure, nevertheless enables it to function as a transformation and a transition.
The formula itself indicates what it is without explaining it because it simply functions to articulate the law of the group of
the permutations of the various variants of the myth.  This articulation, of course, is paramount, showing not only how the law
is embodied in its elements but also introducing the additional
content by which the myth is constituted as mediatorial.  Within
the structure, then, an additional story appears to which it cannot be realized, that is not required by the structure but without
which the structure cannot function.  In the structure of the Passion narrative, as analyzed by Marin, the negation of man as the
function of life introduces the role of Judas Iscariot, the traitor,
who is the man who stands over and against God while simultaneously
representing the negation of man.  At the Last Supper that Judas
exchanges the sign, the person of Jesus, for an empty sign, the
coinage of treachery, uniting in himself two functions that cannot be integrated at the semantic level, the negative act of betrayal and the positive function of making the mediatorial work of
Jesus possible.  Usually, a traitor is discovered after his treachery or denounced beforehand; in Judas' case, however, he is discovered before and only denounced after his act.  At the level of
the surface of the text this underscores his uselessness, the fact
that Jesus could have been arrested without his intervention.  His
role, in a sense, has also been emptied of real significance by
the discovery of it on the part of Jesus.

At the level of the deep structure, however, relating to the
functions, Judas occupies the role of the sujet-operateur who effects the exchange, a role that is indispensable in the transmission
of any object between opposing parties.  This role is a necessary
one for two reasons.  First, the mediation is realized in a structure of exchange and inversion of terms that has as its prere-
quisite a traitor.  Second, Jesus cannot effect the transformation

himself and still remain the sign of God. If he did, the meaning
of the modal signs, cognition and power, would be expressed, and
he would cease to be for that moment and from then on the sign of
God; the tension between history and eschatology would be broken.
Thus, the betrayal of Judas Iscariot is that element which, without being integrally a part of the structure, is the supplement
that permits it to function. In an apparently unmotivated act
Judas delivers Jesus, the sign, to his death and thus enables him
by this act to realize the meaning of the sign. Symbolically,
this signifies the nullification of time, the body of Jesus being
given as the continuing Passover feast, representing the unifi-
cation of knowledge and power in him. It is also that moment when
the deliberate choice of Jesus sets in motion an irreversible train
of events leading to his struggle and his victory in death, the
moment in which Jesus becomes the historical sign filling the negative modalities with a positive meaning.

At this point one other important question relating to the
structure of the Passion narrative needs to be raised. If the
principal test is that point at the center of the structure that
is without structure, where there is only an inversion or negation
of sign, what are the objects in the narrative structure of the
Gospel that are exchanged? What is originally denied to Jesus that
is, as a result of the principal struggle, attributed to him? According to the temptation narratives in Matthew and Luke, the exchange involves three objects, the word, the knowledge of the transformational power of signs (cognition), the force that can validate
the message of Jesus by preserving him from any and every evil (power), and the person as the will to redeem the world (volition),
corresponding to the three modalities appearing in the correlated
content of the narrative structure.[31] In reality, however, what
is originally offered to Jesus is only a sign without its corresponding content, the three modal powers that are offered by Satan
being "a form of godliness without the power thereof."

Moreover, the three modalites are disjoined from one another,
and they cannot be integrated except by a transformation accomplished by God. The point or place in which the sign is exchanged
for its meaning and the three modalites are integrated, already,
by implication, embodied in the person of Jesus, is the principal
test. In the narrative sequence the act of betrayal appears isolated, unmotivated, interrupting the metonymic contiguity of the
functions in the story, and therefore violates the narrative structure as a kind of irruption that neutralizes the negative. In this
struggle the negative signs are annulled and united in the person
of Jesus as positive powers effected through an exchange by the
traitor, Judas Iscariot. In contrast to Karl Barth, who refers
to Judas role as a "planned" one and who seeks to root Judas'
motivation in his unwillingness to glorify God without exploitation,
as Mary did in her prodigal act of annointing Jesus at Bethany,
Marin seeks to distinguish between the deep structure of the narrative, where some such role in required, and the manifestation
of the text, where the role of Judas in the story appears as a
contingent element in the story because of its revalorization in
a theological context.[32] Thus, he distinguishes between the function, which is essential, and its realization at the surface of
the text, which, in his view, is integrated more fully into the
theological perspective of the various Gospels than into the development of the narrative.

Although Marin analyses the Passion narrative from a semiotical perspective that includes the formula of Lévi-Strauss,
his interpretation is controlled by a model of exchange.[33] Since
an operator is necessary in an exchange model, Marin modifies the
mythical formula to incorporate Judas Iscariot into it. The last
element of the formula, representing the inverse function as a
term value (life eternal), itself involves a transformational
story that has as its function the negation of the first element
of the structure (man). To this function (NON-man) Marin attaches

the story of Judas Iscariot as an element that is not required by the mythical structure but that enables it to function as such. In this way the model of exchange is complete. Judas causes the death of God, and the ensuing eternal life has as its function the negation of the traitor.

In a similar way, utilizing the actantial model of Greimas, Marin interprets the essential structure of the Gospels as an exchange, located on the axis of communication.[34] On this axis the Sender, God, gives the Object, the body of Jesus as the power of life, to the Receiver, mankind. The body of Jesus is the material manifestation of the ultimate sign, and it is given in his death to be consumed as food that signifies eternal life. As the bearer of the message of God, Jesus embodies the salvation that God will give to mankind through him. In Marin's semiotics of the Passion, the mythical formula and the actantial model are subordinated to the model of exchange. It is on the basis of this model that Marin constructs his eucharistic theology of the Passion narrative.

An evaluation of Marin's type of structural analysis will depend in large part upon the perspective by which it is judged. On the one hand, his method has a certain heuristic value for theological study. It reveals the way in which one particular theological understanding can be utilised to build a structure from materials that are compatible with it and thus provide a theological understanding of the life of Jesus. On the other hand, since his own intention, to work back from the Passion narrative in order to show the way in which the other struggles of Jesus are related to it, is carried out only very partially, the question concerning the viability of this structure and its theological vaidity in the face of a more complete semiotical analysis of one or several Gospels is a serious one. Of even greater import, however, is the fact that Marin ignores vital issues related to the question of the historical Jesus. This implies that semiotics does not have its own contribution to make in the field of historical studies. Actually, this is not the case. Even though the first gropings of this new discipline in the field of biblical studies will need to be refined and brought more directly into relation to traditional methods, semiotics is a vehicle of research that can assist in clarifying the nature of historical discourse.

## V.  History and Diachrony

The analysis of the narrative structure, accomplished by Propp and refined by Greimas, provides an important interpretive vehicle that can be utilized in the study of history. The historical task, of course, involves the creation and use of an operational set of concepts different from the object under study.[35] By these concepts, whether specifically elaborated or merely implied in the descriptive language used, the object of the historical investigation is defined. Also, it is through these categories that the historian is able to apprehend the object that is the aim of his study. For example, the distinction between nature and history is not one that the historiographers of the ancient Near East developed. They did not distinguish between human actions and natural events in some cases, since both of them could be considered to embody supernatural agencies. The modern historian, however, makes this distinction as a means of defining his object. This raises the important question concerning the scope of historical investigation. Is the historian responsible to account for natural disasters and under what conditions? Or is his task to be defined more narrowly as pertaining to human history? Unless significant restrictions are introduced into history as a distinct field of study, historical discourse will become encyclopedic, and history will dissolve into any number of phenomena, many of them unrelated to human events as such.

Beginning with the definition of history as "deeds," i.e., that which has been done, brought into a relation to each other,

the semiotician proceeds from a purely semantic and non-realistic
perspective to propose a canonical statement of a logical kind as
a linguistic representation of what constitutes a "deed" or action.[36]
Suspending reference to the past and considering the action as a
function of a logical statement, he postulates a Subject (S) and
Object (O) of the action (F), linked by a function-relation. A
canonical historical statement in this sense would be a sentence
signifying simply "someone does something," written as follows:

$$F (S \longrightarrow O).$$

This permits the formulation of all historical events in a consistent manner and envisages, according to the investment of this
formula with appropriate but different semantic contents, the construction of a typology of historical statements. This simple model
also defines clearly the object under investigation. It involves
events, not states, and excludes natural events as such. Of course,
these intentional restrictions are regarded as metalinguistic con-
structions that enable the historian to focus upon particular dimensions of the object that he is investigating.

This distinction between a metalinguistic construction and
reality and between function and past action has as its goal a
more profound understanding of historical statements by an analysis
of their constituent elements within the scope of a logical perspective. This includes a study of the way in which these statements are organized into sequences and narrative programs. Viewed
from the perspective of the Object, what in the formulaic description represents the fulfillment of the desire of the Subject, it
involves an oriented relation that gives important clues pertaining to the aim of the Subject to attain something. When the Subject is represented by a collective body, such as the multitude
of Israelite slaves that escaped from Egypt, this orientation
expresses the will of a social class and leads to foundational
history where motivations arise in the context of social structures that represent systems of economic and social exchange. It
is the actual expression of this in the function, however, that

determines interpretation of the historian. A report concerning a series of events brings into play important aspects of the narrative structure as a means of reconstructing specific narrative programs and linking events to one another in a sequence. Utilizing a logic of presuppositions that can reconstruct the constitutive relations of historical statements, the historian can begin with the results of specific narrative programs and penetrate backwards into the deeper dimensions of history, whether it is history as event or foundational history.

Although this non-realistic understanding of the historical task represents the concerns of the semiotician about the construction of historical discourse, it also provides a vehicle by which the historian can discover what is truly diachronic.[37] The two fundamental problems facing the historian are to determine what events are actually intrusions that effect changes in successive historical states and how these events are related by implication to other events in the temporal sequence. The first issue requires the historian to make two judgments about an event. He must decide that it does not simply represent an extension of the functions of a structure into other realms. He must also conclude from his study that the historical model explaining the existing state cannot account for the event. By the description of static structures, such as Lévi-Strauss has done, and by the comparison of successive structural states he can determine what event or events truly are transformational. Of course, both the descriptive and the comparative task are metalinguistic operations with respect to the historical contents that are studied. The operational set of concepts or the metalangue by which this decision is made may be provided by an immanental understanding of the transformational action at the level of the deep structure. Working at the level of foundational history, Lévi-Strauss has studied the contents and transformational models of myth immanent within the manifestation of history. Without denying history as such, he has sought to provide a repertoire of models of transformation by positing a logic of the concrete to explain mythological transformations.

> Far from constituting an a-historical or even an anti-
> historical method, the structuralist methodology has
> probably made possible a resumption of historical re-
> search. For a better knowledge of the general laws of
> structural transformations is necessary before one can
> render a judgment with some certainty on the specific
> nature of the diachronic transformations.[38]

By discovery of what is reversible within given historical states,
the historian is enabled to focus upon what is irreversible. Also,
by an awareness of compatibilities between the structures of
foundational history that permit the operation of freedom, he can
locate the exercise of original choices within the historical
process.

With respect to the interrelation of events, it has already
become evident that interlocking events that effect changes of
historical states can be related to each other syntactically. Using
a logical model, some may be included within others as sub-groups
of the same event. From a semiotical perspective the three tests,
which represent competence, performance, and effects, provide categories that enable the historian to isolate the transformational
event and its relation to the two states involved, what, viewed
from a chronological perspective, are the "before" and "after" of
history. Although the subject of the relation between the three
levels is too complicated to be analyzed at this point, the effects
of events upon states does not rule out the reverse possibility,
even in terms of the assessment of the factor of human freedom.
Nor does the establishment of an autonomous level of history as
event necessarily imply the abandonment of the search for structures
within foundational history. If the study of history does involve
the construction of a metalangue by which the object at which the
historian aims can be realized, semiotics is a valuable resource
in the search to discover what is truly diachronic, the once-for-all
events that embody human freedom and choice.

Finally, in the context of the Judaeo-Christian tradition, the discovery of history as event leads to a _faire interprétatif_ in which certain events are viewed as paradigmatic. Within the biblical tradition these events shape, formulate, and interpret the movement of history. Their meaning is not exhausted in their diachronic status nor is it entirely absorbed in the immediate change of state that they effect. They emerge from the historical process provided with an interpretation that embodies the meaning and destiny of a people transcending the culture-bound forms in which they are given. In this respect what is unique about Israel's witness to the meaning of these events is the fact that they are validated as vehicles of revelation. Where they appear in the form of the narrative, textual semiotics can play an important role in clarifying the relationship between the narrative structure, history, and theology. For between what the historian discovers to be truly syntagmatic and what the theologian perceives to be truly paradigmatic is the elaborate set of mechanisms realized in the structure of language itself. By an analysis of the "form" and substance of the narrative, the relation between the narrative as history and the narrative as theology can be approached at a more profound level. It is at this deeper level that the discoveries of the semiotician can assist in clarifying the relation between synchrony and diachrony, a dimension that is critical to the understanding of the divine self-disclosure that occurred "in, through, and by means of history."

FOOTNOTES

1. A. Cohen, *The Myth of the Judeo-Christian Tradition* (New York: Harper, 1957) 159-64, 193-217; E. Berkovits, "Judaism in the Post-Christian Era," *Disputation and Dialogue* (ed. F.E. Talmage; New York: KTAV, 1975) 291.

2. J. Coert Rylaarsdam, "Jewish-Christian Relationship: The Two Covenants and the Dilemmas of Christology," *Journal of Ecumenical Studies* 9 (1972) 249-70.

3. R. G. Collingwood, *The Idea of History* (Oxford: Clarendon, 1946) 126-33, 321-34; H. Meyerhoff, *The Philosophy of History in Our Time* (Garden City, New York: Doubleday, 1959) 291-345; H. B. Acton, "Historical Materialism," *The Encyclopedia of Philosophy* (ed. P. Edwards; New York: Macmillan, 1967) 4. 12-15; A. J. Greimas, "Sur l'histoire événementielle et l'histoire fondamentale," *Sémiotique et sciences sociales* (Paris: Seuil, 1976) 161-74.

4. Collingwood, *The Idea of History*, 314-20; R. Bultmann, *History and Eschatology* (Edinburgh: University, 1957) 138-55; C. Lévi-Strauss, *The Savage Mind* (Chicago: University, 1966) 231-37; *Race et histoire* (France: Gonthier, 1961) 41-50.

5. E. Meyer, *Die Israeliten und ihre Nachbarstämme* (Halle: Max Niemeyer, 1906) 486-87. Referring to Meyer's essay, *Zur Theorie und Methodik der Geschichte*, published in 1902, Collingwood comments, "Here, as in Bury but far more clearly thought out, we find an attempt to disentangle history from errors and fallacies due to the influence of natural science: an anti-positivistic view of its task, which in the long run fails to rise decisively above the atmosphere of positivism" (*The Idea of History*, 177). H. Gunkel traced the origins of history-writing in Israel to the awareness of the Israelite historiographers that a history was contained in the political events that involved the king and the people. However, Gunkel also accepted the immanental understanding of history as its distinguishing mark: "The historiographer speaks about God and divine things very reservedly; he knows nothing of miracles, quite different in this respect from the näiveté of the legend (*Sage*)." "Die israelitische Literatur," *Die orientalischen Literatur* (ed. P. Hinneberg; Berlin: Teubner, 1906) 1. 7. 74.

6. J. A. Wilson, "The Journey of Wen-Amon to Phoenicia," *ANET* (2d ed.; Princeton: University, 1955) 25-29; E. F. Wente, "The Report of Wenamon," *The Literature of Ancient Egypt* (ed. W. K. Simpson; New Haven: Yale, 1972) 142. Following Gunkel, G. Hölscher connects the origins of Hebrew historiography to the emergence of the nation of Israel and to the consciousness of

national traditions that originated with this event ("Die Anfänge
der hebräischen Geschichtsschreibung," *Sitzungsberichte der Heidel-
berger Akademie der Wissenschaften: Philosophisch-historische
Klasse* [1941-42] 3. 101-02, 113-15).

7. G. E. Wright, *Biblical Archaeology* (Philadelphia: Westminster, 1962) 133, 83; M. Noth, *The Old Testament World* (Philadelphia: Fortress, 1966) 144.

8. A. J. Greimas, "Structure et histoire," *Du sens* (Paris:
Seuil, 1970) 105-09; *Sémiotique et sciences sociales,* 164-67.

9. The interrelationships between the three levels of history, developed by C. Lévi-Strauss (*Structural Anthropology* [Garden
City, New York: Doubleday, 1967] 9, 22-24, 31), are discussed by
Greimas in *Sémiotique et sciences sociales,* 165, 168. For ex-
plications of the terms related to the root chronos see F. de
Saussure, "On the Nature of Language," *Introduction to Structural-
ism* (ed. M. Lane; New York: Basic Books, 1970) 54-56; Lévi-Strauss,
*Structural Anthropology,* 88; A. J. Greimas, *Sémantique structurale,*
149-50, 204-05. General discussions may be found in Oswald Ducrot
and Tzvetan Todorov, *Dictionnaire encyclopédique des sciences du
langage* (Paris: Seuil, 1972) 179-87; J. Lyons, *Introduction to
Theoretical Linguistics* (Cambridge: University, 1968) 46-52; R.
Barthes, "Eléments de sémiologie," *Communications* 4 (1964) 113;
H. Gardner, *The Quest for Mind* (New York: Random, 1974) 24.

10. L. Hjelmslev, *Prolégomènes à une théorie du langage* (Paris:
Minuit, 1971) 70-85 (=*Prolegomena to a Theory of Language* [Madison,
Wisconsin: University, 1963]); Greimas, "La structure sémantique,"
*Du sens,* 41-43; Ducrot and Todorov, *Dictionnaire,* 36-41; M. Teţescu,
*Précis de sémantique française* (Paris: Klincksieck, 1975) 18-19.

11. C. Lévi-Strauss, *Structural Anthropology* (Garden City, New
York: Doubleday, 1967) 1-26; *The Savage Mind,* 256-63; *Race et
histoire,* 79-85; E. N. Hayes and T. Hayes, eds., *Claude Lévi-Strauss:
The Anthropologist as Hero* (Cambridge, Mass.: M.I.T., 1970) 230-32,
20-21.

12. Lévi-Strauss, *Structural Anthropology,* 19.

13. Ibid., 5.

14. Lévi-Strauss, *The Savage Mind,* 237.

15. Lévi-Strauss, *Structural Anthropology,* 209-227; E. Leach,
*Claude Lévi-Strauss* (New York: Viking, 1970) 65.

16. Lévi-Strauss, *Structural Anthropology,* 221.

17. Ibid., 225.

18. Ibid., 211; E. Leach, *Claude Lévi-Strauss*, 62-68.

19. C. Lévi-Strauss, *Anthropologie structurale deux* (Paris: Plon, 1973) 157-59.

20. C. Lévi-Strauss, "Réponses à quelques questions," *Esprit* (1963) 631-32.

21. Ibid., 632.

22. *Morphology of the Folktale* (Austin: University of Texas, 1970). A survey of research in this field is found in the French edition of this work. E. Mélétinski, "L'étude structurale et typologique du conte," *Morphologie du conte* (Paris: Seuil, 1965) 202-54.

23. H. Gunkel, *Die Kultur der Gegenwart*, 1.7.53.

24. Greimas, *Sémantique structurale*, 194-98, 208-10; *Du sens*, 168-76, 180-92.

25. Greimas, *Sémantique structurale*, 208.

26. Greimas, *Sémiotique et sciences sociales*, 173.

27. A. H. Gardiner, *Late Egyptian Stories* (Bibliotheca Aegyptiaca, 1; Brussels: La Fondation égyptologique, 1932) 61-76.

28. Greimas, *Sémantique structurale*, 185.

29. *Sémiotique de la passion* (Aubier: Cerf, 1971) 106-19. In the footnotes to this section Marin's interpretations and modifications of the approach of Greimas are discussed.

30. Ibid., 109.

31. Ibid., 114-117. In the schema given above they are the modalities marked a, b, c.

32. K. Barth, *Church Dogmatics* (Edinburgh: Clark, 1957) 2.2. 462. The annointing of Jesus at Bethany functions as the qualifying test in Marin's interpretation of the narrative sturcture (*Sémiotique de la passion*, 144).

33. "It is necessary that the betrayer exist in order to make fortuitous and contingent that which is necessary" (Marin, *Sémiotique de la passion*, 105).

34. *Sémantique structurale*, 180; *Sémiotique de la passion*, 112-13. Explanations of the actantial model of Greimas in English

may be found in R. Scholes, *Structuralism in Literature* (New Haven: Yale, 1974) 103-11; J. Culler, *Structuralist Poetics* (Ithaca: Cornell University, 1975) 233-34; D. Patte, *What is Structural Exegesis?* (Philadelphia: Fortress, 1976) 42.

35. Greimas, *Sémiotique et sciences sociales,* 161-62.

36. Ibid., 170-74.

37. Greimas, *Du Sens,* 113-14.

38. Ibid., 113.

# CHRISTOLOGY IN SCRIPTURE AND EXPERIENCE: THE CASE OF PROCESS THEOLOGY

William A. Beardslee

The role of Scripture as a norm for experience has always been a difficult problem for liberal theologies. By their strong emphasis on a "highest" form of experience, these theologies have tended to look away from a past originating point toward a systematic classification of present forms of experience. When they do turn to the past, liberal Christian theologies have tended to concentrate on the figure of Jesus rather than on Scripture as a whole, but their concentration on Jesus has tended to "liberate" Jesus from the Scripture so as to see him as the model of a perennial possibility. By their strong confidence that the vision of faith may become actual in the world, liberal theologies have turned to a human figure and to personal growth, and away from the "judgmental" aspect of Scriptural norms.

All these aspects of liberal theology were subjected to severe scrutiny in the theological debates of the past two generations. The work of theology is now carried on in a post-modern culture which brings home to us the polymorphous or amorphous qualities of experience, so that it is not easy to speak of a highest form of experience. The study of the Bible has fragmented the figure of Jesus or made this figure difficult to access. And the situation in our world has brought home the gap between the vision of faith and the opportunities of making it actual; in particular, the emphasis on the play of chance in so many aspects of the contemporary way of perceiving the world challenges the earlier liberal hope that rational models could set directions for action.

343

This paper is written from within a perspective of liberal theology and specifically as an exploration of process Christologies. It will examine the Christologies of John B. Cobb, Jr. and Schubert M. Ogden as responses to the situation sketched above, and will then explore the relation of Christology to Scripture from the vantage point of some questions posed by J. Coert Rylaarsdam about tensions within the Scripture itself. Thus it will appear that the issues with which we are grappling are not unique to liberal theology, but are modern representatives of issues which were already part of the make-up of the earliest Christological reflection.

Rylaarsdam himself has expressed (in conversation with the author) a severe doubt that a process interpretation of the NT can be viable, though he has been much more sympathetic to process interpretation of the Hebrew Scriptures. The problem which he sees in the NT is that Christ is such a fixed point, such an absolute, that it is difficult to see how this fixed point can be incorporated into a pattern of process.

Cobb is keenly aware of this problem.[1] On the one hand, he opens a vision of Christ or the logos as creative transformation, so that Christian faith does not have a fixed essence, but is characterized (when it is true to itself) precisely by its opening us to new forms of life; faith is a matter of attending to the "call forward" in each particular situation.[2] In this way Cobb takes a position in a long-continuing discussion within liberal historical study about the difficulty of discovering an essence of Christianity. But he avoids the historical relativism that so often attends the denial of essence by developing a definite criterion of value with which to scrutinize change: creative transformation. What Jesus incarnated was the logos of a process of continual self-surpassing which contradicts the effort to define a stable essence. It should be said that by his careful correlation of creative transformation with love, Cobb finds an element of contact between the stability which Christians have usually tried to

find in their faith and the movement of creative transformation.
He rightly says that love itself constantly requires us to question established frameworks of judgment.  It is creative transformation as love which is Cobb's equivalent of the highest form
of experience which has been a mark of liberal theology.  His
version goes far to overcome the "triumphalism" of much liberal
theology, for though he does not give up the effort to rank types
of experience, he holds that there is more than one line of development, so that there is not one highest form of experience.

Cobb also stands in the liberal tradition with its emphasis
on the historical Jesus.  He grounds his own interest in Jesus in
the Whiteheadian conviction that important changes arise from actual
events; the new presence of God which the early Christians experienced "was somewhere"; was fully incarnated in the selfhood
of Jesus.  Jesus' decisions were made in so full an attention to
the concrete will of God for each occasion that the sense of tension between the self and the call of God which we commonly experience was overcome; Jesus' "I" was "co-constituted by the in-
carnate Logos."[3]  From this new selfhood sprang his own sense of
authority, and still today it is our confidence in the transcendence by Jesus of our ordinary struggle to respond to God's will
which opens our attention to his words and deeds, and delivers us
from the quest for self-salvation which would dominate us if we
responded to him only for the pragmatic reason that paying serious
heed to his words had good results in our own development.  Thus
his theory of Jesus' uniqueness is a central moment in Cobb's
Christology, expressing the primacy of grace in the experience of
Christ.

At the same time, the new fluid understanding of the logos
as creative transformation provides the background for Cobb's
approach to the question of making the vision of faith actual.
It is no longer a question of the extent to which a pre-established
pattern of the Kingdom of God can be realized in human experience
or social life.  His recognition that each new achievement of a

more complex order brings with it the possibility of greater evil as well as greater good signals the full recognition of the precariousness of human existence. But Cobb refuses to fall into the stance of irony or that of resignation, which so often characterize the post-modern consciousness. Like the older liberal theologians, he holds that one of the valid tests of any theological perspective is its potential for changing behavior. The link between creative transformation as the meaning of Christ and the changing of behavior is a twofold one: on the one hand, this view of Christ opens the way for full commitment to ventures where Christ is not explicitly named; and on the other hand, creative transformation as the logos opens the door to hope, to the hope that the relevant future can be different. Seeing that "the world produced by the older notion of the credible is in shambles...,"[4] he calls for a more venturesome and pluralistic exercise of the imagination to open new possibilities of existence. "What exists does not fully determine what will be"; our hope for the future is based on its partial undeterminedness.[5] Thus Cobb meets the new cultural perception of rootlessness and chance by an appeal to the power of Christ as the power of the future, as the dimension that can still give direction to our choices and actions.

Cobb's Christological positions are directly related to the theses of the older liberalism; he has modified these in the framework of process theology to take account of the less rational, pluralistic world that we perceive today. Ogden follows a different path, developing his Christology from a perspective of liberalism modified by the neo-Reformation critique of liberalism.[6]

As a basis for his Christology, Ogden establishes that the question about God is "at bottom, the existential question about the ultimate meaning of our own existence."[7] Ogden does not mean to eliminate language about God. What he does affirm is that the path to the recognition of Christ is identified theologically by finding that there is for humans ultimately an existential question with, in faith, an answer. In other words, the liberal quest for a highest form of existence has been reformulated in terms of the Heideggerian analysis of existence. Heidegger's understanding of authentic existence offers a less speculative, more existential way of understanding what it is that faith in Christ responds to. Though he speaks with approval of Cobb's exploration of a possible mutual enrichment of Christianity and Buddhism,[8] Ogden does not develop a pluralistic view of types of authentic existence as Cobb does. Rather he is concerned to separate the existential and the speculative ways of grasping life, so that the distinctiveness of faith and the Christ faith responds to may be sharply separated from theoretical knowledge; an old Reformation theme.

The originating point of faith is also handled very differently by Ogden. He sharply dissents from Cobb's effort to describe Jesus' personal response to God. He marshals the evidence for the difficulties of speaking of Jesus' own experience, and insists that the NT makes no positive claims about the historical Jesus. Rather than affirming anything about Jesus' existence, the NT "takes" Jesus' existence and personal commitment as an assumption on the basis of which it makes its proper assertions about faith. Should these assumptions actually be unfounded, this conclusion would no more disconfirm NT faith than would a metaphysical theory be disconfirmed by the discovery that one of the presumed empirical facts was not true, on the basis of which the theory had been constructed. For Ogden, here following a major trend of modern Reformation theology, faith is not grounded in the message of Jesus but in the message about Jesus.

Though the forms in which this message is presented are extremely varied,[9] it is essentially one message, in which "man's authentic possibility of self-understanding" is re-presented.[10] This message is essentially the Pauline-Augustinian-Lutheran message of judgment, acceptance, and love. Christ is the predicate by which you and I are definitively interpreted. This means that statements about Christ are at bottom statements about God, since

God is "the ultimate reality in which the norms of existence have
their ground and end."[11] One sees at once that the point of contact
with Cobb's treatment is the centrality of God's love to both.  But
Ogden develops this central insight in terms of a fixed structure
of human existence and in terms of a message about Christ, the
early forms of which serve as a constant norm for the church's reflection.[12]

If we turn to the third motif which we cited as characteristic
of liberal theology, the confidence that the message of Christ can
be made actual, Ogden again displays a modified liberalism.  He
insists that application is one of the essential aspects of the
whole movement of theology, and emphasizes this point by following
a traditional division of theology in which "practical theology"
is one of the three branches of theology (along with historical
and systematic theologies), and by stressing the ethical and social
dimensions of practical theology.[13]  But it is noteworthy that in
describing the task of practical theology he mentions first the
"limitations" that thinking faith must identify as it moves into
action.[14]  He is very reluctant to submit faith to the traditional
liberal empirical test, for he sees a sharp disjunction between
empirical and existential statements, but above all he is eager to
preserve the privacy of faith between a person and God, a relationship which is not to be measured by someone else or even by the
person himself, but to be known only to God.[15]  This concern to
separate faith from that which can be empirically tested by observation — again a Reformation motif — is so strong with Ogden that
it prevents him from dealing more directly with the question of the
expected impact of faith in Christ.

Each of these Christologies displays a tension between the
effort to perceive Christ in ways that are continuous with the
rest of experience, and the effort to affirm the uniqueness of
Christ.  We can clarify what is at issue in this tension by referring to Rylaarsdam's presentation of the two covenants as sources
of Christological symbolism.[16]  Neither Cobb nor Ogden gives much

attention to the OT roots of their Christologies; both are more
interested in discussions that arose later in the church. But the
contrast between the symbolism of the covenant with Israel and
that of the covenant with David was a constitutive factor in the
early Christologies, and the elements which were in tension then
are, many of them, still apparent in these contemporary Christological reflections.

In Rylaarsdam's presentation, the covenant with Israel was
historical, relative, and mutual. It promised nothing beyond what
could be given in this spatio-temporal world, and, equally important, its promises were joined to requirements; grace and demand
were inextricably interwoven. This covenant has been the predom-
inant organizing center of Jewish faith. The covenant with David,
in contrast, was static rather than historical; it was absolute,
and its absoluteness forced those who used its symbolism to project a future beyond this historical world, where its promises
could be realized. It focused on an individual and his line rather
than upon a people. Most important, the promise to David was understood as absolute in such a way that the reciprocal interplay of
promise and responsibility was not a part of this covenant. In
Rylaarsdam's interpretation, the covenant with David provided the
major occasion for the development of apocalyptic. Though Christians used covenant-with-Israel symbolism, they drew predominantly
from the symbolism of the covenant with David and its apocalyptic
developments to find categories in which to express the absoluteness of the coming of Christ which was central to the early Christian faith.

We do not need to commit ourselves to the details of Rylaarsdam's thesis about the narrow connections between the covenant
with David and apocalyptic (which may indeed have developed from
much more diffuse and complex factors) to see how useful and important his typology is for understanding the dynamics of Christological symbolism. He notes that while the early church and
classical Christologies were strongly "Davidic," modern theology

has striven to eliminate the Davidic symbolism and to develop Christologies that in effect use covenant-with-Israel symbolism. Process theology would be an example of this reformulation; its rejection of supernaturalism and its explication of reality in terms of events is highly coordinate with the covenant-with-Israel symbolism as Rylaarsdam sets it forth.

We shall concentrate on the elements or equivalents of covenant-with-David symbolism in the authors we are studying. Factors in the covenant with David which are relevant to the Christologies under discussion are: the focus of the promise on a person rather than on a people; the consequent limitation of the locus where transcendence is perceived to elements associated with that person; a universalistic claim (arising from the royal symbolism); a sense of the totality or finality of revelation, which cannot be surpassed, though it can and must be completed in the future; and a definitiveness of grace which tends to thrust responsibility into the background.

Cobb's recasting of the meaning of Christ to be creative transformation shows many analogies to the historical-processive covenant with Israel as Rylaarsdam sketches it, and Cobb's concept of the interplay of grace and responsibility (with grace primary) is closer to that of the covenant with Israel than to the absoluteness of the promise to David. The "Davidic" elements that appear in Cobb's Christology are particularly two. First, his emphasis on the unique personal constitution of Jesus, which corresponds to the Davidic theme of the divine representative, the king, as the bearer of salvation, and second, his conviction that, once the logos is perceived in Christ, all forms of creative transformation can be seen to be coherent with what is revealed in Jesus. Cobb has set these convictions in a highly processive framework, in which Christian faith can cling to no fixed forms.

In the case of Ogden, the absoluteness of the Davidic symbolism shows itself in the assertion that "nothing is more striking about the New Testament witnesses to Jesus the Christ than the extent to which they emphatically place Jesus on the _divine_, rather than the human, side of the God-man relationship."[17]  Of course, for Ogden this is the Christ who is re-presented in the Christian message.  The existentialist reading of this message by Ogden only strengthens its claim to be decisive of any and all human existence, for the kerygma is _the_ answer to _the_ human question -- a stance typical of a universal religion which Christianity became, and used Davidic symbolism to do so.  Odgen's insistence on _the_ question and _the_ answer is his way of resisting the pluralism and relativism of contemporary culture.

This brief sketch has well substantiated Rylaarsdam's suggestion of the usefulness of the Israel and Davidic covenant symbolisms as a way of identifying problematic areas in Christology.  He is right both that modern Christologies have moved strongly toward categories that are coherent with the covenant with Israel, and also that they cannot eliminate the Davidic type of symbolism altogether.

The way forward in Christology will also be determined largely by how one understands and deals with the tension between the two symbolic complexes.  My own path in Christology will be the resolutely liberal one of constantly questioning the "Davidic" elements in the conviction that they can be transformed without being eliminated, to make them more appropriate to the pluralistic situation in which faith must understand itself -- a theme strongly articulated by Cobb.  Ogden's effort to maintain central Reformation emphases is gained at the price of restricting the flow of Christian reflection, by his insistence on an existential/ speculative dichotomy which does not correspond to the experience of reflection as I understand it.  Faith must be more self-reflective than I understand him to allow it to be; that is, it must be able to question the very forms in which it appears.  Ogden's desire to affirm the enduring oneness of the re-presentation of Christ represents a concern that I share; but I cannot recognize this oneness in the actual diversity of the proclamations.  I believe

that we must think of early Christianity and of Christianity in
general as constituted by the coming-together of a variety of
commitments. No one of these remains constantly in the focus of
all the forms of faith. Rather, reflection about the different
styles of Christian faith will lead us to construct a grid with
various squares filled in for various forms of faith. This will
be true even for the very earliest stages, for the notion of a
uniform early Christianity is not supported by the sources. Normative judgments will be judgments about various clusters of
commitments rather than judgments about the effectiveness of
realization of a single essence.

Further, Ogden's unquestioning acceptance of the claim of
faith to be the decisive answer to the human question also needs
to be scrutinized by faith itself. This claim is part of the
structure of a universal religion; we need to ask what it means
to be moved beyond the stage of the universal religion. As we
pass into a situation where genuine encounter with other faiths
is possible in a way never before actual in Christian history,
faith must reformulate its unreflective understanding of its own
absoluteness, in the hope for a more comprehensive faith yet to
come.

Thus, a further exploration of the more speculative methods
followed by Cobb holds the greater promise. But here, too, it
is precisely the most "Davidic" elements which are the most questionable. To understand the logos as creative transformation is
a major advance in Christological thinking. But creative transformation comes into our field of experience from a complex set
of sources. One might think that Plato, moving from his early
theory of ideas toward his later view of the quest for truth as
a dialectic movement often without final conclusion, has been a
model of creative transformation for many modern as well as ancient theologians, parallel to Jesus. Cobb would not question
the variety of the sources through which we may encounter cre-

ative transformation. The question is whether the different types of creative transformation can be seen as coherent, as one logos. I would doubt this, and would hold that the convergence of different movements of creative transformation has to be regarded as a hope, a part of eschatology -- an essential part of Christian hope even though it will, probably, never be fully realized.

Secondly, Jesus' selfhood as co-constituted by the logos is a questionable thesis. We need to recognize that the Jesus to whom we respond in faith is a "constructed" figure, constructed in the imagination of believers. Elements contributing to the construction of this figure are the power of symbols from the Hebrew Scriptures and from the Hellenistic world, the experiences of early Christians, and our own experiences, as well as the impact of the selfhood of Jesus himself, made manifest through his words and deeds. We can indeed know something about Jesus, and that knowledge, for all its tentativeness, is relevant to faith. A part of the basis for our trust is his commitment to God and to his task. But we cannot rigorously distinguish his sense of vocation from that of others who understood themselves to be authoritative representatives of God, by making the distinction that Jesus was responding fully to the call of God, while others were exaggerating their responsiveness. Rather, it is the setting in which he acted and spoke and was perceived that enabled the first Christians, and enables us, to fuse his person with the symbols drawn from the two covenants and elsewhere and to see in him the full representation of God and the fulfillment of our hopes.

We have seen that the various forms of process theology considered here take seriously the tension between the historical-mutual-processive symbolism originally mediated by the covenant with Israel, and the absolute-personal-universal symbolism of the covenant with David. Putting the stress on the former type, in various ways they recognize the necessity for some equivalent of the latter. Since the strongest statements of the Davidic themes occur in the Psalms, and the highest Christologies of early Christianity in hymnic passages in the NT, the tension we have been studying is an instance of the problem of poetic language versus discursive language. So far this way into our problem has not been much explored by process theologies, which have tended to be weighted toward discursive, rational thought. Cobb's exploration of Christ as an "image" is an opening into this further line of exploration.

Finally, what light has our sketch of process Christologies cast on our original question about the relation between Scripture and experience? Rylaarsdam has shown that in contrast to some earlier versions of Scripture as a norm, it is precisely the tensions within the Scripture that have made it fruitful in deepening our understanding of new issues. Both Cobb and Ogden take Scripture very seriously as a norm. Ogden thinks of it as in some sense, at the existential level of interpretation after the lengendary elements have been discounted, a fixed norm. He takes the view that the community of the church simply finds it to be the case that "the New Testament contains the original as well as the finally normative witness of Christian faith."[18] Cobb follows the path of seeking for an explanation of how it is that the early witness can still be a shaping power. His view of Jesus' person is developed largely to meet this question.[19] Neither theologian is much concerned with the outer limits of the canon; these theologies will be adequate for those who find the heart of the question of Scripture to be the finding of a center of the Scripture. It is the merit of Rylaarsdam's essay to have taken this starting-point presupposed by most liberal theology, and shown how important for the clarification of it large reaches of the Scripture actually are.

FOOTNOTES

1.  John B. Cobb, Jr., *Christ in a Pluralistic Age* (Philadelphia:  Westminster Press, 1969).

2.  See also John B. Cobb, Jr., *God and the World* (Philadelphia:  Westminster Press, 1969).

3.  *Christ*, 144.

4.  Ibid., 181.

5.  Ibid., 182-83.

6.  Schubert M. Ogden, "The Point of Christology," JR 55 (1975) 375-95; *The Reality of God* (New York:  Harper, 1966).

7.  "The Point of Christology," 377.

8.  Schubert M. Ogden, "Christology Reconsidered:  John Cobb's 'Christ in a Pluralistic Age,'" *Process Studies* 6(1976) 118.

9.  Schubert M. Ogden, "What Is Theology?," JR 52 (1972) 22-40, esp. p. 24.

10.  "The Point of Christology," 382.

11.  Ibid., 378.

12.  Ibid., 380.

13.  "What Is Theology," 24.

14.  Ibid.

15.  "Christology Reconsidered," 118-22; "What Is Theology," 36-37.

16.  J. Coert Rylaarsdam, "The Two Covenants and the Dilemmas of Christology," JES 9 (1972) 249-70.

17.  "The Point of Christology," 388.

18.  Ibid., 380; "What Is Theology," 29-30.

19.  *Christ*, 136-46.

# STORY AND CELEBRATION

Harry M. Buck


"A wandering Aramean was my father; and he went down into Egypt.
. . ." And when "I bring the first of the fruit of the ground, which
thou, O Lord, has given me" and "set it down before the Lord . . .
and worship before the Lord . . ."[1] this story becomes my story.
Its narratives link the sequences of events that form the background of my life--if I am a psychic part of the community whose
story this is.[2]

The community of Israel--in the United Kingdom, in deuteronomic times, in the Exile, in the days of Antiochus or Bar Cocheba,
in the Diaspora, in a Warsaw ghetto or the ovens of Auschwitz,
and in our present postholocaust age--has found its unity not in
a common theology but in common stories. Theologies demand acceptance; stories cry out for participation, the acting out of a
community. Perhaps such stories preserve little that a modern
historian would find useful. It does not matter; the story has a
reality of its own. Its truth lies in its power to regenerate.
Recollection and imitation of the "old, old story" releases spiritual power.


## I. Story


There are two approaches which divide academic studies of
religion into opposing camps. Those disciplines that prescribe
precision and order, that purvey an identifiable body of knowledge
consisting of doctrines, dogmas, and intellectual ideas to be mas-
tered (and tested and graded), are currently in the ascendency.

But more basic is human experience itself. To stand aside and let centuries of human experience speak to us is difficult. The data are not orderly (i.e., our tools for measurement and calculation are not sufficiently precise, and we cannot reduce our materials to a series of "objective" examination "questions"). To appreciate this more basic part of our studies, we must listen to story and, at least vicariously, participate. We must go down with the "wandering Aramean" into Egypt and march along when "the Lord brought us up out of Egypt with a mighty hand and an outstretched arm, with signs and wonders . . ." (Deut 26:8).

Religious structures that endure grow out of fundamental human needs, for in the fullest sense the experience of religious living encompasses a total commitment to matters seen as of ultimate concern, lived out with such intensity that it transforms the lives of the devotees, conditioning their relations with all other persons and with each other—and with the planet on which they live. There is, thus, no single area of life to be labeled religious, for religion is the unifying dimension of depth in which all human experience is to be contemplated. It is a way of discovering meaning in our existence and organizing our lives into significant patterns. Beyond this, I do not know any more useful definition.

Questions about God or the gods are less important than they appear to be at first glance. Even attempts to validate truth claims of religious traditions recede into insignificance. Indeed, the question, "Do you believe in the existence of God?" may have little religious significance. But there are other questions: "In what experiences—mine personally or those of my people—do I ground my life? For what am I willing to give up anything else?" To ask these questions is to inquire about religion in its most fundamental sense. Answers are never in words alone, certainly not in abstract words. These answers are lived out, danced out, acted out—only later are they reduced to the sterility of theological formulas.

Religious experience is not abstract. It happens to someone, somewhere, sometime, and it has little to do with the structures

that we build to encase it.  Hence, there is something quite artificial about the way in which most courses about the study of religion are structured.  To compare one system of faith with another,
e.g., Buddhism with Christianity, is to miss the point of both of
them.  Except in the most theoretical way, these "systems" never
encounter each other; conflict or cooperation, alienation or
understanding is between flesh-and-blood men and women.  To see
"Yahwism" and "Ba'alism" as two irreconcilable ways of life is
to probe Hebrew scriptures at one level, but it will miss the
creative interchange that did take place as human persons experienced wholeness, drawing from both traditions and from others.

The Form of the Story.  Theological thought is by definition linear and logical.  A story zigzags, oscillating between
contradictories, for there is no plot without conflict.  The religious story lives because the Word (debir, logos) is an act,
and the words that count are spoken words.  When one utters them
in context one sets power in motion.

Written accounts are poor substitutes.  Once reduced (and
the word reduced is used advisedly) to writing, the story has become fixed, no longer able to respond livingly and lovingly to new
occasions which must teach new duties.  The spoken word, "Tell me
a story!," requires participation; the Word cannot be spoken in
isolation.

In a living story there is both rigidity and flexibility.  Because the story deals with events that are interpreted as having
cosmic significance, ordinary, historical language will not suffice.
When, for example, the ancient poet exalted,

Lord, when thou didst go forth from Seir,
    when thou didst march from the region of Edom,
the earth trembled,
    and the heavens dropped water.
The mountain quaked before the Lord,
    yon Sinai before the Lord, the God of Israel.

. . . . .

> The torrent Kishon swept them away,
>      the onrushing torrent, the torrent Kishon.
> March on, my soul, with might!  (Judg 5:4,5,21)

he had no concern to reconstruct what one might have seen from a
modern helicopter pausing above the battlefield of Megiddo.  He
was retelling the struggle of YHWH on behalf of his people and
calling on them to give themselves totally to YHWH.  The repetition of his story, and its oral nature is altogether evident even
in its written versions, recalled an experience and permitted hearer and speaker to share that experience, even as the formula of
the first fruits, which we cited earlier, concludes,

> . . . and the Egyptians treated us harshly, and afflicted
> us, and laid upon us hard bondage . . . and the Lord
> brought us out of Egypt . . . and gave us this land . . .
> (Deut 26:6-9)

even though not one of "us" was historically present.

The first criterion, then, of the religious story is involvement of the teller and the hearer (already a community) in events
that transcend historical time.  The story is not true simply because it may contain elements of "history," in many cases there is
little if any factual history, but because it places events into a
scheme that expresses our views about ourselves, our relations with
others, with God, and with the world.  What difference if nobody
ever "saw" YHWH ride across the clouds to the Kishon River or if
nobody ever "saw" Marduk slay Ti'amat?  The story told is the power
of the Word itself.  Its very repetition creates its own history.[3]

Israel's collective memory reaches far back into deep recesses
of time, recalling one event after another out of the past.  More
than simple memory was involved as the people made their heritage
come alive.  Even though such stories were proudly proclaimed as
history and not myth,[4] when they were told and retold, embellished
tales and legends took on mythic character, flourishing without

effective control until a suitable authoritative scripture provided a canonical frame of reference. The sacred story, alive and ever-changing to meet the shifting needs of the people, supplied a means for Israel to know herself by recalling a series of primordial events in which the community saw the hand of their "living God" ordaining his people's existence.

We can isolate three elements in most such stories: banish-ment, struggle, and reintegration, or they can be termed descent, conflict, and ascent.[5] We can begin with descent/banishment. Until a way of life is shattered, nothing happens. Virtually all ancient traditions trace the beginnings of Israel's story to that nameless "wandering Aramean" who "went down to Egypt." After that the strug-gle begins, the conflict which is the central focus of the story.

In postexilic days this story was supplanted by one told against a larger, cosmic frame of reference. The later story began with creation itself and the molding of the humankind (ha ꜣadam)[6] from the earth itself. The real story begins, however, when the man and the woman were expelled from their idyllic life in Eden. Struggle and conflict mark the story from that point on. Sinai and the Exodus is a kind of ascent, but in postexilic times these powerful stories had become symbols of the reintegration that was yet to come. The developed Christian myth sees this expulsion from Eden as a "fall," and the Christian Bible is bounded by the primordial event of banishment (told in the character of "Once upon a time") and the appearance of a new heaven and a new earth (Revelation 21), the final reintegration ("And they lived happily ever after"), the end of the story.

The pattern is nearly universal. There is no real Muslim com-munity until the Hijra, the flight of Muhammad from Mecca to Madinah, and there is no Islamic story until the night of Power and Excel-lence, when the Angel appeared to Muhammad and commanded: "Recite!"

In the ever-popular Hindu story of Rāma action begins when Rāma is banished to the forest for fourteen years. His struggles in Dandaka forest occupy all but the opening and closing chapters

of the Rāmāyana. During this period his brother Bharata is suppose
to rule in Ayodhyā, but instead he took Rāma's sandals (pāduka) and
placed them on the throne, symbols of the expected advent of the
true ruler. During Pādukarājya ("the reign of the sandals") the
real king was absent. At the end of the exile, Rāma returns to
ascend the throne and establish Rāmarājya ("the rule of Rāma"),
the righteous, eschatological reign. This hope is similar to the
expectation of the Kingdom of God to end this present, evil age.

As a devout Hindu, if I tell the story of Rāma, I can identify
with the period of Pādukarājya. The righteous age is clearly not
upon us as yet. We remain in the midst of struggle, and by align-
ing myself with righteous Rāma, I fight against the evil symbolized
by his demonic enemy Rāvana, anticipating the coming age of Rāmarājya. Likewise in telling the story of Israel, I can identify
with the struggle; the Messianic Age has not yet arrived. Or as
a Christian, the struggle continues until the Second Advent, the
new heaven and the new earth.

We have seen two prominent characteristics of the saving story
its involvement with metahistorical time so that its events are not
simply past episodes but contemporary realities, and a struggle to
bring about a righteous reintergration.

The Story of Israel. Quite simply, Hebrew scripture presents
just the story of Israel. This collection of hymns and poems,
diaries and records, laws and sermons, fact, folklore, and fiction
was written for and by the Hebrews to mirror their national hopes,
to chronicle the rise and fall of a Palestinian kingdom, but most
of all they express the self-understanding of a people with a profound sense of both heritage and destiny. But is this all? Hardly.
The story of Israel was told and retold by those who saw in a particular series of events the hand of One whom they called the living
God. Ancient Israel and modern Judaism both are people with common
stories, told with countless variation but with common elements of
existential significance nonetheless.

In the Bible we have a story, not a statement. Verbs, rather
than nouns are the value-laden words, expressing an ontology that
is difficult for English speaking people to grasp. English sentences presuppose a different sense of reality. In elementary school
we are taught that "nouns are naming words; they name persons, places,
or things. Verbs are action words; they describe what nouns do."
Our grammatical structure complements the materialistic view of
life we have been taught to value. Things are real, objects are
important. They can be named, described, measured, and above all
dealt with. Actions by themselves are inconceivable.

In many other languages this is not so, including some languages within the Indo-Aryan family. In Sanskrit, if a personal
pronoun is used it separates the doer from the act in an artificial
fashion. In Japanese one goes to great lengths to avoid expressing
subjects and objects, but one takes pains to express precise relationships. In Japanese thought, persons, places, and things are
not ultimately real; relationships endure. One of the most important Hindu "sins" is ahaṁkara (lit. "I-making"), i.e., regarding
a person or place or thing as having intrinsic reality.

In biblical Hebrew, likewise, the strength of the nominal subject and object is weak; the living God expresses himself in action.
In the Bible virtually nothing is said about the "nature of God"
(Gott-an-sich), but God's actions are prominent: what he has done,
is doing, and yet will do. There is also no explicit anthropology,
what or who man is in himself. The stories carefully describe man
in relation to God. To translate the religious experience of Israel into nominalistic terms, to stress nouns at the expense of
verbs, is to lose its very essence. The story, therefore, is the
only way to appropriate Israel's basic experience, and whenever
the story is subordinated to abstractions, this unique relationship with a living God cannot be transmitted.

Without altering the basic apprehension of reality that is a
perennial note in Hebrew-Jewish life, the story can shift its focus

from time to time, and it is a mark of maturity that our stories
can so change. So far as we can tell, the earliest story to emerge
with clarity told of a journey from Egypt to Canaan. Later ages
so idealized this event that it became the vehicle for Israel's
legislation: "Because I, YHWH, brought you out of the land of
Egypt and the house of bondage, therefore . . ."

To describe the Exodus simply as an episode in history, the
escape of some slaves from Egypt and their eventual settlement in
Palestine, even to make as precise an historical reconstruction of
dates, places, and numbers as possible (and not much precision has
proved possible) is to miss the point. The Exodus is an eternal
event. The shekinah shines forth whenever a person senses the
call of God to himself, and the promised land continually beckons.
But never in a simple, literal fashion.

In the Exile, the Exodus took on still more significance, and
the Book of Deuteronomy was coupled to a four-volume history of
Israel: Joshua, Judges, Samuel, and Kings, telling the story from
the Exodus to the end of the kingdom period, but in the light of
the then-present Exile from which YHWH's deliverance was again expected.

Stories enlarge their frame of reference. The Christian story
of Jesus the Christ was enlarged from his break with his family at
the time of his baptism to the cosmic story of the Prince who "didst
leave thy throne and thy kingly crown when thou camest to earth for
me." The Rāma story, which once began with banishment from Ayodhyā
is now told as the descent of Lord Visnu from heaven.

The completed Torah goes back to the cosmic events of God's
structuring the earth at creation, the formation of man and woman
from the earth, and God's breathing into his new creation the
nefesh of life so that man becomes a living nefesh. This exciting
story tells vividly of the establishment of a vital relationship
between men, women, and God. But nothing really happens until
there is a break in that relationship, a break that allows the re-

lationship itself to mature. In the Yahwist tradition, Genesis
2-4 does not tell about a fall from a state of moral perfection
but of the rise to new, adult responsibilities. The innocent (i.e.,
ignorant) man and woman acquire knowledge and with knowledge power,
and embark from the garden to "till the ground from which he had
been taken" (Gen 3:23). Adam does not "know" his wife until after
the separation (Gen 4:1).

As Thomas Aquinas emphasized, the number 5 does not negate
the numbers 1, 2, 3, and 4, but includes them, so this more cosmic
vision does not negate the Exodus; it incorporates it into a larger
frame of reference. Medieval Christian mystery plays expand the
horizon again, setting their story against their understanding of
the history of the world, past, present, and future. In every case,
following the initial banishment, struggle ensued in a life and
death conflict. Human action became vitally important, viewed
against the backdrop of the story. Abraham Heschel once said,

> [Man] undertook to build a paradise by his own might,
> and he is driving God from this paradise . . . Now we
> have discovered . . . that the paradise . . . may turn
> out to be a vast extermination camp.[7]

In contemporary times there is yet another Exodus, the journey of many Jews from a modern Exile all over the earth to that
same land to which Moses led earlier tribes to form a new nation,
a nation presently engaged in a bitter struggle for existence,[8]
growing out of an experience far more dreadful than the first Exodus, the Exile, or the persecutions of Antiochus. Auschwitz is
part of the story of every thinking and feeling Jew in the world
today, and problems of Jewish identity and personal integrity arise
whenever a Jew thinks of himself in terms of his relationship with
his historic and ongoing community. "Who am I as a Jew?" must
include a consideration of the Holocaust. It has caused some Jews
to renounce central elements of their previous story and deny a

relationship with a YHWH who has "chosen" his people.  It has caused
others to search their ancient stories more carefully, entrenching
themselves still more firmly in the historic community.  Both reactions are story, much more than explicit theology.

In the Holocaust, as in the Exile, the Exodus, or the explusion
from the Garden, the way is barred, the gate is closed, and you cannot go back home.  But this is the beginning not the end of the story
When the way is barred, one must go forward, not back, and seek not
a re-entry to the old life of innocence, the fleshpots of Egypt,
or Germany before the Nazis.  In maturity and knowledge, one must
search for a new integration.

The religion of the Bible is not simple.  Israel did not bring
its unique faith from the desert just to set up a pure religion
in Canaan any more than Theodor Herzl envisioned modern Zion as a
theological monument.  Israel has never recalled history for its
own sake, neither the Exodus, the Exile, or Auschwitz.  She told
and retold stories of her past because in them she saw the hand of
the living God at work.  Neither Jews nor Christians really look
for a new heaven to drop out of the sky; we know that it can come
only through the struggle involved as we honestly resolve our own
integrity crises.  Return to the womb or the Garden is out of the
question.  We must enter into our own appropriation of our own story,
and to this we now turn our attention.


## II.  Celebration


However we understand it, we have come to see that religious
experience in its varied manifestations is the outward expression
of a human search for wholeness.  We attempt to invest our varied
activities with a sense of significance and meaning.  Words like
holy, whole, and wholeness are related to the idea of health, as
is the German word for salvation, Heil.  What is sought is restoration to health, wholeness.

The religious experience, whether it is something sui generis, as Rudolph Otto contended, or contiguous with other aspects of human life, as his detractors urged, involves total persons responding with their total beings to ultimate concerns. Total needs cannot be met through partial responses. The body instructs the soul, and what we do with our hands, our legs, and our lungs is closely related to what we do with our souls. Cultus is, therefore, important.

Doctrines and rituals, the observable phenomena of religion studies, point beyond themselves to a depth of meaningful encounter. The self that lives in realistic depth lives also in creative tension, never altogether comfortable about his theological expression, his cultic life, or his community fellowship, even though plateaus let him come to rest occasionally. True peace of mind includes an existential restlessness.

How, then, shall we study such complex phenomena? To describe externalia with objective precision is to miss the point of both ideas and rituals. Small wonder that in academic circles, we have always chosen the safe way, falling prey to what Maurice Friedman calls "the universal misconception that one becomes educated through learning to abstract what others say from the ground from which they speak." Friedman's reply is that "what is at stake is not the names of things—God, church, society, respect for the family, 'dialogue'— but the wind of the spirit that once blew over them and gave them life."[9]

Rites and Ceremonies. In its primal manifestations, religion is not so much thought out as danced out. Intellectual expressions follow; they do not precede. When a religious tradition has been active and meaningful, when it has succeeded in bringing salvation to thousands, it has maintained its active earth tie. Reduced to abstractions, it becomes sterile. Therefore, the story is appropriated not by its textual analysis, its basic presuppositions, nor even a catalogue of its symbolism, but by remembrance and patterning, or as we shall call it, anamnesis and paradigm.

In apprehending religious experience, one has the feeling of encountering power, and there can be an immanent sense of danger. To deal with such power taboos are needed, ritualized procedures, safe and approved methods, just as no one would presume to handle radioactive materials, splice an electric wire, or touch surgical instruments without learning proper procedures. To do otherwise can be a fatal error.

Rites and ceremonies, indeed the entire concept of "service," grow out of the felt necessity of applying proper taboos. Offerings are presented, and the presentation of offerings precedes any theories about their significance. Gifts of value express the awareness that one does not get something for nothing. The earth gives life; to it life must be returned. Hence, the festival of the first fruits and, in extreme cases, the sacrifice of the first born son. Initiation ceremonies which offer a part of the body, circumcision, defloration, filing of teeth, also express the feeling that life cannot be lived without establishing a harmonious relation with the powers about us.

In Israel, however, rites and ceremonies were not directed toward a vague sense of power. They celebrated YHWH's redemptive power and were appropriated through the story.

The Religious Community. Words must accompany offerings, and the words develop into mantras, chants or hymns. Petition and supplication (prayer) may also be present. Of course, there will be a place set aside for the performance of these rituals, a temple, and someone designated to aid in their performance, a priest. All this grows up in the context of a community telling its story.

Even though in many instances, these rites can be performed by one person in solitude, they are not solitary acts. They are part of a community of understanding. There is a tension between the collective aspects of religious living and its individual aspects; nonetheless, the religious life demands participation in a group with shared experiences. With the exception of the private mass of a Roman Catholic priest, the mass is always celebrated in congregation. The third "refuge" in Buddhism is the Sangha ("congregation"). A minion (a minimum of ten adult males) is required for Jewish services. Muslims find extreme difficulty practicing Islam apart from a Muslim society. Throughout history, religious loyalties outweigh all other loyalties, and a common bond to God is the strongest of all bonds.

Those things we regularly do together constitute a silent binding force in any community, for our actions speak louder, even to ourselves, than do our words. In time, an elaborate list of special days and observances grew up to celebrate the story of Israel.

The Sabbath. No cultic celebration was more prominent than the weekly participation in God's creative act and the election of his people, the Sabbath. Deuteronomists used it to celebrate the Exodus. Placed first in the priestly Torah (cf. Gen 2:3), the Sabbath quickly became the touchstone of loyalty to the faith of the fathers.

Passover (Pesach). In an annual celebration in the spring at the time of the first full moon, Nisan 15, two services came to be combined, the Passover and the Feast of Unleavened Bread. The former was originally a shepherd festival; the latter, agricultural. Both traditions, however, were assimilated to Israel's central story, the celebration of the Exodus.

Pentecost (Shabouoth). Sometimes called the Feast of the Weeks, this ceremony took place fifty days after Pesach and was originally associated with the harvest. In postexilic Judaism it came to commemorate the divine gift of the Torah, the literary expression of Israel's story.

Tabernacles (Sukkoth). Doubtless of Canaanite origin, this feast of ingathering, observed in the autumn, came to be associated not with the powers of renewal in the earth, although it never lost this emphasis, but with the journey through the wilderness from Egypt to the promised land.

The Sabbath had at one time been associated with the Exodus but came to celebrate the total ordering of the earth and the heavens at Creation. Passover, Shabouoth, and Sukkoth were celebrations of the Exodus. Two other celebrations retained their ties with recurring seasons. Rosh Hashanah (New Year) combined a celebration of creation with the renewal of the year. A solemn ten-day period of penance was concluded with Yom Kippur (Day of Atonement), when the sound of the shofar ("ram's horn") called to repentance and rededication.

Hanukkah and Purim were joyous deliverance festivals, celebrating not the central story of deliverance but other stories of YHWH's deliverance of his people. The first celebrated the conquest of the Temple by Judas Maccabeus, and it was coupled with the Feast of Lights. Purim celebrated the deliverance of the Jews in the days of Esther.

Anamnesis and Paradigm. Why, then, these celebrations? They do not recount mere history, and they contain many elements that seem mythical. But the events celebrated constitute God's action in the life of the believing community, and they recall the events to mind. The stories become paradigmatic, i.e., they provide patterns on which to fashion life, an archetype for thought and action, as did the story of Romulus for the Romans. Romulus was not merely the first Roman in point of time. He was the first (archē) Roman, the paradigm of what all good Romans should be, the epitome of the glory of Rome itself.

These stories, then, serve two important functions: anamnesis and paradigm. Anamnesis, untranslated, is a better term than memory in describing the functions of a shared story, for it connotes the timeless repetition of an event. The narratives are not simple memory. One recounts them in order to make them happen all over again, quite outside the ordinary time sequence in which we live out our lives.

Paradigm is the other side. If these stories have a timeless character about them, they become patterns for action. In the dual function of anamnesis and paradigm, we may approach Israel's stories anew.

# FOOTNOTES

1. From Deut 26:5-11. The word translated "worship" is
šohoh ("bow down") and it implies primarily a bodily posture.
On worship in the Hebrew tradition see my "Worship, Idolatry, and
God" in *A Light unto My Path* (ed. by Howard Bream et al.; [Phila-
delphia: Temple University Press, 1964]) 67-82.

2. This chapter is by no means based on Michal Novak's
brilliant book, *Ascent of the Mountain, Flight of the Dove* (New
York: Harper & Row, 1971), but that I have been refreshingly
nourished by his insights will be obvious.

3. I have dealt with this at greater length in my essays,
"Saving Story and Sacred Book," in *Search the Scriptures* (ed. by
J. M. Myers et al.; [Leiden: Brill, 1969]) 79-94, and "From His-
tory to Myth: A Comparative Study," JBR 29 (1961) 219-26.

4. This was a point of pride among Christian theologians in
their struggle against Gnosticism. Note their warnings not to
"occupy themselves with myths and endless genealogies," nor to
"turn aside from listening to the truth and wander into myths"
(cf. 1 Tim 1:4; 4:7; 2 Tim 4:4).

5. The monumental study of Joseph Campbell, *Hero with a
Thousand Faces* (Cleveland: World Publishing Co., 1956) cites the
formula of what he calls the "monomyth" as separation, initiation,
and return.

6. Ha-adam is not a masculine being from whom woman was derived. The word in context indicates mankind; "Male and female
created he them." Primal "man" is androgynous. In the Yahwist
tradition, the separation into male and female beings implies neither inferiority nor superiority.

7. In *Christian Century*, December 11, 1957.

8. This is not meant as a political statement, certainly not
to endorse all the actions of the current State of Israel.

9. Maurice Friedman, *Touchstones of Reality* (New York: E. P.
Dutton, 1974) 14-15.

# THE CONTEMPORANEITY OF THE BIBLE

George W. Schreiner

"Most Americans are Baal-worshippers. It's unfortunate that
they can't enjoy their religion without a bad conscience." This
comment was made by J. Coert Rylaarsdam in a class on OT Theology
in the autumn of 1949. Such a statement is open to all kinds of
criticism by historians. The religion of Baal was part of an
ancient agricultural milieu and so has vanished with that milieu.
Today we hear no hymns to Baal and we see no altars on the high
hills or under the green trees. Moreover, is not modern man non-
religious and has he not come of age? Nevertheless, there is reflected in this remark a central concern of all of Rylaarsdam's
work: the contemporaneity of the Bible. For him, biblical exposition carries on a dialogue with modernity through which the
present age illuminates the Bible, and the Bible interprets the
present.

The Church and theology are in serious trouble today on this
very issue, particularly in America. In his usual uncompromising
way, William Stringfellow charges:

> The Bible has been closed in preaching in American con-
> gregations, for one thing, for a very long time. It has
> been my fortune to circulate widely among the churches
> of Protestantism in all parts of the nation and in all
> sectors of the confessional spectrum, in churches rich
> and poor, rural and urban, segregated and integrated,
> conservative and liberal, small and large. I can barely
> recall having heard in them Biblical preaching . . .
> Very seldom is there the confident and responsible ex-
> posure of God's own Word in a manner in which the people
> may know and rejoice in the event of the Word of God and
> (to refute those who stupidly suppose that Biblical preach-
> ing has no contemporary significance) be so enlightened
> in the Biblical Word that they discern and celebrate that
> very Word present and militant in modern society.[1]

It is supposed that the Bible "has no contemporary significance."

My thesis here is that the contemporaneity of biblical interpretation depends primarily upon the question that is asked. That is, whether or not Biblical exposition can open up an effective dialogue with the modern world depends upon that initial spoken or unspoken question which provides perspective, vantage point, orientation. Much else, of course, is involved, biblical scholarship and knowledge of society's dynamics, but that question, that basic orientation, will finally be the determining factor. Here answers, though not without significance, are not as important as questions. The possible questions relating to biblical contemporaneity are many and can be formulated in many different ways. We will consider three which have been historically important.

The first question can be dealt with briefly: Is the Bible factually accurate? That is, did what is said to have taken place actually take place; was what is said to have been spoken actually spoken by those to whom such words are attributed? This question has caused barrels of ink to flow, and has initiated innumerable archaeological expeditions. It has obviously an apologetic bearing because the assumption behind it is that modern man with his scientific bent demands that the problem of objective truth be elucidated. If the Bible represents authority, the issue of its historical trustworthiness must be dealt with. This question has been with us for a long time, but it is by no means obsolete: consider the struggles of the Missouri Synod and the "Battle for the Bible."

If the answer given to this question is yes, interpretation moves in the direction of fundamentalism. This option should not be denigrated. Churches which have adopted this position are growing; within them are often found genuine reverence for the Bible and careful searching of the Scriptures. Their leaders are quick to detect the illusions of the standard denominations. Yet the old problem exposed by Kierkegaard so long ago remains: faith becomes the acceptance of guaranteed past facts instead of the present passionate relationship to an objective uncertainty. The Bible loses its contemporary character and disappears into the past; for man can enter into it only by leaving behind his rational, critical powers. A widening gap opens up between the Bible and the present.

If the answer to the question of factual historicity is no, difficulties less obvious but just as real emerge. The most radical no given by a theologian in this century is that of Rudolph Bultmann. This no moved him and his followers in the direction of demythologization and existential interpretation. The originality, depth, and lucidity of Bultmann's work, his capacity to use philosophy in the service of theology, cannot be questioned. Yet, as Cullmann pointed out, the weight given to that original no causes history in his theology to be volatilized. "The appearance of Christ 'when the time had fully come' (Gal 4:4) signifies the eschatological event that puts an end to the old aeon. Henceforth, there can be no more history and also no more history of salvation, for the latter has reached its end precisely in him."[2] Also, the historical element of the Incarnation and Resurrection becomes a matter of no import.

The question concerning historical accuracy has thrown valuable light upon the history of tradition and has shown that the Biblical writers were not disinterested chroniclers but witnesses of faith. But when this question becomes central in exposition, when it provides orientation, no matter how the question is answered, a split appears separating the Bible from the present. History is a major concern of modern man, yet Bultmann is very ambiguous concerning the meaning of history. This question then cannot provide the standpoint (in spite of its original apologetic intent) by means of which the contemporaneousness of the Bible can appear. It cannot bring the dialogue into being.

The second question might seem more promising: Is the Bible relevant? Indeed, relevance and contemporaneity are often treated as synonyms. In other words, is the Bible related to, does it speak to, the psychological, sociological, and political condition of the modern human being? Or, can the Bible be a resource for dealing with the problems of the modern world? Here again, we find an apologetic impulse: if the Bible can be shown to throw light upon modern man's problems, he will see its relevance and be moved to take it seriously. In this context the contemporaneity of the Bible seems definitely at stake.

If the answer to this question is no, the interpreter of the modern age relies upon principles drawn from one or another system; depth psychology, existentialism, structuralism, Marxism. These will be taken to be far more helpful than the Bible in arriving at an understanding of the modern situation.

An example of a yes answer given to this question is today's theology of liberation, to which the theology of hope is closely related. Gutierrez, Cone, and Moltmann are representative. The starting point in this theology, the issue to which the Bible is related, is that of justice in the modern world. Gutierrez describes his A Theology of Liberation as "a theological reflection born of the experience of shared efforts to abolish the current unjust situation and to build a different society, freer and more human."[3] The struggle is for liberation from racist, sexist, and economic oppression in the United States, from colonialism and its aftermath in Africa, from imperialist structures in South America. This entails the breaking of multifarious forms of domination with the recognition and exercise of human rights. Self-affirmation and the fulfillment of human personality are required. Human autonomy over against the world and history is stressed:

> It is the behavior of man ever more conscious of being an
> active subject of history; he is ever more articulate in
> the face of social injustice and of all repressive forces
> which stand in the way of his fulfillment; he is ever
> more determined to participate both in the transformation
> of social structures and in effective political action. . .

But they are all based on the profound aspiration of man, who wants to take hold of the reins of his own life and be the artisan of his own destiny.[4]

Liberation is that process by which man becomes free to build up the world, carry on the creative process in the world and in himself. "By working, transforming the world, breaking out of servitude, building a just society, and assuming his destiny in history, man forges himself."[5] We find a similar theme in Moltmann:

> This world is not the hell of self-estrangement, as it is said to be in romanticist and existentialist writing. The world is not yet finished, but is understood as engaged in a history. It is therefore the world of possibilities, the world in which we can serve the future, promised truth and righteousness and peace.[6]

Liberation drives forward to the just and free society.

This theology is performing a valuable service for the church. It is demonstrating that ecclesiastical and scholarly business as usual is not enough in a revolutionary world. And that privatized pietism that does nothing but wait upon the Lord is simply irresponsibility. Liberation theology, which uses sociological and political analysis, reveals that a Christianity which uncritically accepts American capitalism is prostitution of the Gospel. It illustrates the contemporary bearing of the prophetic demand for justice. The theme of hope points to the future and to the promised new earth, negating all forms of docetism. The theology of liberation reminds us that a reflection which has no consequences for action is sterile.

That serious problems arise concerning liberation theology is due to its basic orientation and to the influence of the unspoken inquiry: Is the Bible relevant? When all is said and done, despite the brilliance and penetration of its insights, this theology uses the Bible as a resource for present problems. The result is that biblical concepts are taken out of their original context and made to serve another world of meaning. Bonhoeffer's distinction

between ultimate and penultimate is useful in getting at the heart
of the difficulty. He writes:

> What is this penultimate? It is everything that precedes
> the ultimate, everything that precedes the justification
> of the sinner by grace alone, everything which is to be
> regarded as leading up to the last thing when the last
> thing has been found. It is at the same time everything
> which follows the ultimate and yet again precedes it.
> There is, therefore, no penultimate in itself; as though
> a thing could justify itself in itself as being a thing
> before the last thing; a thing becomes penultimate only
> through the ultimate, that is to say, at the moment when
> it has already lost its own validity. . . Concretely,
> two things are called penultimate in relation to the
> justification of the sinner by grace; namely, being man
> and being good. . . That which has been cast down into
> the depths of human wretchedness, that which has been
> abased and humbled, is now to be raised up. There is
> a depth of human bondage, of human poverty, of human
> ignorance, which impedes the merciful coming of Christ.
> "The mountains and hills shall be made low" (Isa 40:4).
> If Christ is to come, then all that is proud and haughty
> must bow down.[7]

In liberation theology, again and again, the penultimate --
justice and freedom, key factors in "being man and being good" --
takes the place of the ultimate, acceptance of grace by faith.
Justice becomes the sole issue, the chief characteristic of the
new age to come, and the means for bringing in that future. This
would be expected and appropriate in a purely political analysis,
but not in a theology which calls upon the Bible. The Exodus is
referred to as the paradigmatic event of liberation, creating a
new just situation. Then this event is generalized and universal-
ized. Political revolution, the destruction of old structures and
the creation of new, becomes Exodus, an instance of the latter and
justified by it. Political revolution, whether violent or non-
violent, is assimilated to Exodus in the Old Testament and to the
coming of the Celestial Jerusalem in the New. In the biblical Exodus Yahweh's action does not have justice as its primary end. The

end and purpose is to bring into being a people who know him, trust
in him, receive his grace, and are his witnesses and servants -- a
covenant people. The deliverance from Egypt and the gift of the
land, instances of justice, are instrumental to this end. Justice,
then, is penultimate, a thing before the last; necessary, essential,
but secondary.

In the Bible this original action and intent determines the
subsequent struggle: will Israel continue to trust Yahweh or turn
to other gods?, this is the dominant issue through the judges and
the prophets. In liberation theology the issue is different: can
man build a just society and can his religion help him to do so?
Development and liberation become assimilated to salvation. "To
work, to transform this world, is to become a man and to build the
human community; it is also to save. Likewise, to struggle against
misery and exploitation and to build a just society is already to
be part of the saving action, which is moving toward its complete
fulfillment."[8] The biblical transcendent dimension in salvation
all but disappears. The tragic aspect of man's revolutionary
struggle against misery (delineated so well by Hannah Arendt) is
lost sight of. That the net result of revolution today is increased
state power and new forms of oppression is ignored. Reinhold Nie-
buhr's "the Christ and the Anti-Christ march together through history" is forgotten. Gutierrez writes:

> The concerns of the so-called Third World countries revolve
> around the social injustice -- justice axis, or, in con-
> crete terms, the oppression-liberation axis. In contra-
> distinction to a pessimistic approach to this world which
> is so frequent in traditional Christian groups and which
> encourages escapism, there is proposed in these other
> countries an optimistic vision which seeks to reconcile
> faith and the world and to facilitate commitment.[9]

It is true that the tragic element in Christian theology can en-
courage escapism: man can always twist the Bible to his own ends.
But optimism can lead to the escapism of false hopes and to the

use of means which produce results diametrically opposed to the
original intent. The vision of man creating his future requires
a particular ideal type of man: the autonomous personality free
from all alienating pressures. "Moreover, man becomes aware -- as
we have noted above -- that he is an agent of history, responsible
for his own destiny."[10] "Nevertheless, it is necessary to recall
that the revolutionary process now under way is generating the kind
of man who critically analyzes the present, controls his destiny,
and is oriented towards the future."[11] The man of Exodus, of Second Isaish, and of Acts is not autonomous man; he is in communion
with a Power who bestows freedom as a gift, a freedom always dependent upon that communion.

A critique of liberation theology is vulnerable to the oft-
repeated charge of desiring a return to an individualized piety,
a compartmentalized religion in a comfortable social status quo.
A critique of this kind, that "religion should stay out of politics,"
cannot be taken seriously; Christianity is revolutionary or it is
unfaithful. But a theology which in the name of liberation puts
the penultimate in the place of the ultimate, understands man as
saving himself by building up the world and controlling his destiny, uses the Bible as a convenient resource by conforming biblical
themes to a very different view of history, and envisions a continuous unbroken line between political action and the New Jerusalem must be called in question for the sake of revolution itself.
Man is called to fight the wrong war at the wrong place. He fights
for political power instead of for freedom from Baal and the prin-
cipalities and powers. Here we have something quite different from
the contemporaneity of the Bible: Biblical ideas emptied of their
original meaning. The distortion begins when the original apologetic
question is asked: Is the Bible relevant?

The third orienting question moves in a direction opposite to
the first two; it moves from the Bible to man, rather than from man
to the Bible. It is the question which enables the contemporaneity
of the Bible to become evident, which can bring about real dialogue

between the Scriptures and modern man in the modern world. It has no apologetic character. One way to phrase this question is simply: Will you believe or not?

In the Bible this question is formulated in many ways and is found in various contexts. It is heard in the garden when the Lord God calls, "Where are you?" It is present in the summons to Abraham before the trial: "After these things God tested Abraham and said to him 'Abraham!' And he said, 'here am I.'" It is raised by Joshua, "Choose this day whom you will serve . . ." In the New Testament it is, "What do you think of the Christ?" and "Who do men say that I am?" John puts the issue clearly: "Then they said to him, 'What must we do, to be doing the works of God?' Jesus answered them, 'This is the work of God, that you believe in him whom he has sent.'" The governing question is that of faith or unbelief.

There are many ways of saying, "No, I choose not to believe." By far the most common way is to ignore the question, or to claim that actually there is no such question. Pharaoh and Pilate both take this course. Another way is to admit that there may indeed be such a question, but that it makes no difference, is not related to reality. Many thinkers whose works are of great value assume this answer.

When this question is heard, when the answer is Abraham's "Here am I," the human being is situated in his world. He knows and recognizes himself as one who is addressed. But he also perceives himself to be one who, like Adam, resists that address. Moses argues and Jeremiah appeals to his youth. Peter asks Jesus to depart (Luke 5:8). Man wants to escape this grasp, to fashion his own life, to decide for himself what is right and wrong, to create his own image of God, to control his own destiny, in a word, to be autonomous. He wants to choose the temporal rather than the eternal and he can do this by choosing himself or some power (or combination of powers) that it seems he can control to make himself secure and happy. Baal, nature and her forces, is one of these powers. Even when he believes and responds to the Word, the resistance continues; he relies on pardon and justification.

The question of faith/unbelief provides the setting and context for the ethical and for justice. To serve justice is a way of being faithful over against idolatry. Justice is penultimate, but essential because it prepares the way for faith. Judgment falls upon those who trample the poor because this profanes the holy name in Israel and among the nations. Bonhoeffer writes, "If the hungry man does not attain to faith, then the guilt falls on those who refused him bread. To provide the hungry man with bread is to prepare the way for the coming of grace."[12]

At the same time justice is made secondary and relativized. Jeremiah does not support the war effort against the Chaldeans, though this is a just effort against an oppressor. More important than the struggle for justice is the acknowledgment in trust and repentance of Yahweh's judgment against Israel's idolatry. Faith here supersedes justice.

In Luke 12:13 a man asks Jesus to help him get justice: "Bid my brother divide the inheritance with me." Jesus' answer sounds rude, "Man, who made me a judge or divider over you? Take heed, and beware of all covetousness." It is far better to be cheated than to be unfaithful, to fall victim to covetousness and the false god Mammon. What might seem like weakness or indifference to justice is actually faithfulness. Justice is only relatively important.

The same point is present in "Render to Caesar the things that are Caesar's and to God the things that are God's." Justice might be served by refusing to pay taxes to an occupying power. But since to God belongs man himself, heart, soul, mind, and strength, compared to this the issue of taxes and justice is secondary. Let Caesar have the money.

The fact that in the New Testament the poor have an advantage over the rich presents a problem to liberation theology, whose proponents see poverty as the chief enemy. In the Gospels the poor are blessed and the gospel is preached particularly to them. After many convolutions Gutierrez finally decides that, "They are blessed because the coming of the Kingdom will put an end to their poverty by creating a world of brotherhood,"[13] a perfect example of making the Bible relevant at all costs. Why the poor are blessed can be easily understood from the warning that it is harder for a rich man to enter the Kingdom than for a camel to go through the eye of a needle. He trusts in his wealth, is in the grip of Mammon, and so like the young ruler cannot respond to the summons to faith. The poor have the advantage of being without the stumbling block of wealth. They can hear the gospel. Matthew realizes, however, that even the poor can fall victim to greed and alters the beatitude to "poor in spirit." Paul touches upon the same point when reminding the believers that not many are wise, powerful, or noble (1 Cor 1:26). On the other hand, sometimes those poor in material goods, such as the Pharisees, have other stumbling blocks such as learning, reputation and adherence to the Law. The tax collectors, rich in material wealth, will enter the Kingdom before them. Here again, the central issue is faith, answering "Here am I" to the question and the summons. Justice and getting one's fair share is entirely secondary to this. Poverty presents less of an obstacle to faith than wealth. Slavery also is a matter of relative indifference (1 Cor 7:21-24). The slave can have faith, so he has that which ultimately matters. If he can gain his freedom, he should do so; but he is already a "freedman of the Lord." This "realized eschatology" is also the point of the parable of the laborers in the vineyard.

The decisive character of the choice faith/unbelief does not change from age to age up to the end: "Nevertheless, when the Son of man comes, will he find faith on earth?" It is always possible to choose Baal, even when one supposes that the choice is for Yahweh. Baal can be given the name of Yahweh. But Baal can be seen, recognized in the present, discerned for what he is, only when the choice is made for Yahweh -- only from the standpoint of faith. From any other standpoint Baal appears as a power bestowing happiness. For Baal is a temporal force to which is attributed saving efficacy, a sacred power. Baal takes many forms today, the most

revered being technology. Around the technological center is
woven an ideology of happiness through consumption, the end and
aim of life. Man is homo faber, the technician, whose task is
to understand and put to use the materials and forces of the
earth. Human existence consists of problems to be solved by
techniques, including political and psychological techniques.
The derived virtues are conscientiousness in work, adaptability,
normality, ambition, and optimism. History is moving toward a
time when all human problems will be solved by technology and mankind will be happy and at peace. This end is to be accomplished
by using energetically all available means: if anything can be
done, it should be done. Great importance is attached to the
economic sphere of life. It is assumed that all spiritual, cultural, and intellectual development is dependent upon economic and
technological development. Seek first technological evolution and
all these things shall be yours as well. Justice in this context
is empowerment to participate in the technological process and to
share in the happiness which consumption bestows. The religion
of Baal is simple but extensive, penetrating into every aspect of
personal and social life.

A serious question facing Christians (and theologians) today
is whether to view technology as a good under man's control whose
benefits, in love and justice, are to be distributed as widely as
possible; or as a sacred dehumanizing power to be resisted, exposed, desacralized and relativized. (Two able exponents of the
latter view are Jacques Ellul and William Stringfellow, both influenced by Barth. There are, of course, other related powers
such as the state, sex, the corporation, etc.)

To resist doesn't mean to try to abolish technology, money,
or the state; it means to attack and expose the ideology of happiness and security. Obviously, justice must be a concern; world
hunger must be dealt with; the health care system in the United
States must be made accessible to everyone. But resistance to
this ideology on the basis of faith entails renunciation. Ellul
writes:

If I speak of rupture with the society of consumption,
it is because this is one of the concrete ways of liberation for modern man.  Psychic liberation, liberation
in the sphere of work.  Liberation in belonging to this
society.  This is, in addition, one of the most important
revolutionary means:  to reduce consumption attacks this
absurd society much more vigorously than all the present
revolutionary movements (which are definitely conformist,
because it is always a matter of enabling more people to
participate in the great consumption.[14]

t is noteworthy that Ivan Illich, from the standpoint of Catholic
umanism, and working on the sociological plane, arrives at a po-
ition similar to Ellul's.  He represents the third world in a
ay very different from Gutierrez.  Illich calls for resistance
o technological development because it is counter-productive,
nherently unjust, and because of the religious aura attached to
t.  Describing the medical establishment (a cadre of the tech-
ological system) he writes:

Organized medicine has practically ceased to be the art
of healing the curable, and consoling the hopeless has
turned into a grotesque priesthood concerned with salvation and has become a law unto itself.  The policies
that promise the public some control over the medical
endeavor tend to overlook the fact that to achieve their
purpose, they must control a church, not an industry.[15]

When man responds to the question of faith, when he replies
"here am I," he situates himself in relation to the Power that
as summoned him and in relation to the world given to him.  The
3ible becomes contemporary because it provides the perspective for
eyes of faith.  He looks forward in hope to the coming of Christ
and to the New Creation.  The believer's task, derived from faith,
is to resist the false gods and to love his neighbor as Christ has
loved him.  Through faith and love Christ is present here and now
in the midst of the fallen powers.  The expression of faith involves
preparing the way for grace.  Bonhoeffer writes:

> Certainly one would have misunderstood all this if one
> were to say that before he can become a Christian, the
> slave must have received his liberty, the outcast his
> rights, and the hungry man his bread; in other words,
> that values must first be set in order. This is refuted
> by the evidence of the New Testament and of Church his-
> tory . . . It is quite certain that the preparation of
> the way is a matter of concrete interventions in the
> visible world, and it is certain that hunger and the
> satisfaction of hunger are concrete and visible matters;
> yet everything depends on this activity being a spiritual
> reality, precisely because ultimately it is not indeed
> a question of the reform of earthly conditions, but it
> is a question of the coming of Christ.[16]

When the question is, will you believe?, the Bible engages the
present world and modern man.

We have attempted to show that whether or not biblical exposition manifests the contemporaneity of the Bible, brings about
a genuine dialogue with the modern world, depends upon the original, governing, orienting question. When man questions the Bible,
nothing happens; when the Bible questions him, he sees reality.
The question concerning historicity is preparatory; it clarifies
the text. The question concerning relevance is deceitful: in answering this question, the Bible is used as a source book to justify
actions and views foreign to it. This is the problem with liberation
theology, some versions of the theology of hope, and with much teaching and preaching in the church. The Bible is "closed" so much of
the time, not because there is failure to quote it or refer to it,
but because it is used for alien ends -- to establish the status
quo, to provide happiness, or to bring about social reform. Only
when the question of faith, originating in the Scripture, becomes
primary can engagement take place.

This does not mean that biblical exposition is limited to only
"religious" matters. It can call upon the whole range of human existence, for everything human relates to faith's consequences and
to "preparing the way." The interpreter can draw upon any discipline: Tillich's use of depth psychology and Fritz Kunkel's use of

reud are examples. This third perspective is not the property of
ome particular theological school. It is found in Luther, Kier-
egaard, and in the work of Thomas Merton. It is present below the
urface in the literary works of T. S. Eliot and e. e. cummings.
ut the issue of the Bible and the modern world, the contempora-
eity of the Bible, is more than an intellectual matter. The Church
nd human freedom are at stake.

388

FOOTNOTES


1. *Count It All Joy* (Grand Rapids: William B. Eerdman's, 1967) 13.

2. *Existence and Faith, Shorter Writings of Rudolf Bult-mann* (trans. S. M. Ogden; New York: Living Age Books, Meridian Boo Inc., 1960) 237.

3. *A Theology of Liberation* (trans. and ed. by Sister Caridad Inda and John Eagleson; New York: Orbis Books, 1973) IX.

4. Ibid., 46, 47.

5. Ibid., 159.

6. *Theology of Hope* (trans. J. W. Leitch; New York: Harper and Row, 1967) 338.

7. *Ethics* (ed. E. Bethige, trans. N. Horton Smith; New York: Macmillan, 1961) 91-93.

8. Gutierrez, *A Theology of Liberation,* 159.

9. Ibid., 174.

10. Ibid., 67.

11. Ibid., 213.

12. *Ethics,* 95.

13. *A Theology of Liberation,* 298.

14. *Ethique de la Liberte* (Tome II; Geneva: Editions Labor et Fides, Librarie Protestante, 1973) 152.

15. *Medical Nemesis* (New York: Pantheon Books, Random House, 1976) 247.

16. *Ethics,* 96.

PART FOUR

BIBLIOGRAPHY

# THE WRITINGS OF J. COERT RYLAARSDAM

Compiled by Arthur L. Merrill

## BOOKS AND COMMENTARIES

*Revelation in Jewish Wisdom Literature.*
 Chicago: University of Chicago Press, 1946

*Introduction and Exegesis of the Book of Exodus.*
 *(The Interpreter's Bible,* Vol. 1. Edited by George A.
 Buttrick)
 Nashville: Abingdon Press, 1952

*Hebrew Wisdom* and *The Proverbs.*
 *(Peake's Commentary on the Bible.* Edited by M. Black and
 H. H. Rowley)
 London: Thomas Nelson and Sons, Ltd., 1962

*Proverbs, Ecclesiastes, Song of Solomon.*
 *(Layman's Bible Commentary,* Vol. 10. Edited by Balmer H.
 Kelly)
 Richmond: John Knox Press, 1964

*Transitions in Biblical Scholarship.* Editor.
 *(Essays in Divinity,* Vol. 6. Edited by Jerald C. Brauer)
 Chicago: University of Chicago Press, 1968

## CONTRIBUTIONS TO DICTIONARIES AND ENCYCLOPAEDIAS

*Encyclopaedia Britannica.*
 Chicago: Encyclopaedia Britannica, 1973

 Abel

 Bathsheba

 David

 Exodus

 Mercy Seat

 Nazirite

 Proverbs

 Shewbread (in part)

*Encyclopaedia Britannica,* 15th Edition, 1975

    Biblical Literature (in part), Vol. 2, Macropaedia

    David, Vol. 5, Macropaedia

*Interpreter's Dictionary of the Bible,* Edited by George A. Buttrick, 4 Vols.
New York, Nashville:  Abingdon Press, 1962

    Atonement, Day of

    Booths, Feast of

    Convocation

    Dedication, Feast of

    Feasts and Fasts

    New Moon

    Passover and Feast of Unleavened Bread

    Pentecost

    Purim

    Solemn Assembly

    Unleavened Bread

    Weeks, Feast of

*Dictionary of the Bible,* Edited by James Hastings.  Rev. ed. by F. C. Frant and H. H. Rowley.
New York:  C. Scribner's Sons, 1963

    John the Baptist

CONTRIBUTIONS TO BOOKS

"Intertestamental Studies since Charles' Apocrypha and Pseudepigrapha," in *The Study of the Bible Today and Tomorrow,* ed. by Harold R. Willoughby, Chicago Society of Biblical Research, Chicago:  University of Chicago Press, 1947, pp. 32-51.

"The Matrix of Worship in the Old Testament" in *Worship in Scripture and Tradition,* edited by Massey H. Shepherd, Jr. New York:  Oxford University Press, 1963, pp. 44-76.

"Judaism and Christian Biblical Studies," in *Conference on Judaism and the Christian Seminary Curriculum, Chicago, 1965,* edited by J. B. Long. Chicago: Loyola University Press, 1966, pp. 85-89.

"The Work of Our Hands: Three Responses to the Crisis of Death," in *Rockefeller Chapel Sermons,* edited by Donovan E. Smucker, Chicago: University of Chicago Press, 1967, pp. 188-196.

"Introduction: The Chicago School - and After," in *Transitions in Biblical Scholarship,* edited by J. Coert Rylaarsdam, Chicago: University of Chicago Press, 1968, pp. 1-16.

"The Old Testament and the New; theocentricity, continuity, finality," in *The Future as the Presence of Shared Hope,* edited by Sister Maryellen Muckenhirn, New York: Sheed and Ward, 1968, pp. 59-83.

"Editor's Foreword," in *Form Criticism of the Old Testament,* by Gene M. Tucker, (Guides to Biblical Scholarship: O.T. Series) Philadelphia: Fortress Press, 1971, pp. iii-viii.

"Editor's Foreword," in *Literary Criticism of the Old Testament,* by Norman C. Habel, (Guides to Biblical Scholarship: O.T. Series) Philadelphia: Fortress Press, 1971, pp. iii-ix.

"Editor's Foreword," in *Tradition History and the Old Testament,* by Walter E. Rast, (Guides to Biblical Scholarship: O.T. Series) Philadelphia: Fortress Press, 1972, pp. iii-x.

"Foreword," in *The Threshing Floor: An Interpretation of the Old Testament,* by John F. X. Sheehan. New York: Paulist Press, 1972, pp. ix-x.

"Jewish-Christian Relationship: The Two Covenants and the Dilemmas of Christology," *Grace Upon Grace:* Essays in Honor of Lester J. Kuyper, edited by James I. Cook. Grand Rapids: William B. Eerdmans, 1975, pp. 70-84.

CONTRIBUTIONS TO PERIODICALS AND JOURNALS

"Prophets or Planners?"
    *Christian Century* 63 (1946) 1211-12

"Hitler and the Jews"
    *Open Door* 581 (1946) 1-2

"The Divinity School of the University"
*Divinity School News* 14 (1947) 1-5

"The Apocrypha and the Bible"
*Journal of Bible and Religion* 17 (1949) 175-180

"Preface to Hermeneutics"
*Journal of Religion* 30 (1950) 79-89

"The Freedom of the Christian Man"
*Open Door* 716 (1950) 4-6

"The Christian Man is Free"
*Divinity School News* 17 (1950) 7-11

"The Doctrine of the Church and the Problem of Culture"
*Christianity and Society* 18 (1953) 7-15

"The Security of Faith"
*Divinity School News* 20 (1953) 1-6

"Justification by Faith"
*Divinity School News* 21 (1954) 1-8

"Present Status of Pentateuchal Criticism"
*Journal of Bible and Religion* 22 (1954) 242-47

"Arab State of Mind"
*Christian Century* 73 (1956) 612-14

"The Biblical Field Today"
*Divinity School News* 23 (1956) 16-21

"The Recovery of the Bible"
*Chicago Theological Seminary Register* 46 (1956) 1-7

"The Problem of Faith and History in Biblical Interpretation"
*Journal of Biblical Literature* 77 (1958) 26-32

"The Joy and Dread of Advent"
*Frontiers* 11 (1959) 3-6

"The Religious Issue of Israel"
*Land Reborn* 12:1 (1961) 16-19

"Common Ground and Difference"
*Journal of Religion* 43 (1963) 261-70

"The Song of Songs and Biblical Faith"
  *Biblical Research* 10 (1965) 7-18

"What is the Ought in Race?"
  *Criterion* 4 (1965) 10-14

"Recovery of Revelance"
  *Criterion* 5 (1966) 13-16

"Disavowal of the curse; a new beginning"
  *Dialog* 6 (1967) 190-99

"Is Dialogue Between Jew and Christian Possible?"
  *Criterion* 6 (1967) 33-35

" Catholicism Today"
  *Commentary* 45 (1968) 79-80

"Poverty and the Poor in the Bible"
  *Pastoral Psychology* 19 (1968) 13-24

". . . of Old Testament Theology"
  *Criterion* 11 (1971) 24-31

"Jewish-Christian Relationship:  The Two Covenants and the
  Dilemmas of Christology"
  *Journal of Ecumenical Studies* 9 (1972) 249-70

PAMPHLETS

"The Challenge of Christian Faith."  An NBC Radio discussion
  by Bernard Loomer, J. Coert Rylaarsdam and John Thompson.
  *University of Chicago Round Table,* No. 578, April 17, 1949,
  pp. 1-10.

"The Present-Day Meaning of Easter."  An NBC Radio discussion
  by Joseph M. Kitagawa, Wilhelm Pauck and J. Coert Rylaarsdam, with a Special Opening Statement by Lawrence A. Kimp-
  ton.  *University of Chicago Round Table,* No. 733, April
  13, 1952, pp. 1-10.

"Judaism and Christianity."  An NBC Radio discussion by
  Louis Binstock, Bernard Loomer, J. Coert Rylaarsdam and
  Edgar Siskin.  *University of Chicago Round Table,* No. 813,
  November 8, 1953, pp. 1-10.

"Biblical Faith and Liberal Education"
  Pella, Iowa:  Central College, 1957.

"Historical Criticism and an Historical Faith"
Appleton, Wisconsin: Lawrence College, 1965.

EDITORSHIPS

*The Journal of Religion,* Co-editor, 1953-1972

*Encyclopaedia Britannica*
Department Editor and Advisor, Religion, 1958-

*Studia Post-Biblica*
Editorial Board 1959-1969

*Biblical Research*
Editorial Board: O.T. Reader, 1963-1972

*Guides to Biblical Scholarship;* Old Testament Series,
Editor, 1971-1973

UNPUBLISHED MANUSCRIPTS

*Hebrew Wisdom with special reference to the concept of the
Spirit.* University of Chicago: Ph.D. Dissertation, 1944

"God and History"

    I. Revelation in History
   II. Purpose in History
  III. Death & Resurrection in History
Rauschenbusch Lectures, 1957
Rochester, New York: Colgate Rochester Divinity
School.

398

## I. Old Testament

## II.  New Testament

## V.  Early Christian Writings

VI.  Early Jewish Writings